THE
GATES OF INDIA

THE GATES OF INDIA

BEING
AN HISTORICAL NARRATIVE

BY
COLONEL SIR THOMAS HOLDICH
K.C.M.G., K.C.I.E., C.B., D.Sc.

AUTHOR OF
'THE INDIAN BORDERLAND,' 'INDIA,' 'THE COUNTRIES OF THE KING'S AWARD'

WITH MAPS

GYAN

Published by

Gyan Publishing House
5, Ansari Road
Daryaganj, New Delhi-110002
Phone: 011-47034999, 9811692060
E-mail: books@gyanbooks.com

Distribution Network
gyanbooks.com
India, USA, Canada, UK, Australia, France

ISBN : 978-81-212-3423-8 (PB)
First Published, 1910

2nd Impression 2020

Printed at: Gyan Press, Delhi.

The Gates of India
Author: Colonel Sir Thomas Holdich

THE

GATES OF INDIA

BEING

AN HISTORICAL NARRATIVE

BY

COLONEL SIR THOMAS HOLDICH

K.C.M.G., K.C.I.E., C.B., D.Sc.

AUTHOR OF

'THE INDIAN BORDERLAND,' 'INDIA,' 'THE COUNTRIES OF THE KING'S AWARD'

WITH MAPS

MACMILLAN AND CO., LIMITED

ST. MARTIN'S STREET, LONDON

1910

PREFACE

As the world grows older and its composition both physical and human becomes subject to ever-increasing scientific investigation, the close interdependence of its history and its geography becomes more and more definite. It is hardly too much to say that geography has so far shaped history that in unravelling some of the more obscure entanglements of historical record, we may safely appeal to our modern knowledge of the physical environment of the scene of action to decide on the actual course of events. Oriental scholars for many years past have been deeply interested in reshaping the map of Asia to suit their theories of the sequence of historical action in India and on its frontiers. They have identified the position of ancient cities in India, sometimes with marvellous precision, and have been able to assign definite niches in history to historical personages with whose story it would have been most difficult to deal were it not intertwined with marked features of geographical environment. But on the far frontiers of India, beyond the Indus, these geographical conditions have only been imperfectly known until recently. It is only within the last thirty years that the geography of the hinterland of India—Tibet, Afghanistan, and Baluchistan—have been in any sense brought under scientific examination, and at the best such examination has been partial and incomplete. It is unfortunate that recent years have added nothing to our knowledge of Afghanistan, and it seems hopeless to wait for detailed information as to some of the more remote (and most interesting) districts of that historic country. As, therefore, in the course of twenty years of official wanderings I have amassed certain notes which may help to throw some light on the ancient highways and cities of those trans-frontier regions which contain the landward gates of India, I have thought it better to make some use of these notes now, and to put together the various theories that I may have formed from time to time bearing on the past history of that country, whilst the opportunity lasts. I have endeavoured to present my own impressions at first hand as far as possible, unbiased by the views already expressed by far more eminent writers than myself, believing that there is a certain value in originality. I have also endeavoured to keep the descriptive geography of such districts as form the theatre of historical incidents on a level with the story itself, so that the one may illustrate the other.

Whilst investigating the methods of early explorers into the hinterland of India it has, of course, been necessary to appeal to the original narratives of the explorers themselves so far as possible. Consequently I am indebted to the assistance afforded by quite a host of authors for the basis of this compilation. And I may briefly recount the names of those to whom I am under special obligation. First and foremost are Mr. M'Crindle's admirable series of handy little volumes dealing with the Greek period of Indian history, the perusal of which first prompted an attempt to reconcile some of the apparent discrepancies between classical story and practical geography, with which may be included Sir A. Cunningham's *Coins of Alexander's Successors in Kabul.* For the Arab phase of commercial exploration I am indebted to Sir William Ouseley's translation, *Oriental Geography of Ibn Haukel*, and the *Geographie d'Edrisi*; *traduite par P. Aimedée Joubert.* For more modern records the official reports of Burnes, Lord, and Leech on Afghanistan; Burnes' *Travels into Bokhara, etc.*; *Cabul*, by the same author; Ferrier's *Caravan Journeys*; Wood's *Journey to the Sources of the Oxus*; Moorcroft's *Travels in the Himalayan Provinces*; Vigne's *Ghazni, Kabul, and Afghanistan*; Henry Pottinger's *Travels in Baloochistan and Sinde*; and last, but by no means least, Masson's *Travels in Afghanistan, Beluchistan, the Panjab, and Kalat*, all of which have been largely indented on. To this must be added Mr. Forrest's valuable compilation of Bombay records. It has been indeed one of the objects of this book to revive the records of past generations of explorers whose stories have a deep significance even in this day, but which are apt to be overlooked and forgotten as belonging to an ancient and superseded era of research. Because these investigators belong to a past generation it by no means follows that their work, their opinions, or their deductions from original observations are as dead as they are themselves. It is far too readily assumed that the work of the latest explorer must necessarily supersede that of his predecessors. In the difficult art of map compilation perhaps the most difficult problem with which the compiler has to deal is the relative value of evidence dating from different periods. Here, then, we have introduced a variety of opinions and views expressed by men of many minds (but all of one type as explorer), which may be balanced one against another with a fair prospect of eliminating what mathematicians call the "personal equation" and arriving at a sound "mean" value from combined evidence. I have said they are all of one type, regarded as explorers. There is only one word which fitly describes that type—magnificent. We may well ask have we any explorers like them in these days? We know well enough that we have the raw material in plenty for fashioning them, but alas! opportunity is wanting. Exploration in these days is becoming so professional and so scientific that modern methods hardly admit of the dare-devil, face-to-face intermixing with savage breeds and races that was such a distinctive feature in the work of these heroes of an older age. We get geographical results with a rapidity and a precision that were undreamt of in the early years (or even in the middle) of the last century. Our instruments are incomparably better, and our equipment is such that we can deal with the hostility of nature in her more savage moods with comparative facility. But we no longer live with the people about whom we set out to write books—we don't wear their clothes, eat their food, fraternize with them in their homes and in the field, learn their language and discuss with them their religion and politics. And the result is that we don't *know* them half as well, and the ratio of our knowledge (in India at least) is inverse to the official position towards them that we may happen to occupy. The missionary and the police officer may know something of the people; the high-placed political administrator knows less (he cannot help himself), and the parliamentary demagogue knows nothing at all. My excuse for giving so large a place to the American explorer Masson, for instance, is that he was first in the field at a critical period of Indian history. Apart from his extraordinary gifts and power of absorbing and collating information, history has proved that on the whole his judgment both as regards Afghan character and Indian political ineptitude was essentially sound. Of course he was not popular. He is as bitter and sarcastic in his unsparing criticisms of local political methods in Afghanistan as he is of the methods of the Indian Government behind them; and doubtless his bitterness and undisguised hostility to some extent discounts the value of his opinion. But he knew the Afghan, which we did not: and it is most instructive to note the extraordinary divergence of opinion that existed between him and Sir Alexander Burnes as regards some of the most marked idiosyncrasies of Afghan character. Burnes was as great an explorer as Masson, but whilst in Afghanistan he was the emissary of the Indian Government, and thus it immediately became worth while for the Afghan Sirdar to study his temper and his weaknesses and to make the best use of both. Thus arose Burnes' whole-hearted belief in the simplicity of Afghan methods, whilst Masson, who was more or less behind the scenes, was in no position to act as prompter to him. It was just preceding and during the momentous period of the first Afghan war (1839-41) that European explorers in Afghanistan and Baluchistan were most active. Long before then both countries had been an open book to the Ancients, and both may be said geographically to be an open book to us now. There are, however, certain pages which have not yet been properly read, and something will be said later on as to where these pages occur.

CONTENTS

CHAPTER XIV

CHAPTER XV

CHAPTER XVI

CHAPTER XVII

CHAPTER XVIII

LIST OF MAPS

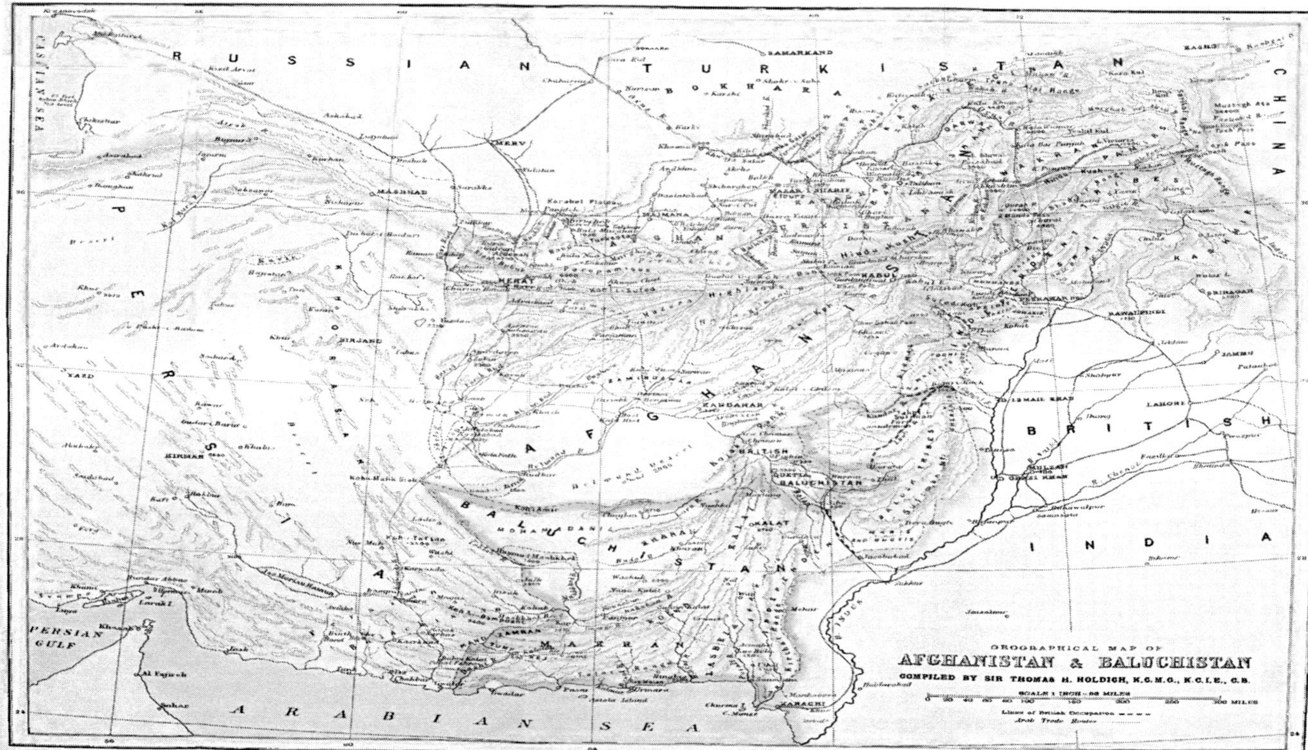
GEOGRAPHICAL MAP OF
AFGHANISTAN & BALUCHISTAN
COMPILED BY SIR THOMAS H. HOLDICH, K.C.M.G., K.C.I.E., C.B.
Lines of British Occupation
Arab Trade Routes
RUSSIAN TURKISTAN
CHINA
PERSIA
AFGHANISTAN
BALUCHISTAN
BRITISH INDIA
ARABIAN SEA
PERSIAN GULF
CASPIAN SEA
KABUL
HERAT
KANDAHAR
QUETTA
KARACHI
LAHORE
MERV
MASHHAD
SAMARKAND

INTRODUCTION

SINCE the gates of India have become water gates and the way to India has been the way of the sea, very little has been known of those other landward gates which lie to the north and west of the peninsula, through which have poured immigrants from Asia and conquerors from the West from time immemorial. It has taken England a long time to rediscover them, and she is even now doubtful about their strategic value and the possibility of keeping them closed and barred. It is only by an examination of the historical records which concern them, and the geographical conditions which surround them, that any clear appreciation of their value can be attained; and it is only within the last century that such examinations have been rendered possible by the enterprise and activity of a race of explorers (official and otherwise) who have risked their lives in the dangerous field of the Indian trans-frontier. In ancient days the very first (and sometimes the last) thing that was learned about India was the way thither from the North. In our times the process has been reversed, and we seek for information with our backs to the South. We have worked our way northward, having entered India by the southern water gates, and as we have from time to time struggled rather to remain content within narrow borders than to push outward and forward, the drift to the north has been very slow, and there has never been, right from the very beginning, any strenuous haste in the expansion of commercial interests, or any spirit of crusade in the advance of Conquest.

So late as the early years of the sixteenth century England was but a poor country, with less inhabitants than are now crowded within the London area. There was not much to spare, either of money or men, for ventures which could only be regarded in those days as sheer gambling speculations. The splendid records of a successful voyage must have been greatly discounted by the many dismal tales of failure, and nothing but an indomitable impulse, bred of international rivalry, could have led the royal personages and the few wealthy citizens who backed our earliest enterprises to open their purse-strings sufficiently wide to find the necessary means for the equipment of a modest little fleet of square-sailed merchant ships. National tenacity prevailed, however, in the end. The hard-headed Islander finally succeeded where the more impetuous Southerner failed, and England came out finally with most of the honours of a long commercial contest. It was in this way that we reached India, and by degrees we painted India our own conventional colour in patches large enough to give us the preponderating voice in her general administration. But as we progressed northward and north-westward we realized the important fact that India—the peninsula India—was insulated and protected by geographical conformations which formed a natural barrier against outside influences, almost as impassable as the sea barriers of England. On the north-east a vast wilderness of forest-covered mountain ranges and deep lateral valleys barred the way most effectually against irruption from the yellow races of Asia. On the north where the curving serrated ramparts of the north-east gave place to the Himalayan barrier, the huge uplifted highlands of Tibet were equally impassable to the busy pushing hordes of the Mongol; and it was only on the extreme north-west about the hinterland of Kashmir, and beyond the Himalayan system, that any weakness could be found in the chain of defensive works which Nature had sent to the north of India. Here, indeed, in the trans-Indus regions of Kashmir, sterile, rugged, cold, and crowned with gigantic ice-clad peaks, there is a slippery track reaching northward into the depression of Chinese Turkestan, which for all time has been a recognised route connecting India with High Asia. It is called the Karakoram route. Mile upon mile a white thread of a road stretches across the stone-strewn plains, bordered by the bones of the innumerable victims to the long fatigue of a burdensome and ill-fed existence—the ghastly debris of former caravans. It is perhaps the ugliest track to call a trade route in the whole wide world. Not a tree, not a shrub, exists, not even the cold dead beauty which a snow-sheet imparts to highland scenery, for there is no great snowfall in the elevated spaces which back the Himalayas and their offshoots. It is marked, too, by many a sordid tragedy of murder and robbery, but it is nevertheless one of the northern gates of India which we have spent much to preserve, and it does actually serve a very important purpose in the commercial economy of India. At least one army has traversed this route from the north with the prospect before it of conquering Tibet; but it was a Mongol army, and it was worsted in a most unequal contest with Nature.

India (if we include Kashmir) runs to a northern apex about the point where, from the western extension of the giant Muztagh, the Hindu Kush system takes off in continuation of the great Asiatic divide. Here the Pamirs border Kashmir, and here there are also mountain ways which have aforetime let in the irrepressible Chinaman, probably as far as Hunza, but still a very long way from the Indian peninsula. Then the Hindu Kush slopes off to the south-westward and becomes the divide between Afghanistan and Kashmir for a space, till, from north of Chitral, it continues with a sweep right into Central Afghanistan and merges into the mountain chain which reaches to Herat. From this point, north of Chitral, commences the true north-west barrier of India, a barrier which includes nearly the whole width of Afghanistan beyond the formidable wall of the trans-Indus mountains. It is here that the gates of India are to be found, and it is with this outermost region of India, and what lies beyond it, that this book is chiefly concerned.

As the history of India under British occupation grew and expanded and the painting red process gradually developed, whilst men were ever reaching north-westward with their eyes set on these frontier hills, the countries which lay beyond came to be regarded as the "ultima thule" of Indian exploration, and Afghanistan and Baluchistan were reckoned in English as the hinterland of India, only to be reached by the efforts of English adventurers from the plains of the peninsula. And that is the way in which those countries are still regarded. It is Afghanistan in its relations to India, political, commercial, or strategic, as the case may be, that fills the minds of our soldiers and statesmen of to-day; and the way to Afghanistan is still by the way of ships—across the ocean first, and then by climbing upward from the plains of India to the continental plateau land of Asia. It was not so twenty-five centuries ago. One can imagine the laughter that would echo through the courts and palaces of Nineveh at the idea of reaching Afghanistan by a sea route! Think of Tiglath Pilesur, the founder of the Second Assyrian Empire, seated, curled, and anointed, surrounded by his Court and flanked by the sculptured art of his period (already losing some of the freshness and vigour of First Empire design) in the pillared halls of Nineveh, and counting the value of his Eastern satrapies in Sagartia, Ariana, and Arachosia, with outlying provinces in Northern India, whilst meditating yet further conquests to add to his almost illimitable Empire! No shadow of Babylon had stretched northward then. No premonition of a yet larger and later Empire overshadowed him or his successors, Shalmaneser and Sargon. Northern Afghanistan was to these Assyrian kings the dumping ground of unconsidered companies of conquered slaves, a bourne from whence no captive was ever likely to return. No record is left of the passing of those bands of colonists from West to East. We can only gather from the writings of subsequent historians in classical times that for centuries they must have drifted eastward from Syria, Armenia, and Greece, carrying with them the rudiments of the arts and industries of the land they had left for ever, and providing India with the germs of an art system entirely imitative in design, colour, and relief. The Aryan was before them in India. Already the foundations were laid for historic dynasties, and

Rajput families were dating their origin from the sun and moon, whilst somewhere from beneath the shadow of the Himalayas in the foothills of Nipal was soon to arise the daystar of a new faith, a "light of Asia" for all centuries to come.

It is impossible to set a limit to the number and variety of the people who, in these early centuries, either migrated, or were deported, from West to East through Persia to Northern Afghanistan, or who drifted southwards into Baluchistan. Not until the ethnography of these frontier lands of India is exhaustively studied shall we be able to unravel the influence of Assyrian, Median, Persian, Arab, or Greek migrations in the strange conglomeration of humanity which peoples those countries. Baktra (Balkh), in Northern Afghanistan, must have been a city of consequence in days when Nineveh was young. Farah, a city of Arachosia in Western Afghanistan on the borders of Seistan, must have been a centre from whence Assyrian arts and industries were passed on to India for ages; for Farah lies directly on the route which connects Seistan with the southern passes into the Indus valley. The Indus itself seems to have been the boundary which limited the efforts of migration and exploration. Beyond the Indus were deserts in the south and wide unproductive plains of the Punjab in the north, and it is the deserts of the world's geography which, far more than any other feature, have always determined the extent of the human tidal waves and influenced their direction. They are as the promontories and capes of the world's land perimeter to the tides of the ocean. Beyond these parched and waterless tracts, where now the maximum temperatures of sun-heat in India are registered, were vague uncertainties and mythical wonders, the tales of which in ancient literature are in strange contrast to the exact information which was obtained of geographical conditions and tribal distributions in the basins of the Kabul or Swat rivers, or within the narrow valleys of Makran.

A recent writer (Mr. Ellsworth Huntington) has expressed in picturesque and convincing language the nature of the relationship which has ever existed between man and his physical environments in Asia, and has illustrated the effect of certain pulsations of climate in the movement of Asiatic history. The changing conditions of the climate of High Asia, periods of desiccation and deprivation of natural water-supply alternating with periods of cold and rainfall, acting in slow progression through centuries and never ceasing in their operation, have set "men in nations" moving over the face of that continent since the beginning of time, and left a legacy of buried history, to be unearthed by explorers of the type of Stein, such as will eventually give us the key to many important problems in race distribution. But more important even than climatic influence is the direct influence of physical geography, the actual shaping of mountain and valley, as a factor in directing the footsteps of early migration. Nowadays men cross the seas in thousands from continent to continent, but in the days of Egyptian and Assyrian empire it was that straight high-road which crossed the fewest passes and tapped the best natural resources of wood and water which was absolutely the determining factor in the direction of the great human processions; and although change of climate may have set the nomadic peoples of High Asia moving with a purpose more extensive than an annual search for pasturage, and have led to the peopling of India with successive nations of Central Asiatic origin, it was the knowledge that by certain routes between Mesopotamia and Northern Afghanistan lay no inhospitable desert, and no impassable mountain barrier, that determined the intermittent flow from the west, which received fresh impulse with every conquest achieved, with every band of captives available for colonizing distant satrapies. To put it shortly, there was an easy high-road from Mesopotamia through Persia to Northern Afghanistan, or even to Seistan, and not a very difficult one to Makran; and so it came about that migratory movements, either compulsory or voluntary, continued through centuries, ever extending their scope till checked by the deserts of the Indian frontier or the highlands of the Pamirs and Tibet, or the cold wild wastes of Siberia.

Thus Afghanistan and Baluchistan, the countries with which we are more immediately concerned, were probably far better known to Assyrian and Persian kings than they were to the British Intelligence Office (or its equivalent) of a century ago. The first landward explorations of these countries are lost in pre-historic mists, but we find that the first scientific mission of which we have any record (that which was led by Alexander the Great) was well supplied with fairly accurate geographical information regarding the main route to be followed and the main objectives to be gained.

In tracing out, therefore, or rather in sketching, the gradual progress of exploration in Afghanistan and Baluchistan, and the gradual evolution of those countries into a proper appanage of British India, we will begin (as history began) from the north and west rather than from the south and the plains of Hindustan.

CHAPTER I

EARLY RELATIONS BETWEEN EAST AND WEST. GREECE AND PERSIA AND EARLY TRIBAL DISTRIBUTIONS ON THE INDIAN FRONTIER.

IT is unfortunately most difficult to trace the conditions under which Europe was first introduced to Asia, or the gradual ripening of early acquaintance into inter-commercial relationship. Although the eastern world was possessed of a sound literature in the time of Moses, and although long before the days of Solomon there was "no end" to the "making of books," it is remarkable how little has been left of these archaic records, and it is only by inference gathered from tags and ends of oriental script that we gradually realize how unimportant to old-world thinkers was the daily course of their own national history. India is full of ancient literature, but there is no ancient history. To the Brahmans there was no need for it. To them the world and all that it contains was "illusion," and it was worse than idle—it was impious—to perpetuate the record of its varied phases as they appeared to pass in unreal pageantry before their eyes. We know that from under the veil of extravagant epic a certain amount of historical truth has been dragged into daylight. The "Mahabharata" and the "Ramayana" contain in allegorical outline the story of early conflicts which ended in the foundation of mighty Rajput houses, or which established the distribution of various races of the Indian peninsula. Without an intimate knowledge of the language in which these great epics are written it is impossible to estimate fully the nature of the allegory which overlies an interesting historical record, but it has always appeared to be sufficiently vague to warrant some uncertainty as to the accuracy of the deductions which have hitherto been evolved therefrom. Nevertheless it is from these early poems of the East that we derive all that there is to be known about ancient India, and when we turn from the East to the West strangely enough we find much the same early literary conditions confronting us.

About 950 years before Christ, two of the most perfect epic poems were written that ever delighted the world, the *Iliad* and *Odyssey* of Homer. The first begins with Achilles and ends with the funeral of Hector. The second recounts the voyages and adventures of Ulysses after the destruction of Troy. With our modern intimate knowledge of the coasts of the Mediterranean it is not difficult to detect, amidst the fabulous accounts of heroic adventures, many references to geographical facts which must have been known generally to the Greeks of the Homeric period, dealing chiefly with the coasts and islands of the Western sea. There is but little reference to the East, although many centuries before Homer's day there was a sea-going trade between India and the West which brought ivory, apes, and peacocks to the ports of Syria. The obvious inference to be derived from the general absence of reference to the mysteries of Eastern geography is that there was no through traffic. Ships from the East traded only along the coast-lines that they knew, and ventured no farther than the point where an interchange of commodities could be established with the slow crawling craft of the West, the navigation of the period being confined to the hugging the coast-line and making for the nearest shelter when times were bad. The interchange of commodities between the rough sailor people of those days did not tend to an interchange of geographical information. Probably the language difficulty stood in the way. If there was no end to the making of books it was not the illiterate and rough sailor men who made them. Nor do sailors, as a rule, make them now. It is left to the intelligent traveller uninterested in trade, and the journalistic seeker after sensation, to make modern geographical records; and there were no such travellers in the days of Homer, even if the art of writing had been a general accomplishment. In days much later than

Homer we can detect sailors' yarns embodied in what purport to be authentic geographical records, but none so early. We have a reference to certain Skythic nomads who lived on mare's milk, and who had wandered from the Asiatic highlands into the regions north of the Euxine, which is in itself deeply interesting as it indicates that as early as the ninth century B.C. Milesian Greek colonies had started settlements on the shores of the Black Sea. As the centuries rolled on these settlements expanded into powerful colonies, and with enterprising people such as the early Greeks there can be little doubt that there was an intermittent interchange of commerce with the tribes beyond the Euxine, and that gradually a considerable, if inaccurate, knowledge of Asia, even beyond the Taurus, was acquired. The world, for them, was still a flat circular disc with a broad tidal ocean flowing around its edge, encompassing the habitable portions about the centre.

Africa extended southward to the land of Ethiop and no farther, but Asia was a recognised geographical entity, less vague and nebulous even than the western isles from whence the Phœnicians brought their tin. There were certain fables current among the Greeks touching the one-eyed Arimaspians, the gold-guarding griffins, and the Hyperboreans, which in the middle of the sixth century were still credited, and almost indicate an indefinite geographical conception of northern

Asiatic regions. But it is probable that much more was known of Asiatic geography in these early years than can be gathered from the poems and fables of Greek writers before the days of Herodotus and of professional geography. There were no means of recording knowledge ready to the hand of the colonist and commercial traveller then; even the few literary men who later travelled for the sake of gaining knowledge were dependent largely on information obtained scantily and with difficulty from others, and the expression of their knowledge is crude and imperfect. But what should we expect even in present times if we proceeded to compile a geographical treatise from the works of Milton and Shakespere? What indeed would be the result of a careful analysis of parliamentary utterances on geographical subjects within, say, the last half century? Would they present to future generations anything approaching to an accurate epitome of the knowledge really possessed (though possibly not expressed) by those who have within that period almost exhausted the world's store of geographical record? The analogy is a perfectly fair one. Geographers and explorers are not always writers even in these days, and as we work backwards into the archives of history nothing is more astonishing than the indications which may be found of vast stores of accurate information of the earth's physiography lost to the world for want of expression.

It was between the sixth century B.C. and the days of Herodotus that Miletus was destroyed, and captive Greeks were transported by Darius Hystaspes from the Lybian Barké to Baktria, where we find traces of them again under their original Greek name in the northern regions of Afghanistan. It was long ere the days of Darius that the hosts of Assyria beat down the walls of Samaria and scattered the remnants of Israel through the highlands of Western Asia. Where did they drift to, these ten despairing tribes? Possibly we may find something to remind us of them also in the northern Afghan hills.

It was probably about the same era that some pre-Hellenic race, led (so it is written) by the mythical hero Dionysos, trod the weary route from the Euxine to the Caspian, and from the southern shores of the Caspian to the borderland of modern Indian frontier, where their descendants welcomed Alexander on his arrival as men of his own faith and kin, and were recognised as such by the great conqueror. Now all this points to an acquaintance with the geographical links between East and West which appears nowhere in any written record. Nowhere can we find any clear statement of the actual routes by which these pilgrims were supposed to have made their long and toilsome journeys. Just the bare facts are recorded, and we are left to guess the means by which they were accomplished. But it is clear that the old-world overland connection between India and the Black Sea is a very old connection indeed, and further, it is clear that what the Greeks may not have known the Persians certainly did know. When Herodotus first set solidly to work on a geographical treatise which was to embrace the existing knowledge of the whole world, he undoubtedly derived a great deal of that knowledge from official Persian sources; and it may be added that the early Persian department for geographical intelligence has been proved by this last century's scientific investigations to have collected information of which the accuracy is certainly astonishing. It is only quite recently, during the process of surveys carried on by the Government of India through the highlands and coast regions of Baluchistan and Eastern Persia, that anything like a modern gazetteer of the tribes occupying those districts has been rendered possible. Twenty-five years ago our military information concerning ethnographic distributions in districts lying immediately beyond the north-western frontier was no better than that which is contained in the lists of the Persian satrapies, given to the world by Herodotus nearly 500 years before the Christian era. Twenty-five years ago we did not know of the existence of some of the tribes and peoples mentioned by him, and we were unable to identify others. Now, however, we are at last aware that through twenty-four centuries most of them have clung to their old habitat in a part of the Eastern world where material wealth and climatic attractions have never been sufficient to lead to annihilation by conquest. Oppressed and harried by successive Persian dynasties, overrun by the floatsam and jetsam of hosts of migratory Asiatic peoples from the North, those tribes have mostly survived to bear a much more valuable testimony to the knowledge of the East entertained by the West in the days of Herodotus than any which can be gathered from written documents.

The Milesian colonies founded on the southern and western shores of the Euxine in the sixth and seventh centuries B.C., whilst retaining their trade connection with the parent city of Miletus (where sprang that carpet-making industry for which this corner of Asia has been famous ever since), found no open road to the further eastern trade through the mountain regions that lie south of the Black Sea. Half a century after Herodotus we find Xenophon struggling in almost helpless entanglement amongst these wild mountains comparatively close to the Greek colonies; and it was there that he encountered the fiercest opposition from the native tribes-people that he met with during his famous retreat from Persia. It is always so. Our most active opponents on the Indian frontier are the mountaineers of the immediate borderland—the people who *know* us best, and therefore fear us most. It was chiefly through Miletus and the Cilician gates that Greek trade with Persia and Babylon was maintained. There were no Greek colonies on the rugged eastern coasts of the Black Sea—sufficient indication that no open trade route existed direct to the Caspian by any line analogous to that of the modern railway that connects Batum with Baku. On the north of the Euxine, however, there were great and flourishing colonies (of which Olbia at the mouth of the Borysthenes, or Dneiper, was the most famous) which undoubtedly traded with the Skythic peoples north and west of the Caspian. From these sources came the legends of Hyperobeans and Griffins and other similar tales, all flavoured with the glamour of northern mystery, but none of them pointing to an eastern origin. Recent investigations into the ethnography of certain tribes in Afghanistan, however, seem to prove conclusively that even if there was no recognised trade between Greece and India before Miletus was destroyed by Darius Hystaspes, and Greek settlers were transported by the Persian conqueror to the borders of the modern Badakshan, yet there must have been Greek pioneers in colonial enterprise who had made their way to the Far East and stayed there. For instance, we have that strange record of settlements under Dionysos amongst the spurs and foothills of the Hindu Kush, which were clearly of Greek origin, although Arrian in his history of Alexander's progress through Asia is unable to explain the meaning of them.

There is more to be said about these settlements

later. The first actual record of settlement of Greeks in Baktria is that of Herodotus, to which we have referred as being affected by Darius Hystaspes in the sixth century before Christ, and the descendants of these settlers are undoubtedly the people referred to by Arrian as "Kyreneans," who could be no other than the Greek captives from the Lybian Barke. Their existence two centuries later than Herodotus is attested by Arrian, and they were apparently in possession of the Kaoshan pass over the Hindu Kush at the time of Alexander's expedition. Another body of Greeks is recorded by Arrian to have been settled in the Baktrian country by Xerxes after his flight from Greece. These were the Brankhidai of Milesia, whose posterity are said to have been exterminated by Alexander in punishment for the crimes of their grandfather Didymus. The name Barang, or Farang, is frequently repeated in the mountain districts of Northern Afghanistan and Badakshan, and careful inquiry would no doubt reveal the fact that surviving Greek affinities are still far more widely spread through that part of Asia than is generally known. All these settlements were antecedent to Alexander, but beyond these recorded instances of Greek occupation there can be little doubt that (as pointed out by Bellew in his *Ethnography of Afghanistan* and supported by later observations) the Greek element had been diffused through the wide extent of the Persian sovereignty for centuries before the birth of

Alexander the Great. It is probable that each of the four great divisions of the ancient Greeks had contributed for a thousand years before to the establishment of colonies in Asia Minor, and from these colonies bands of emigrants had penetrated to the far east of the Persian dominions, either as free men or captives. Amongst the clans and tribal sections of Afghans and Pathans are to be found to this day names that are clearly indicative of this pre-historic Greek connection.

Persia at her greatest maintained a considerable overland trade with India, and Indian tribute formed a large part of her revenues. All Afghanistan was Persian; all Baluchistan, and the Indian frontier to the Indus. The underlying Persian element is strong in all these regions still, the dominant language of the country, the speech of the people, whether Baluch or Pathan, is of Persian stock, whilst the polite tongue of Court officials, if not the Persian of Tehran or Shiraz, is at least an imitation of it. It is hardly strange that the Greek language should have absolutely disappeared. We have the statement of Seneca (referred to by Bellew in his *Inquiry*) that the Greek language was spoken in the Indus valley as late as the middle of the first century after Christ; "if indeed it did not continue to be the colloquial in some parts of the valley to a considerably later period." As this is nearly two centuries after the overthrow of Greek dominion in Afghanistan, it at least indicates that the Greek settlements established four centuries earlier must have continued to exist, and to be reinforced by Greek women (for children speak their mother's tongue) to a comparatively late period; and that the triumph of the Jat over the Greek did not by any means efface the influence of the Greek in India for centuries after it occurred. It is probable that when the importation of Greek women (who were often employed in the households of Indian chiefs and nobles at a time when Greek ladies married Indian Princes) ceased, then the Greek language ceased to exist also. The retinue and followers of Alexander's expedition took the women of the country to wife, and it is not, as is so often supposed, to the results of that expedition so much as to the long existence of Greek colonies and settlements that we must attribute the undoubted influence of Greek art on the early art of India.

Thus we have a wide field before us for inquiry into the early history of ethnographical movement in Asia, as it affected the relation between Europe and Afghanistan. Afghanistan (which is a modern political development) has ever held the landward gates of India. We cannot understand India without a study of that wide hinterland (Afghan, Persian, and Baluch) through which the great restless human tide has ever been on the move: now a weeping nation of captives led by tear-sodden routes to a land of exile; now a band of merchants reaching forward to the land of golden promise; or perchance an army of pilgrims marching with their feet treading deep into narrow footways to the shrines of forgotten saints; or perchance an armed host seeking an uncertain fate; a ceaseless, waveless tide, as persistent, as enterprising, and infinitely more complicated in its developments than the process of modern emigration, albeit modern emigration may spread more widely.

Living as we do in fixed habitations and hedged in not merely by narrow seas but by the conventionalities of civilized existence, we fail to realize the conditions of nomadic life which were so familiar to our Asiatic ancestors. Something of its nature may be gathered to-day from the Kalmuk and Kirghiz nomads of Central Asia. A day's march is not a day's march to them—it is a day's normal occupation. The yearly shift in search of fresh pasture is not a flitting on a holiday tour; it is as much a part of the year's life as the change of raiment between summer to winter. Everything moves; the home is not left behind; every man, woman, and child of the family has a recognised share in the general shift. Perhaps that of the Kirghiz man is the easiest. He smokes a lazy pipe in the bright sunshine and watches his boys strip off the felt covering of his wicker-built "kibitka," whilst his wife with floating bands of her white headdress fluttering in the breeze, and her quilted coat turned up to give more freedom to her booted legs, gets together the household traps in compact bundles for the great hairy camel to carry. Her efforts are not inartistic; long experience has taught her exactly where every household god can be stowed to the best advantage. Meanwhile the happy, good-looking Kirghiz girls are racing over the grass country after sheep, and ere long the little party is making its slow but sure way over the breezy steppes to the passes of the blue mountains, which look down from afar on to the warmer plains. And who has the best of it? The free-roving, untrammelled child of the plain, quite godless, and taking no thought for the morrow, or the carefully cultured and tight-fitted product of civilization to whom the motor and the railway represent the only thinkable method of progression? That, however, is not the point. What we wish to emphasize is the apparent inability on the part of many writers on the subject of ancient history and geography to realize the essential difference between then and now as regards human migratory movement.

There is often an apparent misconception that there is more movement in these days of railways and steamers and motors than existed ten centuries before Christ. The difference lies not in the comparative amount of movement but in the method of it. In one sense only is there more movement—there are more people to travel; but in a broader sense there is much less movement. Whole nations are no longer shifted at the will of the conqueror across a continent, trade seekers no longer devote their lives to the personal conduct of caravans; armies swelled to prodigious size by a tagrag following no longer (except in China) move slowly over the face of the land, devouring, like a swarm of locusts, all that comes in their way. Colonial emigration perhaps alone works on a larger scale now than in those early times; but taking it "bye and large," the circulation of the human race, unrestricted by political boundaries, was certainly more constant in the unsettled days of nomadic existence than in these later days of overgrown cities and electric traffic. If little or nothing is recorded of many of the most important migrations which have changed the ethnographic conditions of Asia, whilst at the same time we have volumes of ancient philosophy and mythology, it is because such changes were regarded as normal, and the current of contemporary history as an ephemeral phenomenon not worth the labour of close inquiry or a manuscript record.

Such a gazetteer as that presented to us by Herodotus would not have been possible had there not been free and frequent access to the countries and the people with whom it deals. It is impossible to conceive that so much accuracy of detail could have been acquired without the assistance of personal inquiry on the spot. If this is so, then the Persians at any rate knew their way well about Asia as far east as Tibet and India, and the Greeks undoubtedly derived their knowledge from Persia. When Alexander of Macedon first planned his expedition to Central Asia he had probably more certain knowledge of the way thither than Lord Napier of Magdala possessed when he set out to find the capital of Theodore's kingdom in Abyssinia, and it is most interesting to note the information which was possessed by the Greek authorities a century and a half before Alexander's time.

One notable occurrence pointing to a fairly comprehensive knowledge of geography of the Indian border by the Persians, was the voyage of the Greek Scylax of Caryanda down the Indus, and from its mouth to the Arabian Gulf, which was regarded by Herodotus as establishing the fact of a continuous sea. This voyage, or mission, which was undertaken by order of Darius who wished to know where the Indus had its outlet and "sent some ships" on a voyage of discovery, is most instructive. It is true that the accounts of it are most meagre, but such details as are given establish beyond a doubt that the expedition was practical and real. The Persian dominions then extended to the Indus, but there is no evidence that they ever extended beyond that river into the peninsula of India. The Indus of the Persian age was not the Indus of to-day, and its outlet to the sea presumably did not differ materially from that of the subsequent days of Alexander and Nearkos.

Thanks to the careful investigations of the Bombay Survey Department, and the close attention which has been given to ancient landmarks by General Haig during the progress of his surveys, we know pretty certainly where the course of the Lower Indus must have been, and where both Scylax and Nearkos emerged into the Arabian Sea. The Indus delta of to-day covers an area of 10,000 square miles with 125 miles of coast-line, and it presents to us a huge alluvial tract which is everywhere furrowed by ancient river channels. Some of these are continuous through the delta, and can be traced far above it; others are traceable for only short distances. Without entering into details of the rate of progression in the formation of Delta (which can be gathered not only from the abandoned sites of towns once known as coast ports, but from actual observation from year to year), it may be safely assumed that the Indus of Alexander and Scylax emptied itself into the Ran of Kach, far to the south of its present debouchment. The volume of its waters was then augmented by at least one important river (the Saraswati), which, flowing from the Himalayas through what is now known as the Rajputana desert, was the source of widespread wealth and fertility to thousands of square miles where now there is nothing to be met with but sandy waste. As far as the Indus the Persian Empire is known to have extended, but no farther; and it was important to the military advisers of

Darius that something should be known of the character of this boundary river.

Wherever the ships sent by Darius may have gone it is quite clear that they did not sail *up* the Indus, or there would have been no objective for an expedition which was organised to determine where the Indus met the sea by the process of sailing down that river. Moreover, the voyage up the Indus would have been tedious and slow, and could only have been undertaken in the cold weather with the assistance of native pilots acquainted with the ever-shifting bed of the river, which, so far as its liability to change of channel is concerned, must have been much the same in the days of Darius as it is at present. The possibility, therefore, is that Scylax made his way to the Upper Indus overland, for we are told that the expedition *started* from the city of Carpatyra in the Pactyan country. This in itself is exceedingly instructive, indicating that the Pactyans, or Pathans, or Pukhtu speaking peoples have occupied the districts of the Upper Indus for four-and-twenty centuries at least; and coincident with them we learn that the Aprytæ or Afridi shared the honour of being resident landowners. Nor need we suppose that the beginning of this history was the beginning of their existence. The Afridi may have rejoiced in his native hills ten or twenty centuries before he was written about by Herodotus. We need not stay to identify the site of Carpatyra. The Upper Indus valley is full of ancient sites. A century and a half later Taxilla was the recognized capital of the Upper Punjab, and Carpatyra meanwhile may have disappeared. Anyhow we hear of Carpatyra no more, nor has the ingenuity of modern research thrown any certain light on its position. It is, however, probably near Attok that we must look for it. Scylax made his way down the Indus in native craft that from long before his day to the present have retained their primitive form, a form which was not unlike that of the coast crawling "ships" of Darius. He proved the existence of an open water-way from the Upper Punjab to the Persian Gulf, and incidentally his expedition shows us that the chief lines of communication through the width of the Persian Empire were well known, and that the road from Susa to the Upper Indus was open. The outlying satrapies of the Persian Empire could never have been added one by one to that mighty power without definite knowledge of the way to reach them. It was not merely a spasmodic expedition, such as that of Scylax, which pointed the way to the conquests of the Far East; it was the gathered information of years of experience, and it was on the basis of this experience (unwritten and unrecorded so far as we know) that Alexander founded his plans of campaign.

The detailed list of peoples included in the satrapies of the Persian Empire, whilst it is more ethnographical than geographical in its character, is sufficient proof in itself of the existence of constant movement between Persia and the borderland of Afghanistan, which assuredly included commercial traffic. This enumeration has been compared with a catalogue of tribal contingents which swelled the great army of Xerxes, an independent statement, and therefore a valuable test to the general accuracy of Herodotus; and it is still further confirmed by the list of nations subject to the Persian king found in the inscriptions of Darius at Behistan and Persepolis. We are not immediately concerned with the satrapies included in Western Asia and Egypt, but when Herodotus makes a sudden departure from his rule of geographical sequence and introduces a satrapy on the remotest east of the Persian Empire, we immediately recognize that he touches the Indian frontier.

The second satrapy most probably corresponds with that part of Central Afghanistan south of the Kabul River, which lies west of the Suliman Hills and north of the Kwaja Amran or Khojak. Every name mentioned by Herodotus certainly has its counterpart in one or other of the tribes to be found there to this day, excepting the Lydoi (whose history as Ludi is fairly well known) and the Lasonoi, who have emigrated, the former into India and the latter to Baluchistan.

The seventh satrapy, again, comprised the Sattagydai, the Gandarioi, the Dadikai, and the Aparytai ("joined together"), an association of names too remarkable to be mistaken. The Sattag or Khattak, the Gandhari, the Dadi, and the Afridi are all trans-Indus people, and without insisting too strongly on the exact habitat of each, originally there can be little doubt that the seventh satrapy included a great part of the Indus valley.

The eleventh satrapy is also probably a district of the Indian trans-frontier, although Bunbury associates the name Kaspioi with the Caspian Sea. It is far more likely that the Kaspioi of Herodotus are to be recognized as the people of the ancient Kaspira or Kasmira, and the Daritæ as the Darad-desa (Dards) of the contiguous mountains. All Kashmir, even to the borders of Tibet (whence came the story of the gold-digging ants), was well enough known to the Persians and through them to Herodotus.

The twelfth satrapy comprised Balkh and Badakshan—what is now known as Afghan Turkistan. It was here that, generations before Alexander's campaign, those Greek settlements were founded by Darius and Xerxes which have left to this day living traces of their existence in the places originally allotted to them. In Afghan Turkistan also was founded the centre of Greek dominion in this part of Asia after the conquest of Persia, and it is impossible to avoid the conviction that there was a connection between these two events. The Greeks took the country from the Bakhi; but there are no people of this name left in these provinces now.

They may (as Bellew suggests) be recognized again in the Bakhtyari of Southern Persia, but it seems unlikely; and it is far more probable that they were obliterated by Alexander as his most active opponents after he passed Aria (Herat) and Drangia (Seistan).

The sixteenth satrapy was north of the Oxus, and included Sogdia and Aria (Herat). South of Aria was the fourteenth satrapy, represented by Seistan and Western Makran, with "the islands of the sea in which the King settles transported convicts"; and east of this again was the seventeenth satrapy covering Southern Baluchistan and Eastern Makran. It is only during the last twenty-five years that an accurate geographical knowledge of these uninviting regions has been attained. The gradual extension of the red line of the Indian border, with the necessity for preserving peace and security, has gradually enveloped Makran and Persian Baluchistan, the Gadrosia and Karmania of the Greeks, and has brought to light many strange secrets which have been dormant (for they were no secrets to the traveller of the Middle Ages) for a few centuries prior to the arrival of the British flag in Western India. It is an inhospitable country which is thus included. "Mostly desert," as one ancient writer says; marvellously furrowed and partitioned by bands of sun-scorched rocky hills, all narrow and sharp where they follow each other in parallel waves facing the Arabian Sea, or massed into enormous square-faced blocks of impassable mountain barrier whenever the uniform regularity of structure is lost. And yet it is a country full not only of interest historical and ethnographical, such as might be expected of the environment of a series of narrow passages leading to the western gates of India, but of incident also. There are amongst these strange knife-backed volcanic ridges and scarped clay hills valleys of great beauty, where the date-palms mass their feathery heads into a forest of green, and below them the fertile soil is moist and lush with cultured vegetation. But we have described elsewhere this strangely mixed land, and we have now only to deal with the aspect of it as known to the Greeks before the days of Alexander. That knowledge was ethnographical in its quality and exceedingly slight in quantity. Herodotus mentions the Sagartoi, Zarangai, Thamanai, Uxoi, and Mykoi. These are Seistan tribes. The Sagartoi were nomads of Seistan, mentioned both amongst tribes paying tribute and those who were exempt. The Zarangai were the inhabitants of Drangia (Seistan), where their ancient capital fills one of the most remarkable of all historic sites. The Zarangai are said to be recognizable in the Afghan Durani. No Afghan Durani would admit this. He claims a very different origin (as will be explained), and in the absence of authoritative history it is never wise to set aside the traditions of a people about themselves, especially of a people so advanced as the Duranis. More probable is it that the ancient geographical appellation Zarangai covers the historic Kaiani of Seistan supposed to be the same as the Kakaya of Sanscrit.

The Uxoi may be the modern Hots of Makran —a people who are traditionally reckoned amongst the most ancient of the mixed population which has drifted into the Makran ethnographic cul-de-sac, and who were certainly there in Alexander's time. In eastern Makran, Herodotus mentions only the Parikanoi and the Asiatic Ethiopian. Parikan is the Persian plural form of the Sanscrit Parva-ka, which means "mountaineer." This bears exactly the same meaning as the word Kohistani, or Barohi, and is not a tribal appellation at all, although the latter may possibly have developed into the Brahui, the well-known name of a very important Dravidian people of Southern Baluchistan (highlanders all of them) who are akin to the Dravidian races of Southern India. The Asiatic Ethiopian presents a more difficult problem. During the winter of 1905 careful inquiries were made in Makran for any evidence to support the suggestion that a tribe of Kushite origin still existed in that country. It is of interest in connection with the question whether the earliest immigrants into Mesopotamia (these people who, according to Accadian tradition, brought with them from the South the science of civilization) were a Semitic race or Kushites. It is impossible to ignore the existence of Kushite races in the east as well as the south. We have not only the authority of the earliest Greek writings, but Biblical records also are in support of the fact, and modern interest only centres in the question what has become of them. Bellew suggests that it was after the various Kush or Kach, or Kaj tribes that certain districts in Baluchistan are called Kach Gandava or Kach (Kaj) Makran, and that the chief of these tribes were the Gadara, after whom the country was called Gadrosia. This seems mere conjecture. At any rate the term Kach, sometimes Kachchi, sometimes Katz, is invariably applied to a flat open space, even if it is only the flat terrace above a river intervening between the river and a hill, and is purely geographical in its significance. But it was a matter of interest to discover whether the Gadurs of Las Bela could be the Gadrosii, or whether they exhibited any Ethiopian traits. The Gadurs, however, proved to be a section of the Rajput clan of Lumris, a proud race holding themselves aloof from other clans and never intermarrying with them. There could be no mistake about the Rajput origin of the red-skinned Gadur. He was a Kshatrya of the lunar race, but he might very possibly represent the ancient Gadrosii, even though he is no descendant of Kush. The other Rajput tribes with whom the Gadurs coalesce have apparently held their own in Las from a period quite remote, and must have been there when Alexander passed that way.

Asiatic negroes abound in Makran: some of them fresh importations from Africa, others bred in the slave villages of the Arabian Sea coast, as they have been for centuries. They are a fine, brawny, well-developed race of people, and some of the best of them are to be found as stokers in the P. & O. service; but they do not represent the Asiatic Ethiopian of Herodotus, who could hardly compile a gazetteer for the Greeks which should include all the ethnographical information known to the Persians, any more than our Intelligence Department could compile a complete gazetteer of the whole Russian Empire. To the maritime Greek nation the overwhelming preponderance of the huge Empire which overshadowed them must have created the same feeling of anxious suspicion that the unwieldy size of Russia presents to us, and it is not very likely that military intelligence of a really practical nature was offered gratis to the Greeks by the Persian geographers and military leaders. It is not surprising, therefore, that Herodotus did not know all that existed on the far Persian frontier. There are tribes and peoples about Southern Baluchistan who are as ancient as Herodotus but who are not mentioned. For instance, the ruling tribe in Makran until quite recently (when they were ousted by certain Sikh or Rajput interlopers called Gichki) were the Boledi, and their country was once certainly called Boledistan. The Boledi valley is one of the loveliest in a country which is apt to enhance the loveliness of its narrow bands of luxuriance by their rarety and their narrowness. It is a sweet oasis in the midst of a barren rocky sea, and must always have been an object of envy to dwellers outside, even in days when a fuller water-supply, more widely spread, turned many a valley green which is now deep drifted with sand. Ptolemy mentions the Boledis, so that they can well boast the traditional respectability of age-long ancestry. The Boledis are said to have dispossessed the Persian Kaiani Maliks, who ruled Makran in the seventeenth century, when they headed what is known as the Baluch Confederation. This may be veritable history, but their pride of race and origin, on whatever record it is based, has come to an end now; it has been left to the present generation to see the last of them. A few years ago there was living but one representative of the ruling family of the Boledis, an old lady named Miriam, who was exceedingly cunning in the art of embroidery, and made the most bewitching caps. She was, I believe, dependent on the bounty of the Sultan of Muscat, who possesses a small tract of territory on the Makran coast. Herodotus apparently knew nothing about the Boledis, nor can it be doubted that the Greek knowledge of Makran was exceedingly scanty.

Thus, whilst Alexander marched to the Indian frontier, well supplied with information as to the ways thither when once he could make Persia his base, he was almost totally ignorant of the one route out of India which he eventually followed, and which so nearly enveloped his whole force in disaster.

CHAPTER II

ASSYRIA AND AFGHANISTAN—ANCIENT LAND ROUTES —POSSIBLE SEA ROUTES

WITH the building up of the vast Persian Empire, and the gradual fostering of eastern colonies, and the consequent introduction of the manners and methods of Western Asia into the highlands of Samarkand and Badakshan, other nationalities were concerned besides Persians and Greeks. Captive peoples from Syria had been deported to Assyria seven centuries before Christ. The House of Israel had been broken up (for Samaria had fallen in 721 B.C. before the victorious hosts of Sargon), and some of the Israelitish families had been deported eastwards and northwards to Northern Mesopotamia and Armenia. With the vitality of their indestructible race it is at least possible that a remnant survived as serfs in Assyria, preserving their own customs and institutions—secretly if not openly—intermarrying, trading, and money-making, yet still looking for the final restoration of Israel until the final break-up of the Assyrian Kingdom.

They were never absolutely absorbed, and never forgot to recount their historic pedigree to their children.

With the final overthrow of the Assyrian Kingdom we lose sight of the tribes of Israel, who for more than a century had been mingled with the peoples of Northern Mesopotamia and Armenia. At least history holds no record of their further national existence. From time immemorial in Asia it had been customary for the captives taken in war to be transported bodily to another field for purposes of colonization and public labour. When the world was more scantily peopled such methods were natural and effectual; the increase of working power gained thereby being of the utmost importance in days when enormous irrigation canals were excavated, and bricks had to be fashioned for the construction of walled cities.

The extent and magnificence of Assyrian building must have demanded an immense supply of such manual labour for the purpose of brickmaking. All the mighty works of ancient Egypt, Assyria, and Babylon were literally "the work of men's hands." In Mesopotamia was captured labour especially necessary. Stone was indeed available at Nineveh, but the barrenness of the soil which stretches flatly from the rugged hills of Kurdistan across Mesopotamia rendered the country unproductive unless enormous works of irrigation were undertaken for the distribution of water. Mesopotamia is a country of immense possibilities, but the wealth of it is only for those who can distribute the waters of its great rivers over the productive soil. The yearly inundations of the Euphrates and Tigris are but sufficient for the needs of a narrow strip of land on either side the rivers, and the crops of the country undeveloped by canals can only support a scattered and scanty population. Towards the south there is another difficulty. The flat soil becomes water-logged and marshy and runs to waste for want of drainage. There is no stone for building purposes near Babylon. Approaching Babylon over the windy wastes of scrub-powdered plain there is nothing to be seen in the shape of a hill. Long, low, flat-topped mounds stretch athwart the horizon and resolve themselves on nearer approach into deeply scarred and weather-worn accretions of debris, or else they are banks of ancient water-ways winding through the steppe, the last remnants of a stupendous system of irrigation. Then there breaks into view the solitary erection which stands in the open plain overlooking a wide vista of marsh and swamp to the west, which represents the ruins called Birs Nimrud, the Ziggurat or temple which, in successive tiers devoted to the powers of heaven, supported the shrine of Mercury. It is by far the most conspicuous object in the Babylonian landscape; huge, dilapidated, and unshapely, it mounts guard over a silent, stagnant, swampy plain.

Now the remarkable feature in all these gigantic remains of antiquity is that they are built of brick. In the wide expanse of Mesopotamia plain around there is not a stone quarry to be found. Of Nineveh, we learn from the masterly records of Xenophon that as he was leading the surviving 10,000 Greeks in their retreat from the disastrous field of Babylon back to the sunny Hellespont, some 200 years after the destruction of Nineveh, he came upon a vast desert city on the Tigris. The wall of it was 25 feet wide, 100 feet high, with a 20-foot basement of stone. This was all that was left of Kalah, one of the Assyrian capitals. A day's march farther north he came on another deserted city with similar walls. These were the dry bones of Nineveh, already forgotten and forsaken. Two centuries had in these early ages been sufficient to blot out the memory of Assyrian greatness so completely that Xenophon knew not of it, nor recognized the place where his foot was treading. Barely seventy years ago was the memory of them restored to man, and tokens of the richness and magnificence of the art which embellished them first given to the world. The mounds representing Nineveh and Babylon are some of them of enormous size. The mound of Mugheir (the ancient Ur) is the ancient platform of an Assyrian palace, which is faced with a wall 10 feet thick of red kiln-dried bricks cemented with bitumen. Some of these platforms were raised from 50 to 60 feet above the plain and protected by massive stone masonry carried to a height exceeding that of the platform. But the Babylonian mound of Birs-Nimrud, which rises from the plain level to the blue glazed masonry of the upper tier of the Ziggurat, is altogether a brick construction. The debris of the many-coloured bricks now forms a smooth slope for many feet from its base; but above, where the square blocks of brickwork still hold together in scattered disarray, you may still dig out a foot-square brick with the title and designations of Nebuchadnezzar imprinted on its face. These artificial mounds could only have been built at an enormous cost of labour. The great mound of Koyunjik (the palace of Nineveh) covers an area of 100 acres and reaches up 95 feet at its highest point. It has been calculated that to heap up such a pile would "require the united efforts of 10,000 men for twelve years, or 20,000 men for six years" (Rawlinson, *Five Monarchies*), and then only the base of the palace is reached; and there are many such mounds, for "it seems to have been a point of honour with the Assyrian Kings that each should build a new palace for himself" (Ragozin, *Chaldaea*).

Only conquering monarchs with whole nations as prisoners could have compassed such results. This, indeed, was one of the great objectives of war in these early times. It was the amassing of a great population for manual labour and the creation of new centres of civilization and trade. Thus it was that the peoples of Western Asia—Egyptians, Israelites, Jews, Phœnicians, Assyrians, Babylonians, and even Greeks—were transported over vast distances by land, and a movement given to the human race in that part of the world which has infinitely complicated the science of ethnology. The peopling of Canada by the French, of North America by the English, of Brazil by the Portuguese, of Argentina and Chile by Spaniards and Italians, is perhaps a more comprehensive process in the distribution of humanity and more permanent in its character. But ancient compulsory movement, if not as extensive as modern voluntary emigration, was at least wholesale, and it led to the distribution of people in districts which would not naturally have invited them. The first process in the consolidation of a district, or satrapy, was the settlement of inhabitants, sometimes in supercession of a displaced or annihilated people, sometimes as an ethnic variety to the possessors of the soil. Tiglath Pileser was the first Assyrian monarch to consolidate the Empire by its division into satrapies. Henceforward the outlying provinces of the dominions were convenient dumping places for such bodies of captives as were not required for public works at home.

Nothing would be more natural than that Sargon should deport a portion of the Israelitish nation to colonize his eastern possessions towards India, just as

Darius Hystaspes later employed the same process to the same ends when he deported Greeks from the Lybian Barke to Baktria. There is nothing more astonishing in the fact that we should find a powerful people claiming descent from Israel in Northern Afghanistan than that we should find another people claiming a Greek origin in the Hindu Kush.

Nor was the importance of peopling waste lands and raising up new nations out of well-planted colonies overlooked ten centuries before Christ any more than it is now. Then it was a matter of transporting them overland and on foot to the farthest eastern limits of these great Asiatic empires. Always east or south they tramped, for nothing was known of the geography of the North and West. Eastwards lay the land of the sun, whence came the Indians who fought in the armies of Darius, and where gold and ivory, apes and peacocks were found to fill Phœnician ships. To-day it is different. The peopling of the world with whites is chiefly a Western process. Emigrants go out in ships, not as captives, but almost equally in compact bodies—the best of our working men to Canada, and many of the best of our much-wanted domestic servants to South Africa. It is a perpetual process in the world's economy, and perhaps the chief factor in the world's history; but in the old, old centuries before the Christian era it was necessarily a land process, and the geographical distribution of the land features determined the direction of the human tide. Some twenty years before the fall of Samaria and the deportation of the ten tribes of Israel, Tiglath Pileser had effected conquests in Asia which carried him so far east that he probably touched the Indus. Why he went no farther, or why Alexander subsequently left the greater part of the Indian peninsula unexplored, is fully explicable on natural grounds, even if other explanations were wanting.

The Indus valley would offer to the military explorers from the West the first taste of the quality of the climate of the India of the plains which they would encounter. The Indus valley in the hot weather would possess little climatic attraction for the Western highlander. Alexander's troops mutinied when they got far beyond the Indus. Any other troops would mutiny under such conditions as governed their outfit and their march. It is more than possible that the great Assyrian conqueror before him encountered much the same difficulty. It is clear, however, historically, that the Assyrian knew and trod the way to Northern Afghanistan (or Baktria), and if we examine the map of Asia with any care we shall see that there is no formidable barrier to the passing of large bodies of people from Nineveh to Herat (Aria), or from Herat to the Indus valley, until we reach the very gates of India on the north-west frontier. Four centuries later than Tiglath Pileser the battle of Arbela was fought to a finish between Alexander and Darius (who possessed both Greek and Indian troops in his army) on a field which is not so very far to the east of Nineveh, and which is probably represented more or less accurately by the modern Persian town of Erbil. The modern town may not be on the exact site of the action, and we know that the ancient town was some sixty miles away from the battlefield. However that may be, we learn that in the general retreat of the Persians which followed the battle, Darius made his way to Ecbatana, the ancient capital of the Medes. There he remained for about a year, but hearing of Alexander's advance from Persepolis in the spring of 330 B.C. he fled to the north-east, with a view to taking refuge with his kinsman Bessos, who was then satrap of Baktria. This gives us the clue to the general line of communication between Northern Mesopotamia and Baktria (or Afghanistan) in ancient days; and the twenty-five centuries which have rolled by since that early period have done little to modify that line.

Until the beginning of the nineteenth century A.D. from the earliest times with which we can come into contact through any human record, this high-road (not the only one, but the chief one) must have been trodden by the feet of thousands of weary pilgrims, captives, emigrants, merchants, or fighting men—an intermittent tide of humanity exceeding in volume any host known to modern days—bringing East into touch with the West to an extent which we can hardly appreciate. It may be said that the straightest road to Baktria did not lie through Ecbatana. It did not; but independently of the fact that Ecbatana was a city of great defensive capacity, and of reasons both political and military which would have impelled Darius to take that route, we shall find if we examine the latest Survey of India map of Western Persia that the geographical distribution of hill and valley make it the easiest, if not the shortest, route. The configuration of Western Persia, like that of Makran and Southern Baluchistan extending to our own north-west frontier, mainly consists of long lines of narrow ridges curving in lines parallel to the coast, rocky and mostly impassable to travellers crossing their difficult ridge and furrow formation transversely, but presenting curiously easy and open roads along the narrow lateral valleys. Ecbatana once stood where the modern Hamadan now stands. The road from Arbil (or Erbil) that carries most traffic follows this trough formation to Kermanshah and then bends north-eastward to Hamadan. From Hamadan to Rhagai and the Caspian gates, which was the route followed by Darius in his flight from Ecbatana, the road was clearly coincident with the present telegraph line to Tehran from Hamadan, which strikes into the great post route eastward to Mashad and Herat, one of the straightest and most uniformly level roads in all Asia. It must always have been so. Remarkable physical changes have occurred in Asia during these twenty-five centuries, but nothing to alter the relative disposition of mountain and plain in this part of Persia, or to change the general character of its ancient highway. All this part of Persia was under the dominion of the Assyrian king when the tribes of Israel left Syria for Armenia. He had but recently traversed the road to India, and he knew the richness of Baktria (of Afghan Turkistan and Badakshan) and could estimate what a colony might become in these eastern fields.

What more natural than that he should draft some of his captives eastward to the land of promise? There is not an important tribe of people in all that hinterland of India that has not been drafted in from somewhere. There is not a people left in India, for that matter, that can safely call themselves indigenous. From Persia and Media, from Aria and Skythia, from Greece and Arabia, from Syria and Mesopotamia they have come, and their coming can generally be traced historically, and their traditions of origin proved to be true. But there is one important people (of whom there is much more to be said) who call themselves Ben-i-Israel, who claim a descent from Kish, who have adopted a strange mixture of Mosaic law and Hindu ordinance in their moral code, who (some sections at least) keep a feast which strangely accords with the Passover, who hate the Yahudi (Jew) with a traditional hatred, and for whom no one has yet been able to suggest any other origin than the one they claim, and claim with determined force; and these people rule Afghanistan. It may be that they have justification for their traditions, even as others have; they may yet be proved to stand in the same relationship to the scattered remnants of Israel as some of the Kafir inhabitants of Northern Afghanistan can be shown to hold to the Greeks of pre-Alexandrian days. It is difficult to account for the name Afghan: it has been said that it is but the Armenian word Aghvan (Mountaineer). If this is so, it at once indicates a connection between the modern Afghan and the Syrian captives of Armenia.

But whilst "men in nations" were thus traversing the highlands of Persia from Mesopotamia to Northern Afghanistan by highways so ancient that they may be regarded almost as geographical fixtures as everlasting as the hills, we do not find much evidence of traffic with the Central Asian States north of the Oxus.

Early military excursions into the land of the Skyths were more for the purpose of dealing with the predatory habits of these warlike tribes, who afterwards peopled half of Europe as well as India, than of promoting either trade or geographical inquiry; and it was the route which led to Northern Afghanistan and Baktria through

Northern Persia which was most attractive from its general accessibility and promise of profit. It was this way that Northern Kashmir and the gold-fields of Tibet were touched. The Indian gold which formed so large a part of the Persian revenues in the time of Darius undoubtedly came from Northern India and Tibet. Old as are the workings of the Wynaad gold-fields in the west, and Kolar in the east, of the peninsula, it is unlikely that either of these sources was known to Persia.

The more direct routes to India from Ecbatana, passing through Central Persia *via* Kashan, Yezd, and Kirman, terminated on the Helmund or in Makran, and there is no evidence that the mountain system which faces the Indus was ever crossed by invading Persian hosts. There was, indeed, a tradition in Alexander's time that an attempt had been made to traverse Makran and that it had failed. This, says Arrian, was one of the reasons why Alexander obstinately chose that route on his retirement from India. In spite, however, of the geographical difficulties which render it improbable that the hosts of Tiglath Pileser (who could have dealt with the Skythians of the north readily enough) ever broke across the north-western gateways of India's mountain borderland, there was undoubtedly a close connection between Assyria and India of which the evidence is still with us.

Throughout the golden age of the Second Empire

of Assyria, after the subjugation of Babylon and the consolidation of the Empire by Tiglath Pileser, during the reigns of Sargon and Senacherib (who fought the first Assyrian naval fight), Esar Haddon (who destroyed Sidon and removed the inhabitants) and Assur-bani-pal (Sardanapalus), to the final overthrow of Assyria by Babylon in 625 B.C., when the star of Nebuchadnezzar arose on the southern horizon, Assyria held the supreme command of Eastern commerce, and Nineveh dictated the cannons of art to the world. No event more profoundly affected the commerce of Asia than the destruction of Sidon and the bodily transfer of its commercial inhabitants to Assyria. This was the age of Assyrian art, of literature, and of architecture; Assyrian culture realized its culminating point in the reign of Assur-bani-pal, when the library at Nineveh far surpassed any library that the world had ever seen. It was then that intercourse between Assyria and India became unbroken and intimate. Then public works of the largest dimensions were undertaken, and colonies formed for the purpose of developing the riches of the newly acquired lands in the East. Assyrian art found its way to India, and the affinity between Assyrian and Indian art is directly traceable still in spite of the impress subsequently effected by Greece and Rome.

The carpets that are spread on the floors of every Anglo-Indian home and which, as Turkish,

Persian, Central Asian, or Indian, are to be found in every carpet shop in London, usually possess in the intricacies of their pattern some trace of ancient Assyrian art. As Sir George Birdwood has long ago pointed out, general similarities between Assyrian and Indian design in carpet patterns may possibly be due to a common Turanian origin, pre-Semitic and pre-Aryan; but there are details of architectural plan in the Southern Indian temples which, quite as much as the reproduction of the ancient Assyrian "knop and flower" in its infinite variety of form (all expressing more or less conventionally the cone and the lotus of the original idea), testify to an infinitely old art affinity, and at the same time witness to the wonderful vitality of intelligent design.

The tree of life so largely interwoven into Eastern fabrics was the "Asherah" or "grove" sacred to Asshur the supreme god of the Assyrians, the Lord and Giver of life; and it appears to have been the development of the "Hom" or lotus, which, although it is a Kashmir valley plant, is always admirably rendered in Assyrian sculpture. Eventually the date palm took the place of the Hom in the Euphrates valley, just as the vine replaced it in Asia Minor and Greece. In Central Asian rugs we find the cone replaced by the pomegranate, and the tree of life becomes a pomegranate tree. There is too much intricacy in such similarity of ornamental detail between Assyrian and Indian art for the result to have been merely developments from a common pre-historic stock along separate lines. They are clearly imitations one of the other, and the similarity is but another link in the chain of evidence which proves that the highways of Asia connecting Assyria with India through Persia were well-trodden ways seven centuries at least before Christ, even if the sea route from the Red Sea and Euphrates had not then reached the Indus and western coast of India.

Whilst all historical evidence points to the Tehran-Mashad route as the great highway which linked Mesopotamia with Baktria in past ages, there are certain curious little indications that the southern road through Persia, viz. Yezd and Kirman, was also well known, for it is a remarkable fact (which may be taken for what it is worth) that it is in the villages and bazaars of Sind that the potters may be found whose conservative souls delight in the reproduction of a class of ornamental decoration which most clearly indicates an Assyrian origin. The direct route to Sind from Mesopotamia is not by way of Herat. It is (as will be subsequently explained) *via* Kirman and Makran, but there is absolutely no historical evidence to support the suggestion that this was a route utilized by the Assyrians; and there is, on the other hand, Arrian's statement that roads through Makran were unknown or but legendary.

It is impossible, however, to ignore the fact that

the sea route to North-western India was utilized in very ancient times; and although its connection with the northern landward gates of India may appear to be rather obscure, that connection is a matter which actually concerns us rather nearly in the present day. For it is by this ancient sea route that Persia and Baluchistan, Seistan and Afghanistan derive those supplies of small arms and ammunition which are abundant in those countries, but which never pass through India. Muskat is the chief depot for distribution, and the Persian ports of Bandar Abbas, Jask, or Pasni on the Makran coast are utilized as ports for the interior, leading by routes which are quite sufficiently good for caravan traffic towards the point where Afghan territory meets that of Persia and Baluchistan just south of Seistan. Once in Seistan they are well behind the passes which split our nearer line of defence in the trans-Indus hills. Even our command of the sea fails to suppress this traffic, which has led to such a general distribution of arms of precision (chiefly of German manufacture), that these countries may fairly claim to be able to arm their whole population. No recent researches in the Persian Gulf or on the Persian coast have added much to the sum of our knowledge respecting the early navigation of these Eastern seas, but there can be no question as to its immense antiquity. The Phœnician settler in Syria and Mesopotamia has been traced back to his primeval home in the Bahrein Islands, which, if Herodotus is correct in his estimated date for the founding of Tyre (2756 years B.C.), takes us back to very early times indeed for the coast navigation of the Persian Gulf and the Indian Seas. Hiram, King of Tyre, could look back through long ages to the days when his Phœnician forefathers started their well-packed vessels (the Phœnicians were famous for their skill in stowing cargo) to crawl along the coasts of Makran and Western India for the purpose of acquiring those stores of spices and gold which first made commerce profitable, or else to make their way westward, guided by the headlands and shore outlines of Southern Arabia, to gather the riches from African fields. Makran is full of strange relics of immense age for which none can account. Since Egyptology has become a recognized science, who will lay the foundations of such a science for Southern Arabia and Makran? When will some one arise with the wisdom and the leisure to write of the power of ancient Arabia, and to trace the impressions left on the whole world of commerce, of art, of architecture, and literature by the ancient races who hailed from the South?

We cannot tell when the first sea-borne trade passed to and fro between India and the Erythrean Sea, a creeping, slow-moving trade making the best shift possible of wind and tide, and knowing no guide but the pole star of that period, and the rocky headlands and islands of the Makran coast. Many of the ancient islands exist no more, but the coast is a peculiarly well-marked one for the mariner still. Probably the coast trade was earlier than the overland caravan traffic; but the latter was certainly co-existent with the Assyrian monarchy when Persia and Central Asia lay at the feet of the conqueror Tiglath Pileser.

CHAPTER III

GREEK EXPLORATION—ALEXANDER—MODERN BALKH—THE BALKH PLAIN AND BAKTRIA

TWENTY-TWO centuries have rolled away since the first military expedition from Europe was organized and led into the wilds of an Asia which was probably as civilized then as it is now. Two thousand two hundred years, and yet along the wild stretches of the Indian frontier, where a mound here and there testifies to the former existence of some forgotten camp, or where in the slant rays of the evening sun faint indications may be traced on the level Punjab flats of the foundation of a city long since dead, the name of the great Macedonian is uttered with reverence and awe as might be the name of a god who can still influence the lives of men, yet qualified by an affix which indicates a curious survival of the mythological conception of gods as human beings. You may wander through some of the valleys cleft through the western frontier hills, where an intermittent rivulet of water spreads a network of streamlets on the boulder-covered bed of the nullah, and where the stony hills rise in barren slopes on either side, and find, perchance half hidden by weather-worn debris and tufts of stringy verdure, the remains of what was once an artificial water-channel, stone built and admirably graded, and you may ask who was responsible for this construction. Not a man can say. There is no history, no tradition even, connected with it. It passes their understanding. Doubtless it was the work of "Sekunder" (Alexander)—that prehistoric, mythological, incomprehensible, and yet beneficent being who lives in the minds of the frontier people as the apotheosis of the Deputy Commissioner. Yet the impression left on India by the Greeks is marvellously small. It is chiefly to be found in the architecture and the sculpture of the Punjab. The Greek language disappeared from the Indus valley about the end of the tenth century A.D., and there is hardly a Greek place-name now to be recognized anywhere on the Indus banks. But any unusual relic of the past, the story of which has passed beyond the memory of the present tribes-people (even though it may be obviously of mediæval Arabic origin), is invariably attributed to Alexander. It is, however, chiefly in the sculpture and decorations of Buddhist buildings (which never existed in Alexander's day) that clear evidence exists of Greek art conception. The classical features and folded raiment of the sculptured saints and buddhas, which are found so freely in certain parts of the Punjab, are obviously derived from original Greek ideals which may very possibly have been transmitted through Rome.

With Alexander in India we have nothing to do in these pages. It is as the first explorer in the regions beyond India, the Afghan and Baluchistan hinterlands, that he at present concerns us; and it may fairly be stated that no later expedition combining scientific research with military conquest ever added more to the sum of the world's knowledge of those regions than that led by Alexander. For centuries after it no light arises on the geographical horizon of the Indian border. Indeed, not until political exigencies caused by Russia's steady advance towards India compelled a revision of political boundaries in Persia, Baluchistan, Afghanistan, and India, was any very accurate idea obtained of the geographical conditions of Northern and Western Afghanistan, or of Baluchistan, or of Southern Persia. The mapping of these countries has been recent, and the progress of it, as year by year the network of Indian triangulation and topography spread westward and northward, has reopened many sources of light which, if not altogether new, have lain hidden ever since the Macedonian conqueror passed over them. Long before the Greek army mustered on the banks of the Hellespont we have seen that the highways to the East were well trodden and well known. It was not likely that Alexander's intelligence department was lacking in information. For many centuries subsequent to that expedition the rise of the Parthian power absolutely cut off these old-world trade communications and set the restless tides of human emigration into new channels. But in Alexander's time there was nothing in Persia to interrupt the interchange of courtesies between East and West.

The great Aryan tide had already flowed from the Central Asian highlands into India, but Jutes and Skyths had yet to make that great drift westward which peopled half of Europe with nomadic tribes speaking kindred tongues—a drift which never rested in its westward advance till, as Anglians and Saxons, it had enveloped England and faced its final destiny in an American continent. Assyria had passed by with arts and commerce rather than with arms, and Persia had followed in Assyrian tracks. Both had established colonies half-way to India in the Afghan highlands, Persia with the aid of captive Greeks, and Assyria with people taken from the Syrian land. The list of Assyrian and Persian satrapies included all those lands which we now call the hinterland of India, and which in Alexander's time must have been absolutely Persianized. But beyond the historical evidence which can be collected to prove the early, the constant, traffic which ensued between Mesopotamia, or Asia Minor, and India, after the consolidation of those two great empires, there is the tradition which certain Greek writers (notably Arrian) treat rather scornfully, of the conquest of Upper India by the mythical hero Bacchus. It is never wise to treat any tradition scornfully, and Arrian is himself obliged to admit the difficulty of explaining certain records connected with Alexander's history, without assuming that the tradition was not groundless.

Writing of the city of Nysa, Arrian says that "it was built by Dionysos or Bacchus, when he conquered the Indians; but who this Bacchus was, or at what time or from whence he conquered the Indians is hard to determine, whether he was that Theban who from Thebes, or he who from Timolus, a mountain of Lydia, undertook that famous expedition into India is very uncertain." There is a Greek epic poem in hexameter verse, called the "Dionysiaka," or "Bassarika," which tells of the conquest of India by Bacchus, the greatest of all his achievements. The author is Nonnus of Panoplis in Egypt, who wrote about the beginning of the fifth century of our era. Bacchus is said to have received a command from Zeus to turn back the Indians, who had extended their conquests to the Mediterranean, and in the execution of this command he marched through Syria and Assyria. In Assyria he was entertained with magnificent hospitality. Nothing further is said of the route he took to reach India. The first battle which took place in India was on the banks of the Hydaspes, where the Indians were routed. Then followed as an incident in the war the destruction of the Indian fleet in a naval battle, which is instructive. It took the assistance of the goddess of war, Pallas Athene, to bring the campaign to a conclusion, which terminated with the death of the Indian leader Deriades. Here, then, is crystallized in verse the tradition to which Arrian refers, and remembering that we are indebted to two great epics of India, the "Ramayana" and the "Mahabharata," for such glimmering of the ancient history of the Aryan occupation of India as we possess, we may very well conceive that the germs of real historical fact lie half-concealed in this poem of Nonnus. However that may be, it is tolerably certain that Alexander found a people in Northern India who claimed a Greek origin when he arrived there, quite apart from the colonists of Baktria who had been transported there by Darius Hydaspes, and that he recognized their claim to distant relationship.

When Alexander, then, mustered his army in the sunny fields of Macedon he was preparing for an expedition over no uncertain ways between Greece and Baktria or Arachosia (Northern and Western Afghanistan). He knew what lay before him if he could once break through the Persian barrier; and the strength of that barrier he must have been well aware lay as much in the stern fighting qualities of the mercenary Greek legions in the pay of Persia as in the hosts of Persian and Indian troops which the Persian monarch could array against him. We have lists of the component forces on both sides. The Macedonian legions were homogeneous and patriotic. The Persian army was partly European, but chiefly Asiatic, with a mixed company of Asiatic troops such as has probably never taken the field since. The opposing forces, indeed, partook of the nature of the two armies which fought out the issue of the Russo-Japanese campaign, and the result was much the same. There was no tie of national sentiment to bind together the unwieldy cohorts of Persia. They fought for their pay, and they fought well; but when big battalions are divided in religious sentiment and unswayed by patriotism, they are no match for Macedonian cohesion, Mahomedan Jehad, or Japanese Bushido.

It is quite interesting to examine the details of Alexander's army. The main body consisted of six brigades of 3000 men, each united to form an irresistible phalanx. Heavily armoured, with a long shield, a long sword, and a four-and-twenty foot spear (sarina), the infantryman of the phalanx must have possessed a powerful physique to enable him to carry himself and his weapons in the field. The depth of the phalanx was sixteen ranks, and the first six ranks were so placed that they could all bring their spears into action at once. The bulk of the phalanx consisted of Macedonians only. The light infantry, bowmen, and dartsmen numbered about 6000. A third corps of 6000 men more lightly armed, but with longer swords than the phalangists (called Hypaspists), were intermediate. The cavalry consisted of three classes, light, heavy, and medium, 3000 Macedonian and Thessalian horsemen, heavily armoured, forming its main strength. The light cavalry were Thracian lancers. The Royal Horse Guard included eight Macedonian squadrons of horsemen picked from the best families in Greece. It is useful to note that there were mounted infantry and artillery (*i.e.* balistai and katapeltai) with the force. More useful still to note that none of Alexander's victories were won by the solid strength of his phalanx; it was the sweeping and resistless force of his cavalry charges (often led by himself) that gained them.

Perhaps the most notable feature about this Greek expedition to India was the fact that it was the first military expedition of which there is any record which included scientific inquiry as one of its objects. Alexander had on his personal staff men of literary if not of scientific acquirements, and it is to them doubtless that we owe a comparatively clear account of the expedition, although unfortunately their records have only been transmitted to us by later authors. If we could but recover originals what a host of doubtful points might be cleared up! It is true that previous to the date of Alexander one man of genius, Xenophon, had kept a record of a magnificent military achievement, and had proved himself to be master of literature as he was of the science of leading; but Xenophon stands alone, and it may be doubted whether, during the many centuries which have passed away since the era of Greek supremacy, any practical leader of men has ever attained such a splendid position in the ranks of writers of military history. Alexander appears, at any rate, to have been no historian, but his staff of cultivated literary assistants and men of letters included many notable Greek names.

Alexander crossed the Hellespont in the spring of the year 334 B.C., and first encountered the Persians near the Granikos River. The battle was decisive although the losses on either side do not appear to have been heavy. It was but the augury of what was to follow. The subsequent advance of the Macedonian troops southward through the lovely land of Iona, and the reduction of Miletus and Helikarnassos, brought the first year's campaign to a close. The second year opened with the conquest of Pamphyllia and Phrygia, the passage of the Tauros ranges being made in winter. On the return of spring he recrossed the Tauros and reduced the western hill-tribes of Kilikia. Part of his force, meanwhile, had occupied the passes into Syria known as the Syrian gates. Within two days march of the Syrian gates the Persian hosts again were massed in an open plain under Darius, who had advanced from the east, waiting to fall upon the Macedonian troops and crush them as they debouched from the defile. Tired of waiting, however, Darius moved forward into Kilikia by the Amanian passes to look for Alexander, and thus it happened that when Alexander finally emerged from the Syrian gates into the plains of Syria he found his enemy behind him. He partially retraced his steps and regained the pass by midnight, and there from one of the adjoining summits he "beheld the Persian watch-fires gleaming far and wide over the plain of Issos." The rapidity of Alexander's movements was only equalled by the fierce energy of his onslaught when he led his cavalry against the unwieldy formations of his Persian enemy. It was his own hand that gained the victory both then and afterwards.

There is no more stirring story in all history than this progress of the Macedonian force. Step by step it has been traced out from Granikos to Issos and from Issos to Arbela; but this is not the place to recapitulate that part of the story which applies only to Western Asia. It is not until after the final decisive battle at Arbela, when Darius fled in hot haste along the south-eastern road to Ecbatana, the former capital of Media, and thence in the spring of 330 B.C. retreated with a disorganized force and an intriguing court towards Baktria, where he hoped to find a refuge with his kinsman Bessos the satrap of that province, that we really touch on the subject with which we wish to deal in this book, viz. the high-roads to Afghanistan in those long past days. Alexander, meanwhile, had received the submission of Babylon and restored the temple of Belus, and made himself master of a more spacious empire than the world had yet seen. It was then that the amazing results of his military success began to turn his head. From this point the severe simplicity of the Macedonian soldier is exchanged for the luxury, arrogance, and intolerance of the despot and conqueror. As Alexander advanced in material strength so did he slide down the easy descent of moral retrogression, and whilst we can still admire his magnificence as a military leader we find little else left to admire about him. From Babylon to the lovely valley wherein lies Susa, and from Susa to Persepolis, was more or less of a triumphal march in spite of the fierce opposition of the satrap Artobaizanes. Of Persepolis we are taught to believe that Alexander left nothing behind him but blackened ruins—the result of a drunken orgy. During the winter, amidst snow and ice, he subdued the Mardians in their mountain fastnesses (for he never left an active foe on the flank or rear), and with the return of the sweet Persian spring he renewed his hunt after Darius, turning his face to the north and east.

There are two high-roads through Persia to the East—one leading to Northern Afghanistan and the Oxus regions over Mashad, the other to Kirman, Seistan, and Kandahar. Along both of them there now runs a telegraph line connecting with the Russian system *via* Mashad, and the Indian system *via* Kirman. They must always have been high-roads—the great trade routes to Central Asia and India. Where the orderly line of telegraph poles now stretches in unending regularity to mark the dusty highway, there, through more ages than we can count, the padded foot of the camel must have worn the road into ridges and ruts as he plodded his weary way with loads of merchandise and fodder. No geological evolution can have disturbed those tracks since the Assyrian kings first drew riches from the East and started colonies on the Baktrian highlands; they are now as they were 1000 years before Christ, and it is only natural that in the ordinary course of the same unresting spirit of enterprise the telegraph posts will sooner or later cast long shadows over a passing railway. The desert regions of Persia separate these two roads: the wide flat spaces of sand or "Kavir"; an unending procession of sand-hills on the glittering fields of salt-bound swamp. The desert is crossable—it has been fairly well exploited—but nothing so far has been found in it to justify the expectation of great discoveries of dead and buried cities, or traces of a former civilization such as once occupied the deserts of Chinese Turkistan.

We may well believe that the central deserts of Persia were the same in Alexander's time as they are in ours. Consequently any large company of people would have been more or less forced into one or other of the well-known routes which the geographical configuration of the country presented to them. In his pursuit of Darius Alexander followed the northern route to Baktria which strikes a little north of east from Ecbatana (Hamadan), and in these days leads direct to Tehran the modern capital of Persia. The tragical fate of Darius, and Alexander's crocodile grief thereat, belongs to another story. It is only when he touches the regions beyond Mashad that he figures as one of the earliest explorers of Afghanistan, and certainly the earliest of whom we have any certain record. Unfortunately these records say very little of the nature of those cities and centres of human life which he found on the Afghan border; nor is there any definite allusion to be found in the writings of Alexander's historians to the colonial occupation of Afghanistan which must have preceded the Persian conquests. We have seen that Assyrian influence was strongly and continuously felt in India for many centuries after the consolidation of the Second Assyrian Empire, and the probability that between the Tigris and the Oxus there must have been intercommunication from the earliest days of the rise of Assyrian power.

There is one ragged and time-worn city in Afghan Turkistan which certainly belongs to the centuries preceding the era of Alexander—it was the capital of Baktria, the city of Bessos, and it has been a great centre of commerce, a city of pilgrimage, Buddhist and Mahomedan, for many a century since. This is Balkh, traditionally known as the "Mother of cities," whose foundation is variously ascribed to Nimrud, or to "Karomurs the Persian Romulus," Assyrian or Persian as the fancy strikes the narrator. Of its extreme antiquity there can be no doubt. It is certain that at a very early date it was the rival of Ecbatana, of Nineveh, and of Babylon. Bricks with inscriptions are said to have been found there some seventy years ago, and similar bricks should certainly be there still. Officers of the Russo-Afghan Boundary Commission passed through modern Balkh in 1884, but no such bricks were found during the very cursory and entirely superficial examination which was all that could be made of the place; square bricks, without inscription, of the size and quality of those which may any day be dug out of the Birs Nimrud at Babylon were certainly found, and point to a similarity of construction in a part of the ancient walls, which is surely not accidental. Modern Balkh consists of about 500 houses of Afghan settlers, a colony of Jews, and a small bazaar set in the midst of a waste of ruins and many acres of debris. The walls of the city are 6½ or 7 miles in perimeter; in some places they are supported by a rampart like the walls of Herat. These, of course, are modern, as is the fort and citadel, or Bala Hissar, which stands on a mound to the north-east. The green cupola of the Masjid Sabz and the arched entrance to the ruined Madrasa testify to modern Mahomedan occupation, as do the Top-i-Rustam and the Takht-i-Rustam (two ancient topes) to the fervour of religious zeal with which its Buddhist inhabitants invested it in the early centuries of our era. Balkh awaits its Layard, and not only Balkh, for there are mounds and ruins innumerable scattered through the breadth of the Balkh plain.

As one approaches Balkh by the Akcha road from the west, one looks anxiously around for some outward signs of its extreme antiquity. They are not altogether wanting, but time and the mellowing hand of Nature have rounded off the edges of the mounds of debris which lie scattered over miles of the surrounding country, brushing them over with the fresh green of vegetation, and leaving no sign by which to judge of the age of them. It is difficult in this part of Asia to get back farther than the age of the great destroyer Chenghiz Khan. His time has passed by long enough to leave but little evidence that the hand of the destroyer was his hand; but probably nothing visible on the surface dates back further than the six centuries which have come and gone since his Mongol hordes were set loose. Beyond these surface ruins and below them there must be cities arranged, as it were, in underground flats, one piled on another, strata below strata, till we reach the debris of the pre-Semitic days of Western and Central Asia, when the Turanian races who supplied Arcadian civilization to Mesopotamia peopled the land. Just as we cannot tell exactly when Babylon first became a city, so are we confounded by the age of Balkh. Babylon belongs to the time when myths were grouped around the adventures of a solar hero. Ultimately, however, the Ca-dimissa of the Accad became the Bab-ili (the "gate of God") of the Semite. It was always the "gate of God," but whether the presiding deity was always the Accadian Merodach seems doubtful. Fourteen or fifteen centuries before Christ there was probably a Balkh as there was a Babylon; and from time immemorial and a date unreckoned Balkh and Babylon must have been the two great commercial centres of Asia. What a history to dig out when its time shall come!

As the Akcha road leads into the city it passes the outer wall, which is about 30 feet high, by a gateway which is frankly nothing more than a gap in the partially destroyed wall. It then skirts along, past a ziarat gay with red flags, to a gateway in the second wall under the citadel leading to an avenue of poplars ending with a garden. Here is a pretentious and fairly comfortable caravanserai, facing a court which is shaded by magnificent plane trees. At first sight Balkh appears to consist of nothing but ruins, but ascending the mound, which is surrounded by the dilapidated fort walls, one can see from this vantage of about 70 feet how many new buildings are grouped round the remnants of the old Mahomedan mosque, of which the dome and one great gateway are all that is left.

The plain of the ancient Baktria, of which Balkh represents the capital, lies south of the Oxus River, extending east and west for some 200 miles parallel to the river after its debouchment from the mountains of Badakshan. It is flat, with a scattering of prominences and mounds at intervals denoting the site of some village or fortress of sufficient antiquity to account for its gradual rise on the accumulations of its own debris, probably assisted in the first instance by some topographical feature. Looking south it appears to be flanked by a flat blue wall of hills, presenting no opportunity for escalade or passage through them, a blue level line of counterscarp, which is locally known as the Elburz. This great flanking wall is in reality very nearly what it appears to be—an unassailable rampart; but there are narrow ways intersecting it not easily discernible, and through these ways the rivers of the highlands make a rough passage to the plains. Wherever they tumble through the mountain gateways and make placid tracks in the flats below, they are utilized for irrigation purposes, and so there exists a narrow fringe of cultivation under the hills, which extends here and there along the banks of the rivers out into the open Balkh plain. But these rivers never reach the Oxus. This is not merely because the waters of them are absorbed in irrigation, but because there is a well-ascertained tectonic action at work which is slowly raising the level of the plain. Thus it happens that whilst big affluents from the north bring rushing streams of much silt-stained water to the great river, no such affluents exist on the south. The waters of the Elburz streams are all lost in the Oxus plain ere they reach the river. Nevertheless there are abundant evidences of the former existence of a vast irrigation system drawn from the Oxus. The same lines of level mounds which break the horizon of the plains of Babylon are to be seen here, and they denote the same thing. They are the containing walls of canals which carried the Oxus waters through hundreds of square miles of flat plain, where they never can be carried again because of the alteration in the respective levels of plain and river. Ten centuries before Christ, at least, were the plains of Babylon thus irrigated, and just as the arts of Greece and India rose on the ashes of the arts of Nineveh, so doubtless was the science of irrigation carried into the colonial field of Baktria from Assyria, and thus was the city of "Nimrud" surrounded with a wealth of cultivation which rendered it famous through Asia for more centuries than we can tell. Whether or no the science of irrigation drifted eastwards from the west it seems more than probable that the ruined and decayed water-ways which intersect the Balkh plain were primarily due to the introduction of Syrian labour, and account for the presence in that historic region of a people amongst others who claim descent from captive Israelites. There are no practical irrigation engineers in the world (excepting perhaps the Chinese) who can rival the Afghans in their knowledge of how to make water flow where water never flowed before. It is of course impossible, on such evidence as we possess as yet, to claim more than the appearance of a probability based on such an undeniable possibility as this.

After the death of Darius his kinsman Bessos escaped into his own satrapy (probably to Balkh), and there assumed the upright tiara, the emblem of Persian royalty, taking at the same time the name of Artaxerxes.

True to his invariable principle of leaving no unbeaten enemy on the flank of his advance, Alexander proceeded to subjugate Hyrkania, from which country he was separated by the Elburz (Persian) mountains. He crossed those mountains in three divisions by separate passes, and effected his purpose with his usual thoroughness and without much difficulty. Having crushed the Mardians he shaped a straight course eastward to Herat on his way to Baktria, marching by the great highway which connects Tehran with Mashad. The country around Mashad (part of Khorasan) was a satrapy of Persia under Satibarzanes, who submitted without apparent opposition and was confirmed in his government. The capital of this province was Artakoana, described as a city situated in a plain of exceptional fertility where the main roads from north to south and from west to east crossed each other. To no place does such a description apply so closely as Herat, and it has consequently been assumed that Herat indicates more or less closely the site of the ancient city Artakoana, which, indeed, is most probable. But Alexander had not long passed that city in his march towards Baktria when the news of the revolt of Satibarzanes reached him with the story of the loss of the Macedonian escort which had been left with that satrap and had been massacred to a man. He immediately turned on his tracks, captured Artakoana, routed the satrap, and by way of leaving a permanent monument of his victory founded a new city in the neighbourhood which he called Alexandreia. This is probably the actual origin of the modern Herat, and it is a tribute to the sagacity of the Macedonian King that from that time to this it has abundantly proved its importance as a strategical and commercial centre.

The forward march to Baktria would have

taken the Greek army *via* Kushk, Maruchak, and Maimana along the route which is practically the easiest and safest for a large body of troops. It is the route followed by the Afghan Boundary Commission in 1885. Alexander, however, instead of resuming his march on Baktria, elected to crush another of the Persian satraps who was concerned in the murder of Darius and who ruled a province to the south of Herat. Crossing the Hari Rud he therefore marched straight on Farah (Prophthasia), then the capital of Seistan (Drangiana). Farah is considerably to the north of any part of the Afghan province of Seistan at present, but it was undoubtedly Alexander's objective, and the Drangiana of those times was considerably more extensive than the Seistan of to-day—a fact which will go some way to account for the exaggerated reports of the ancient wealth and fertility of that province. Farah is a great agricultural centre still, and would add enormously to the restricted cultivable area of Seistan, even if one allows for the effects of sand encroachment in that unpleasant region. Then occurred the plot against Alexander's life which was detected at Prophthasia, and the consequent torture and death of Philotas, who probably had no part in it. It is one of the many actions of Alexander's life which reveals the ferocity of the barbarian beneath the genius of the soldier. It was but the barbarity of his age—a barbarity for the matter of that which lasted in England till the time of the Georges, and which still survives in Afghanistan. After a halt in Seistan, probably whilst waiting for reinforcements, he struck north-eastwards again for Baktria. As it is generally assumed that the Macedonian force now followed the Helmund valley route to the Paropamisos, *i.e.* the Hindu Kush and its extension westwards, it is as well to consider what sort of a country it is that forms the basin of Helmund.

It is worth remarking in the first place that the Ariaspian inhabitants of the Helmund valley had received from Cyrus the name of Euergetai, or benefactors, because they had assisted him at a time when he had been in great difficulties. This is enough to satisfy us that the district was known and had been traversed by a military force long before Alexander entered it, and that he was making no venturesome advance in ignorance of what lay before him. The valley of the Helmund (or Etymander) could not have differed greatly in its geographical features 300 years before Christ from its present characteristics. The Helmund of the Seistan basin then occupied a different channel to its present outlets into the Seistan swamps. How different it is difficult to tell, for it has frequently changed its course within historic times, silting up its bed and striking out a new channel for itself, splitting into a number of streams and wandering uncontrolled in loops or curves over the face of the flat alluvial plains to which it brought fertility and wealth. It has been a perpetual source of political discussion as a boundary between Afghanistan and Persia, and it has altered the face of the land so extensively and so often that there is nothing in ancient history referring to the vast extent of agricultural wealth and the immensity of its population which can be proved to be impossible, although it seems likely enough that false inferences have been drawn from the widespread area of ruined and deserted towns and villages which are still to be seen and may almost be counted. It is not only that the water-supply and facilities for irrigation, by shifting their geographical position, have carried with them the potentialities for cultivation. Other forces of Nature which seem to be set loose on Seistan with peculiar virulence and activity have also been at work. The sweeping blasts of the north-west wind, which rage through this part of Asia with a strength and persistence unknown in regions more protected by topographical features, carrying with them vast volumes of sand and surface detritus, piling up smooth slopes to the windward side of every obstruction, smoothing off the rough angles of the gaunt bones of departed buildings, and sometimes positively wearing them away by the force of attrition, play an important part in the kaleidoscopic changes of Seistan landscape. Villages that are flourishing one year may be sand-buried the next. Channels that now run free with crop-raising water may be choked in a month, and all the while the great Helmund, curving northward in its course, pours down its steady volume of silt from the highlands, carrying tons of detritus into open plains where it is spread out, sun-baked, dried, wind-blown, and swirled back again to the southward in everlasting movement. Thus it is that the evidence of hundreds of square miles of ruins is no direct evidence of an immense population at any one period. Nor can we say of this great alluvial basin, which is by turns a smiling oasis, a pestilential swamp, a huge spread of populous villages, or a howling desert smitten with a wind which becomes a curse and afflicted with many of the pests and plagues of ancient Egypt, that at any one period of its history more than another it deserved the appellation of the "granary of Asia." The Helmund of Seistan, however, is quite a different Helmund from the same river nearer its source. Its character changes from the point where it makes its great bend northward towards its final exit into the lagoons and swamps of the Hamún. At Chaharburjak, where the high-road to Seistan from the south crosses the river into Afghan territory, the Helmund is a wide rippling stream (when not in flood), distinguished, if anything, for the clearness of its waters. From this point eastwards it parts two deserts. To the north the great, flat, windswept Dasht-i-Margo, about as desolate and arid a region as fancy could depict. To the south the desert of Baluchistan, by no means so absolutely devoid of interest, with its marshalled sand-dunes answering to the processes of the winds, its isolated but picturesque peaks like islands in a sand sea, a few green spots here and there showing where water oozes out from the buried feet of the rocky hills, decorated with bunches of flowering tamarisk and perchance a palm or two—a modified desert, but still a desert. Between the two deserts is the Helmund, running in a cliff-sided trough which is never more than a mile or two wide, intensely green and bright in the grass and crop season, with flourishing villages at reasonable intervals and a high-road connecting them from which can be counted that strange multitude of departed cities of the old Kaiani Kingdom, which are marked by a ragged crop of ruins still upstanding in a weird sort of procession. Sometimes the high-road sweeps right into the midst of a roofless palace, through the very walls of the ancient building, and outside may be found spaces brushed clean by the wind leaving masses of pottery, glass, and other common debris exposed.

One constant surprise to modern explorers is the extraordinary quantity of domestic crockery the remains of which surround old eastern cities; and almost yet more of a surprise it is how far and how widespread are certain easily recognized specialities, such, for instance, as the so-called "celadon." Chips and fragments of celadon are to be found from Babylon to Seistan, from Seistan to India, in Afghanistan, Kashmir, Burma, Siam. In Siam are all that remains of what were probably the original furnaces. Every shower of rain that falls in this extended cemetery of crumbling monuments reveals small treasures in the way of rings, coins, seals, etc. Much of the cultivation and of the extent of population indicated by the ruins in this narrow valley must have existed in the times of Alexander of Macedon and the Ariaspians, and we find no difficulty in accepting the Helmund (or Etymander) as the line of route which he followed for a certain distance. Indeed, there is much more than a passing probability that he followed the line which gave him water and supplies as far as the junction of the Argandab and Helmund, for the problem of crossing the desert from the Helmund valley to Nushki and the cultivated districts of Kalat is a serious one—one, indeed, which gave the Russo-Afghan Boundary Commissioners much anxious thought. But beyond the Argandab junction it is extremely improbable that Alexander followed the Helmund. The Helmund and its surroundings have been carefully surveyed from this point through the turbulent districts of Zamindawar for 100 miles or more, and again from its source near Kabul for some fifty miles of its downward flow. The Zamindawar section of the river affords an open road, although the river, as we follow it upward, gradually becomes enclosed in comparatively narrow (yet still fertile) valleys, and rapidly assumes the character of a mountain stream. North of Zamindawar and south of its exit from the Koh-i-Baba mountain system to the west of Kabul, no modern explorer has ever seen the Helmund. It there passes through the Hazara highlands, and although we have not penetrated that rugged plateau we know very well its character by repute, and we have seen similar country to the west where dwell cognate tribes—the Taimani and the Firozkohi. This upland basin of the Helmund to the west of Kabul and Ghazni, this cradle of a hundred affluents pouring down ice-cold water to the river, is but a huge extension southwards of the Hindu Kush, and from it emerge many of the great rivers of Afghanistan. To the north the rivers of Balkh and Khulm take a hurried start for the Oxus plains. Westward the Hari Rud streams off to Herat. South-westward extends the long curving line of the Helmund, and eastward flow the young branches of the Kabul. A rugged mountain mass called the Koh-i-Baba, the lineal continuation of the Hindu Kush, dominates the rolling plateau from the north and continues westward in an almost unbroken wall to the Band-i-Baian looking down into the narrow Hari Rud valley. It is a part of the continental divide of Asia, high, rugged, desolate, and almost pathless.

No matter from which side the toiler of the mountains approaches this elevated and desolate region, whether emerging from the Herat drainage he essays to reach Kabul, or from the small affluents of the Helmund he strikes for the one gap which exists between the Hindu Kush and the Koh-i-Baba which will lead him to Balkh and Afghan Turkistan, he will have enormous difficulties to encounter. It can be done, truly, but only with the pains and penalties of high mountaineering attached. Taken as a whole, the highest uplands above the sources of the minor rivers which water the bright and fertile valleys of Ghur, Zamindawar, and Farah may be described much as one would describe Tibet —a rolling, heaving, desolate tableland, wrinkled and intersected by narrow mountain ranges, whose peaks run to 13,000 and 14,000 feet in altitude, enclosing between them restricted spaces of pasture land. The Mongol population, who claim to have been introduced as military settlers by Chenghiz Khan, live a life of hard privation. They leave their barren wastes which the wind wipes clear of any tree growth, for the lower valleys in the winter months, merely resorting to them in the time of summer pasturage. The winter is long and severe. It is not the altitude alone which is accountable for its severity; it is the geographical position of this Central Afghan upheaval which exposes it to the full blast of the ice-borne northern winds which, sweeping across Turkistan with destructive energy, reduce the atmosphere of Seistan to a sand-laden fog, and penetrate even to the valley of the Indus where for days together they wrap the whole landscape in a dusty haze. For many months the Hazara highlands are buried under successive sheets of snowdrift. In summer, like the Pamirs, they emerge from their winter's sleep and become a succession of grass-covered downs. There are then open ways across them, and travellers may pass by many recognizable tracks. But in winter they are impassable to man and beast. Yet we are asked to believe that Alexander, who had the best of guides in his pay, and who knew the highways and byways of Asia as well, if not better, than they are known now to any military authorities, took his army *in winter* up the Helmund valley till it struck its sources somewhere under the Koh-i-Baba!

There was no madness in Alexander's methods. His withdrawal from India through the defiles and deserts of Makran was most venturesome and most disastrous, but he had a distinct object to gain by the attempt to pass into Persia that way. Here there was no object. The Helmund route does not, and did not, lead directly to his objective, Baktria, and there was another high-road always open, which must have been as well known then as, indeed, it is well known to-day. There can be very little doubt that he followed the Argandab to the neighbourhood of the modern Kandahar (in Arachosia), and from Kandahar to Kabul he took the same historic straight high-road which was followed by a later General (Lord Roberts) when he marched from Kabul to Kandahar. This would give him quite difficulties enough in winter to account for Arrian's story of cold and privations. It would lead him direct to the plains of the Kohistan north of Kabul, where there must have ever been the opportunity of collecting supplies for his force, and where, separated from him by the ridges of the Hindu Kush, were planted those Greek colonies of Darius Hystaspes whose assistance might prove invaluable to his onward movement. It was here, at any rate, not far from the picturesque village of Charikar, that he founded that city of Alexandreia, the remains of which appear to have been recently disturbed by the Amir, and to which we shall make further reference. Military text-books still speak of the Unai, or Bamian, as a pass which was traversed by the Greeks. It is most improbable that they ever crossed the Hindu Kush that way, and the question obviously arises in connection with this theory of his march—How was it possible for Alexander to spend the rest of the winter near the sources of the Helmund? It was not possible. His next step was to cross the Hindu Kush. This he attempted with difficulty in the spring, and reached a fertile country in fifteen days. He might have crossed by the Kaoshan Pass (which local tradition assigns as the pass which he really selected), or by the Panjshir, which is longer, but in some respects easier. The Panjshir is the pass usually adopted for the passage of large bodies of troops by the Afghans themselves, and there is reported to be, in these days, a well-engineered Khafila road, which is kept open by forced labour in snow-time, connecting Kabul with Andarab by this route. The pass of the Panjshir is about 11,600 feet high, whereas the Kaoshan, though straighter, is 14,300. Considering the slow rate of movement (fifteen days) it is more probable that he took the easier route *via* Panjshir. In either case he would reach the beautiful and fertile valley of Andarab, and from that base he could move freely into Baktria. The country had been ravaged and wasted by Bessos, but that did not delay Alexander. The chief cities of Baktria surrendered without opposition, and he pushed forward to the Oxus in his pursuit of Bessos.

All this would be more interesting if we could trace the route more closely which was followed to the Oxus. We know, however, that for previous centuries Balkh had been the capital city, the great trade emporium of all that region. There is therefore no difficulty in accepting Balkh as the Greek Baktria. Between Balkh and the Oxus the plains are strewn with ruins, some of them of vast extent, whilst other evidences of former townships are to be found about Khulm and Tashkurghan farther to the east, and on the direct route from Andarab to the Oxus. Bessos had retreated to Sogdiana of which Marakanda was capital, and the straight road to Marakanda (Samarkand) crosses the Oxus at Kilif. The description of the river Oxus at that point tallies fairly well with Arrian's account of it. It is deep and rapid, and the hill fortress of Kilif on the right bank, and of Dev Kala and other isolated rocky hills on the left, hedges in the river to a channel which cannot have changed through long ages. Elsewhere the Oxus is peculiarly liable to shift its channel, and has done so from time to time, forming new islands, taking fresh curves, and actually changing its destination from the Caspian to the Aral Sea; but at Kilif it must have ever been deep and rapid, covering a breadth of about three-quarters of a mile. Across the breadth nowadays is about as peculiar a ferry as was ever devised. Long, shallow, flat-bottomed boats, square as to bow and stern, are towed from side to side of the river by swimming horses. This would not be a matter of so much surprise if the horses employed for the purpose were powerful animals from fourteen to fifteen hands in height, but the remarkable feature about the Kilif stud is the diminutive and ragged crew of underfed ponies which it produces. And yet two, or even one, of these inefficient-looking little animals will tow across a barge of twenty feet or so in length, crowded with weighty bales of Bokhara merchandise, and filled as to interstices with its owners and their servants. The ponies are attached to outriggers with a strap from a surcingle or belly-band buckled to their backs, thus supporting their weight in the water at the same time that it takes the haulage. With their heads just above stream, snorting and blowing, they swim with measured strokes and tow the boat (advancing diagonally in crab-like fashion to meet the current) straight across the river. The inadequacy of the means to the end is the first thing which strikes the beholder, but he is, however, rapidly convinced of the extraordinary hauling capacity of a swimming horse when properly trained. Alexander crossed on rafts supported on skins stuffed with straw, and it took him five days to cross his force in this primitive fashion.

On the right bank of the river, Bessos was given up by traitors in his camp and was sent south to "Zariaspa" to await his doom. Zariaspa is identified with Balkh by some authorities, but the name is probably a variant on Adraspa which almost certainly was Andarab. Andarab was the fertile and promising district into which Alexander descended from the slopes of the Hindu Kush, by whichever route (Kaoshan or Panjshir) he crossed those mountains. Directly on the route between Andarab and Balkh is a minor province called Baglan, and a little less than half-way (after crossing a local pass of no great significance called Kotal Murgh) is a village or township, nowadays called Zardaspan, which is sufficiently like Zariaspa to suggest an identity which is at least plausible though it may be deceptive. But it is the fact that the town of Baraki which lies farther on the same route is on the outskirts of Baglan; and in this connection a reference to the theory put forward by Dr. Bellew in his *Ethnography of Afghanistan* (*Asiatic Quarterly*, October 1891) is at least interesting. He points out that the captive Greeks who were transported in the sixth century B.C. by Darius Hystaspes from the Lybian Barké to Baktrian territory were still occupying a village called Barké in the time of Herodotus. A century later again during the Macedonian campaign, Kyrenes, or Kyreneans, existed in that region according to Arrian, and it is difficult to account for them in that part of Asia unless they were the descendants of those same exiles from Barké, a colony of Kyrene whom Darius originally transported to Baktria. They were in possession of the Kaoshan Pass too, and might have rendered very effective aid to Alexander during his passage across the mountains. Another body of Greek colonists are recorded to have been settled in this same part of Baktria by Xerxes after his flight from Greece, namely, the Brankhidai, whose original settlement appears to have been in Andarab. As we shall see later, people from Greece or from Grecian colonies undoubtedly drifted across Asia to Northern Afghanistan in even earlier times than those of the Persian Empire. There can, indeed, be very little doubt that Ariaspa, or Andarab, was an important position for the Greeks to occupy from its strategic value as commanding the most practicable of the Hindu Kush passes.

When Bessos, therefore, was deported across the Oxus to Zariaspa it is probable that he was sent to Andarab; and here too Alexander returned to winter towards the close of the year 329 B.C. after his extraordinary success in Sogdia (Bokhara). With his trans-Oxus campaign we have nothing to do; it is another history, and deeply interesting as it would be to follow it in detail we must return to Afghanistan. Nothing in all his Eastern campaign is more remarkable than the facility with which Alexander recruited his army from Greece during its progress. Gaps in the ranks were constantly filled up, and the fighting strength of his force maintained at a high level. His army was re-organized during the winter, and with the returning spring he again started expeditions across the Oxus, in the course of which he captured Roxana, the most beautiful woman in Asia (after the wife of Darius) and married her. The particular fortress which held this charming lady was perched on the top of an isolated craggy hill, and the story of its capture is as thrilling as that of Aornos subsequently. But, like Aornos, it is difficult to locate it. It might have been Dev Kala, or Kilif, or any of a dozen such rock-crowned hills which border the Oxus River. It is about this period that we read first of his encounters with the Skythic races of

Central Asia, who gave him great trouble at the time and who subsequently subverted the Greek power in Baktria altogether. In the spring of 327 B.C. he moved out to invade a mountain district to the "East of Baktria" (probably modern Badakshan), and subdued the hill-tribes under Khorienes whom he confirmed in the government of his own country. It was summer ere he set out finally from Baktria on his Indian expedition. He recrossed the Paropamisos in ten days and halted at Alexandreia near Charikar. Then commences the first recorded expedition of the Kabul River basin.

CHAPTER IV

GREEK EXPLORATION—ALEXANDER—THE KABUL VALLEY TO THE INDUS

ALEXANDER passed the next winter at the city of his own founding, Alexandreia, in the Koh Daman to the north of Kabul. And from thence in two divisions he started for the Indus, sending the main body of his troops by the most direct route, with Taxila (the capital of the Upper Punjab) for its objective, and himself with lighter brigades specially organized to subdue certain tribes on the northern flank of the route who certainly would imperil the security of his line of communication if left alone. This was his invariable custom, and it was greatly owing to the completeness with which these flanking expeditions were carried out that he was able to keep open his connection with Greece. There have been discussions as to the route which he followed. Hyphæstion, in command of the main body, undoubtedly followed the main route which would take him most directly to the plains of the Punjab, which route is sufficiently well indicated

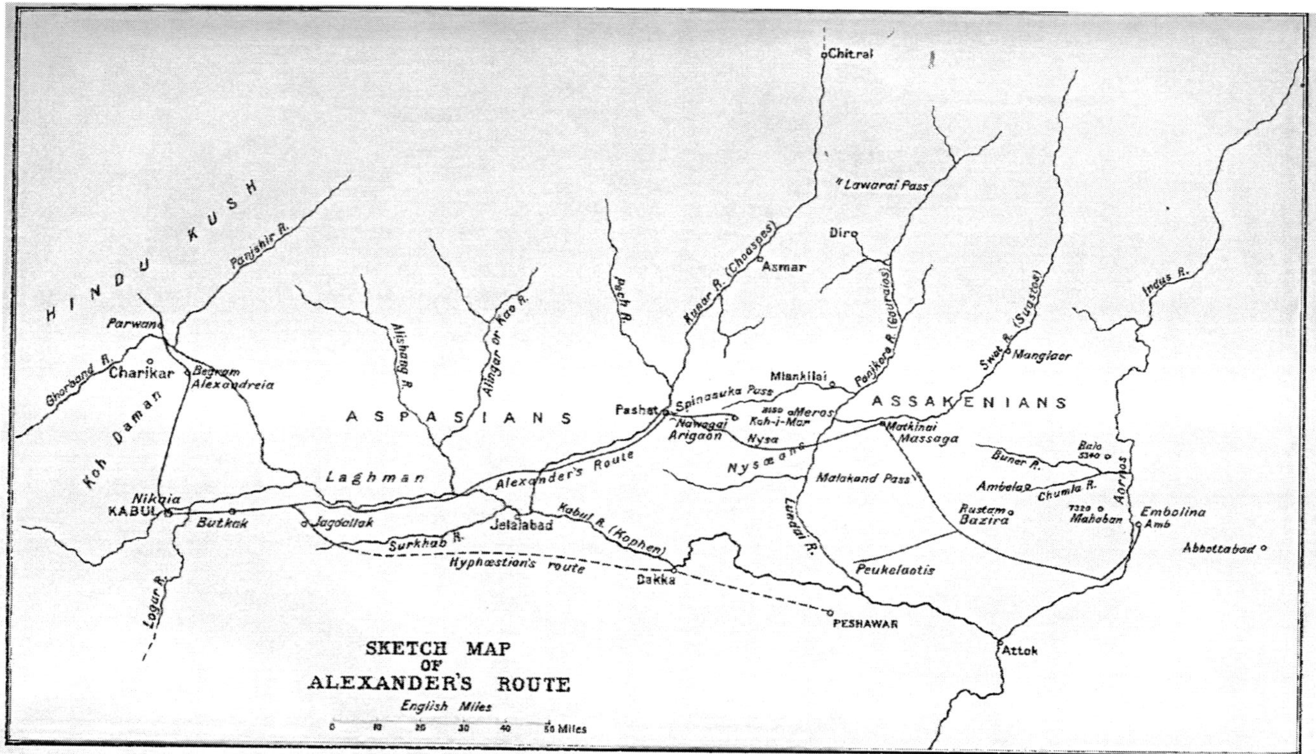

SKETCH MAP OF ALEXANDER'S ROUTE

in these days as the "Khaibar." We hear very little about his march eastwards.

In the days preceding the use of fire-arms the march of a body of troops through defiles such as the Khurd Kabul or the Jagdallak was comparatively simple. So far from such defiles serving as traps wherein to catch an enemy unawares and destroy him from the cliffs and hills on either side, these same cliffs and hills served rather as a protection. The mere rolling down of stones would not do much mischief, even if they could be rolled down effectively, which is not usually the case; and in hand-to-hand encounters the tribespeople were no match for the armoured Greeks. Alexander's operations would preserve his force from molestation on its northern flank, and the rugged ridges and spread of desolate hill-slopes presented by the Safed Koh and other ranges on the south has never afforded suitable ground for the collection of fighting bodies of men in any great strength. General Stewart marched his force from Kabul to Peshawur in 1880 with his southern flank similarly unprotected with the same successful result, his movements being so timed as to give no opportunity for a gathering of the Ghilzai clans. On the northern flank of the Khaibar route, however, there had been large tribal settlements from the very beginning of things, and it was most important that these outliers should feel the weight of Alexander's mailed fist if the road between

Kabul and the Indus were ever to be made secure. He accordingly directed his attention to a more northerly route to India which would bring him into contact with the Aspasians, Gauraians, and Assakenians.

We need not follow the ethnologists who identify these people with certain tribes now existing with analogous names. There may very possibly be remnants of them still, but they are not to be identified. They obviously occupied the open cultivable valleys and alluvial spaces which are interspersed amongst the mountains of the Kabul River basin, the Kohistan and Kafiristan of modern maps. The Gauraians certainly were the people of the Panjkora valley, and there is no difficulty in assigning to the Aspasians the first great fertile tract of open valley which would be encountered on the way eastwards. This is Laghman (or Lamghan) with its noble reach of the Kabul River meeting a snow-fed affluent, the Alingar, from the Kafir hills. There is, indeed, no geographical alternative. Similarly with even a cursory knowledge of the actual geographical conformation of the country, it is impossible to imagine that Alexander would choose any other route from Alexandreia towards Laghman than that which carries him past Kabul. The Koh Daman (the skirts of the hills) which intervene between Alexandreia (or Bagram) and Kabul is one of the gardens of Afghanistan. There one may wander in the sweet springtide amidst the curves and folds of an undulating land, neither hill nor plain, with the scent of the flowering willow in the air, and the rankness of a spring growth of flower and grass bordering narrow runlets and irrigation channels; an unwinking blue above and a varied carpet beneath, whilst the song of the labourer rises from fields and orchards. Westward are the craggy outlines of Paghman (a noble offshoot of the Hindu Kush hiding the loveliness of the Ghorband valley behind it), down whose scarred and wrinkled ribs slide waterfalls and streams to gladden the plain. Piled up on steep and broken banks from the very foot of the mountains are scattered white-walled villages, and it is here that you may find later in the year the best fruit in Afghanistan.

In November a gentle haze rests in soft indecision upon the dust-coloured landscape—heavier and bluer over the low-lying fields from which all vegetation has been lifted, lighter and edged with filmy skirts where it rises from the sun-warmed brow of the hills. It is a different world from the world of spring—all utterly sad-coloured and dust-laden; but it is then that the troops and strings of fruit-laden donkeys take their leisurely way towards the city, where are open shops facing the narrow shadowed streets with golden bulwarks of fruit piled from floor to roof. A narrow band of rugged hills shuts off this lovely plain on the east from the only valley route which could possibly present itself to an inexperienced eye as an outlet from the Charikar region to the Kabul River bed, ere it is lost in the dark defiles leading to the Laghman valley. The hills are red in the waning light, and when the snow first lays its lacework shroud over them in network patches they are inexpressibly beautiful. But they are also inexpressibly rough and impracticable, and the valley beyond is but a walled-in boulder-strewn trough, which no general in his senses would select for a military high-road. Alexander certainly did not march that way; he went to where Kabul is, and there, at the city of Nikaia, he made sacrifice to the goddess Athena. If Nikaia was not the modern Kabul it must have been very near it. Does not Nonnus tell us that it was a stone city near a lake? There is but one lake in the Kabul valley, and it is that at Wazirabad close to the city. It is usual to regard Nonnus as a most untrustworthy authority, but here for once he seems to have wandered into the straight and narrow path of truth. So far there can be no reasonable doubt about the direction of this great Pioneer's explorations in Afghanistan. Beyond this, once again, we prefer to trust to the known geographical distribution of hill and valley, and the opportunities presented by physical features of the country, rather than to any doubtful resemblance between ancient and modern place, or tribal, names, for determining the successive actions of the expedition. After the summons to

Taxiles, chief of Taxila (itself the chief city of the Upper Punjab), and the satisfactory reply thereto, there was nothing to disturb the even course of Alexander's onward movements but the activity of the mountain tribespeople who flanked the line of route.

The valley of Laghman must always have been a populous valley. From the north the snow-capped peaks of Kafiristan look down upon it, and from among the forest-clad valleys at the foot of these peaks two important river systems take their rise, the Alingar and the Alishang, which, uniting, join the Kabul River in the flat plain, where villages now crowd in and dispute each acre of productive soil. It is difficult to reach the Laghman valley from the west. The defiles of the Kabul River are here impassable, but they can be turned by mountain routes, and Alexander's force, which included the Hyspaspists, who were comparatively lightly armed, with the archers, the "companion" cavalry and the lancers, was evidently picked for mountain warfare. The heavier brigades were with Hyphæstion who struck out by the straightest route for Peukelaotis, which has been identified with an ancient site about 17 miles to the north-east of Peshawur on the eastern bank of the Swat River, and was then the capital of the ancient Gandhara. We are told that Alexander's route was rugged and hilly, and lay along the course of the river called Khoes. Rugged and hilly it certainly was, but the Khoes presents a difficulty. He could not actually follow the course of the Kabul River (Kophen) from the Kabul plain because of the defiles, but he could have followed that river below Butkak to the western entrance of the Laghman valley where it unites with the Alingar, or Ḳao, River. It is impossible to admit that he reached the Kao River after crossing the Kohistan and Kafiristan, and then descended that river to its junction with the Kabul. No cavalry could have performed such a feat. Geographical conditions compel us to assume that he followed the Kabul River, which is sometimes called Kao above the junction of the Kao River.

It is far more impossible to identify the actual sites of Alexander's first military engagements than it is to say, for instance, at this period of history, where Cæsar landed in Great Britain, as we have no means of making exhaustive local inquiries; but subsequent history clearly indicates that his next step after settling the Lughman tribes was to push on to the valley of the Choaspes, or Kunar. It was in the Kunar valley that he found and defeated the chief of the Aspasians. The Kunar River is by far the most important of the northern tributaries of the Kabul. It rises under the Pamirs and is otherwise known as the Chitral River. The Kunar valley is amongst the most lovely of the many lovely valleys of Afghanistan. Flanked by the snowy-capped mountains of Kashmund on the west, and the long level water parting which divides it from Bajaor and the Panjkora drainage on the east, it appears, as one enters it from Jalalabad, to be hemmed in and constricted. The gates of it are indeed somewhat narrow, but it widens out northward, where the ridges of the lofty Kashmund tail off into low altitudes of sweeping foothills a few miles above the entrance, and here offer opportunity for an easy pass across the divide from the west into the valley. This is a link in the oldest and probably the best trodden route from Kabul to the Punjab, and it has no part with the Khaibar. It links together these northern valleys of Laghman, Kunar, and Lundai (*i.e.* the Panjkora and Swat united) by a road north of the Kabul, finally passing southwards into the plains chequered by the river network above Peshawur.

The lower Kunar valley in the early autumn is passing beautiful. Down the tawny plain and backed by purple hills the river winds its way, reflecting the azure sky with pure turquoise colour—the opaque blue of silted water—blinking and winking with tiny sun shafts, and running emerald green at the edges. Sharp perpendicular columns of black break the landscape in ordered groups. These are the cypresses which still adorn in stately rows the archaic gardens of townlets which once were townships. The clustering villages are thick in some parts—so thick that they jostle each other continuously. There is nothing of the drab Punjab about these villages. They are white-walled and outwardly clean, and in at least one ancient garden there is a fair imitation of a Kashmir pavilion set at the end of a white eye-blinding pathway, leading straight and stiff between rows of cypress, and blotched in spring with inky splashes of fallen mulberries. The scent of orange blossoms was around when we were there, luscious and overpowering. It was the oppressive atmosphere of the typical, sensuous East, and the free, fresh air from the river outside the mud walls of that jealously-guarded estate was greatly refreshing when we climbed out of the gardens. All this part of the river must have been attractive to settlers even in Alexander's time, and it requires no effort of imagination to suppose that it was here that his second series of actions took place. Higher up the river the valley closes, until, long before Chitral is reached, it narrows exceedingly. Here, in the north, the northern winds rage down the funnel with bitter fury and make life burdensome. The villages take to the hill-slopes or cluster in patches on the flat terraces at their foot. The revetted wall of small hillside fields outline the spurs in continuous bands of pasture, and at intervals quaint colonies of huts cling to the hills and seem ready to slither down into the wild rush of the river below. Such as a whole is the Kunar valley, which, centuries after Alexander had passed across it, was occupied by Kafir tribes who may have succeeded the

Aspasian peoples, or who may indeed represent them. All the wild mountain districts west of the Kunar are held by Kafirs still, and there is nothing remarkable in the fact (which we shall see later on) that just to the east of the Kunar valley Alexander found a people claiming the same origin there that the Kafirs of Kashmund and Bashgol claim now.

It was during the fighting in the Kunar valley that we hear so much of that brilliant young leader Ptolemy, the son of Lagos, who was then shaping his career for a Royal destiny in Egypt. With all the thrilling incidents of the actual combat we have no space to deal, and much as they would serve to lighten the prosaic tale of the progress of Alexander's explorations, we must reluctantly leave them to Arrian and the Greek historians. We are told that after the Kunar valley action Alexander crossed the mountains and came to a city at their base called Arigaion. Assuming that he crossed the Kunar watershed by the Spinasuka Pass, which leads direct from Pashat (the present capital of Kunar) into Bajaor, he would be close to Nawagai, the present chief town of Bajaor. Arigaion would therefore be not far from Nawagai. The place was burnt down; but recognizing the strategic importance of the position, he left Krateros to fortify it and make it the residence not only of such tribespeople as chose to return to their houses, but also of such of his own soldiers as were unfit for further service. This seems to have been his invariable custom, and accounts for the traditions of Greek origin which we still find so common in the north-western borderland of India. The story of this part of his expedition reads almost as if it were journalistic. Then, as now, the tribesmen took to the hills. Then, as now, their position and approximate numbers could be ascertained by their camp-fires at night. Ptolemy was intelligence officer and conducted the reconnaissance, and on his report the plan of attack was arranged. This was probably the most considerable action fought by Alexander in the hills north of India. The conflict was sharp but decisive, and the Aspasians, who had taken up their position on a hill, were utterly routed. According to Ptolemy 40,000 prisoners and 230,000 oxen were taken, and the fact that the pick of the oxen were sent to Macedonia to improve the breed there shows how complete was the line of communication between Greece and Upper India. The next tribe to be dealt with were the Assakenians, and to reach them it was necessary to cross the Gauraios, or Panjkora, which was deep, swift as to current, and full of boulders. As we find no mention in Arrian's history of the passage of the Suastos (Swat River) following on that of the Gauraios, we must conclude that Alexander crossed the Panjkora *below* its junction with the Swat, where the river being much enclosed by hills would certainly afford a most difficult passage. There are other reasons which tend to confirm this view.

The next important action which took place was the siege and capture of the city called Massaga, which was only taken after four days' severe fighting, during which Alexander was wounded in the foot by an arrow. M'Crindle[1] quotes the various names given in Sanscrit and Latin literature, and agrees with Rennel in adopting the site of Mashanagar, mentioned by the Emperor Baber in his memoirs as lying two marches from Bajaor on the river Swat, as representing Massaga. M. Court heard from the Yasufzais of Swat that there was a place called by the double name of Mashkine and Massanagar 24 miles from Bajaor. It is not to be found now, but there is in the survey maps a place on the Swat River about that distance from Nawagai (the chief town in Bajaor) called Matkanai, close to the Malakand Pass, and this is no doubt the place referred to. It is very difficult even in these days to get a really authoritative spelling for place-names beyond, or even within, the British Indian border; and as these surveys were made during the progress of the Tirah expedition when the whole country was armed, such information as could be obtained was often unusually sketchy. If this is the site of Massaga it would be directly on the line of Alexander's route from Nawagai eastwards, as he rounded the spurs of the Koh-i-Mor which he left to the north of him, and struck the Panjkora some miles below its

[1] *Ancient India*, "Invasion by Alexander the Great." Appendix.

junction with the Swat. There can be little doubt that it was near this spot that the historic siege took place. His next objective were two cities called Ora and Bazira, which were obviously close together and interdependent. Cunningham places the position of Bazira, at the town of Rustam (on the Kalapani River), which is itself built on a very extensive old mound and represents the former site of a town called Bazar. Rustam stands midway between the Swat and Indus, and must always have been an important trade centre between the rich valley of Swat and the towns of the Indus. Ora may possibly be represented by the modern Bazar which is close by. Geographically this is the most probable solution of the problem of Alexander's movements, there being direct connection with the Swat valley through Rustam which is not to be found farther north. Alexander would have to cross the Malakand from the Swat valley to the Indus plains, but would encounter no further obstacles if he moved on this route. Bazira made a fair show of resistance, but the usual Greek tactics of drawing the enemy out into the plains was resorted to by Koenos with a certain amount of success; and when Ora fell before Alexander, the full military strength of Bazira dispersed and fled for refuge to the rock Aornos.

So far we have followed this Greek expedition into regions which are beyond the limits of modern Afghanistan, but the new geographical detail acquired during the most recent of our frontier campaigns enables new arguments to be adduced in favour of old theories (or the reverse), and this departure from the strict political boundaries of our subject leads us to regions which are at any rate historically and strategically connected with it. With Aornos, however, our excursion into Indian fields will terminate. Round about Aornos historical controversy has ebbed and flowed for nearly a century, and it is not my intention to add much to the literature which already concerns itself with that doubtful locality. I believe, however, that it will be some time yet before the last word is said about Aornos. Of all the positions assigned to that marvellous feat of arms performed by the Greek force, that which was advanced by the late General Sir James Abbott in 1854 is the most attractive—so attractive, indeed, that it is hard to surrender it. The discrepant accounts of the capture of the famous "rock" given by Arrian (from the accounts of Ptolemy, one of the chief actors in the scene), Curtius, Diodoros, and Strabo obviously deal with a mountain position of considerable extent, where was a flattish summit on which cavalry could act, and the base of it was washed by the Indus. All, however, write as if it were an isolated mountain with a definite circuit of, according to Arrian, 23 miles and a height of 6200 feet (according to Diodoros of 12 miles and over 9000 feet). The "rock" was situated near the city of Embolina, which we know to have been on the Indus and which is probably to be identified more or less with the modern town of Amb. The mountain was forest-covered, with good soil and water springs. It was precipitous towards the Indus, yet "not so steep but that 220 horse and war engines were taken up to the summit," all of which Sir James Abbott finds compatible with the hill Mahaban which is close to Amb, and answers all descriptions excepting that of isolation, for it is but a lofty spur of the dividing ridge between the Chumla, an affluent of the Buner River, and the lower Mada Khel hills, culminating in a peak overlooking the Indus from a height of 7320 feet. The geographical situation is precisely such as we should expect under the circumstances. The tribes-people driven from Bazira (assuming Bazira to be near Rustam) following the usual methods of the mountaineers of the Indian frontier, would retreat to higher and more inaccessible fastnesses in their rugged hills. There is but one way open from Rustam towards the Indus offering them the chance of safety from pursuit, and undoubtedly they followed that track. It leads up to the great divide north of them and then descends into the Chumla valley leading to that of Buner, and the hills which were to prove their salvation might well be those flanking the Chumla on the south, rising as they do to ever higher altitudes as they approach the Indus. This, in fact, is Mahaban. By all the rules of Native strategy in Northern India this is precisely the position which they would take up.

Aornos appears to have been a kind of generic name with the Greeks, applied to mountain positions of a certain class, for we hear of another Aornos in Central Asia, and the word translated "rock" seems to mean anything from a mountain (as in the present case) to a sand-bank (as in the case of the voyage of Nearkos). No isolated hill such as would exactly fit in with Arrian's description exists in that part of the Indus valley, and no physical changes such as alteration in the course of the Indus, or such as might be effected by the tectonic forces of Nature, are likely to have removed such a mountain. Abbott's identification has therefore been generally accepted for many years, and it has remained for our latest authority to question it seriously.

The latest investigator into the archæological interests of the Indian trans-frontier is Dr. M. A. Stein, the Inspector-General of Education in India. The marvellous results of his researches in Chinese Turkistan have rendered his name famous all over the archæological world, and it is to him that we owe an entirely new conception of the civilization of Indo-China during the Buddhist period. Dr. Stein's methods are thorough. He leaves nothing to speculation, and indulges in no romance, whatever may be the temptation. He takes with him on his archæological excursions a trained native surveyor of the

Indian survey, and he thus not only secures an exact illustration of his own special area of investigation, but incidentally he adds immensely to our topographical knowledge of little known regions. This is specially necessary in those wild districts which, are more immediately contiguous to the Indian border, for it is seldom that the original surveys of these districts can be anything more than topographical sketches acquired, sometimes from a distance, sometimes on the spot, but generally under all the disadvantages and disabilities of active campaigning, when the limited area within which survey operations can be carried on in safety is often very restricted. Thus we have very presentable geographical maps of the regions of Alexander's exploits in the north, but we have not had the opportunity of examining special sites in detail, and there are doubtless certain irregularities in the map compilation. This is very much the case as regards those hill districts on the right bank of the Indus immediately adjoining the Buner valley both north and south of it. Mahaban, the mountain which in Abbott's opinion best represents what is to be gathered from classical history of the general characteristics of Aornos, is south of Buner, overlooking the lower valley close to the Indus River. Dr. Stein formed the bold project of visiting Mahaban personally, and taking a surveyor with him. It was a bold project, for there were many difficulties both political and physical. The tribespeople immediately connected with Mahaban are the Gaduns—a most unruly people, constantly fighting amongst themselves; and it was only by seizing on the exact psychological moment when for a brief space our political representative had secured a lull in these fratricidal feuds, that Stein was enabled to act. He actually reached Mahaban under most trying conditions of wind and weather, and he made his survey. Incidentally he effected some most remarkable Buddhist identifications; but so far as the identification of Mahaban with Aornos is concerned he came to the conclusion that such identification could not possibly be maintained. This opinion is practically based on the impossibility of fitting the details of the story of Aornos to the physical features of Mahaban. It is unfortunate (but perhaps inevitable) that even in those incidents and operations of Alexander's expedition where his footsteps can be distinctly traced from point to point, where geographical conformation absolutely debars us from alternative selection of lines of action, the details of the story never do fit the physical conditions which must have obtained in his time.

As the history of Alexander is in the main a true history, there is absolutely no justification for cutting out the thrilling incident of Aornos from it. There *was* undoubtedly an Aornos somewhere near the Indus, and there was a singularly interesting fight for its possession, the story of which includes so many of the methods and tactics familiar to every modern north-west frontiersman, that we decline to believe it to be all invention. But the story was written a century after Alexander's time, compiled from contemporary records it is true, but leaving no margin for inquiry amongst survivors as to details. If, instead of ancient history, we were to turn to the century-old records of our own frontier expeditions and rewrite them with no practical knowledge of the geography of the country, and no witness of the actual scene to give us an *ex parte* statement of what happened (for no single participator in an action is ever able to give a correct account of all the incidents of it), what should we expect? Some furtive investigator might study the story of the ascent of the famous frontier mountain, the Takht-i-Suliman (a veritable Aornos!), during the expedition of 1882-83, and find it impossible to recognize the account of its steep and narrow ascent, requiring men to climb on their hands and knees, with the fact that a very considerable force did finally ascend by comparatively easy slopes and almost dropped on to the heads of the defenders. Such incidents require explanation to render them intelligible, and at this distance of time it is only possible to balance probabilities as regards Aornos.

Alexander's objective being India, eventually, and the Indus (of India, not of the Himalayas) immediately, he would take the road which led straightest from Massaga to the Indus; it is inconceivable that he would deliberately involve himself and his army in the maze of pathless mountains which enclose the head of Buner. He would certainly take the road which leads from Malakand to the Indus, on which lies Rustam. It has always been a great high-road. One of the most interesting discoveries in connection with the Tirah campaign was the old Buddhist road, well engineered and well graded, which leads from Malakand to the plains of the Punjab—those northern plains which abound with Buddhist relics. If we identify Bazar, or Rustam, with Bazireh we may assume with certainty that a retreating tribe, driven from any field of defeat on the straight high-road which links Panjkora with the Indus, would inevitably retire to the nearest and the highest mountain ridge that was within reach. This is certainly the ridge terminating with Mahaban and flanking the Buner valley on the south, a refuge in time of trouble for many a lawless people. Probability, then, would seem to favour Mahaban, or some mountain position near it. The modern name of this peak is Shah Kot, and it is occupied by a mixed and irregular folk. Here Dr. Stein spent an unhappy night in a whirling snow-storm, but he succeeded in examining the mountain thoroughly. He decided that that position of Mahaban could not possibly represent Aornos, for the following reasons:—The hill-top is too narrow for military action; the ascent, instead of being difficult, is easy from every side; and there is no spring of water on the summit, which summit must have been a very considerable plateau to admit of the action described; finally, there is no great ravine, and therefore no opportunity for the erection of the mound described by Arrian, which enabled the Greeks to fusilade the enemy's camp with darts and stones. Can we reconcile these discrepancies with the text of history?

After the reduction of Bazira Alexander marched towards the Indus and received the submission of Peukelaotis, which was then the capital of what is now, roughly speaking, the Peshawur district. The site of this ancient capital appears to be ascertained beyond doubt, and we must regard it as fixed near Charsadda, about 17 miles north-east (not north-west as M'Crindle has it) from Peshawur. From this place Alexander marched to Embolina, which is said to be a city close adjoining the rock of Aornos. On the route thither he is said by Arrian to have taken "many other small towns seated upon that river," *i.e.* the Indus; two princes of that province, Cophæus and Assagetes, accompanying him. This sufficiently indicates that his march must have been up the right bank of the Indus, which would be the natural route for him to follow. Arrived at Embolina, he arranged for a base of supplies at that point, and then, with "Archers, Agrians, Cænus' Troop" and the choicest, best armed, and most expeditious foot out of the whole army, besides 200 auxiliary horse and 100 equestrian archers, he marched towards the "rock" (8 miles distant), and on the first day chose a place convenient for an encampment. The day after, he pitched his tents much higher. The ancient Embolina may not be the modern Amb, but Amb undoubtedly is an extremely probable site for such a base of supplies to be formed, whether the final objective were Mahaban or any place (as suggested by Stein) higher up the river. The fact that there is a similarity in the names Amb and Embolina need not militate against the adoption of the site of Amb as by far the most probable that any sagacious military commander would select. A mere resemblance between the ancient and modern names of places may, of course, be most deceptive. On the other hand it is often a most valuable indication, and one certainly not to be neglected. Place-names last with traditional tenacity in the East, and obscured as they certainly would be by Greek transliteration (after all, not worse than British transliteration), they still offer a chance of identifying old positions such as nothing else can offer excepting accurate topographical description. Once again, if Embolina were not Amb it certainly ought to have been.

Alexander's next movements from Embolina most clearly indicate that he had to deal with a mountain position. There is no getting away from it, nor from the fact that the road to it was passable for horsemen, and therefore not insuperably difficult. At the same time he had to move as slowly as any modern force would move, for he was traversing the rough spurs of a hill which ran to 7800 feet in altitude. Further, the mountain was high enough to render signalling by fire useful. The "rock" was obviously either a mountain itself or it was perched on the summit of a mountain. Ptolemy as usual had conducted the reconnaissance. He established himself unobserved in a temporary position on the crest, within reach of the enemy, who attempted to dispossess him and failed; and it was he who (according to the story) signalled to Alexander. Ptolemy had followed a route, with guides, which proved rough and difficult, and Alexander's attempt to join him next day was prevented by the fierce activity of the mountaineers, who were plainly fighting from the mountain spurs. Then, it is said, Alexander communicated with Ptolemy by night and arranged a combined plan of attack. When it "was almost night" of the following day Alexander succeeded in joining Ptolemy, but only after severe fighting during the ascent. Then the combined forces attacked the "rock" and failed. All this so far is plain unvarnished mountain warfare, and the incidents follow each other as naturally as in any modern campaign. It becomes clear that the "rock" was a position on the crest of a high mountain, the ascent of which was rendered doubly difficult by fierce opposition. But it was practicable. Nothing is said about cavalry ascending. Why, then, did Alexander take cavalry? This question leads to another. Why do our frontier generals always burden themselves with cavalry on these frontier expeditions? They cannot act on the mountain-sides, and they are useless for purposes of pursuit. The answer is that they are most valuable for preserving the line of communication. Without the cavalry Alexander had no overwhelming force at his disposal, and it would not be very hazardous if we assumed that the force which actually reached the crest of the mountain was a comparatively small one — much of the original brigade being dispersed on the route.

Dr. Stein found the ascent too easy to reconcile with history. This might possibly be the effect of long weather action of the slopes of mountains subject to severe snow-falls. Twenty-three centuries of wind and weather have beaten on those scarred and broken slopes since Alexander's day. Those twenty-three centuries have had such effect on the physical outlines of land conformation elsewhere as absolutely to obliterate the tracks over which the Greek force most undoubtedly passed. What may have been the exact effect of them on Mahaban, whether (as usual) they rounded off sharp edges, cut out new channels, obliterated some water springs and gave rise to others, smoothing down the ruggedness of spurs and shaping the drainage, we cannot say. Only it is certain that the slopes of Mahaban—and its crest for that matter—are not what they were twenty-three centuries ago. We shall never recognize Aornos by its superficial features. Then, in the Greek story, follows the episode of filling up the great ravine which yawned between the Greek position and the "rock" on which the tribes-people were massed, and the final abandonment of the latter when, after three days' incessant toil, a mound had been raised from which it could be assailed by the darts and missiles of the Greeks. Arrian tells the story with a certain amount of detail. He states that a "huge rampart" was raised "from the level of that part of the hill where their entrenchment was" by means of "poles and stakes," the whole being "perfected in three days." On the fourth day the Greeks began to build a "mound opposite the rock," and Alexander decided to extend the "Rampart" to the mound. It was then that the "Barbarians" decided to surrender.

In the particular translation from which I have quoted (Rookes, 1829) there is nothing said about the "great ravine" of which Stein writes that it is clearly referred to by "all texts," and a very little consideration will show that it could never have existed. No matter what might have been the strength of Alexander's force it could only have been numbered by hundreds and not by thousands, when it reached the summit of the mountain. We might refer to the modern analogy of the expedition to the summit of the Takht-i-Suliman, where it was found quite impossible to maintain a few companies of infantry for more than two or three days. Numbers engaged in action are proverbially exaggerated, especially in the East; but the physical impossibility of keeping a large force on the top of a mountain must certainly be acknowledged. Even supposing there were a thousand men, and that no guards were required, and no reliefs, and that the whole force could apply themselves to filling up a "large ravine" with such "stakes and poles" as they could carry or drag from the mountain-slopes, it would take three months rather than three days to fill up any ravine which could possibly be called "large." General Abbott, as a scientific officer, was probably quite correct in his estimate of the "Rampart" as some sort of a "trench of approach with a parapet." There could not possibly have been a "great mound built of stakes and poles for crossing a ravine." It may be noted that Ptolemy's defensive work on his first arrival on the summit is called (or translated) "Rampart," and yet we know that it could only have been a palisade or an abattis. The story told by Arrian (and possibly maltreated by translators) is doubtless full of inaccuracies and exaggerations, but we decline to believe that it is pure invention. There is nothing in it, so far, which absolutely militates against the Mahaban of to-day (that refuge for Hindustani fanatics at one time, and for the discontented tribesfolk of the whole countryside through all time) being the Aornos of Arrian. No appearance of "precipices" is, however, to be found in the survey of the summit which accompanied Dr. Stein's report, and no opportunity for the defeated tribesmen to fall into the river. The story runs that the defeated mountaineers retreating from the victorious Greeks fell over the precipices in their hot haste, and that many of them were drowned in the Indus. This is indeed an incident which might be added as an effective addition to any tall story of a fight which took place on hills in the immediate neighbourhood of a river; but under no conceivable circumstances could it be adjusted to the formation of the Mahaban hill, even if it were admitted that armoured Greeks were any match in the hills for the fleet-footed and light-clad Indians. Probably the incident is purely decorative, but we need not therefore assume that the whole story is fiction. It has been pointed out by Sir Bindon Blood, who commanded the latest expedition to the Buner valley, that failing Mahaban there is north of the Buner River, immediately overlooking the Indus, a peak called Baio with precipitous flanks on the river side, which would fit in with the tale of Aornos better even than Mahaban. The Buner River joins the Indus through an impassable gorge steeply entrenched on either side, and a mile or two above it is the peak of Baio. So far as the Indus is concerned, that river presents no difficulties, for boats can be hauled up it far beyond Baio—even to Thakot. Looking northward or westward from above Kotkai one sees the river winding round the foot of the lower spurs of the Black Mountain on its left or eastern bank. Beyond is Baio on its right bank, towering (with a clumsy fort on its summit) over the Indus and forming part of a continuous ridge, beyond which again in the blue distance is the line of hills over which is the Ambela Pass at the head of the Chumla valley. (It is curious how the nomenclature hereabouts echoes faintly the Greek Embolina.) Above Baio is the ford of Chakesar, from which runs an old-time road westward to Manglaor, once the Buddhist capital of Swat. It would be all within reach of either Indians or Greeks, so we need not quite give up the thrilling tale of Aornos yet, even if Dr. Stein defeats us on Mahaban.

Then follows the narrative of an excursion into the country of the Assakenoi and the capture of the elephants, which had been taken for safety into the hills. The scene of this short expedition must have been near the Indus, and was probably the valley of the Chumla or Buner immediately under Mahaban, to the north. There was in those far-off days a different class of vegetation on the Indus banks to any which exists at present. We know that a good deal of the Indus plain below its debouchment from the hills was a reedy swamp in Alexander's time, and it was certainly the haunt of the rhinoceros for centuries subsequently, and consequently quite suitable for elephants, and it is probable that for some little distance above its debouchment the same sort of pasturage was obtainable. Most interesting perhaps of all the incidents in Arrian's history is that which now follows. We are told that "Alexander then entered that part of the country which lies between the Kophen and the Indus, where Nysa is said to be situate." Other authorities, however, Curtius (viii. 10), Strabo (xv. 697), and Justin (xii. 7), make him a visitor to Nysa before he crossed the Choaspes and took Massaga. All this is very vague; the river he crossed immediately before taking Massaga was certainly the Gauraios or Panjkora.

There is a certain element of confusion in classical writings in dealing with river names which we need not wait to investigate; nor is it a matter of great importance whether Alexander retraced his steps all the way to the country of Nysa (for no particular reason), or whether he visited Nysa as he passed from the Kunar valley to the Panjkora. The latter is far more probable, as Nysa (if we have succeeded in identifying that interesting relic of pre-Alexandrian Greek occupation) would be right in his path. Various authorities have placed

Nysa in different parts of the wide area indicated as lying between the Kophen (Kabul) and the Indus, but none, before the Asmar Boundary Commission surveyed the Kunar valley in the year 1894, had the opportunity of studying the question *in loco*. Even then there was no possibility of reaching the actual site which was indicated as the site of Nysa; and when subsequently in 1898 geographical surveys of Swat were pushed forward wherever it was possible for surveyors to obtain a footing, they never approached that isolated band of hills at the foot of which Nysa once lay. The result of inquiries instituted during the progress of demarcating the boundary between Afghanistan and the independent districts of the east from Asmar have been given in the *R.G.S. Journal*, vol. vii., and no subsequent information has been obtained which might lead me to modify the views therein expressed, excepting perhaps in the doubtful point as to *when*, in the course of his expedition, Alexander visited Nysa. In the first engraved Atlas sheet of the Indian Survey dealing with the regions east of the Kunar River, the name of Nysa, or Nyssa, is recorded as one of the most important places in that neighbourhood, and it is placed just south of the Koh-i-Mor, a spur, or extension, from the eastern ridges of the Kunar valley. From what source of information this addition to the map was made it is difficult to say, now that the first compiler of those maps (General Walker) has passed away. But it was undoubtedly a native source. Similarly the information obtained at Asmar, that a large and scattered village named *Nusa* was to be found in that position, was also from a native (Yusufzai) source. No possible cause can be suggested for this agreement between the two native authorities, and it is unlikely that the name could have been invented by both. At the same time Nysa, or Nusa, is not now generally known to the borderland people near the Indian frontier, and it is certainly no longer an important village. It is probably no more than scattered and hidden ruins. Above it towers the three-peaked hill called the Koh-i-Mor, whose outlines can be clearly distinguished from Peshawur on any clear day, and on that hill grows the wild vine and the ivy, even as they grow in glorious trailing and exuberant masses on the scarped slopes of the Kafiristan hills to the west.

We may repeat here what Arrian has to say about Nysa. "The city was built by Dionysos or Bacchus when he conquered the Indians, but who this Bacchus was, or at what time or from whence he conquered the Indians is hard to determine. Whether he was that Theban who from Thebes or he who from Tmolus, a mountain of Lydia, undertook that famous expedition into India . . . is very uncertain." So here we have a clear reference to previous invasions of India from Greece, which were regarded as historical in Arrian's time. However, as soon as Alexander arrived at Nysa a deputation of Nysæans, headed by one Akulphis, waited on him, and, after recovering from the astonishment that his extraordinary appearance inspired, they presented a petition. "The Nysæans entreat thee O King, for the reverence thou bearest to Dionysos, their God, to leave their city untouched . . . for Bacchus . . . built this city for an habitation for such of his soldiers as age or accident had rendered unfit for military service. . . . He called this city Nysa (Nuson) after the name of his nurse . . . and the mountain also, which is so near us, he would have denominated Meros (or the thigh) alluding to his birth from that of Jupiter . . . and as an undoubted token that the place was founded by Bacchus, the ivy which is to be found nowhere else throughout all India, flourishes in our territories." Alexander was pleased to grant the petition, and ordered that a hundred of the chief citizens should join his camp and accompany him. It was then that Akulphis, with much native shrewdness, suggested that if he really had the good of the city at heart he should take two hundred of the worst citizens instead of one hundred of the best—a suggestion which appealed at once to Alexander's good sense, and the demand was withdrawn. Alexander then visited the mountain and sacrificed to Bacchus, his troops meanwhile making garlands of ivy "wherewith they crowned their heads, singing and calling loudly upon the god, not only by the name of Dionysos, but by all his other names." A sort of Bacchic orgy!

But who were the Nysæans, and what became of them? In Arrian's *Indika* he says: "The Assakenoi" (who inhabited the Swat valley east of Nysa) "are not men of great stature like the Indians . . . not so brave nor yet so swarthy as most Indians. They were in old times subject to the Assyrians; then after a period of Median rule submitted to the Persians . . . the Nysaioi, however, are not an Indian race, but descendants of those who came to India with Dionysos"; he adds that the mountain "in the lower slopes of which Nysa is built" is designated Meros, and he clearly distinguishes between Assakenoi and Nysaioi. M. de St. Martin says that the name Nysa is of Persian or Median origin; but although we know that Assyrians, Persians, and Medes all overran this part of India before Alexander, and all must have left, as was the invariable custom of those days, representatives of their nationality behind them who have divided with subsequent Skyths the ethnographical origin of many of the Upper Indian valley tribes of to-day, there seems no sound reason for disputing the origin of this particular name.

Ptolemy barely mentions Nysa, but we learn something about the Nysæans from fragments of the *Indika* of Megasthenes, which have been collected by Dr. Schwanbeck and translated by M'Crindle. We learn that this pre-Alexandrian

Greek Dionysos was a most beneficent conqueror. He taught the Indians how to make wine and cultivate the fields; he introduced the system of retiring to the slopes of Meros (the first "hill station" in India) in the hot weather, where "the army recruited by the cold breezes and the water which flowed fresh from the fountains, recovered from sickness. . . . Having achieved altogether many great and noble works, he was regarded as a deity, and obtained immortal honours."

Again we read, in a fragment quoted by Strabo, that the reason of calling the mountain above Nysa by the name of Meron was that "ivy grows there, and also the vine, although its fruit does not come to perfection, as the clusters, on account of the heaviness of the rains, fall off the trees before ripening. They" (the Greeks) "further call the Oxydrakai descendants of Dionysos, because the vine grew in their country, and their processions were conducted with great pomp, and their kings, on going forth to war, and on other occasions, marched in Bacchic fashion with drums beating," etc.

Again we find, in a fragment quoted by Polyænus, that Dionysos, "in his expedition against the Indians, in order that the cities might receive him willingly, disguised the arms with which he had equipped his troops, and made them wear soft raiment and fawn-skins. The spears were wrapped round with ivy, and the thyrsus had a sharp point.

He gave the signal for battle by cymbals and drums instead of the trumpet; and, by regaling the enemy with wine, diverted their thoughts from war to dancing. These and all other Bacchic orgies were employed in the system of warfare by which he subjugated the Indians and the rest of Asia."

All these lively legends point to a very early subjugation of India by a Western race (who may have been of Greek origin) before the invasions of Assyrian, Mede, or Persian. It could not well have been later than the sixth century B.C., and might have been earlier by many centuries. The Nysæans, whose city Alexander spared, were the descendants of those conquerors who, coming from the West, were probably deterred by the heat of the plains of India from carrying their conquests south of the Punjab. They settled on the cool and well-watered slopes of those mountains which crown the uplands of Swat and Bajaur, where they cultivated the vine for generations, and after the course of centuries, through which they preserved the tradition of their Western origin, they welcomed the Macedonian conqueror as a man of their own faith and nation. It seems possible that they may have extended their habitat as far eastward as the upper Swat valley and the mountain region of the Indus, and at one time may have occupied the site of the ancient capital of the Assakenoi, Massaga, which there is reason to suppose stood near the position now occupied by the town of Matakanai; but they were clearly no longer there in the days of Alexander, and must be distinguished as a separate race altogether from the Assakenoi. As the centuries rolled on, this district of Swat, together with the valley of Dir, became a great headquarters of Buddhism. It is from this part of the trans-frontier that some of the most remarkable of those sculptures have been taken which exhibit so strong a Greek and Roman influence in their design. They are the undoubted relics of stupas, dagobas, and monasteries belonging to a period of a Buddhist occupation of the country, which was established after Alexander's time. Buddhism did not become a State religion till the reign of Asoka, grandson of that Sandrakottos (Chandragupta) to whom Megasthenes was sent as ambassador; and it is improbable that any of these buildings existed in the time of the Greek invasion, or we should certainly have heard of them.

But along with these Buddhist relics there have been lately unearthed certain strange inscriptions, which have been submitted by their discoverer, Major Deane,[1] to a congress of Orientalists, who can only pronounce them to be in an unknown tongue. They have been found in the Indus valley east of Swat, most of them being engraved on stone slabs which have been built into towers, now in ruins. The towers are comparatively modern, but it by no means follows that these inscriptions are so. It is the common practice of Pathan builders to

[1] The late Sir H. Deane.

preserve any engraved or sculptured relic that they may find, by utilizing them as ornamental features in their buildings. It has probably been a custom from time immemorial. In 1895 I observed evidences of this propensity in the graveyard at Chagan Sarai, in the Kunar valley, where many elaborately carved Buddhist fragments were let into the sides of their roughly built "chabutras," or sepulchres, with the obvious purpose of gaining effect thereby. No one would say where those Buddhist fragments came from. The Kunar valley appears at first sight to be absolutely free from Buddhist remains, although it would naturally be selected as a most likely field for research. These undeciphered inscriptions may possibly be found to be vastly more ancient than the towers they adorned. It is, at any rate, a notable fact about them that some of them "recall a Greek alphabet of archaic type." So great an authority as M. Senart inclines to the opinion that their authors must be referred to the Skythic or Mongolian invaders of India; but he refers at the same time to a sculptured and inscribed monument in the Louvre, of unknown origin, the characters on which resemble those of the new script. "The subject of this sculpture seems to be a Bacchic procession." What if it really is a Bacchic procession, and the characters thereon inscribed prove to be an archaic form of Greek—the forgotten forms of the Nysæan alphabet?

Whilst surveying in the Kunar valley along

the Kafiristan borderland, I made the acquaintance of two Kafirs of Kamdesh, who stayed some little time in the Afghan camp, in which my own tent was pitched, and who were objects of much interest to the members of the Boundary Commission there assembled. They submitted gracefully enough to much cross-examination, and amongst other things they sang a war-hymn to their god Gish, and executed a religious dance. Gish is not supreme in their mythology, but he is the god who receives by far the greatest amount of attention, for the Kafir of the lower Bashgol is ever on the raid, always on the watch for the chance of a Mahomedan life. It is, indeed, curious that whilst tolerant enough to allow of the existence of Mahomedan communities in their midst, they yet rank the life of a Mussulman as the one great object of attainment; so that a Kafir's social position is dependent on the activity he displays in searching out the common enemy, and his very right to sing hymns of adoration to his war-god is strictly limited by the number of lives he has taken. The hymn which these Kafirs recited, or sang, was translated word by word, with the aid of a Chitrali interpreter, by a Munshi, who has the reputation of being a most careful interpreter, and the following is almost a literal transcript, for which I am indebted to Dr. MacNab, of the Q.O. Corps of Guides:—

O thou who from Gir-Nysa's (lofty heights) was born
Who from its sevenfold portals didst emerge,

On Katan Chirak thou hast set thine eyes,
Towards (the depths of) Sum Bughal dost go,
In Sum Baral assembled you have been.
Sanji from the heights you see; Sanji you consult?
The council sits. O mad one, whither goest thou?
Say, Sanji, why dost thou go forth?

The words within brackets are introduced, otherwise the translation is literal. Gir-Nysa means the mountain of Nysa, Gir being a common prefix denoting a peak or hill. Katan Chirak is explained to be an ancient town in the Minjan valley of Badakshan, now in ruins; but it was the first large place that the Kafirs captured, and is apparently held to be symbolical of victory. This reference connects the Kamdesh Kafirs with Badakshan, and shows these people to have been more widespread than they are at present. Sum Bughal is a deep ravine leading down to the plain of Sum Baral, where armies are assembled for war. Sanji appears to be the oracle consulted before war is undertaken. The chief interest of this verse (for I believe it is only one verse of many, but it was all that our friends were entitled to repeat) is the obvious reference in the first line to the mountain of Bacchus, the Meros from which he was born, on the slopes of which stood the ancient Nysa. It is, indeed, a Bacchic hymn (slightly incoherent, perhaps, as is natural), and only wants the accessories of vine-leaves and ivy to make it entirely classical.

That eminent linguistic authority, Dr. Grierson, thinks that the language in which the hymn was recited is derived from what Sanscrit writers said was the language of the Pisacas, a people whom they dubbed "demons" and "eaters of raw flesh," and who may be represented by the "Pashai" dwellers in Laghman and its vicinity to-day. Possibly the name of the chief village of the Kunar valley Pashat may claim the same origin, for Laghman and Kunar both spread their plains to the foot of the mountains of Kafiristan.

The vine and the ivy are not far to seek. In making slow progress through one of the deep "darras," or ravines, of the western Kunar basin, leading to the snow-bound ridges that overlook Bashgol, I was astonished at the free growth of the wild vine, and the thick masses of ivy which here and there clung to the buttresses of the rugged mountain spurs as ivy clings to less solid ruins in England. The Kafirs have long been celebrated for their wine-making. Early in the nineteenth century, when the adventurer Baber, on his way to found the most magnificent dynasty that India has ever seen at Delhi, first captured the ancient city of Bajaor, and then moved on to the valley of Jandoul—now made historic by another adventurer, Umra Khan—he was perpetually indulging in drinking-parties; and he used to ride in from Jandoul to Bajaor to join his cronies in a real good Bacchic orgy more frequently than was good for him. He has a good deal to say about the Kafir wine in that inimitable Diary of his, and his appreciation of it was not great. It was, however, much better than nothing, and he drank a good deal of it. Through the kindness of the Sipah Salar, the Amir's commander-in-chief, I have had the opportunity of tasting the best brand of this classical liquor, and I agree with Baber—it is not of a high class. It reminded me of badly corked and muddy Chablis, which it much resembled in appearance.

English Miles 10 0 10 20 30 40 50 Natural Scale. 1:4,530,000.

London: Macmillan & Co. Ltd.

Stanford's Geog.l Estab.t, London.

CHAPTER V

GREEK EXPLORATION—THE WESTERN GATES OF INDIA

SOUTH of the Khaibar route from Peshawur to Kabul and separated from it by the remarkable straight-backed range of Sufed Koh, is an alternative route *via* the Kuram valley, at the head of which is the historic Peiwar Pass. From the crest of the rigid line of the Sufed Koh one may look down on either valley, the Kabul to the north or the Kuram to the south; and but for the lack of any convenient lateral communications between them, the two might be regarded as a twin system, with Kabul as the common objective. But there is no practicable pass across the Sufed Koh, so that no force moving along either line could depend on direct support from the other side of the mountains. It will be convenient here to regard the Kuram as an alternative to the Kabul route, and to consider the two together as forming a distinct group.

The next important link between Afghanistan and the Indian frontier south of the Kuram, is the open ramp of the Tochi valley. The Tochi does not figure largely in history, but it has been utilized in the past for sudden raids from Ghazni in spite of the difficulties which Nature has strewn about its head. The Tochi, and the Gomul River south of it, must be regarded as highways to Ghazni, but there is no comparison between the two as regards their facilities or the amount of traffic which they carry. All the carrying trade of the Ghazni province is condensed into the narrow ways of the Gomul. Trade in the Tochi hardly extends farther than the villages at its head. About the Gomul there hangs many a tale of adventure, albeit adventure of rather ancient date, for it is exceedingly doubtful if any living European has ever trod more than the lower steps of that ancient staircase. Then, south of the Gomul, there follows a whole series of minor passes and byways wriggling through the clefts of the mountains, scrambling occasionally over the sharp ridges, but generally adhering closely to the line of some fierce little stream, which has either split its way through the successive walls of rock offered by the parallel uptilted ridges, or else was there, flowing gently down from the highlands, before these ridges were tilted into their present position. There are many such streams, and the history of their exploration is to be found in the modern Archives of the Survey of India. They may have been used for centuries by roving bands of frontier raiders, but they have no history to speak of. South of the Gomul, they all connect Baluchistan with India, for Baluchistan begins, politically, from the Gomul; and they are of minor importance because, by grace of the determined policy of the great maker of the Baluch frontier, Sir Robert Sandeman, their back doors and small beginnings in the Baluch highlands are all linked up by a line of posts which runs from Quetta to the Gomul *via* the Zhob valley. Whoever holds the two ends of the Zhob holds the key of all these back doors. There is not much to be said about them. No great halo of historical romance hangs around them; and yet the stern grandeur of some of these waterways of the frontier hills is well worth a better descriptive pen than mine. I know of one, in the depths of a fathomless abyss, whose waters rage in wild fury over fantastic piles of boulders, tossing up feathers of white spray to make glints of light on the smooth apron of the limestone walls which enclose and overshadow it, which is matchless in its weird beauty. From rounded sun-kissed uplands, where olive groves shelve down long spurs, the waters come, and with a gradually deepening and strengthening rush they swirl into the embrace of the echoing hills, passing with swift transition from a sunny stream to a boiling fury of turgid water under the rugged cliffs of the pine-clad Takht-i-Suliman. Then the stream sets out again, babbling sweetly as it goes, into the open, just a dimpled stream, leaving lonely pools in silent places on its way, and breaking up into a hundred streamlets to gladden the mountain people with the gift of irrigation.

It is impossible to describe these frontier waterways. There is nothing like them to be found amidst scenes less wild and less fantastic than their frontier cradles. But full of local light and colour (and local tragedy too) as they surely are, they are unimportant in the military economy of the frontier, and their very wildness and impassability have saved them from the steps of the great horde of Indian immigrants. When, however, we reach still farther southward to the straight passes leading to Quetta, we are once again in a land of history. It is there we find by far the most open gates and those most difficult to shut, although the value of them as military approaches is very largely discounted by the geographical conditions of Western India at the point where they open on to the Indus frontier.

Quetta, Kalat, and Las Bela, standing nearly in line from north to south, are the watch-towers of the western marches. Quetta and Kalat stand high, surrounded by wild hill country. Magnificent cliff-crowned mountains overlooking a wilderness of stone-strewed spurs embrace the little flat plain on which Quetta lies crumpled. Here and there on the plain an isolated smooth excrescence denotes an extinct volcano. Such is the Miri, now converted into the protecting fort of Quetta. The road from Quetta to the north-west, *i.e.* to Kandahar and Herat, has to pass through a narrow hill-enclosed space some eight miles from Quetta; and this physical gateway is strengthened and protected by all the devices of which military engineering skill is capable, whilst midway between Quetta and Kandahar is the formidable Khojak range which must always have been a trouble to buccaneers from the north-west. From Quetta to the south-east extends that road and that railway which, intersecting the complicated rampart of frontier hills, finally debouches into the desert plains round Jacobabad in Sind. Kalat is somewhat similarly situated. High amongst the mountains, Kalat also commands the approaches to an important pass to the plains, *i.e.* the Mula, a pass which in times gone by was a commercial high-road, but which has long been superseded by the Quetta passes of Harnai and Bolan (or Mashkaf). Las Bela is an insignificant Baluch town in the valley of the Purali, and at present commands nothing of value. But it was not always insignificant, as we shall see, and if its military value is not great at present, Las Bela must have stood full in the tide of human immigration to India for centuries in the past. It is a true gateway, and the story of it belongs to a period more ancient than any.

Owing to the peculiar geographical conformation of the country, Quetta holds in her keeping all the approaches from the west, thus safeguarding

Kalat. The Kalat fortress is only of minor importance as the guardian of the Mula stairway to the plains of India. It is the extraordinary conformation of ridge and valley which forms the great defensive wall of the southern frontier. Only where this wall is traversed by streams which break through the successive ridges gathering countless affluents from left and right in their course—affluents which are often as straight and rectangular to the main stream as the branches of a pear-tree trained on a wall are to the parent stem—is it possible to find an open road from the plains to the plateau.

For very many miles north of Karachi the plains of Sind are faced by a solid wall of rock, so rigid, so straight and unscalable (this is the Kirthar range) as to form a veritably impracticable barrier. There is but one crack in it. For a short space at its southern end, however, it subsides into a series of minor ridges, and it is here that the connection between Karachi and Las Bela is to be found. These southern Las Bela approaches (about which there is more to be said) are not only the oldest, but they have been the most persistently trodden of any in the frontier, and they would be just as important in future as they have been in the past but for their geographical position. They are commanded from the sea. No one making for the Indus plains can again utilize these approaches who does not hold command of the Arabian Sea. In this way, and to this extent, the command of the Arabian Sea and of the Persian Gulf beyond it becomes vitally important to the security of India. Omitting for the present the Gomul gateway (the story of the exploration of which belongs to a later chapter), and in order to preserve something of chronological sequence in this book, it is these most southern of the Baluchistan passes which now claim our attention.

Until quite lately these seaboard approaches to India have been almost ignored by historians and military strategists (doubtless because so little was known about them), and the pages of recent text-books are silent concerning them. They lead outwards from the lower Indus valleys through Makran, either into Persia or to the coast ports of the Arabian Sea. From extreme Western Persia to the frontiers of India at Quetta, or indeed to the Indus delta, it is possible for a laden camel to take its way with care and comfort, never meeting a formidable pass, never dragging its weary limbs up any too steep incline, with regular stages and more or less good pasturage through all the 1400 or 1500 miles which intervene between Western Persia and Las Bela. From the pleasant palm groves of Panjgur in Makran to India, it might indeed be well to have an efficient local guide, and indeed from Las Bela to Karachi the road is not to be taken quite haphazard; nevertheless, if the camel-driver knew his way, he could not only lead his charge comfortably along a well-trodden route, but he might turn chauffeur at the end of his long march and drive an exploring party back in a motor.

In the illimitable past it was this way that Dravidian peoples flocked down from Asiatic highlands to the borderland of India. Some of them remained for centuries either on the coast-line, where they built strange dwellings and buried each other in earthen pots, or they were entangled in the mass of frontier hills which back the solid Kirthar ridge, and stayed there till a Turco-Mongol race, the Brahuis (or Barohis, *i.e.* "men of the hills"), overlaid them, and intermixing with them preserved the Dravidian language, but lost the Dravidian characteristics. According to their own traditions a large number of these Brahuis were implanted in their wild and almost inaccessible hills by the conqueror Chenghiz Khan, and some of them call themselves Mingals, or Mongols, to this day. This seems likely to be true. It is always best to assume in the first instance that a local tradition firmly held and strongly asserted has a basis of fact to support it. Here are a people who have been an ethnological puzzle for many years, talking the language of Southern Indian tribes, but protesting that they are Mongols. Like the degenerate descendants of the Greeks in the extreme north-west, or like the mixed Arab peoples of the Makran coast and Baluchistan, these half-bred

Mongols have preserved the traditions of their fathers and adopted the tongue of their mothers. It is strange how soon a language may be lost that is not preserved by the women! What we learn from the Brahuis is that a Dravidian race must once have been where they are now, and this supports the theory now generally admitted, that the Dravidian peoples of India entered India by these western gateways.

No more interesting ethnographical inquiry could be found in relation to the people of India than how these races, having got thus far on their way, ever succeeded in getting to the south of the peninsula. It could only have been the earliest arrivals on the frontier who passed on. Later arrivals from Western Persia (amongst whom we may reckon the Medes or Meds) remained in the Indus valley. The bar to frontier progress lies in the desert which stretches east of the Indus from the coast to the land of the five rivers. This is indeed India's second line of defence, and it covers a large extent of her frontier. Conquerors of the lower Indus valley have been obliged to follow up the Indus to the Punjab before striking eastwards for the great cities of the plains. Thus it is not only the Indus, but the desert behind it, which has barred the progress of immigration and conquest from time immemorial, and it is this, combined with the command given by the sea, which differentiates these southern gates of

India from the northern, which lead on by open roads to Lahore, Delhi, and the heart of India.

The answer to the problem of immigration is probably simple. There was a time when the great rivers of India did not follow their courses as they do now. This was most recently the case as regards the Indus and the rivers of Central India. In the days when there was no Indus delta and the Indus emptied itself into the great sandy depression of the Rann of Katch, another great lost river from the north-east, the Saraswati, fed the Indus, and between them the desert area was immensely reduced if it did not altogether disappear. Then, possibly, could the cairn-erecting stone-monument building Dravidian sneak his way along the west coast within sight of the sea, and there indeed has he left his monuments behind him. Otherwise the Dravidian element of Central Southern India could only have been gathered from beyond the seas; a proposition which it is difficult to believe. However, never since that desert strip was formed which now flanks the Indus to the east can there have been a right-of-way to the heart of India by the gateways of the west. The earliest exploration of these western roads, of which we can trace any distinct record, was once again due to the enterprise of the Greeks. We need not follow Alexander's victorious footsteps through India, nor concern ourselves with the voyage of his fleet down the Indus, and from the mouth of the Indus to Karachi.

General Haig, in his pamphlet on the Indus delta, has traced out his route[1] with patient care, demonstrating from observations taken during the course of his surveys the probable position of the coast-line in those early days.

From Karachi to the Persian Gulf, a voyage undertaken 300 years B.C., of which a log has been kept from day to day, is necessarily of exceeding interest, if only as an indication of a few of the changes which have altered the form of that coast-line in the course of twenty-two centuries. This old route from Arabia to the west coast of India can hardly be left unnoticed, for it illustrates the earliest beginning of those sea ways to India which were destined finally to supplant the land ways altogether. I have already pointed out that, judged by the standard of geographical aptitude only, there is no great difficulty in reaching Persia from Karachi. But geographical distribution of mountain, river, and plain is not all that is necessary to take into account in planning an expedition into new territory. There is also the question of supplies. This was the rock on which Alexander's enterprise split. In moving out of India towards Persia he adopted the same principle which had stood him in good stead on the Indus, viz. the maintenance of communication between army and fleet. Naturally he elected to retire from India by a route which as far as possible touched

[1] *Indus Delta Country*, 1894.

the sea. This was his fatal mistake, and it cost him half his force.

We need not trouble ourselves further with the ethnographical conditions of that extraordinary country, Makran, in Alexander's time; nor need we follow in detail the changes which have taken place in the general configuration of the coast-line between India and the Persian Gulf during the last 2000 years, references to which will be found in the *Journal of the Royal Society of Arts* for April 1901. Apart from the enormous extension of the Indus delta, and in spite of the disappearance of many small islands off the coast, the general result has been a material gain by the land on the sea in all this part of the Asiatic coast-line.

Alexander left Patala about the beginning of September 326 B.C. to push his way through the country of the Arabii and Oritæ to Gadrosia (or Makran) and Persia. The Arabii occupied the country between Karachi and the Purali (or river of Las Bela), and the Oritæ and Gadrosii apparently combined with other tribes to hold the country that lay beyond the Purali (or Arabius). He had previously done all that a good general can do to ensure the success of his movements by personally reconnoitring all the approaches to the sea by the various branches of the Indus; by pacifying the people and consolidating his sovereignty at Patala so as to leave a strong position behind him entirely subject to Greek authority; and by dividing his force so as to utilize the various arms with the best possible effect. This force was comprised in three divisions; one under Krateros included the heavy transport and invalids, and this was despatched to Persia by a route which was evidently as well known in that day as it is at present. It is never contended by any historian that Alexander did not know his way out of India. On the contrary, Arrian distinctly insinuates that it was the perversity of pride, the "ambition to be doing something new and astonishing" which "prevailed over all his scruples" and decided him to send his crank Indus-built galleys to the Euphrates by sea, and himself to prove that such an army led by "such a general" could force a passage through the Makran wilderness where the only previous records were those of disaster. He had heard that Cyrus and Semiramis had failed, and that decided him to make the attempt.

We can follow Krateros no farther than to point out that his route was by the Mulla (and not the Bolan) Pass to Kalat and Quetta. Thence he must have taken the Kandahar route to the Helmund, and following that river down to the fertile and well-populated plains of lower Seistan (or Drangia) he crossed the Kirman desert by a well-known modern caravan route, and joined Alexander at or near Kirman; for Alexander was "on his way to Karmania" at the time that Krateros joined him, and not at Pura (the capital of the Gadrosii) as suggested by St. John. One interesting little relic of this march was dug up by Captain Mackenzie, R.E., during the construction of the fort on the Miri at Quetta. A small bronze figure of Hercules was brought to light, and it now rests in the Asiatic Society's Museum at Calcutta.

Alexander, as we have said, left Patala about the beginning of September. But where was Patala? Probably it was neither Hyderabad (as suggested by General Cunningham) nor Tatta (as upheld by other authorities), but about 30 miles S.E. of the former and 60 miles E.N.E. of the latter, in which locality, indeed, there are ruins enough to satisfy any theory. From Patala we are told by Arrian that he marched with a sufficient force to the Arabius; and that is all. But from Quintus Curtius we learn that it was nine marches to Krokala (a point easier of identification than most, from the preservation of the name which survived through mediæval ages in the Karak—the much-dreaded pirate of the coast—and can now be recognized in Karachi) and five marches thence to the Arabius. He started in cool monsoon weather. His route, after leaving Krokala, is determined by the natural features of the country as then existing. There was no shore route in these days. Alexander followed the subsequent mediæval route which connected Makran with Sind in the days of Arab ascendancy, a route that has been used as a highway into India for nearly eight centuries. It is not the route which now connects Karachi and Las Bela, but belongs to the later mediæval phase of history. As the sea then extended at least to Liari, in the basin of the Purali or Arabius, we are obliged to locate the position of his crossing that river as being not far south of Las Bela; where in Alexander's time it was "neither wide nor deep," and in these days is almost entirely absorbed in irrigation. This does not, I admit, altogether tally with the five marches of Quintus Curtius. It would amount to over a hundred miles of marching, some of which would be heavy, though not very much of it; but the discrepancy is not a serious one. The Arabius may have been far to the east of its present channel—indeed, there are old channels which indicate that it was so, and it does not follow that the river was crossed at the point at which it was struck. The reason for placing this crossing so far north is that room is required for subsequent operations. After crossing, we are told that Alexander "turned to his left towards the sea" (from which he was evidently distant some space), and with a picked force he made a sudden descent on the Oritæ. He marched one night only through desert country and in the morning came to a well-inhabited district. Pushing on with cavalry only, he defeated the Oritæ, and then later joining hands with the rest of his forces, he penetrated to their capital city. For these operations he must necessarily have been hedged in between the Purali and Hala range, which he clearly had not crossed as yet. Now we are expressly told by Arrian that the capital city of the Oritæ was but a village that did duty for the capital, and that the name of it was Rambakia. The care of it was committed to Hephæstion that he might colonize it after the fashion of the Greeks. But we find that Hephæstion certainly did not stay long there, and could only have left the native village as he found it, with no very extensive improvements.

It would be most interesting to decide the position of Rambakia. What we want to find is an ancient site, somewhere approaching the sea-coast, say 30 or 40 miles from the crossing of the Purali, in a district that might once have been cultivated and populous. We have found two such sites—one now called Khair Kot, to the north-west of Liari, commanding the Hala Pass; and another called Kotawari, south-west of Liari, and very near the sea. The latter has but recently been uncovered from the sand, but an existing mud wall and its position on the coast indicate that it is not old enough for our purpose. The other, Khair Kot, is an undoubted relic of mediæval Arab supremacy. It is the Kambali of Idrisi on the high-road from Armail (now Bela) to the great Sind port of Debal, and the record of it belongs to another history. Nevertheless, Khair Kot is exactly where we should expect Rambakia to be, and quite possibly where Rambakia was. Amongst the coins and relics collected there, there is, however, no trace of Greek inscription; but that this corner of the Bela district was once flourishing and populous there is ample evidence.

From Rambakia Alexander proceeded with half his targeteers and part of his cavalry to force the pass which the Gadrosii and Oritæ had conjointly seized "with the design of stopping his progress." This pass might either have been the turning pass at the northern end of the Hala, or it might have been on the water-parting from which the Phur River springs farther on. I should think it was probably the former, where there is better room for cavalry to act.

Immediately after defeating the Oritæ (who apparently made little resistance) Alexander appointed Leonatus, with a picked force, to support the new Governor of Rambakia (Hephæstion having rejoined the army), and left him to make arrangements for victualling the fleet when it arrived, whilst he pushed on through desert country into the territory of the Gadrosii by "a road very dangerous," and drawing down towards the coast. He must then have followed the valley of the Phur to the coast, and pushed on along the track of the modern telegraph line till he reached the neighbourhood of the Hingol River. We are indebted to Aristobulus for an account of this track in Alexander's time. It was here that the Phœnician followers of the army gathered their myrrh from the tamarisk trees; here were the mangrove swamps, and the euphorbias, which still dot the plains with their impenetrable clumps of prickly "shoots or stems, so thick set that if a horseman should happen to be entangled therewith he would sooner be pulled off his horse than freed from the stem," as Aristobulus tells us. Here, too, were found the roots of spikenard, so precious to the greedy Phœnician followers. These same products formed part of the coast trade in the days when the Periplus was written, 400 years later, though there is little demand for them now.

It was somewhere near the Hingol River that Alexander made a considerable halt to collect food and supplies for his fleet. His exertions and his want of success are all fully described by Arrian, as well as the rude class of fishing villages inhabited by Ichthyophagi, all the latter of which might well be cut out of the pages of Greek history and entered in a survey report as modern narrative. After this we have but slight indications in Arrian's history of Alexander's route to Pura, the capital of Gadrosia. Three chapters are full of most graphic and lively descriptions of the difficulties and horrors of that march. We only hear that he reached Pura sixty days after leaving the country of the Oritæ, and there is no record of the number of troops that survived. Luckily, however, the log kept by the admiral of the fleet, Nearkhos, comes into our assistance here, and though it is still Arrian's history, it is Nearkhos who speaks.

We must now turn back to follow the ships. I cannot enter in detail into the reasons given by General Haig, in his interesting pamphlet on the Indus Delta Country, for selecting the Gharo creek as the particular arm of the Indus which was finally selected for the passage of the fleet seaward. I can only remark that whilst the nature of the half-formed delta of that period is still open to conjecture, so that I see no reason why the island of Krokala, for instance, should not have been represented by a district which bears a very similar name nowadays, I fully agree that the description of the coast as given by Nearkhos can only possibly apply to that section of it which is embraced between the Gharo creek and Karachi.

It is only within very recent times that the Gharo has ceased to be an arm of the Indus. For the present, at any rate, we cannot do better than follow so careful an observer as General Haig in his conclusions. There can be little doubt that Alexander's haven, into which the fleet put till the monsoon should moderate, and where it was detained for twenty days, was *somewhere near* Karachi. That it was the modern Karachi harbour seems improbable. Of all parts of the western coast of India, that about Karachi has probably changed its configuration most rapidly, and there is ample room for conjecture as to where that haven of refuge of 2000 years ago might actually have been. Let us accept the fleet of river-built galleys, manned with oars, and open to every phase of wind and weather, as having emerged from it about the beginning of October, and as having reached the island of Domai, which I am inclined to identify with Manora.

Much difficulty has been found in making the estimate of each day's run, as given in stadia, tally with the actual length of coast. I think the difficulty disappears a good deal if we consider what means there were of making such estimates. Short runs in the river between known landmarks are very fairly consistent in the Greek accounts. On the basis of such short runs, and with a very vague idea of the effect of wind and tide, the length of each day's run at sea was probably reckoned at so much per hour. There could hardly have been any other way of reckoning open to the Greeks. They recognized no landmarks after leaving Karachi. Even had they been able to use a log-line it would have told them but little. Wind and current (for the currents on this part of the sea mostly follow the monsoon wind) were either against them or on their beam all the way to the Hingol, and they encountered more than one severe storm which must have broken on them with the full force of a monsoon head wind. From the point where the fleet rounded Cape Monze and followed the windings of the coast to the harbour of Morontobara the estimates, though excessive, are fairly consistent; but from this point westward, when the full force of monsoon wind and current set against them, the estimates of distance are very largely in excess of the truth, and continue so till the pilot was shipped at Mosarna who guided them up the coast of Persia. Thenceforward there is much more consistency in their log. It must not be supposed that Nearkhos was making a voyage of discovery. He was following a track that had often been followed before. It was clear that Alexander knew the way by sea to the coasts of Persia before he started his fleet, and it is a matter of surprise rather than otherwise that he did not find a pilot amongst the Malli, who, if they are to be identified with the Meds, were one of the foremost sea-going peoples of Asia. His Phœnician and Greek sailors evidently were strangers to the coast, and some of his mixed crew of soldiers and sailors had subsequently to be changed for drafts from the land forces.

We cannot now follow the voyage in detail, nor could we, even if we would, indicate the precise position of those islands of which Arrian writes between Cape Monze and Sonmiani; some of them may now be represented by shoals known to the coasting vessels, whilst others may be connected with the mainland. I have no doubt myself that Morontobara (the "woman's haven") is represented by the great depression of the Sirondha lake. Between Morontobara and Krokala (which about answers to Ras Kachari) they touched at the mouth of the Purali, or Arabius, not far from Liari, having an island which sheltered them from the sea to windward, which is now part of the mainland. Near by the mouth of the Arabius was another island "high and bare" with a channel between it and the mainland. This, too, has been linked up with the shore formation, and the channel no longer exists, but there is ample evidence of the ancient character of this corner of the coast. Between the Arabius and Krokala (three days' sail) very bad weather was made, and two galleys and a transport were lost. It was at Krokala that they joined hands with the army again. Here Nearkhos formed a camp, and it was "in this part of the country" that Leonatus defeated the Oritæ and their allies in a great battle wherein 6000 were slain. Arrian adds that a full account of the action and its sequel, the crowning of Leonatus with a golden crown by Alexander, is given in his other work, but as a matter of fact the other account is so entirely different (representing the Oritæ as submitting quietly) that we can only suppose this to have been a separate and distinct action from the cavalry skirmish mentioned before.

It must be noted that the coast hereabouts has probably largely changed. A little farther west it is changing rapidly even now, and it is idle to look for the names given by the Greeks as marking any positive locality known at present. Hereabouts at any rate was the spot where Alexander with such difficulty had collected ten days' supplies for the fleet. This was now put on board, and the bad or indifferent sailors exchanged for better seamen. From Krokala, a course of 500 stadia (largely over-estimated) brought them to the estuary of the Hingol River (which is described a winter torrent under the name of Tomeros), and from this point all connection between the fleet and the army appears to have been lost. It was at the mouth of the Hingol that a skirmish took place with the natives which is so vividly described by Nearkhos, when the Greeks leapt into the sea and charged home through the surf. Of all the little episodes described in the progress of the voyage this is one of the most interesting; for there is a very close description given of certain barbarians clothed in the skins of fish or animals, covered with long hair, and using their nails as we use fish-knives, armed with wooden pikes hardened in the fire, and fighting more like monkeys than men. Here we have the real aboriginal inhabitants of India. Not so very many years ago, in the woods of Western India, a specimen almost literally answering to the description of Nearkhos was caught whilst we were in the process of surveying those jungles, and he furnished a useful contribution to ethnographical science at the time. Probably these barbarians of Nearkhos were incomparably older even than the Turanian races which we can recognize, and which succeeded them, and which, like them, have been gradually driven south into the fastnesses of Central and Southern India.

Makran is full of Turanian relics connecting it with the Dravidian races of the south; but there is no time to follow these interesting glimpses into prehistoric ethnography opened up by the log of Nearkhos. Nor, indeed, can we follow the voyage in detail much farther, for we have to take up the route of Alexander, about which very much less has hitherto been known than can be told about the voyage of Nearkhos. We may, however, trace the track of Nearkhos past the great rocky headland of Malan, still bearing the same name that the Greeks gave it, to the commodious harbour of Bagisara, which is likely enough the Damizar, or eastern bay, of the Urmara headland. The Padizar, or western bay, corresponds more nearly with the name Bagisara, but as they doubled a headland next day it is clear they were on the eastern side of the Isthmus. The Pasiris whom he mentions have left frequent traces of their existence along the coast. Kalama, reached on the second day from Bagisara, is easily recognizable in the Khor Khalmat of modern surveys, and it is here again that we can trace a very considerable extension of the land seawards that would completely have altered the course of the fleet from the coasting track of modern days. The island of Karabine, from which they procured sheep, may very well have been the projecting headland of Giaban, now connected by a low sandy waste with the mainland. It could never have been the island of Astola, as conjectured by M'Crindle and others. From Kalama to Kissa (now disappeared) and Mosarna, along the coast called Karbis (now Gazban), the course would again be longer than at present, for there is much recent sand formation here; and when we come to Mosarna itself, after doubling the headland of Jebel Zarain, we find the harbour completely silted up. It may be noted that this western bay of Pasni was probably exactly similar to the Padizar of Urmara or of Gwadur, and that there is a general (but not universal) tendency to shallowing on the western sides of all the Makran headlands. Here they took the pilot on board, and after this there was little difficulty.

In three more days they made Barna (or Badara), which answers to Gwadur, where were palm trees and myrtles, and we need follow them for the present no farther. Colonel Mockler, who was well acquainted with the Makran coast, but hardly, perhaps, appreciated all the changes which the coast-line has undergone (neither, indeed, did I till the surveys were complete), has traced the course of that historic fleet with great care. He has pointed out correctly that two islands (Pola and Karabia) have disappeared from the eastern neighbourhood of the Gwadur headland and one (Derenbrosa) from its western extremity; and he might have added that yet another is breaking up, and rapidly disappearing off the headland of Passabandar, near, Gwadur. He has identified Kyiza (or Knidza), the small town built on an eminence not far from the shore, which was captured by stratagem, beyond doubt, and has traced the fleet from point to point with a careful analysis of all existing records that I cannot pretend to imitate. We cannot, however, leave Nearkhos without a passing reference to that island on the coast of the Ichthyophagi, and which was sacred to the sun, and which was, even in those days, enveloped in such a halo of mystery and tradition that even Arrian holds Nearkhos up to contempt for expending "time and ingenuity in the not very difficult task of proving the falsehood" of these "antiquated fables." I have been to that island, the island of Astola, and the tales that were told to Nearkhos are told of it still. There, off the southern face of it, is the "sail rock," the legendary relic of a lost ship which may well have been the transport which Nearkhos did undoubtedly lose off its rocky shores. There, indeed, I did not find the Nereid of such fascinating manners and questionable customs as Nearkhos describes on the authority of the inhabitants of the coast, but sea-urchins and sea-snakes abounded in such numbers as to make the process of exploration quite sufficiently exciting; and there were not wanting indications of those later days when the Meds (now an insignificant fish-eating people scattered in the coast hamlets) were the dreaded pirates of the Arabian Sea, and used to convey the crews of the ships they captured to that island, where they were murdered wholesale. It is curious that the name given by Nearkhos is Nosala, or Nuhsala. In these days it is Astola, or more properly Hashtala, sometimes even called Haftala. I am unable to determine the meaning of the termination to which the numerals are prefixed. Another name for it is Sangadip, which is also the mediæval name for Ceylon. There can be no doubt about the identity of this island of sun worship and historic fable.

We must now turn to Alexander. We left him near the mouth of the Hingol, then probably four or five miles north of its present position, and nearer the modern telegraph line. So far he had almost step by step followed out the subsequent line of the Indo-Persian telegraph, and at the Hingol he was not very far south of it. Near here Leonatus had had his fight with the Oritæ, and Alexander had spent much time (for it must be remembered that he started a month before his fleet, and that the fleet and Leonatus at least joined hands at this point) in collecting supplies of grain from the more cultivated districts north, and was prepared to resume his march along the coast, true to his general tactical principle of keeping touch with his ships. But an obstacle presented itself that possibly he had not reckoned on. The huge barrier of the Malan range, abutting direct on the sea, stopped

M

his way. There was no "Buzi" pass (or goat track) in those days, such as finally and after infinite difficulty helped the telegraph line over, though there was indeed an ancient stronghold at the top, which must have been in existence before his time, and was likely enough the original city of Malan. He was consequently forced into the interior, and here his difficulties began.

We should be at a loss to follow him here, but for the fact that there is only one possible route. He followed up the Hingol till he could turn the Malan by an available pass westward. Nothing here has altered since his days. Those magnificent peaks and mountains which surround the sacred shrine of Hinglaz are, indeed, "everlasting hills," and it was through them that he proceeded to make his way. It would be a matter of immense interest could one trace any record of the Hinglaz shrine in classical writings, but there is none that I know of. And yet I believe that shrine which, next possibly to Juggernath, draws the largest crowds of pilgrims (Hindu and Mussulman alike) of any in India, was in existence before the days of Alexander. For the shrine is sacred to the goddess Nana (now identified with Siva by Hindus), and the Assyrian or Persian goddess Nana is of such immense antiquity that she has furnished to us the key to an older chronology even than that of Egypt. The famous cylinder of Assurbanipal, King of Assyria, tells us that in the year 645 B.C. he destroyed Susa, the capital of Elam, and from its temple he carried back the Chaldean goddess Nana, and by the express command of the goddess herself, took her from whence she had dwelt in Elam, "a place not appointed her," and reinstated her in her own sanctuary at Urukh (now Warka in Mesopotamia), whence she had originally been taken 1635 years before by a conquering king of Elam, who had invaded Accad territory. Thus she was clearly a well-established deity in Mesopotamia 2280 years B.C. Alexander, however, would have left that Ziarat hidden away in the folds of the Hinglaz mountain on his left, and followed the windings of the Hingol River some forty miles to its junction with a stream from the west, which would again give him the chance of striking out parallel to the coast.

We should be in some doubt at what particular point Alexander left the Hingol, but for the survival of names given in history as those of a people with whom he had to contend, viz. the Parikanoi, the Sagittæ, and the Sakæ, names not mentioned by Arrian. Now, Herodotus gives the Parikanoi and Asiatic Ethiopians as being the inhabitants of the seventeenth satrapy of the Persian Empire, and Bellew suggests that the Greek Parikanoi is a Greek transcript of the Persian form of Parikan, the plural of the Sanscrit Parvá-ka—or, in other words, the *Ba-rohi*—or men of the hills. However this may be, there is the bed of the stream called Parkan skirting the north of the Taloi range and leading westwards from the Hingol, and we need look no farther for the Parikanoi. In support of Bellew's theory it may be stated that it is not only in the heart of the Brahui country, but the Sajidi are still a tribe of Jalawan Brahuis, of which the chief family is called Sakæ, and that they occupy territory in Makran a little to the north of the Parkan. There is every reason why Alexander should have selected this route. It was his first chance of turning the Malan block, and it led most directly westwards with a trend towards the sea. But at the time of the year that he was pushing his way through this low valley flanked by the Taloi hills, which rose to a height of 2000 feet above him on his left, there would not be a drop of water to be had, and the surrounding wilderness of sandy hillocks and scanty grass-covered waste would afford his troops no supplies and no shelter from the fierce autumn heat. All the miseries of his retreat were concentrated into the distance (about 200 miles) between the Hingol and the coast.

The story of that march is well told by Arrian. It was here that occurred that gallant episode when Alexander proudly refused to drink the small amount of water that was offered him in a helmet, because his army was perishing with thirst. It must have been near the harbour of Pasni, once again almost on the line of the present telegraph, that Alexander emerged from the sand-storm with but four horsemen on to the sea-coast at last, and instantly set to work to dig wells for his perishing troops. Thenceforward Arrian tells us only that he marched for seven days along the coast till he reached the well-known highway to Karmania, when he turned inland, and his difficulties were at an end. Now, that well-known highway was almost better known then than it is now. He could only leave the coast near the Dasht River at Gwadur, and strike across into the valley of the Bahu, which would lead him through a country subsequently great in Arabic history, over the yet unsuspected sites of many famous cities, to Bampur, the capital of Gadrosia. From leaving the coast to Bampur the duration of his march with an exhausted force would be little less than a month. Working backward again from that same point (which may be regarded as an obligatory one in his route) the seven days' weary drag through the sand of the coast would carry him no farther than from the neighbourhood of Pasni, and that is why I have selected that point for the historic episode of his guiding his army by chance and emerging on to the shore unexpectedly, rather than the neighbourhood of the Basol River, to which the Parkan route should naturally have led him. He clearly lost his way, as Arrian says he did, or else the estimated number of marches is wrong. We are told by Arrian that he reached Pura, the capital of Gadrosia, on the sixtieth day after leaving the country of the Oritæ.

This is a little indefinite, as he may be considered to have left the country of the Oritæ when he started to collect supplies from the northern district, and we do not know how long he was on this reconnaissance. Probably, however, the date of leaving the coast and striking inland up the Hingol River is the date referred to by Arrian, in which case we may estimate that he spent about twenty-four days negotiating the fearful country opened up to him on the Parkan route ere he touched the seashore again. This is by no means an exaggerated estimate if we consider the distance (something short of 200 miles) and the nature of his army. A half-armed mob, which included women and children, and of which the transport consisted of horses and mules and wooden carts dragged by men, cannot move with the facilities of a modern brigade. Nor would a modern brigade move along that line with the rapidity that has distinguished some of our late manœuvres in South Africa. On the whole, I think the estimate a probable one, and it brings us to Bampur, the ancient capital of Gadrosia.

We have now followed Alexander out of India into Persia. Thenceforward there are no great geographical questions to decipher, or knots to be untied. His progress was a progress of triumph, and the story of his retreat well ends with the thrilling tale of his meeting again with Nearkhos, after the latter had harboured his fleet at the mouth of the Minab River and set out on the search for

Alexander, guided by a Greek who had strayed from Alexander's army. Blackened by exposure and clothed in rags, Nearkhos was unrecognized till he announced himself to the messenger sent to look for him. Even Alexander himself at first failed to recognize his admiral in the extraordinary apparition that was presented to him in his camp, and could only believe that his fleet must have perished and that Nearkhos and Arkias were sole survivors. We can imagine what followed. Those were days of ready recognition of service and no despatches, and all Persia was open to the conquerors to choose their reward.

After Alexander's time many centuries elapsed before we get another clear historic view into Makran, and then what do we find? A country of great and flourishing cities, of high-roads connecting them with well-known and well-marked stages; armies passing and re-passing, and a trade which represented to those that held it the dominant commercial power in the world, flowing steadily century after century through that country which was fatal to Alexander, and which we are rather apt now to consider the fag-end of the Baluchistan wilderness. The history of Makran is bound up with the history of India from time immemorial. Not all the passes of all the frontiers of India put together have seen such traffic into the broad plains of Hindustan as for certainly three, and possibly for eight, centuries passed through the gateways of

Makran. As one by one we can now lay our finger on the sites of those historic cities, and first begin faintly to measure the importance of Makran to India ere Vasco da Gama first claimed the honour of doubling the Cape and opened up the ocean highway, we can only be astonished that for four centuries more Makran remained a blank on the map of the world.

CHAPTER VI

CHINESE EXPLORATIONS—THE GATES OF THE FAR NORTH

THERE are many gateways into India, gateways on the north as well as the north-west and west, and although these far northern ways are so rugged, so difficult, and so elevated that they can hardly be regarded as of political or strategic importance, yet they are many of them well trodden and some were once far better known than they are now. Opinions may perhaps differ as to their practical value as military or commercial approaches under new conditions of road-making, but they never have, so far, been utilized in either sense, and the interest of them is purely historical. These are the ways of the pilgrims, and we are almost as much indebted to Chinese records for our knowledge of them as we are to the researches of modern explorers.

For many a century after Alexander had left the scene of his Eastern conquests historical darkness envelopes the rugged hills and plains which witnessed the passing of the Greeks. The faith of Buddha was strong before their day, but the building age of Buddhism was later. No mention is to be found in the pages of Greek history of the magnificent monuments of the creed which are an everlasting wonder of the plains of Upper India. Such majestic testimony to the living force of Buddhism could hardly have passed unnoticed by observers so keen as those early Greeks; and when next we are dimly lighted on our way to identify the lines of movement and the trend of commerce on the Indian frontier, we find a new race of explorers treading their way with pious footsteps from shrine to shrine, and the sacred books and philosophic teaching of a wide-spreading faith the objects of their quest. The Chinese pilgrim Fa Hian was the first to leave a permanent record of his travels. His date is about A.D. 400, and he was only one of a large number of Chinese pilgrims who knew the road between India and China far better than any one knew it twenty-five years ago.

Although the northern approaches to India from the direction of China are rather far afield, yet recent revelations resulting from the researches of such enterprising travellers as Sven Hedin and Stein, confirming the older records, require some short reference to the nature of those communications between the outside world of Asia and India which distinguished the early centuries of our era. In those early centuries there was to be found in that western extension of the Gobi desert which we call Chinese Turkistan, in the low-lying country, mostly sand-covered, which stretches to a yellow horizon northward beneath the shimmering haze of an almost perpetual dust veil, very different conditions of human existence to those which now prevail. The zone of cultivation fed by the streams of the Kuen Lun was wider, stretching farther into the desert. Rivers ran fuller of water, carrying fertility farther afield; great lakes spread themselves where now there are but marshes and reeds, and cities flourished which have been covered over and buried under accumulating shifting sand for centuries. A great central desert there always has been within historic period, but it was a desert much modified by bordering oases of green fertility, and a spread of irrigated cultivation which is not to be found there now.

Amongst the most interesting relics recovered from some of these unearthed cities are certain writings in Karosthi and Brahmi (Indian) script, which testify to the existence of roads and posts and a regular system of communication between these cities of the plain, which must have been in existence in those early years of the Christian era when Karosthi was a spoken language in Northern India. All this now sand-buried country was Buddhist then, and a great city overlooked the wide expanse of the Lop Lake, and the rivers of the southern hills carried fertility far into the central plain. When the pilgrim Fa Hian trod the weary road from Western China to Chinese Turkistan by way of Turfan and the Buddhist city of Lop, he followed in a groove deep furrowed by the feet of many a pilgrim before him, and a highway for devotees for many a century after.

Strange as it may seem, the ancient people of this desert waste—the people who now occupy the cultivated strip of land at the foot of the Kuen Lun mountains which shut them off from Tibet—are an Indian race, or rather a race of Indian extraction, far more allied to the Indo-European than to any Mongol, Chinese, Tibetan, or Turk race with which they may have been recently admixed. Did they spread northward from India through the rugged passes of Northern Kashmir, taking with them the faith of their ancestors? We do not know; but there can be little doubt that the Chanto of the Lop basin and of Turfan is the lineal successor of the people who welcomed the Chinese pilgrims in their search after truth. Buddhist then and Mahomedan now, they seem to have lost little of their genial spirit of hospitality to strangers.

Khotan (Ilchi) was the central attraction of Western Turkistan, one at least of the most blessed wayside fountains of faith, the ultimate sources of which were only to be found in India. Those ultimate sources have long left India. They are concentrated in Lhasa now, which city is still the sanctuary of Buddhism to the thousands of pilgrims who make their way from China on the east and Mongolia on the north as full of devout aspiration and of patient searching after spiritual knowledge as was ever a Chinese pilgrim of past ages. Not only was Western Turkistan full of the monuments and temples of Buddhism scattered through the length of the green strips of territory which bordered the dry steppe of the central depression watered on the north by the Tarim River, and on the south by the many mountain streams which rushed through the gorges of the Kuen Lun, but there was an evident extension of outward and visible signs of the faith to the northward, embracing the Turfan basin, which in many of its physical characteristics is but a minor repetition of that of Lop, and possibly even as far west as the great Lake Issyk Kul. Thus the old pilgrim route to India from Western China, which was chosen by the devotee so as to include as many sacred shrines as could possibly be made to assist in adding grace to his pilgrimage, was a very different route to that now followed by the pious Mongolian or Western Chinaman to Lhasa.

Avoiding the penalties of the Nan Shan system of mountains which guards the Tibetan plateau on the north-east, these early pilgrims held on their journey almost due west, and, skirting the Mongolian steppe within sight of the Tibetan frontier hills, they reached Turfan; then turning southward, they passed on to the Lop Nor lake region by a well-ascertained route, which at that time intersected the well-watered and fertile land of Lulan. There is water still in the lower Tarim and in the Konche River beds, but it has proved in these late years to be useless for agricultural development owing to the incréasing salinity of the soil. Several recent attempts at recolonizing this area have resulted in total failure. From the Lop Lake to Khotan *via* Cherchen the old-world route was much the same as now, but the width of fertility stretched farther north from the Kuen Lun foothills, and the temples of Buddhism were rich and frequent, and thus were pious pilgrims refreshed and elevated every step of the way through this Turkistan region. Khotan appears to have been the local centre of the faith. No lake spread out its blue waters to catch the sky reflections here, but from the cold wastes of Tibet, through the gorges of the great Kuen Lun range, the waters of a river flowed down past the temples and stupas of Ilchi to find their way northward across the sands to the Tarim.

The high ritual of Buddhism in its ancient form was strange and imposing. When we read Fa Hian's account of the great car procession, we are no longer surprised at the effect which Buddhist symbolism exercised on its disciples. Fa Hian and his fellow-travellers were lodged in a sanghârâma, or temple of the "Great

Vehicle," where were three thousand priests "who assemble to eat at the sound of the *ghantâ*. On entering the dining hall their carriage is grave and demure, and they take their seats in regular order. All of them keep silence; there is no noise with their eating bowls; when the attendants give more food they are not allowed to speak to one another but only to make signs with the hand." "In this country," says Fa Hian, "there are fourteen great sanghârâmas. From the first day of the fourth month they sweep and water the thoroughfares within the city and decorate the streets. Above the city gate they stretch an awning and use every kind of adornment. This is when the King and Queen and Court ladies take their place. The Gomâti priests first of all take their images in the procession. About three or four li from the city they make a four-wheeled image car about 30 feet high, in appearance like a moving palace adorned with the seven precious substances. They fix upon it streamers of silk and canopy curtains. The figure is placed in the car with two Bodhisatevas as companions, while the Devas attend on them; all kinds of polished ornaments made of gold and silver hang suspended in the air. When the image is 100 paces from the gate the King takes off his royal cap, and changing his clothes for new ones proceeds barefooted, with flowers and incense in his hand, from the city, followed by his attendants. On meeting the image he bows down his head and worships at its feet, scattering the flowers and burning the incense. On entering the city the Queen and Court ladies scatter about all kinds of flowers and throw them down in wild profusion. So splendid are the arrangements for worship!"[1] Thus writes Fa Hian, and it is sufficient to testify to the strength of Buddhism and the magnificence of its ritual in the third century of our era, when India still held the chief fountains of inspiration ere the holy of holies was transferred to Lhasa and the pilgrim route was changed.

So far, then, we need not look for the influence exercised by the most recent climatic pulsation of Central Asia which has dried up the water-springs and allowed the sand-drifts to accumulate above many of the minor townships of the Lop basin, in order to account for the trend of Asiatic religious history towards Tibet. It was the gradual decay of the faith, and its final departure from its birthplace in the plains of India in later centuries, which sent pilgrims on another track, and left many of the northern routes to be rediscovered by European explorers in the nineteenth century. Most of the Chinese pilgrims visited Khotan, but from Khotan onward their steps were bent in several directions. Some of them visited Ki-pin, which has been identified with the upper Kabul River basin. Here, indeed, were scattered a wealth of Buddhist records to be studied,

[1] *Buddhist Records of the Western World*, vol. i. p. 27.

shrines to be visited, and temples to be seen. The road from Balkh to Kabul and from Kabul to the Punjab was pre-eminently a Buddhist route. Balkh, Haibak, and Bamian all testify, as does the neighbourhood of Kabul itself, to the existence of a lively Buddhist history before the Mahomedan Conquest, and between Kabul and India there are Buddhist remains near Jalalabad which rival in splendour those of the Swat valley and the Upper Punjab. All these places were objects of devout attention undoubtedly, but to reach Kabul *via* Balkh from Khotan it would be necessary to cross the Pamirs and Badakshan. It is not easy to follow in detail the footsteps of these devotees, but it is obvious that until they entered the "Tsungling" mountains they remained north of the great trans-Himalayan ranges and of the Hindu Kush. The Tsungling was the dreaded barrier between China and India, and the wild tales of the horrors which attended the crossing of the mountains testify to the fact that they were not much easier of access or transit at the beginning of the Christian era than they are now.

The direct distance between Khotan and Balkh is not less than 700 miles, and 700 miles of such a mountain wilderness as would be involved by the passing of the Pamirs into the valley of the Oxus and the plains of Badakshan would represent 900 to 1000 of any ordinary travelling. And yet there appear to be indications of a close connection between these two centres of Buddhism. The great temple a mile or two to the west of Khotan, called the Nava Sanghârâma, or royal new temple, is the same as that to the south-west of Balkh, according to a later traveller, Hiuen Tsiang, while the kings of Khotan were said to be descended from Vaisravana, the protector of the Balkh convent. No modern traveller has crossed Badakshan from the Pamirs to Balkh, but the general conformation of the country is fairly well ascertained, and there can be no doubt that the journey would occupy any pilgrim, no matter how devout and enthusiastic, at least two and a half months, and another month would be required to traverse the road from Balkh *via* Hiabak, or Baiman, over the Hindu Kush to Kabul.

Now we are told that Fa Hian journeyed twenty-five days to the Tsen-ho country, from whence, by marching four days southward, he entered the Tsungling mountains. Another twenty-five days' rugged marching took him to the Kie-sha country, a country "hilly and cold" in "the midst of the Tsungling mountains," where he rejoined his companions who had started for Ki-pin. It is therefore clear that he did not rejoin them at Kabul, nor could they have gone there; and the question arises—Where is Kie-sha? The continuation of Fa Hian's story gives the solution to the riddle. Another month's wandering from Kie-sha across the Tsungling mountains took him to North India. It was a perilous journey. The terrors of it remained engraved on the memory of the saint after his return to his home in China. Great "poison dragons" lived in those mountains, who spat poison and gravel-stones at passing pilgrims, and few there were who survived the encounter. The impression conveyed of furious blasts of mountain-bred winds is vivid, and many travellers since Fa Hian's time have suffered therefrom. "On entering the borders" of India he came to a little country called To-li. To-li seems to be identified beyond dispute with Darel, and with this to guide us we begin to see where our pilgrims must have passed. Fifteen days more of Tsungling mountain-climbing southwards took him to Wuchung (Udyana), where he remained during the rains. Thence he went "south" to Sin-ho-to (Swat), and finally "descended" into Gandara, or the Upper Punjab.

From these final stages of his journey India-ward there is little difficulty in recognizing that Kie-sha must be Kashmir. In the first place, Kashmir lies on the most direct route between Chinese Turkistan and India. Nor is it possible to believe that the wealth of Buddhist remains which now appeal to the antiquarian in that delightful garden of the Himalayas were not more or less due to the first impulse of the devotees of the early faith to plant the seeds of Buddhism where the passing to and fro of innumerable bands of pilgrims would of necessity occur. Through Kashmir lay the high-road to High Asia, at that time included in the Buddhist fold, where Indian language had crystallized and corroborated the faith that was born in India. Thus it was that glorious temples arose amidst the groves and on the slopes of Kashmir hills, and even in the days of Fa Hian, when Buddhism was already nine centuries old, there must have been much to beguile the pilgrim to devotional study. In short, Kashmir could not be overlooked by any devotee, and whether the direct route thither was taken from Khotan, or whether Kashmir was visited in due course from Northern India, we may be certain that it was one of the chief objectives of Chinese pilgrimage.

Fa Hian says so little about the kingdom of Kie-sha which can be made use of to assist us, that it is not easy to identify the part of Kashmir to which he refers. Twenty-five days after entering the Tsungling mountains would enable him to reach the valley of Kashmir by the Karakoram Pass, Leh, and the Zoji-la at the head of the Sind valley. It is not a matter of much consequence for our purposes which route he took, as it is quite clear that all these northern routes were open to Chinese pilgrim traffic from the very earliest times. The alternative route would be to the head of the Tagdumbash Pamir, over the Killik Pass, and by Hunza to Gilgit and Astor. The Hunza country (Kunjut) has always had an attraction for the Chinese. It has been conquered and held by China, and is still reckoned by its inhabitants as part of the Chinese Empire. Hunza and Nagar pay tribute to China to this day.

If we remember that the pains and penalties of a pilgrimage over any of the Hindu Kush passes, or by the Karakoram (the chief trade route through all time), to India, is as nothing to the trials which modern Mongolian pilgrims undergo between China and Lhasa, over the terrible altitudes of the Tibetan plateau, there will be little to surprise us in these earlier achievements. Pioneers of exploration in the true sense they were not, for the Himalayan byways must have been as well known to them as were the Asiatic highways to Alexander ere he attempted to reach India. We may assume, however, that Fa Hian entered the central valley of Kashmir from Leh, for it gives a reasonable pretext for his choice of a route out of it. It is not likely that he would go twice over the same ground. He witnessed the pomp and pageantry of Buddhist ritual in Kie-sha. The King of the country had kept the great five-yearly assembly. He had "summoned Sramanas from the four quarters, who came together like clouds." Silken canopies and flags with gold and silver lotus-flowers figure amongst the ritualistic properties, and form part of the processional arrangements which end with the invariable offerings to the priests. "The King, taking from the chief officer of the Embassy the horse he rides, with its saddle and bridle, mounts it, and then, taking white taffeta, jewels of various kinds, and things required by the Sramanas, in union with his ministers, he vows to give them all to the priests. Having thus given them, they are redeemed at a price from the priests." No mention is made of the price, but as the Kashmiri of the past has been excellently well described by another pilgrim as a true prototype of the Kashmiri of the present, it is unlikely that the King lost much by the deal.

The description of Kie-sha as "in the middle of the Tsungling range" would hardly apply to any country but Kashmir, and the fact is noted that from Kie-sha towards India the vegetation changes in character. Having crossed Tsungling, we arrive at North India, says Fa Hian, but to reach the "little country called To-li" (Darel) he would have to cross by the Burzil Pass into the basin of the Indus, and then follow the Gilgit River to a point under the shadow of the Hindu Koh range, opposite the head-waters of the Darel. Crossing the Hindu Koh, he would then drop straight into this "little country." Remembering something of the nature of the road to Gilgit ere our military engineers fashioned a sound highway out of the rocky hill-sides, one can sympathize with the pious Fa Hian when recalling in after years the frightful experiences of that journey.

A few miles beyond Gilgit the rough evidences of a ruined stupa, and a still rougher outline of a Buddhist figure cut on the rocks which guard a narrow gorge leading up the Hindu Koh slopes, points to the take-off for Darel. No modern explorer has followed that route, except one of the native explorers of the Indian survey who travelled under the soubriquet of "the Mullah." The Mullah made his way through the Darel valley to the Indus, and describes it as a difficult route. There is little variation in the tale of troubled progress, but "the Mullah" makes no mention of Buddhist relics, nor is it likely that they would have appealed to him had he seen them. There can be little doubt, however, that Darel holds some hidden secrets for future enterprise to disclose. "Keeping along Tsungling, they journeyed southward for fifteen days," says Fa Hian. "The road is difficult and broken with steep crags and precipices in the way. The mountain-side is simply a stone wall standing up 10,000 feet. Looking down, the sight is confused and there is no sure foothold. Below is a river called Sintu-ho (Indus). In old days men bored through the walls to make a way, and spread out side ladders, of which there are seven hundred in all to pass. Having passed the ladders, we proceed by a hanging rope bridge to cross the river." All this agrees fairly well with the Mullah's account of ladders and precipices, and locates the route without much doubt. The Darel stream joins the Indus some 30 to 35 miles below Chilas, where the course of the latter river is practically unsurveyed. Crossing the Indus, Fa Hian came to Wuchung, which is identified with Udyana, or Upper Swat, and there he remained during the rains. The Indus below the Darel junction is confined within a narrow steep-sided gorge with hills running high on either side, those on the east approaching 15,000 and 16,000 feet. There are villages, groups of flat-roofed shanties, clinging like limpets to the rocks, but there is little space for cultivation, and no record of Buddhist remains north of Buner. No systematic search has been possible.

Investigations such as led to the remarkable discovery by Dr. Stein of the site of that famous Buddhist sanctuary marking the spot where Buddha, in a former birth, offered his body to the starving tigress on Mount Banj, south of Buner, have never been possible farther north, on account of the dangerous character of the hill-people of those regions. Other Chinese pilgrims, Song Yun (A.D. 520) and Huec Sheng, have recorded that after leaving the capital of ancient Udyana (near Manglaor, in Upper Swat) they journeyed for eight days south-east, and reached the place where Buddha made his body offering. "There high mountains rose with steep slopes and dizzy peaks reaching to the clouds," etc. "There stood on the mountain the temple of the collected bones which counted

300 priests." But there is no mention of other Buddhist sites of importance in the valley of the Indus. Leaving Udyana, Fa Hian and his companions went south to the country of Su-ho-to (Lower Swat), and finally ("descending eastward") in five days found themselves in Gandhara—or the Upper Punjab. Nine days' journey eastward from the point where they reached Gandhara they came to the place of Buddha's body-offering, or Mount Banj. Such, in brief outline, is the story of one pilgrim's journey across the Himalayas to India. Other pilgrims undoubtedly entered India *via* the Kabul River valley, but we need hardly follow them. There were hundreds of them, possibly thousands, and the pains and penalties of the pilgrimage but served to add merit to their devotion.

The point of the story lies in its revelation as regards connection between Central Asia and India in the early centuries A.D. Clearly there was no pass unknown or unvisited by the Chinese. Not merely the direct routes, but all the connecting ways which linked up one Buddhist centre with another were equally well known. What has required from us a weary process of investigation to overcome the difficulties of map-making, was to them, if not exactly an open book, certainly a geographical record which could be turned to practical use, and it is instructive to note the use that was made of it. As a pious duty, bristling with difficulty and danger, travel over the wandering tracks which pass through the northern gates of the Himalayas was regarded with fervour; but it may be taken for granted that less pious-minded adventurers than the Chinese pilgrims would most certainly have made good use of that geographical knowledge to exploit the riches of India had such a proceeding been possible. We know that attempts have been made. From the earliest times the Mongol hordes of China and Central Asia have been directed on India, and no gateway which could offer any possible hope of admittance has been neglected. Baktria (Badakshan), lying beyond the mountain barrier, had been at their mercy. The successors to Alexander's legions in that country were swamped and dispersed within a century or two of the foundation of the Greek kingdom; and the Kabul River way to India has let in army after army. But these northern passes have not only barred migratory Asiatic hordes through all ages, but have proved too much even for small organized Mongol military expeditions.

The Chinese hosts, who apparently thought little of crossing the Tibetan frontier over a succession of Alpine passes such as no Western general in the world's history has ever encountered, failed to penetrate farther than Kunjut. The Mongol invasion of Tibet early in the sixteenth century (which is so graphically described in the Tarikh-i-Rashidi by Mirza Haidar) was tentatively pushed into Kashmir *via* Ladakh, and was defeated by the natural difficulties of the country—not by the resistance of the weak-kneed Kashmiri—much, indeed, as a similar expedition to Lhasa was defeated by cold and starvation. No modern ingenuity has as yet contrived a method of dealing with the passive resistance of serrated bands of mountains of such altitude as the Himalayas. No railway could be carried over such a series of snow-capped ramparts; no force that was not composed of Asiatic mountaineers could attempt to pass them with any chance of success; and these northern lines, these eternal defences of Nature's making may well be left, a vast silent wilderness of peaks, undisturbed by man's puny efforts to improve their strength. Certainly the making of highways in the midst of them is not the surest means of adding to their natural powers of passive obstruction, although such public works may possibly be deemed necessary in the interests of peace and order preservation amongst the "snowy mountain men."

Chinese pilgrims no longer tread those rocky mountain-paths (except in the pages of Rudyard Kipling's entrancing work), and the tides of devotion have set in other directions—to Mecca or to Lhasa; but the fact that thousands of Buddhist worshippers yearly undertake a journey which, for the hardships entailed by cold and starvation between the western borders of China and Lhasa, should surely secure for them a reserve of merit equal to that gathered by their forefathers from the

"Tsungling" mountains, might possibly lead to the question whether the plateau of Eastern Tibet does not afford the open way which is not to be found farther west. If a Chinese force of 70,000 men could advance into the heart of Tibet, and finally administer a severe defeat on the Gurkhas (which surely occurred in 1792) in Nepal, it is clear that such a force could equally well reach Lhasa. It is also certain that the stupendous mountain-chains and the elevated passes, which are the ruling features of the eastern entrance into Tibet from China, far exceed in natural strength and difficulty those which intervene between the plains of India and Lhasa. We are therefore bound to admit that it might be possible for an unopposed Chinese force to invade India by Eastern Tibet; possibly even by the valley of Assam. There is, however, no record that such an attempt has ever been made. The savage and untamable disposition of the eastern Himalayan tribes, and their intense hostility to strangers may have been, through all time, a strong deterrent to any active exploitation of their country; and the density of the forests which close down on the narrow ways which intersect their hills, give them an advantage in savage tactics such as was not possessed by the fighting Gurkha tribe in Nepal. But whatever the reason may be, there is apparently no record of any Chinese force descending through the Himalayas into the eastern plains of India by any of the many ways afforded by the affluents of the Brahmaputra. We may, I think, rest very well assured that no such attempt could possibly be made by any force other than Chinese, and that it is not likely that it ever will be made by them. We do not (at present) look to the north-east (to China) for the shadows of coming events in India. We look to the north, and looking in that direction we are quite content to write down the approach to India by any serious military force across Tibet or through the northern gateways of Kashmir to be an impossibility.

The footsteps of the Buddhist pilgrim point no road for the tread of armies. In the interests of geographical research it is well to follow their tracks, and to learn how much wiser geographically they were in their day than we are now. It is well to remember that as modern explorers we are as hopelessly behind them in the spirit of enterprise, which reaches after an ethical ideal, as we are ahead of them in the process of attaining exact knowledge of the world's physiography, and recording it.

CHAPTER VII

MEDIÆVAL GEOGRAPHY—SEISTAN AND AFGHANISTAN

It was about eight centuries before Buddhism, debased and corrupted, tainted with Siva worship and loaded with all the ghastly paraphernalia of a savage demonology, had been driven from India across the Himalayas, that the Star of Bethlehem had guided men from the East to the cradle of the Christian faith—a faith so like Buddhism in its ethical teaching and so unlike in its spiritual conceptions,—and during those eight centuries Christianity had already been spread by Apostles and missionaries through the broad extent of High Asia. Thereupon arose a new propaganda which, spreading outwards from a centre in south-west Arabia, finally set all humanity into movement, impelling men to call the wide world to a recognition of Allah and his one Prophet by methods which eventually included the use of fire and sword. The rise of the faith of Islam was nearly coincident (so far as India was concerned) with the fall of Buddhism. Thenceforward the gentle life-saving precepts of Gautama were to be taught in the south, and east, and north; in Ceylon, Burma, China, and Mongolia after being first firmly rooted in Tibet and Turkistan, but never again in the sacred groves of the land of their birth. And this raging religious hurricane of Islam swept all before it for century after century until, checked at last in Western Europe, it left the world ennobled by many a magnificent monument, and, by adding to the enlightenment of the dark places of the earth, fulfilled a mission in the development of mankind. With it there arose a new race of explorers who travelled into India from the west and north-west, searching out new ways for their commerce, and it is with them now and their marvellous records of restless commercial activity that we have to deal. Masters of the sea, even as of the land, no military and naval supremacy which has ever directed the destinies of nations was so widespread in its geographical field of enterprise as that of the Arabs. The whole world was theirs to explore. Their ships furrowed new paths across the seas, even as their khafilas trod out new highways over the land; and at the root of all their movement was the commercial instinct of the Semite. After all it was the eternal question of what would pay. Their progenitors had been builders of cities, of roads, of huge dams for water storage and irrigation, and directors for public works in Europe, Asia, and Africa. The might of the sword of Islam but carved the way for the slave-owner and the merchant to follow. Thus it is that mediæval records of exploration in Afghanistan and Baluchistan are mostly Arab records; and it is from them that we learn the "open sesame" of India's landward gates, long ere the seaports of her coasts were visited by European ships.

Nothing in the history of the world is more surprising than the rapid spread of Arab conquests in Asia, Africa, and Western Europe at the close of the seventh century of our era, excepting, perhaps, the thoroughness of the subsequent disappearance of Arab influence, and the absolute effacement of the Arabic language in those countries which Arabs ruled and robbed. In Persia, Makran, Central Asia, or the Indus valley, hardly a word of Arabic is now to be recognized. Geographical terms may here and there be found near the coast, surviving only because Arab ships still skirt those shores and the sailor calls the landmarks by old-world names. Even in the English language the sea terms of the Arab sailor still live. What is our "Admiral" but the "Al mir ul bahr" of the Arabian Sea, or our "Barge" but his "Barija," or warship! But in Sind, where Arab supremacy lasted for at least three centuries, there is nothing left to indicate that the Arab ever was there.

The effacement of the Arab in India is chiefly due to the Afghan, the Turk, and the Mongol. Mahmud of Ghazni put the finishing blow to Arab supremacy in the Indus valley, when he sacked Multan about the beginning of the eleventh century; and subsequently the destroying hordes of Chenghiz Khan and Tamerlane completed the final downfall of the Empire of the Khalifs.

Between the beginning of the eighth century and that of the eleventh the whole world of the Indian north-west frontier and its broad hinterland, extending to the Tigris and the Oxus, was much traversed and thoroughly well known to the Arab trader. In Makran we have seen how they shaped out for themselves overland routes to India, establishing big trade centres in flourishing towns, burying their dead in layers on the hill-sides, cultivating their national fruit, the date, in Makran valleys, and surrounding themselves with the wealth and beauty of irrigated agriculture. The chief impulse to Arab exploration emanated from the seat of the Khalifs in Mesopotamia, and the schools of Western Persia and Bagdad appear to have educated the best of those practical geographers who have left us their records of travel in the East; but there are indications of an occasional influx of Arabs from the coasts of Southern Arabia about whom we learn nothing whatever from mediæval histories. It will be at any rate interesting to discuss the general trend of exploration and travel, associated either with pilgrimage or commerce, which distinguished the days of Arab supremacy, and which throws considerable light on the geography of the Indian borderland before its political features were re-arranged by the hand of Chenghiz Khan and his successors. This has never yet been attempted by the light of recent investigations, and even now it can only be done partially and indifferently from the want of completed maps. The borderland which touches the Arabian Sea—Southern Baluchistan—has been completely explored and mapped, and the more obvious inferences to be derived from that mapping have already been made. But Seistan, Karmania, the highways and cities of Turkistan (Tocharistan) and Badakshan have not, so far as I know, been outlined in any modern work based on Arab writings and collated with the geographical surveys of the Russo-Afghan Boundary Commission and their reports. It was after all but a cursory examination of a huge area of most interesting country that was possible within the limited time devoted to boundary demarcation labours in 1883-85; but the physical features of this part of Asia being now fairly well defined, there is a good deal to be inferred with reasonable probability from the circumstance that highways and cities must ever be dependent for their location on the distributions of topography.

The first impression produced by the general overlook of all the historic area which lies between Eastern Persia and the sources on the Oxus, is one of surprise. There is so little left of this great busy world of Arab commerce. It seems to have dropped out of the world's economy, and certain regions to have reverted to a phase of pristine freedom from sordid competition, which argues much for a decreased population and a desiccated area of once flourishing lands.

There are no forests and jungles in Western Afghanistan, or at least only in restricted spaces on the mountain-slopes, so that there is no wild undergrowth uprooting and covering the evidences of man's busy habitation such as we find in Ceylon and the Nepal Tarai; where may be seen strange staring stone witnesses of the faith of former centuries, half hidden amidst the wild beauty and luxuriance of tropical forest growth. There is nothing indeed quite so interesting. Nature has spread out smooth grass slopes carpeted with sweet flowers in summer, but frozen and wind-swept in winter; and beneath the surface we know for a surety that the buried remains of centuries of busy traffic and marketing lie hidden, but there is frequently no sign whatever above ground. It is difficult to account for the utter want of visible evidence. In the processes of clearing a field for military action, when it becomes essential to remove some obstructive mud-built village and trace a clear and free zone for artillery fire, it is often found that the work of destruction is exceedingly difficult. Only with the most careful management can the debris be so dispersed that it affords no better cover to the enemy than the village which it once represented. As for effacing it altogether, only time, with the assistance of wind and weather, can accomplish that. But it is remarkable with what completeness time succeeds. I have stood on the site of a buried city in Sind—a city, too, of the mediæval era of Arab ascendency—and have recognized no trace of it but what appeared to be the turbaned effigies of a multitude of faithful mourners in various expressive attitudes of grief and despair, who represented the ancient cemetery of the city. The city had been wiped off the land as clean as if it had been swept into the sea, but the burying places remained, and the stone mourners continue mourning through the centuries.

The architectural order of these Khalmat tombs is quite Saracenic, and the vestiges of geometrical design which relieve the plain surface of the stone work and accentuate the lines of arch and moulding, are all clean cut and clear. At the end of each tomb, set up on a pedestal, the folded turban testifies in hard stone to the faith of the occupant beneath. The sharp edges of the slabs and the clearness of the ornamental carving are sufficient to prove that the age of these tombs and monuments cannot be so very remote, although remote enough to have led to the effacement of the township to which they belong. Sometimes a mound, where no mound would naturally occur, indicates the base of one of the larger buildings. Sometimes in the slanting rays of the evening sun certain shadows, unobserved before, take shape and pattern themselves into the form of a basement; and almost always after heavy rain strange little ornaments, beads, and coins, glass bangles, rings, etc., are washed out on the surface which tell their own tale as surely as does the widespread and infinitely varied remnants of household crockery. This last feature is sometimes quite amazing in its variety and extent, and the quality of the local finds is not a bad indication of the quality of the local household which made use of it. "Celadon" ware is abundant from Karachi to Babylon, and some of it is of extraordinary fineness and beauty of glaze. Pale sage green is invariably the colour of it, and the tradition of luck which attaches to it is common from China to Arabia.

In places where vanished towns were in existence as late as the eighteenth century (for instance, in the Helmund valley below Rudbar), debris of pottery may be found literally in tons. In other places, still living, where generations of cities have gradually waxed and waned in successive stages, each in turn forming the foundation of a new growth, it is very difficult to derive any true historical indication from the debris which is to be found near the surface. Nothing but systematic and extensive excavation will suffice to prove that the existing conglomeration of rubbishy bazaars and ruined mosques is only the last and most unworthy phase of the existence of a city the glory of whose history is to be found in the world-wide tradition of past centuries. And so it happens that, moving in the footsteps of these old mediæval commercial travellers, with the story of their travels in one's hand, and the indications of hill and plain and river to testify to the way they went, and a fair possibility of estimating distances according to their slipshod reckoning of a "day's journey," one may possess the moral certainty that one has reached a position where once there stood a flourishing market-town without the faintest outward indication of it. Without facilities for digging and delving, and the time for careful examination, there must necessarily be a certain amount of conjecture about the exact locality of some even of the most famous towns which were centres of Arab trade through High Asia. Some indeed are to be found still under their ancient names, but others (and amongst them many of great importance) are no longer recognizable in the place where once they palpitated with vigorous Eastern life.

The area of Asia which for three or four centuries witnessed the monopoly of Arab trade included very nearly the whole continent. Asia Minor may be omitted from that area, and the remoter parts of China; but all the Indian borderland was literally at their feet; and we can now proceed to trace out some of their principal lines of route and their chief halting-places in those districts of which the mediæval geography has lately become known.

It is not at all necessary, even if it were possible, to follow the records of all the eminent Arab travellers who at intervals trod these weary roads. In the first place they often copied their records from one another, so that there is much vain repetition in them. In the second place they are not all equally trustworthy, and their writing and spelling, especially in place-names, wants that attention to diacritical marks which in Eastern orthography is essential to correct transliteration. It is perhaps unfortunate that the most eminent geographer amongst them should not have been a traveller, but simply a compiler.

Abu Abdulla Mohamed was born at Ceuta in Morocco towards the end of the eleventh century. Being descended from a family named Idris, he came to be known as Al Idrisi. The branch of the family from which Idrisi sprang ruled over the city of Magala. He travelled in Europe and eventually settled at the Court of Roger II. in Sicily. Here he wrote his book on geography. He quotes the various authors whom he consulted in its compilation, and derived further information from travellers whose accounts he compared and tested. The title of his work is *The Delight of those who seek to wander through the Regions of the World*, and it is from the French translation of this work by Jaubert that the following notes on the countries lying beyond the western borders of India are taken. This account may be accepted as representing the condition of political and commercial geography throughout those regions at the end of the eleventh century, some eighty years or so after the borders of India had been periodically harried by Mahmud of Ghazni, and not very long before the Mongol host appeared on the horizon and made a clean sweep of Asiatic civilization.

To the west of the Indian frontier in those early days lay the Persian provinces of Makran and Sejistan (Seistan), which two provinces between them appear to represent a great part of modern Baluchistan. The "Belous" were not yet in Baluchistan; they lived north of the mountains occupied by the "Kufs," with whom they are invariably associated in Arab geography. "The Kufs," says Idrisi, "are the only people who do not speak Persian in the province of Kerman. Their mountains reach to the Persian Gulf, being bordered on the north by the country of Najirman (? Nakirman), on the south and east by the sea and the Makran deserts, on the west by the sea and the 'Belous' country and the districts of Matiban and Hormuz." These are doubtless the "Bashkird" mountains, and the "species of Kurd, brave and savage" which inhabited them under the name of Kufs probably represent the progenitors of the present inhabitants.

The "Bolous" or "Belous" lived in the plains

to the north "right up to the foot of the mountains," and these are the people (according to Mr. Longworth Dames) who, hailing originally from the Caspian provinces, are the typical Baluch tribespeople of to-day.

These mountains, which Idrisi calls the "cold mountains," extend to the north-west of Jirift and are "fertile, productive, and wooded." "It is a country where snow falls every year," and of which "the inhabitants are virtuous and innocent." There have been changes since Idrisi's time, both moral and physical, but here is a strong item of evidence in favour of the theory of the gradual desiccation which has enveloped Southern Baluchistan and dried up the water-springs of Makran. What Idrisi called the "Great Desert" is comprehensive. All the great central wastes of Persia, including the Kerman desert as well as the basin of the Helmund south of the hills, the frontier hills of the Sind border up to Multan, were a part of it, and they were inhabited by nomadic tribes of "thieves and brigands."

Modern Seistan is a flat, unwholesome country, distributed geographically on either side of the Helmund between Persia and Afghanistan. It owes its place in history and its reputation for enormous productiveness to the fact that it is the great central basin of Afghanistan, where the Helmund and other Afghan rivers run to a finish in vast swamps, or lagoons. Surrounded by deserts, Seistan is never waterless, and there was, in days which can hardly be called ancient, a really fine system of irrigation, which fertilized a fairly large tract of now unproductive land on the Persian side of the river. The amount of land thus brought under cultivation was considerable, but not considerable enough to justify the historic reputation which Seistan has always enjoyed as the "Granary of Asia." This traditional wealth was no doubt exaggerated from the fact that the fertility of Seistan (like that of the Herat valley, which is after all but an insignificant item in Afghan territory) was in direct contrast to the vast expanse of profitless desert with which it was surrounded—a green oasis in the midst of an Asiatic wilderness.

The Helmund has taken to itself many channels in the course of measurable time. Its ancient beds have been traced and mapped, and with them have been found evidences of closely-packed townships and villages, where the shifting waters and consequent encroachment of sand-waves leave no sign of life at present.

Century after century the same eternal process of obliteration and renovation has proceeded. Millions of tons of silt have been deposited in this great alluvial basin. Levels have changed and the waters have wandered irresponsibly into a network of channels westward. Then the howling, desiccating winds of the north-west have carried back sand-waves and silt, burying villages and filling the atmosphere for hundreds of miles southward with impalpable dust, crossing the Helmund deserts even to the frontier of India. There is no measurable scale for the force of the Seistan winds. They scoop up the sand and sweep clean the surface of the earth, polishing the rounded edges of the ragged walls of the Helmund valley ruins. It is a notable fact that no part of these ruins face the wind. All that is left of palaces and citadels stands "end on" to the north-west. For a few short months in the year the wind is modified, and then there instantly arises the plague of insects which render life a burden to every living thing. And yet Seistan has played a most important part in the history of Asia, and may play an important rôle again.

Arab records are very full of Seistan. The earliest of them that give any serious geographical information are the records of Ibn Haukel, but there are certainly indications in his account which engender a suspicion that he never really visited the country. He mentions the capital Zarinje (of which the ruins cover an enormous area to the east of Nasratabad, the present capital) and writes of it as a very large town with five gates, one of which "leads to Bist." There were extensive fortifications, and a bazaar of which he reckons the annual revenue to be 1000 direms.

There were canals innumerable, and always the wind and the windmills. It is curious that he traces the Helmund as running to Seistan first and then to the Darya-i-Zarah. This is in fact correct, only the Darya-i-Zarah (or Gaod-i-Zireh, as we know it) receives no water from the Helmund until the great Hamún (lagoons) to the north of Nasratabad are filled to overflow. He also mentions two rivers as flowing into the Zarah—one from Farah (an important place in his time), which is impossible, as it would have to cross the Helmund; and one from Ghur. This indicates almost certainly that the name Zarah was not confined, as it is now, to the great salt swamp south of Rudbar on the Helmund, but it included the Hamúns north of Nasratabad, into which the Farah River and the Ghur River do actually empty themselves. At present these two great lake systems are separated by about 120 miles of Helmund River basin, and are only connected occasionally in flood time by means of the overflow (called Shelag) already referred to. The mention of Bist, and of the bridge of boats across the river at that point, is important, for it is clear that about the year A.D. 950 one high-road for trade eastward was across the desert, *i.e. via* the Khash Rud valley from Zarinje to about the meridian of 63 E.L. and then straight over the desert to Bist (Kala Bist of modern mapping). The further mention of robats (or resting-places) *en route*, indicates that it was well kept up and a much traversed high-road. Subsequently Girishk appears to have become the popular crossing-place of the river, but it is well to remember that the earlier route still exists, and could readily be made available for a flank march on Kandahar.

From Idrisi's writings we learn that a century later, *i.e.* about the end of the eleventh century, the Seistan province extended far beyond its present limits. Bamian and Ghur (*i.e.* the central hills of Afghanistan) were *vis-à-vis* to that province; Farah was included; and probably the whole line of the frontier hills from the Sulimanis, opposite Multan, to Sibi and Kalat. It was an enormous province, and a new light breaks on its traditional wealth in grain and agricultural produce when we understand its vast extent.

The regions of Ghur and Dawar bordered it to the north, and there is a word or two to be said about both hereafter. Ghur in the eleventh century included the valley of Herat and all the wedge of mountainous country south of it to Dawar, but how far Seistan extended into the heart of the mountain system which culminates to the south-west of Kabul it is difficult to say. It is difficult to understand the statement that Bamian, for instance, bordered Seistan, with Ghur in between, unless, indeed, in these early days of Ghur's history (for Ghur was only conquered by the Arabs in A.D. 1020, and was still far from intertwining its history with that of Ghazni when Idrisi wrote) the greatness of Bamian overshadowed the light of the lesser valleys of Ghur, and Bamian was the ruling province of Central Afghanistan. This, indeed, seems possible.

The district of Dawar to the south of Ghur has always been something of a mystery to geographers. Described by Idrisi as "vast, rich, and fertile," and "the line of defence on the side of Ghur, Baghnein, and Khilkh," it would be impossible to place it without a knowledge of the towns mentioned, were it not that we are told that Derthel, one of the chief towns of Dawar, is on the Helmund, and that one crosses the river there "in order to reach Sarwan." This at once indicates the traditional ford at Girishk as the crossing-place, and Zamindawar as the Dawar of Idrisi. Khilkh then becomes intelligible also as a town of the Khilkhi (the people who then occupied Dawar, described as Turkish by Idrisi, and probably identified with the modern Ghilzai), and finds its modern representative in the Kalat-i-Ghilzai which crowns the well-known rock on the road from Kandahar to Kabul. "The country is inhabited by a people called Khilkh," says Idrisi. "The Khilkhs are of a Turkish race, who from a remote period have inhabited this country, and whose habitations are spread to the north of India on the flank of Ghur and in western Seistan." Thus the position of the Ghilzai in the ethnography of Central Afghanistan appears to have been established long before the days of Mongol irruption. Then as now they formed a very important tribal community.

It is, however, sometimes difficult to reconcile Idrisi's account of the routes followed by his countrymen in this part of Asia with existing geographical features. Deserts and mountains must have been much the same as they are now, and the best, if not the only, way to unravel the geographical tangle is to take his itinerary and see where it leads us. Of Baghnein on the southern borders of Seistan, he says it is an "agreeable country, fertile and abundant in fruits." From there (*i.e.* the country, not the town) to Derthel one reckons one day's journey through the nomad tribes of Bechinks, Derthel being "situated on the banks of the Helmund and one of the chief towns of Dawar."

So we have to cross an open uncultivated region for 40 miles or so from Baghnein to reach Derthel, on the Helmund. Again, "one crosses the Helmund at Derthel to reach Sarwan—a town situated about one day's journey off," on which depends a territory which produces everything in abundance. "Sarwan is bigger than Fars, and more rich in fruit and all sorts of productions. Grapes are transported to Bost (or Bist), a town two days distant passing by Firozand, which possesses a big market, and is on the traveller's right as he travels to Benjawai, which is *vis-à-vis* to Derthel." "Rudhan (? Rudbar) is a small town south of the Helmund."

The Helmund valley has been surveyed from Zamindawar to its final exit into the Seistan lagoons, and we know that at Girishk there is a very ancient ford, which now marks, and has always marked, the great highway from Kandahar to Herat. South of Girishk, at the junction of the Arghandab with the Helmund, we find extensive and ancient ruins at Kala Bist; and south of that again there are many ruins at intervals in the Helmund valley; but these latter are comparatively recent, dating from the time of the Kaiani Maliks of the eighteenth century.

Assuming that the Helmund fords have remained constant, and placing Derthel on one side of the river at Girishk and Benjawai on the other, we find on our modern maps that from the ford it is a possible day's journey to Kala Sarwan, higher up the Helmund, where "fruit and grapes are to be had in abundance," and from whence they might certainly have been sent to Bist, where grapes do not grow. Baghnein, separated from Derthel by a strip of nomad country, one day's journey wide, might thus be on either side the Helmund; but its contiguity to Ghur seems to favour a position to the west, rather than to the east, of the river, somewhere east of the plains of Bukwa about Washir.

Now it is certain that no Arab traveller, crossing the Helmund desert from the west by the direct route recently exploited in British Indian interests below Kala Bist and south of the river, could by any possibility have reached a grape-growing and highly-cultivated country in one day's journey. The inference, then, is tolerably clear. Arab traders and travellers never made use of this southern route. Nor should we ourselves make use of such a route as that *via* Nushki and the Koh-i-Malik Siah, were we not forced into it by Afghan policy. The natural high-road from the east of Persia and Herat to India is *via* the plains of Kandahar and the ford of Girishk, and the Arabs, with all Khorasan at their feet, were not likely to travel any other way.

Undoubtedly the system of approach to the Indus valley, open to Arab traffic from Syria and Bagdad, most generally used and most widely recognized was that through the Makran valleys to Karachi and Sind, whilst the inland route, *via* Persia and Seistan, made the well-known ford of the Helmund at Girishk, or the boat bridge at Kala Bist, its objective, and passed over the river to the plains about Kandahar. But it is a very remarkable, and possibly a significant, fact that the continuation of the route to Sind and the Indus valley from the plains about Kandahar is not mentioned by any Arab writer. Did the Arabs descend through any of the well-known passes of the frontier—the Mulla, Bolan, Saki-Sarwar, or Gomul—into the plains of India? Possibly they did so; but in that case it is difficult to account for so important a geographical feature as the frontier passes of Sind being ignored by the greatest geographer of his day.

Following Idrisi's description of the Helmund province we have a brief itinerary from the Hel.

mund ford (Derthel or Benjawai) to Ghazni, said to be nine days' journey inland. None of the places mentioned are to be identified in modern maps except Cariat, which is more than probably Kariut, a rich and fertile district in the Arghandab valley in the direct line to Kalat-i-Ghilzai. This route passes well to the north-east of Kandahar, which was apparently of little account in Idrisi's days. Although there are extensive ruins at Kushk-i-Nakhud, indicated by a huge artificial mound half-way between Girishk and Kandahar, there is nothing in Idrisi's writings by which they can be identified.

Ghazni was then a large town "surrounded by mud walls and a ditch. There are many houses and permanent markets in Ghazni; much business is done there. It is one of the 'entrepots' of India. Kabul is nine days' journey from it." This is not much to say of the city which had been enriched by the spoils carried away from Muttra and Somnath, and by the treasures amassed during seventeen fierce raids of that Mahmud who, by repeated conquests, made all Northern and Western India contribute to his treasury.

Later, in 1332, the Arab traveller, Ibn Batuta, writes of Ghazni as a small town set in a waste of ruins—a description which fits it not inaptly at the present day; but in Idrisi's time, before the wars with Ghur led to its destruction, whilst still the wealth of a great part of India supported its magnificence, and whilst it was still the theme of glowing panegyric by contemporary historians, one would expect a rather more enthusiastic notice. But even Kabul (nine days' journey distant from Ghazni) is only recognized as "*L'une des grandes villes de l'Inde, entourée de murs,*" with a "*bonne citadelle et au dehors divers faubourgs.*"[1]

There is little to interest us, however, in tracing out the routes that linked up Ghazni and Kabul with the Helmund. They have been the same through all time, with just the difference of place-names. Towns and villages, caravanserais and posts, have come and gone, but that historic road has been marked out by Nature as one of the grandest high-roads in Asia, from the days of Alexander to those of Roberts. Two minars tapering to the sky on the plain before Ghazni are all that are left of its ancient glories, and one cannot but contrast the scattered debris of that once so famous city with the solid endurance of the far greater and older architectural efforts in Egypt and Assyria. Southern Afghanistan is indeed singularly poor and empty of historic monuments. Even now were Kabul, Kandahar, and Herat, its three great cities, to be flattened out by a widespread earthquake there would be little that was not of Buddhist origin left for the future archæologist to make a stir about.

Idrisi writes of the Kingdom of Ghur as apart from Herat, although a great part of the long Herat

[1] Joubert's translation.

valley was certainly included. He calls it a country "mountainous and well inhabited, where one finds springs, rivers, and gardens—easy to defend and very fertile. There are many cultivated fields and flocks. The inhabitants speak a language which is not that of the people of Khorasan, and they are not Mohammedans." Who were they? The Khilkhis or Ghilzais we know at that time overspread the southern hills of Dawar; but who were the people speaking a strange language in the land of the Chahar Aimak where now dwell the Taimanis, unless they were the Taimanis themselves whose traditions date from the time of Moses?

More recently the Ghilzais have left Zamindawar, and the Taimanis have been pressed backward and upward into the central hills by the Afghan Durani clans, who circle round westward, forming a fringe on the foothills between Herat and Kandahar, and who have now completely monopolized Zamindawar. Here, indeed, the truculent Nurzai and Achakzai, and other elements of the Durani section of Afghan ethnography, flourish exceedingly, and it is in this corner of Afghanistan, bordering on the Herat highway to India, that nearly all the fanatics and ghazis of the country are bred. They presented so turbulent and uncompromising a front to strangers in 1882 that there was great difficulty in getting a fair survey of the land of the Chahar Aimak or of Zamindawar.

The mediæval provinces of Ghur and Bamain figure so largely in the records of Arab geography, and appear to have been so fully open to commerce during the centuries succeeding the Arab conquests, that one naturally wonders whether there can have been any remarkable change in the physical configuration of those regions which, in these later days, has rendered them more inaccessible and unapproachable. The Arab accounts of trade routes flit easily from point to point, taking little reckoning of long distances and gigantic ice-bound passes, or the perils of a treacherous climate. An itinerary which deals with stupendous mountains and extreme altitudes has little more of descriptive illustration in these Arab records than such as would apply to camel tracks across the sandy desert or over the flat plain. Nor is the distance which figures as a "day's journey" sensibly changed to suit the route. Forty miles or so across the backbone of the Hindu Kush is written of in much the same terms as if it were forty miles over the plains. Giving the Arab travellers all credit for far greater powers of endurance and determination than we moderns possess, we must still believe that there is a great deal of exaggeration (or forgetfulness) in these heroic records of the past. It is unlikely that the physical conditions of the country have materially changed.

So little has been written of this central region of modern Afghanistan (within which lie the ruins of more than one kingdom), so little has it been traversed by modern explorers, that it may be useful to give some slight general description of the country with which these records deal, including Bamain and Kabul and the mountain system occupied by the Taimani and Hazara tribes as well as the prolific region of Zamindawar with the routes which traverse it.

No part of Afghanistan has been subject to more speculative theories, or requires more practical elucidation, than this mountain region in which so large a share of the drama of Afghan history has been played. Before the days of the Anglo-Russian agreement on the subject of the northern boundaries of Afghanistan nothing was known of its geography, beyond what might be gathered from the doubtful records of Ferrier's journey—and that was very little. The geography of a country shapes its history just as surely in the East as in the West, and we have consequently much new light thrown on the interesting story of the rise and fall of the Ghur dynasties by the fairly comprehensive surveys of the region of their turbulent activities which were carried out in 1882-83.

From these sources we obtain a very fair idea of the general conformation of Central Afghanistan, *i.e.* that part of Afghanistan which is occupied by the tribes known as the Chahar Aimak, *i.e.* the Jamshidis, the Hazaras, Firozkohis, and Taimanis. It consists in the first place of a huge irregular tableland—or uplift—which has been deeply scored and eroded by centuries of river action, the rivers radiating from the central mass of the Koh-i-Babar to the west of Kabul and flowing in deep valleys either directly northward towards the Oxus, due west towards Herat (eventually to turn northward), or south-west in irregular but more or less parallel lines to the Helmund lagoons in Seistan.

The Kabul River basin also finds its head near the same group of river sources. The central mountain mass, the Koh-i-Babar, is high, rocky, generally snow-capped and impassable. To the north it sends down long, barren, and comparatively gentle spurs to the main plateau level, which is deeply cut into by the northern system of rivers, including the Murghab and the Balkh Ab. But the strangest feature in this network of hydrography is the long, deep, narrow valley (almost ditch-like in its regularity) which has been eroded by the Hari Rud River as it makes its way due west, cutting off the sources of the northern group from those of the Helmund or south-western group. It is a most remarkable valley, depressed to a depth of 1000 to 2000 feet below the general plateau level, bounded on the north by a comparatively level line of red-faced cliffs, and on the south by another straight flat-backed range called the Band-i-Baian (or farther west, the Sufed Koh), which has been carved into the semblance of a range by the parallel valleys of the Hari Rud on the north and the Tagao

Ishlan on the south, which hug the range between them.

No affluents of any consequence join either stream. Either separate or together they make their way with straight determination westward towards Herat. South of this curious ditch rise the many streamlets which work their way, sometimes through comparatively open valleys where the floor level has been raised by the centuries of detritus, sometimes through steep and narrow gorges where the harder rock of the plateau formation presents more difficulties to erosion, into the great Helmund basin. These are affluents of the Adraskand, the Farah Rud, and the Helmund, all of which have the same bourne in the Seistan depression. High up between the Farah Rud and the Helmund affluents isolated rugged peaks and short ranges crease and crumple the surface of the inhospitable land of the Hazaras, who occupy all the highest of the uplands and all the sources of the streams, a hardy, handy race of Mongols, living in wild seclusion, but proving themselves to be one of the most useful communities amongst the many in Afghanistan. We have some of them as sepoys in the Indian Army. Lower down in the same river basins, where the gentle grass-covered valleys sweep up to the crests of the hills, cultivation becomes possible. Here flocks of sheep dot the hill-sides, and the land is open and free; but there are still isolated and detached ribs of rocky eminence rising to 11,000 and 12,000 feet, maintaining the mountainous character of the scenery, and rivers are still locked in the embrace of occasional gorges which admit of no passing by. This is the land of that very ancient people, the Taimanis.

The fierce and lawless Firozkohis live in the Murghab basin on the plateau north of the Hari Rud, the Jamshidis to the west of them in the milder climate of the lower hills, into which the plateau subsides.

Whilst we are chiefly concerned in tracing out the mediæval commercial routes of Afghanistan, we may briefly summarize the events which prove that those traversed between Herat and the central kingdoms were important routes, worn smooth by the feet of armies as well as by the tread of pack-laden khafilas. They are still very rough and they present solid difficulties here and there, but in the main they are passable commercial roads, although little commerce wends its way about them now.

In the Middle Ages the Kingdom of Ghur included the Herat valley as far as Khwaja Chist above Obeh in the valley of the Hari Rud, as well as all the hill country to the south-east. About the earliest mention of Ghur by any traveller is that of Ibn Haukel, who speaks of Jebel al Ghur, and talks of plains, ring-fenced with mountains, fruitful in cattle and crops, and inhabited by infidels (*i.e.* non-Mussulmans). The later history of Ghur is inextricably intertwined with that of Ghazni.

Mahmud of Ghazni frequently invaded the hills of Ghur which lay to the west of him, but never made any practical impression on the Ghuri tribes-people. In 1020, however, Mahomedans conquered Ghur effectually from Herat. About a century later (this is after the time of Idrisi, whose records we are following) a member of the ruling Ghuri family (Shansabi) was recognized as lord of Ghur, and it was one of his sons (Alauddin) who inflicted such terrible reprisals on Ghazni when he sacked and destroyed that city and its people. It was about this time (according to some authorities) that the kingdom of Bamian was founded by another member of the same family; but we find Bamian distinctly recognized as a separate kingdom by Idrisi a century or so earlier. From 1174 to 1214 Bamian was the seat of government of a branch of this family ruling all Tokharistan (Turkistan), during which period Seistan and Herat were certainly tributary to Ghur. Ghur then became so powerful, that it was said that prayers in the name of the Ghuri were read from uttermost India to Persia, and from the Oxus to Hormuz.

In 1214 Ghur was reduced first by Mahomedans from Khwarezm (Khiva), and shortly afterwards by Chenghis Khan and his Mongol hosts. About the middle of the thirteenth century, however, a recrudescence of power appeared under the Kurt (or Tajik) dynasty subject to the supreme government of the Mongols. Seistan, Kabul, and Tirah were then ruled from Herat as the capital of Ghur. Timur finally broke up Herat and Ghur in 1383, since which time its history has been as obscure as the geography of the region which surrounded it. Such in brief is the stormy tale of Ghur, and it leads to one or two interesting deductions. There was evidently constant and ready communication with Herat, Bamian, and Ghazni. The capital of Ghur must have been an important town, situated in a fertile and fairly populous district, which, although it was mountainous, yet enjoyed an excellent climate. It must have been a military centre too, with fortresses and places of defence. During its later history it is clear that Ghur was often governed from Herat, but in earlier mediæval days Ghur possessed a distinct capital and a separate entity amongst Afghan kingdoms, and was able to hold its own against even so powerful an adversary as Mahmud of Ghazni, whilst its communications were with Bamian on the north-east rather than with Kabul, which was then regarded as an "Indian" city. We can at any rate trace no record of a direct route between Ghur and Kabul.

In the twelfth century we read that the capital of Ghur was known as Firozkohi, which name (says Yule) was probably appropriated by the nomad Aimak tribe now called Firozkohi; but within the limits of what is now recognized as the habitat of the Firozkohi (*i.e.* the plateau which forms the basin of the Upper Murghab), it is impossible to find any place which would answer to what we know of the general condition of the surroundings and climate of the capital of Ghur, and which would justify a claim to be considered a position of commanding eminence. The altitude of the Upper Murghab branches is not more than 6000 to 7000 feet above sea-level, at which height the climate certainly admits of agriculture, but no place that has been visited, nor indeed any position in the valleys of the Upper Murghab affluents, corresponds in any way to what we are told of this capital.

If we look for the best modern lines of communication through Central Afghanistan we shall certainly find that they correspond with mediæval routes, fitting themselves to the conformation of the country. Central Afghanistan is open to invasion from the north, west, and south, but not directly from the east. The invasion of Ghur from Ghazni, for instance, must have been directed by Kalat-i-Gilzai, Kariut, and Musa Kila (in Zamindawar), to Yaman, which lies a little to the east of Ghur (or Taiwara). So far as we know there are no passes leading due west from Ghazni to the heart of the Taimani country.

From the south the Helmund and its affluents offer several openings into the heart of the Hazara highlands to the east of Taimani land, amidst the great rocky peaks of which the positions were fixed from stations on the Band-i-Baian. But there is no certain information about the inhabited centres of Hazara population; and from what we know of that desolate region of winter snow and wind, there never could have been anything to tempt an invader, nor would any sound commercial traveller have dreamt of passing that way from Seistan to Bamian and Kabul. The idea that Alexander ever took an army up the Helmund valley, and over the Bamian passes, must be regarded as most improbable in spite of the description of Quintus Curtius, who undoubtedly describes a route which presented more difficulties than are quite appropriate to the regular Kandahar to Kabul road. On the other hand, from Seistan by the Farah Rud there is a route which is open to wheeled traffic all the way to Daolatyar on the upper Hari Rud. Daolatyar may be regarded as the focus of several routes trending north-eastward from Seistan, with the ultimate objective of Bamian and the populous valleys of Ghur.

One of the chief affluents of the Farah Rud is now known as the Ghur, and we need look no farther than this valley for the central interest of the Ghur kingdom, although the exact position of the capital may still be open to discussion. Between the Tagao Ghur and the Farah Rud are the Park Mountains, which are almost Himalayan in general characteristics and beauty, with delightful valleys and open spaces, terraced fields, well-built two-storied wooden houses, pretty villages, orchards with an abundance of walnuts and vines trailing over the trees; the Ghur valley itself being broad and open with a clear river of sweet water in its midst. This is near its junction with the Farah Rud. Above this, for a space, the valley narrows to a gorge and there is no passing along it, whilst above the gorge again it becomes wide, cultivated, and well populated, and this is where the Taimani headquarters of Taiwara are found. Taiwara is locally known as Ghur, and may be absolutely on the site of the ancient capital, for there are ruins enough to support the theory. Beyond an intervening band of hills to the south are two valleys full of cultivation and trees, wherein are two important places, Nili and Zarni, which likewise boast of extensive ruins, whilst at Jam Kala, hard by, there is perched on a high spur above the road with only one approach, a remarkable stone-built fort. Yaman, to the east of Taiwara, in the Helmund drainage, is a permanent Taimani village. Here also are very ancient ruins, and the people say that they date from the time of Moses. At that time they say that cups were buried with the dead, one at the head and one at the foot of the corpse. Our native surveyor Imám Sharif saw one of these cups with an inscription on it, but was unable to secure the relic.

Nili and Zarni are in direct connection with Farah, with no inconvenient break in the comparatively easy line of communication; and they all (including Taiwara) are in direct communication with Herat, by a good khafila route (*i.e.* good for camels). But the routes differ widely, that from

Herat to Taiwara by Farsi being more direct, whilst the route from Herat to Zarni by Parjuman (which is well kept up between these two places) passes well to the south. All these places, again, are connected with the Hari Rud valley at Khwaja Chist (the Ghur frontier) by a good passable high-road, which first crosses the hills between Zarni and Taiwara, then passes under the shadow of a remarkable mountain called Chalapdalan, or Chahil Abdal (12,700 feet high—about which many mysterious traditions still hover), over the Burma Pass into the Farah Rud drainage, thence over another pass into the valleys of the Tagao Ishlan, and finally over the Band-i-Baian into the Hari Rud valley at Khwaja Chist.

This is the route described by Idrisi as connecting Ghur with Herat, as we shall see. The Ghur district is linked up with Daolatyar and Bamian by the Farah Rud line of approach, or by a route, described as good, which runs east into the Hazara highlands, and then follows the Helmund. The latter is very high. There is therefore absolutely no difficulty in traversing these Taimani mountain regions in almost any direction, and the facility for movement, combined with the beauty and fertility of the country, all point unmistakably to Taiwara and its neighbourhood as the seat of the Ghuri dynasty of the Afghan kings.

The picturesque characteristics of Ghur extend southward to Zamindawar on its southern frontier, the valleys of the Helmund, the Arghandab, the Tarnak, and Arghastan—this is a land of open, rolling watersheds, treeless, but covered with grass and flowers in spring, and crowned with rocky peaks and ridges of rugged grandeur alternating with the rich beauty of pastoral fields. The summer of their existence is in curious contrast to the stern winter of the storm-swept highlands above them, or the dreary expanse of drab sand-dusted desert below. The route upstream to the backbone of the mountains, and so over the divide to the kingdom of Bamian, was once a well-trodden route.

Since so many routes converge on Daolatyar at the head of the Hari Rud valley, one would naturally look for Daolatyar to figure in mediæval geography as an important centre. It is not easy, however, to identify any of the places mentioned by Idrisi as representing this particular focus of highland routes. Between Ghur and Herat, or between Ghur and Ghazni, the difficulty lies in the number and extent of populous towns, any one of which may represent an ancient site, to say nothing of ruins innumerable. Between Taiwara and Herat we get no information from Idrisi till we reach Khwaja Chist on the frontier. He merely mentions the existence of a khafila road, and then he counts seven days' journey between Khwaja Chist and Herat, reckoning the first as "short."

The names of the halting-places between Khwaja Chist and Herat are Housab, Auca, Marabad, Astarabad, Bajitan (or Najitan), and Nachan. Auca I have no hesitation in identifying with Obeh. There is a large village at Marwa which might possibly represent Marabad, and Naisan would correspond in distance with Nachan, but this is mere guesswork; to identify the others is impossible, without further examination than was undertaken when surveying the ground.

The story of the commerce of Central Asia, which centred itself in Herat in the days of Arab supremacy, has a strong claim on the student of Eastern geography, for it is only through the itineraries of these wandering Semetic merchants and travellers that we can arrive at any estimation of the peculiar phase of civilization which existed in Asia in the mediæval centuries of our era; a period at which there is good reason to suppose that civilization was as much advanced in the East as in the West. It is not the professional explorers, nor yet the missionaries (great as are their services to geography), who have opened up to us a knowledge of the world's highways and byways sufficient to lead to general map illustration of its ancient continents, so much as the everlasting pushing out of trade investigations in order to obtain the mastery of the road to wealth.

India and its glittering fame has much to answer for, but India (that is to say, the India we know, the peninsula of India) was so much more get-at-able by sea than by land even in the early days of navigation, that we do not learn so much about the passes through the mountains into India as the way of the ships at sea, and the coast ports which they visited. According to certain Arab writers large companies of Arabs settled in the borderland and coasts of India from the very earliest days. Indeed, there are evidences of their existence in Makran long before the days of Alexander; but there is very little evidence of any overland approach to India across the Indus. Hindustan, to the mediæval Arab, commenced at the Hindu Kush, and Kabul and Ghazni were "Indian" frontier towns; and the invasions and conquests of India dating back to Assyrian times include no more than the Indus basin, and were not concerned with anything farther south. The Indus, with its flanking line of waterless desert, was ever a most effectual geographical barrier.

The Arabs entered India and occupied the Indus valley through Makran, and throughout their writings we find, strangely, little reference to any of the Indian frontier passes which we now know so well. But in the north and north-west of Afghanistan, in the Seistan and the Oxus regions, they were thoroughly at home both as traders and travellers; and with the assistance of their records we can make out a very fair idea of the general network of traffic which covered High Asia. The destroying hordes of the subsequent Mongol invasions, and the everlasting raids of Turkmans and Persians on the border, have clean wiped out the greater number of the towns and cities mentioned by them, and the map is now full of comparatively modern Turkish and Persian names which give no indication whatever of ancient occupation. There are, nevertheless, some points of unmistakable identity, and from these we can work round to conclusions which justify us in piecing together the old route-map of Northern Afghanistan to a certain extent. This is not unimportant even to modern geographers. The roads of the old khafila travellers may again be the roads of modern progress. We know, at any rate, that the Arabs of 1000 years ago were much the same as the Arabs of to-day in their manners and methods. Their routes were camel routes, not horse routes, and their day's journey was as far as a camel could go in a day, which was far in the wider and more waterless spaces of desert or uninhabited country, and very much shorter when convenient halting-places occurred. These Arab itineraries are bare enumeration of place-names and approximate distances. As for any description of the nature of the road or the scenery, or any indication of altitude (which they possibly had no means of judging), there is not a trace of it; and the difficulties of transliteration in place-names are so great as to leave identification generally a matter of mere guesswork.

One of the most interesting geographical centres from which to take off is Herat, and it may be instructive to note what is said about Herat itself and its connections with the Oxus and Seistan. Herat, says Idrisi, is "great and flourishing, it is defended inside by a citadel, and is surrounded outside by 'faubourgs.' It has many gates of wood clamped with iron, with the exception of the Babsari gate, which is entirely of iron. The Grand Mosque of the town is in the midst of the bazaars. . . . Herat is the central point between Khorasan, Seistan, and Fars." Ibn Haukel (tenth century) mentions a gate called the Darwaza Kushk, which is evidence that Kushk was of importance in those days, though no separate mention is made of that place; and he adds that the iron gate was the Balkh gate, and was in the midst of the city. The strategical value of the position was clearly recognized.

That grand edifice, the Mosalla, with its mosques and minars, which stood outside the walls of Herat and was the glory of the town in 1883 (when it was destroyed in the interests of military defence), had no previous existence in any other form than that which was given it when it was built in the twelfth century.

Both Ibn Haukel and Idrisi mention a mountain about six miles from Herat, from which stone was taken for paving (or mill-stones), where there was neither grass nor wood, but where was a place (in

Ibn Haukel's time, but not mentioned by Idrisi) "inhabited, called Sakah, with a temple or Church of Christians." Idrisi says this mountain was "on the road to Balkh, in the direction of Asfaran." This would seem to indicate that Asfaran, "on the road to Balkh," must be Parana (or Parwana), an important position about a day's march north of Herat. Ibn Haukel says nothing about the road to Balkh, which can only be northward from Herat, but merely mentions that the mountain was on the desert or uncultivated side of Herat, where was a river which had to be crossed by a bridge. This could only be *south* of Herat. Asfaran is also stated to be on the road to *Seistan* and to have had four places dependent on it, one of which was Adraskand; and the route to Asfaran from Herat is further described as three days' journey (Idrisi). Ibn Haukel also describes Asfaran as possessing four dependent towns, and places it between Farah and Herat, or *south* of Herat. As Adraskand[1] is a well-known place between Herat and Farah, we must assume that this is either another Asfaran, or that Idrisi has made a mistake in copying Ibn Haukel. It might possibly be represented by

[1] Adraskand is mentioned as "a little place with cultivation, gardens, and plenty of sweet water," and as one of the four towns under the domination of Asfaran. This corresponds fairly well with the modern town of Kila Adraskand of the same name. On the same southern route from Herat, undoubtedly, was "Malin Herat, at one day's journey, a town surrounded by gardens." The picturesque ruins of the bridge called the Pul-i-Malun, across the Hari Rud, on the Kandahar road, is evidence of the former existence of a town of Malun, of which no trace remains to-day, but which must have corresponded very closely with Rozabagh.

Parah, twenty-five miles south-west of Herat, although the limited area of cultivable ground around renders this unlikely. Subzawar would indicate a far more promising position for an important trade centre such as Asfaran must have been, and would accord better with the three days' journey from Herat of Idrisi, or the itinerary from Farah given by Ibn Haukel, while the extensive ruins around testify to its antiquity. Asfaran was almost certainly Subzawar.

Considering the interest which may once again surround the question of communications from Herat to India, it may be useful to point out that the route connecting Farah with Herat 1000 years ago remains apparently unchanged. The bridge called the Pul-i-Malun, over the Hari Rud, must have been in existence then, and there was another bridge over the Farah River one day's march below Farah, on the highway between Herat and Seistan. To the west of Herat, on the ruin-strewn road to Sarakhs, we have one or two interesting geographical propositions.

Idrisi mentions a place possessing considerable local importance "before Herat had become what it is now," about 9 miles west of Herat, called Kharachanabad. This can easily be recognized in the modern Khardozan, a walled but very ancient town, which is about 8½ miles distant. Between it and the walls of the city there is now no place of importance, nor does it appear likely, for local reasons, that there ever could have been any. Another place, called Bousik, or Boushinj (Pousheng, according to Ibn Haukel), is said to be half the size of Sarakhs, built on the flat plain 6 miles distant from the mountains, surrounded with walls and a ditch, with brick houses, and inhabitants who were commercial, rich, and prosperous, and "who drink the water of the river that runs to Sarakhs." This indicates a site on the banks of the Hari Rud. The only modern place of importance which answers this description is the ancient town of Zindajan, which is about 6 miles from the mountains, and which (according to Ferrier) still bears the name of Foosheng. This name, however, was not recognized by the Afghan Boundary Commission. "To the west of Bousik are Kharkerde and Jerkere. One reckons two days' journey to this last town, which is well populated, smaller than Kuseri, but where there is plenty of water and cultivation. From Jerkere to Kharkerde is two days' journey." These two places are obviously on the road to Nishapur. There is an ancient "haoz," or tank, below the isolated hill of Sangiduktar, near the Persian frontier, which might well represent what is left of Jerkere, and Kharkerde lies beyond it, on the road to Rue Khaf (itself a very ancient site, probably representing Rudan), near Karat. Another place which has a very ancient and troubled history is Ghurian, about thirteen miles west of Zindajan.

This is readily identified as the Koure of Idrisi, which is described as twelve miles from Bousik, on the left of the high-road westward, and about three miles from it.

This corresponds exactly with Ghurian, and proves that the high-road has retained its position through ages. Koure is described as an important town, but there is no mention of walls or defences. Another place, second only in importance to Bousik, is Kouseri. It is in fact said to be equal to Bousik, and to possess "running water and gardens." There can be little doubt that this is Kuhsan (or Kusan), one of the most important towns of the Herat valley.

This great high-road, intersecting the plain from the north-west gate of the city, is a pleasant enough road in the spring and summer months. For a space it runs singularly free from crowded villages and close cultivation, and the tread of a horse's hoof is amongst low-growing flowers of the plain, a dwarf yellow rose with maroon centre being the most prominent. Then, as one skirts the Kaibar River as it runs to a junction with the Hari Rud from the northern hills, cultivation thickens and villages increase.

The road next hugs the Hari Rud, and, passing the high-walled town of Zindajan to the south, runs, white and even and hard, with the scarlet and purple of poppies and thistles fringing it, between long gravel slopes of open dasht and the twin-peaked ridge of Doshak, to Rozanak and Kuhsan. Kuhsan is a little to the south of the Kaman-i-Bihist. It was here that the British Commission of the Russo-Afghan Boundary gathered in the late autumn of 1884, one half from England and the other half from India. The drab squares of the cultivated plain were bare then, in November, and the poplars on the banks of the river were scattering yellow leaves to the blasts of the bitter north-west winds of autumn which sweep through Khorasan and Seistan, making of life a daily burden. But there came a marvellous change in the spring-time, when the world was scarlet and green below and blue above; when the sand-grouse began to chatter through the clear sky; then Kaman-i-Bihist (the bow of Paradise) justified its name. The old Arab of the trading days who wandered northward to Sarakhs must have loved this place.

Stretching Sarakhs-ward are the hills, rocky and broken along the river edge, but gradually giving place eastward to easy rounded slopes, softened by rain and snow, and washed into smooth spurs with treacherous waterways between which become quagmires under the influence of a north-western "shamshir." The extraordinary effect of denudation which yearly results from the heavy rain-storms which are so frequent in spring and early summer in these hills must have absolutely changed their outlines during the centuries which have elapsed since the

Semitic trader trod them. A summer storm-cloud charged with electricity may burst on their summits, and the whole surface of the slopes at once becomes soft and pulpy. Mud avalanches start on the steeper grades and carry down thousands of tons of slimy detritus in a crawling mass, and spread it out in fans at their feet. It is not safe to say that the modern passes of the Paropamisus north of Herat—the Ardewan and the Babar—were the passes of mediæval commerce, although the Ardewan is marked by certain wells and ruined caravanserais which show that it has long been used. It seems possible that these passes may have shifted their positions more than once. There was undoubtedly a well-trodden route from Bousik, which carried the traveller more directly to Sarakhs than would the Ardewan or even the Chashma Sabz Pass. This road followed the river more closely than any railway ever will. It turned the river gorge to the east, and probably passed through the hills by the Karez Ilias route, which runs almost due north to Sarakhs. The only certain indication which we can find in Idrisi is the statement that the "silver hill" (*i.e.* the hill of the silver mine) is on the road from Herat to Sarakhs. The Simkoh (silver hill) is still a well-known feature in the broken range of the Paropamisus, near that route. But it is difficult after centuries of disturbing forces, natural and artificial, to identify the sites of many of the towns and markets mentioned by Idrisi, who places Badghis to the west of Bousik, and gives the "silver hill" as one of its "dependencies." There were two considerable towns, Kua (or Kau) and Kawakir, said to have been near the silver hill, and there is mention of a place called Kilrin in this neighbourhood. Probably the ruins at Gulran represent the latter, but Kua and Kawakir are not identified. Gulran was one of the most fascinating camps of the Afghan Boundary Commission. On the open grass slopes stretching in gentle grades northward, bordered by the line of red Paropamisan cliffs to the south and west and by the open desert stretching to Merv on the north, it was, during one or two early months of the year, quite an ideal camping-ground.

It was here that the wild asses of the mountains made a raid on the humble four-footed followers of the Commission, and signified their extreme disgust at the free use which was made of their feeding-grounds; thus witnessing to the condition of primeval simplicity into which that once populous district had subsided after centuries of border raid and insecurity. The remains of an old karez, or underground irrigation channel, not far north of Gulran, testified to a former condition of cultivation and prosperity.

From Gulran (which is connected with the Herat plains directly by the pass called Chashma Sabz) roads stretch northwards and north-eastwards, without obstacle, to the open Turkistan plains, where ancient sites abound. Idrisi's indications, however, are but a very uncertain foundation for identifying most of them. The "dependencies" of Badghis are said to be Kua, Kughanabad, Bast, Jadwa, Kalawun, and Dehertan, the last place being built on a hill having neither vegetation nor gardens; but "lead is found there, and a small stream."

The great trade centres of Turkistan, north of the Paropamisus, in mediæval days were undoubtedly near Panjdeh, at the confluence of the Kushk and Murghab rivers, and at Merv-el-Rud, or Maruchak. Two or three obvious routes lead from the passes above Kaman-i-Bihist, or above Herat, to Panjdeh and Maruchak. One is indicated by the drainage of the Kushk River, and the other by that of the Kashan, which is more or less parallel to the Kushk to the east of it, with desolate Chol country in between. From Herat the most direct route to Panjdeh and Merv is by the Babar Pass, or by Korokh, the Zirmast Pass, and Naratu. Korokh (Karuj) is mentioned both by Ibn Haukel and Idrisi as being situated three marches from Herat, surrounded by entrenchments, and in the "gorge of mountains," with gardens and orchards and vines. The Korokh of to-day is between the mountains, but only some twenty-five miles from Herat. This modern Korokh has, however, many evidences of great antiquity, and it is on the high-road to an important group of passes leading past Naratu to Bala Murghab and Maruchak. The most remarkable feature about Korokh is a grove of pine trees closely resembling the "stone" pine of Italy, which mass themselves into a dark blotch on the landscape and mark Korokh in this treeless country most conspicuously. There are no other trees of the same sort to be found now in this part of Asia, but I was told that they once were abundant in the Herat valley, which renders it possible that the "arar" trees, mentioned by Ibn Haukel as a peculiar source of revenue to Bousik, may have been of this species. Naratu, again, is very ancient, and its position among the hills (for it is a hill-fortress) seems to identify it with Dahertan. Undoubtedly this was one of the most important of the old routes northward, and it is a route of which account should be taken to-day.

In the Kuskh River more than one ancient site was observed, Kila Maur being obviously one of the most important, whilst in the Kashan stream there were evidences of former occupation at Torashekh and at Robat-i-Kashan. Whilst there is a general vague resemblance between the names of certain old Arab towns and places yet to be found in the Herat valley and Badghis, it is only here and there that it has been possible to identify the precise position of a mediæval site. The dependencies of Badghis, enumerated by Idrisi, require the patient and careful researches of a Stein to place them accurately on the basis of such vague definitions as are given. We are merely told that Kanowar and Kalawun are situated at a distance of three miles one from the other, and that between them there is neither running water nor gardens. "The people drink from wells and from rain-water. They possess cultivated fields, sheep, and cattle." Such a description would apply excellently well to any two contiguous villages in the Chol country anywhere between the Kushk and the Kashan. Those rolling, wave-like hills, with their marvellous spread of grass and flowers in summer, and their dreary, wind-scoured bareness in winter, are excellent for sheep and cattle at certain seasons of the year; but water is only to be found at intervals, and there are much wider distances than three miles where not even wells are to be found.

Writing again of Herat, Idrisi says that, starting towards the east in the direction of Balkh, one encounters three towns in the district of Kenef: Tir, Kenef, and Lakshur; and that they are all about equally distant, it being one day's journey to Tir, one more to Kenef, and another to Lakshur (Lacschour). Tir is a rich town where the "prince of the country" resides, larger than Bousik, full of commerce and people, with brick-built houses, etc. Kenef is as large, but more visited by foreigners; and Lakshur is equal to either. They are all of them big towns of commercial importance, Lakshur being bounded on the west by the Merv-el-Rud province, of which the capital is Merv-el-Rud.

Assuming for the present that Maruchak, on the Murghab, represents Merv-el-Rud (Merv of the River), where are we to place these three important sites, so that the last shall be east of the Maruchak province and only three days' journey from Herat? The distance from Herat to Maruchak is not less than 150 miles, and it is called by Idrisi a six days' journey. Starting towards the east can only refer to the Balkh route already referred to, *i.e. via* Korokh and the Zirmast Pass. It cannot mean the Hari Rud valley, for that leads to Bamian rather than Balkh. By the Korokh route, however, it is possible to follow a more direct line to Balkh than any which would pass by Maruchak or Bamian. There is on this route, east of Naratu and south-east of Maruchak, a place called Langar which might possibly correspond to Lakshur, and it is not more than 70 to 80 miles from Herat. From Langar there is an easy pass leading over the Band-i-Turkistan more or less directly to Maimana and Balkh, and it seems probable that this was a recognized khafila route. Tir is an oft-repeated name in the Herat district. The river itself was called Tir west of Herat, and there is the bridge of Tir (Tir-pul) just above Kuhsan. The mountains, again, to the north-east are known as Tir Band-i-Turkistan, and the Tir mentioned as on the road to Balkh must certainly have been east of Herat. Of Kenef I can trace no evidence. It must have been close to Korokh.

That this route, through the Korokh valley and across the water-parting by the Zirmast Pass to Naratu, was the high road between Herat and Balkh I have very little doubt. It was the route selected for mail service during the winter when the Afghan Boundary Commission camp was at Bala Murghab, on the Murghab River, and it was seldom closed by snow, although the Zirmast heights rise to over 7000 feet, and the Tir Band-i-Turkistan (which represents the northern *rebord* or revetment of the uplands which contain the Murghab drainage) cannot be much less. The intense bitterness of a Northern Afghan winter is more or less spasmodic. It is only the dreaded shamshir (the "scimitar" of the north-west) which is dangerous, and travelling is possible at almost every season of the year. The condition of the mountain ways and passes immediately above Bala Murghab is not that of steep and difficult tracks across a rugged and rocky divide. In most cases it is possible to ride over them, or, indeed, off them, in almost any direction; but as these mountains extend eastward they alter the character of their crests. From Herat to Maruchak this is not, however, the direct road; the Kushk River, or the Kashan, offering a much easier line of approach.

All our investigations in 1884 tended to prove beyond dispute that Maruchak represents the famous old city of Merv-el-Rud, the "Merv of the River," to which every Arab geographer refers. Sir Henry Rawlinson sums up the position in the Royal Geographical Society's *Proceedings* (vol. viii.), when he points out that there were two Mervs known to the ancient geographer. One is the well-known Russian capital in trans-Caspia, the "Merv of the Oasis," a city which, in conjunction with Herat and Balkh, formed the tripolis of primitive Aryan civilization. It was to this place that Orodis, the Parthian king, transported the Roman soldiers whom he had taken prisoners in his victory over Crassus, and here they seemed to have formed a flourishing colony.

Merv was in early ages a Christian city, and Christian congregations, both Jacobite and Nestorian, flourished at Merv from about A.D. 200 till the conquest of Persia by the Mahomedans. Merv the greater has as stirring a history as any in Asia, but Merv-el-Rud, which was 140 miles south of the older Merv, is altogether of later date. This city is said to have been built by architects from Babylonia in the fifth century A.D., and was flourishing at the time of the Arab invasion. All this Oxus region (Tokharistan) was then held by a race of Skytho-Aryans (white Huns) called Tokhari or Kushan, and their capital, Talikhan, was not far from Maruchak. Now, Merv-el-Rud is the only great city named in history on the Upper Murghab, above Panjdeh, before the end of the fourteenth century A.D. After that date, in the time of Shah Rokh (Timur's son), the name Merv-el-Rud disappears, and Maruchak takes its place in all geographical works, the inference being that, Merv-el-Rud being destroyed in Timur's wars, Maruchak was built in its immediate neighbourhood. This surmise of Rawlinson's is confirmed by the appearance of Maruchak, which is but an insignificant collection of inferior buildings surrounded by a mud wall, with a labyrinth of deep canal cuttings in front of it and a rough irregular stretch of untilled country around. Merv-el-Rud must have been a much greater place.

There are, however, abundant evidences of grass-covered ruins, both near Maruchak and at the junction of the Chaharshamba River with the Murghab some 10 miles above Maruchak. Sir Henry Rawlinson points out the strategic value of this point, as the Chaharshamba route leads nearly straight into the Oxus plains and to Balkh. At the point of the junction of the two rivers the valley of the Murghab hardly affords room enough for a town of such importance as we are led to believe Merv-el-Rud to have been, even after making all due allowance for Oriental exaggeration. It is only about Maruchak that the valley widens out sufficiently to admit of a large town. It seems probable, therefore, that the site of Maruchak must be near the site of Merv-el-Rud, although it does not actually command the entrance to the Chaharshamba valley and the road to Afghan Turkistan.

On this road, some 30 miles from the junction of the rivers, there is to be seen on the slopes which flank the southern hills, the jagged tooth-edged remains of a very old town (long deserted) which goes by the name of Kila Wali. It is here, or close by, that the Tochari planted their capital Talikan, at one time the seat of government of a vast area of the Oxus basin. There is, however, another Talikan[1] in Badakshan to the east of Balkh, and there are symptoms that some confusion existed between the two in the minds of our mediæval geographers. Ibn Haukel writes of Talikan as possessing more wholesome air than Merv-el-Rud, and he refers to the river running between the two. This is evidently in reference to the capital of Tocharistan at Kila Wali. Again when he writes of Talikan as the largest city in Tocharistan, "situated on a plain, near mountains," he is correct enough as applied to Kila Wali, but this has nothing to do with Andarab and Badakshan with which we find it directly associated in the context.

On the other hand the Talikan in Badakshan was one of a group of important cities whose connection with India lay through Andarab and the northern passes of the Hindu Kush. Between Maruchak and Panjdeh, along the banks of the Murghab, are ruins innumerable, the sites of other

[1] Talikhan in modern maps.

towns which it is impossible to identify with precision. There can be little doubt, however, that the remains of the bridge which once spanned the river at a point between Maruchak and Panjdeh marked the site of Dizek (or Derak, according to Idrisi), which we know to have been built on both sides of the river, and that Khuzan existed near where Aktapa now is (*i.e.* near Panjdeh). The name Dizek is still to be recognized, but it is applied to a curious sequence of ancient Buddhist caves which have been carved out of the cliffs at Panjdeh, and not to any site on the river banks.

The confusion which occasionally exists between places bearing the same name in mediæval geographical annals is very obvious in Idrisi's description of Merv. The greater Merv (the Russian provincial capital) is clearly mixed up in his mind with the lesser Merv when, in describing the latter, he says that Merv-el-Rud is situated in a plain at a great distance from mountains, and that its territory is fertile but sandy; three grand mosques and a citadel adorn an eminence and water is brought to it by innumerable canals, all of which is applicable to Merv but not to Merv-el-Rud. He then continues with a description of the greater Merv, which is quite apropos to that locality, and makes it clear incidentally that Khiva (not Merv) represents the ancient Khwarezm. Again, he enumerates towns and places of Mahomedan origin which are "dependent" on "Merv." Amongst them we find Mesiha, a pretty, well-cultivated place one day's journey to the west of Merv; Jirena (Behvana), a market-town 9 miles from Merv, and 3 from Dorak (? Dizek), a place situated on the banks of the river; then Dendalkan, an important town two days from Merv on the road to Sarakhs; Sarmakan, a large town to the left of Dorak and 3 miles farther, Dorak being situated on the banks of the river at 12 miles from Merv in the direction of Sarakhs; Kasr Akhif (or Ahnef), a little town at one day's distance from Merv on the road to Balkh; Derah, a small town 12 miles from Kasr Ahnef where grapes were abundant. Here, says Idrisi, the river divides the town in two parts which are connected by a bridge. It is quite impossible to straighten out this geographical enumeration, unless we assume that it refers to Merv-el-Rud and not to Merv. Then Mesiha becomes a possibility, and might be looked for among the ruined sites on the Kushk River—possibly at Kila Maur. Dorak, at 12 miles from Merv in the direction of Sarakhs, and Dendalkan at two days' journey in the same direction, would still be on the river banks. Kasr Ahnef we know to have been built after the Arab invasion in the valley of the Murghab, about 12 miles from Khuzan (identified by Rawlinson with Ak Tepe) and 15 from Merv-el-Rud, and must have been situated near the Band-i-Nadir, where the desert road to Balkh enters the hills. Ak Tepe must once have been a place of great importance, both strategically (as it commands the position of the two important highways southward to Herat, the Kushk and the Murghab valleys) and commercially. But apparently its importance did not survive to Arab times. Dendalkan was certainly near Ak Tepe.

In making our surveys of this historic district it was exceedingly difficult to associate the drab and dreary landscape of this Chol (loess) country and its intersecting rivers with such a scene of busy commercial life as the valleys must have presented in Arab times. The Kushk is at best a "dry" river, as its name betokens, an unsatisfactory driblet in a world of sandy desolation. Reeds and thickets hide its narrow ways, and it is only where its low banks recede on either hand as it emerges into the flat plains above Panjdeh that there is room for anything that could by courtesy be called a town. The Murghab River shows better promise.

Below Maruchak, where towns once crowded, it widens into green spaces, and the multiplicity and depth of the astonishing system of canals which distribute the waters of the river on its left bank leave no room to doubt the strength of the former population that constructed them. Where the pheasants breed now in myriads, in reedy swamps and scrubby thickets, there may lie hidden the foundations of many an old town with its caravanserais, its mosques, and its baths. The economic value of the Murghab River is still great in Northern

Afghanistan. No one watching the sullen flood pouring past Bala Murghab in the winter time and looking up to the dark doors of the mountains from whence it seems to emerge, could have any idea of the wealth and fertility and the spread of its usefulness which is to be found on the far side of those doors. From its many cradles in the Firozkohi uplands to its many streamlets reaching out round Merv and turning the desert into a glorious field of fertility, the Murghab does its duty bravely in the world of rivers, and well deserves all that has ever been written in its praise by past generations of geographers.

Amongst the many high-roads of Northern Afghanistan which are mentioned by the Arab writers, none is more frequently referred to than the road from Herat to Balkh, *i.e.* to Afghan Turkistan. Intervening between Herat and Afghan Turkistan there is immediately north the easy round-backed range called by various names which have been lumped under the term Paropamisus, down the northern slopes of which the Kushk and Kashan made a fairly straight way through the sea of rounded slopes and smooth steep-sided hills which constitute the Chol. But this range is but an extension of the southern rampart of the Firozkohi upland, which forms the upper basin of the Murghab and overlooks the narrow valley of the Hari Rud.

The northern rampart or buttress of that upland is the Tir Band-i-Turkistan, the western flank of which is turned by the Murghab River as it makes its way northward. So that there are several ways by which Afghan Turkistan may be reached from Herat. Setting aside the Hari Rud route to Bamian or Kabul, which would be a difficult and lengthy detour for the purpose of reaching Balkh, there is the route we have already mentioned *via* Korokh, Naratu, and Langar, and thence over the Band-i-Turkistan, or down the Murghab. But there is another and probably the most trodden way, *via* the Kashan to the Murghab valley at the junction of the Chaharshamba River, and up that river to the divide at its head, passing over into the Kaisar drainage, and so, either to Andkhui and the Oxus, or to Maimana and Balkh. This was the route made use of generally by the Russo-Afghan Boundary Commission, and the existence of ancient tanks (called "Haoz") and of "robats" (or halting-places) at regular intervals in the Kashan valley, testifies to its use at no very ancient date.

The entrance to the Chaharshamba valley is very narrow, so narrow as to preclude the possibility of any large town ever having occupied this position; but it opens out as one passes the old Kila Wali ruins where there is ample space for the old capital of Tocharistan to have existed. On the north, trailing streams descend from the Kara Bel plateau (a magnificent grass country in summer and a cold scene of windy desolation in winter), and their descent is frequently through treacherous marshes and shining salt pitfalls, making it exceedingly difficult to follow them to the plateau edge. To the south are the harder features of the Band-i-Turkistan foothills, the crest of the long black ridge of this Band being featureless and flat, as is generally the case with the boundary ridges and revetments of a plateau country. Over the Chaharshamba divide (at about 2800 feet) and into the Kaisar drainage is an introduction to a country that is beautiful with the varied beauty of low hill-tops and gentle slopes, until one either by turning north, debouches into the flat desert plains of the Oxus at Daolatabad, or continuing more easterly, arrives at Maimana, the capital of the little province of Almar, the centre of a small world of highly cultivated and populous country, and a town which must from its position represent one or other of the ancient trade centres mentioned by Idrisi. Here we leave behind the long lines of Turkman kibitkas looking like rows of black bee-hives in the snow-spread distance, and find the flat-roofed substantial houses of a settled Uzbek population, with flourishing bazaars and a general appearance of well-being inside the mud walls of the town.

Idrisi writes that Talikan is built at the foot of a mountain which is part of the Jurkan range (Band-i-Turkistan), and that it is on the "paved" route between Merv and Balkh. This at once indicates that route as an important one compared with other routes (there being a desert route across the Karabel plateau from near Panjdeh in addition to those already mentioned), although there is no sign of any serious road-making to be detected at present. Sixty miles from Talikan, on the road to Balkh, Idrisi places Karbat, a town not so large as Talikan but more flourishing and better populated. The distance reckoned along the one possible route here points to Maimana, which is just 60 miles from Talikan, but there is no other indication of identity. Karbat was a dependency of the province of Juzjan (or Jurkan, probably Guzwan), and 54 miles to the east of it was the town of Aspurkan, a small town, itself 54 miles from Balkh. Now Balkh, by any possible route, is at least 130 to 140 miles from Maimana, but if we assume Aspurkan to have been just half-way (as Idrisi makes it) between Maimana and Balkh, we find Sar-i-pul (a small place indifferently supplied with water, and thus answering Idrisi's description of Aspurkan) almost exactly in that position. In support of this identification of Aspurkan with Sar-i-pul there is the name Aspardeh close to Sar-i-pul. Other places are mentioned by Idrisi as flourishing centres of trade and industry in this singularly favoured part of Afghanistan, where the low spurs and offshoots of the Band-i-Turkistan break gently into the Oxus plains. He says that Anbar, one day's march to the south-west of Aspurkan, was a larger place than Merv-el-Rud, with vineyards and gardens surrounding it and a fair trade in cloth. There, both in summer and winter, the chief of the country resided. Two days from Aspurkan, and one from Karbat, was the Jewish colony of Yahudia, a walled town with a good commercial business. This colony is also mentioned by Ibn Haukel as situated in the district of Jurkan. From Yahudia to Shar (a small town in the hills) was one day's march. The main road south-west from Sar-i-pul has probably remained unchanged through the centuries. It runs to Balangur (? Bala Angur) and Kurchi, the former being 10 miles and the latter 30 from Sar-i-pul. Either might represent the site of Anbar. Twenty miles from Kurchi is Belchirag, and Belchirag is about 25 from Maimana. It would thus represent the site of the ancient Yahudia fairly well, whilst 25 to 30 miles from Belchirag we find Kala Shahar, a small town in the mountains, still existing. Jurkan is described as a town by Idrisi (and as a district by Ibn Haukel), built between two mountains, three short marches from Aspurkan, and Zakar is another commercial town two marches to the south-east. I should identify Jirghan of our maps with Jurkan, and Takzar with Zakar.

All this part of Afghan Turkistan is rich in agricultural possibilities. The Uzbek population of the towns and the Ersari Turkmans of the deserts beyond Shibarghan are all agriculturists, and the land is great in fruit. They are a peaceful people, hating the Afghan rule and praying for British or any other alternative. Shibarghan is an insignificant walled town with a small garrison of Afghan Kasidars; always in straits for water in the dry season. The road between Shibarghan and Sar-i-pul is flat, skirting the edge of the rolling Chol to the east of it. Sar-i-pul itself is but a small walled town in rotten repair, sheltering a few Kasidars and two guns, but no regular Afghan troops. There are a few Jews there who make and sell wine, and a few Peshawur bunniahs (shop-keepers).

From Sar-i-pul a direct road runs to Bamian and Kabul *via* Takzar to the south-east, and strikes the hill country almost at once after leaving Sar-i-pul. It surmounts a high divide (about 11,000 feet), and crosses the Balkh Ab valley to reach Bamian. There is another route up the Astarab stream leading to Chiras at the head of the Murghab River and into the Hazara highlands; but these were never trade routes except for local purposes. The Hazaras send down to the plain their camel hair-cloth and receive many of the necessities of life in exchange, but there is no through traffic.

The characteristics of the Astarab road are typical of this part of Afghanistan. After passing Jirghan the valley is shut in by magnificent cliffs from 700 to 1000 feet high. The vista is closed by snow peaks to the south, which, with the brilliancy of up-springing crops on the banks of the river, form a picture of almost Alpine beauty. There is, curiously enough, an entire absence of forest in the valley, but blocks of a soft white clay mixed with mica lend a weird whiteness to its walls, dazzling the eye, and making patchwork of Nature's colouring. Snakes abound in great numbers, mostly harmless, but the deadly "asp-i-mar" is amongst them. There is a yellow variety which is freely handled by the Uzbeks, who call this snake Kamchin-i-Shah-i-Murdan. About eight miles beyond Jirghan the Uzbek population ceases. From this point there are only Firozkohis and some few Taimanis who have been ejected from the Hari Rud valley for their misdeeds. They are all robbers by profession, supporting existence by slave trading. They kidnap girls and boys from the Hazara villages of the highlands and trade them to the Uzbeks in exchange for guns, ammunition, and horses. These Taimani robbers are by no means the only slave dealers. Nearly every well-to-do establishment in Afghan Turkistan has one or two Hazara slaves. The prices paid, of course, vary, but 300 krans each was paid for two girls bought in 1883. Expert native authorities have a very high opinion of the handiness of Hazara slave girls. They are good at needlework, turning out most exquisite embroidery, and they are never idle.

The narrowness of the Astarab gorge renders it impossible to follow the river along the whole of its course. The road finally leaves the valley and strikes up to the plateau on its left bank. One remarkably persistent feature in these valley formations is the existence of two plateau levels, or terraces; that immediately overlooking the valley being sometimes 100 feet lower than the second platform which is thrown back for a considerable distance, leaving a broad terrace formation between the line of its cliff edge and that bordering the stream. Occasionally there is more than one such terrace indicating former geologic floors of the valley.

On gaining the plateau level a very remarkable scene opens out—a broad green dasht, or plain, slopes away to a sharp line westwards bordered by glittering cliffs and intersected by the white line of the road. In the midst of this setting of white and green are the remains of what must once have been a town of considerable importance, which goes by the name locally of the Shahar-i-Wairan, or ancient city. Such buildings as remain are of sun-dried brick; there appears to be no indication of the usual wall or moat surrounding this city, and nothing suggestive of a canal or "karez"; nothing, in short, but scattered ruins covering about one and a half square miles. The kabristan (or graveyard) was easily recognizable, and its vast size furnished some clue to the size of the city. All history, all tradition even, about this remarkable place seems lost in oblivion; but a city of such pretensions must have had a fair place in geography from very early times. It seems improbable, however, that it could have been more than a summer residence in its palmy days, for winter at this elevation (nearly 7000 feet) and in such an exposed locality would be very severe indeed. The only indication which can be derived from Idrisi's writings is the reference to the small town in the mountains called Shah (Shahar) one day's march from the Jewish colony of Yahudia. As already explained there is a Kila Shahar some 25 to 30 miles from Yahudia (if we accept the position of Belchirag as more or less representing that place), but the Shahar-i-Wairan is nearer by some 10 miles, and fits better into the geographical scheme. I should be inclined to identify the Shahar-i-Wairan with the ancient Shahar (or Shah) and the Kila Shahar as a later development of the same place. The point, however, to be specially noted about this geographical theory is that there is no route by which camels can pass either over the Band-i-Turkistan or the mountains enclosing the Balkh Ab from the district of Sangcharak southward. The province of Sangcharak, which corresponds roughly to the ancient district of Jurkan (or Gurkan), is rich throughout, with highly cultivated valleys and a dense population, but it is a sort of geographical cul-de-sac.

Communication with the plains of the Oxus and with Balkh (by the lower reaches of the Balkh Ab) is easy and frequent, but there never could have been a khafila road over the rugged plateau land and mountains which divide it from the basin of the Helmund.

From time immemorial efforts have been made to reach Kabul by the direct route from Herat which is indicated by the remarkable lie of the Hari Rud valley. It was never recognized as a trade route, although military expeditions have passed that way; and it has always presented a geographical problem of great interest. From Herat eastwards, past Obeh as far as Daolatyar, there is no great difficulty to be overcome by the traveller, although the route diverges from the main valley for a space. Between Daolatyar and the head of Sar-i-jangal stream (which is the source and easternmost affluent of the Hari Rud) the valley is well populated and well cultivated, with abundant pasturage on the hills. But the winter here is severe. From the middle of November to the middle of February snow closes all the roads, and even after its disappearance the deep clayey tracks are impassable even for foot travellers. In the neighbourhood of a small fort called Kila Sofarak, about 40 miles from Daolatyar, there is a parting of the ways. Over the water-parting at the head of the stream by the Bakkak Pass a route leads into the Yakulang valley, a continuation of the Band-i-Amir, or river of Balkh, which, in the course of its passage through the gorges of the mountains, here forms a series of natural aqueducts uniting seven narrow and deep lakes. Inexpressibly wild and impressive is the character of the scenery surrounding those deep-set lakes in the depths of the Afghan hills.

Near the lakes are the ruins of two important town or fortresses, Chahilburj, and Khana Yahudi. On a high rock between them are the ruins of Shahr-i-Babar the capital of kings who ruled over a country most of which must have been included in the Hazara highlands, and was probably more or less conterminous with the Bamian of Idrisi. Between the Yakulang and the Bamian valley is a high flat watershed. Looking north-west a vast broken plateau, wrinkled and corrugated by minor ranges, and scored by deep valleys and ravines, fills up the whole space from the mountains standing about the source of the Murghab and Hari Rud to the Kunduz River of Badakshan.

So little is this part of modern Afghanistan known, that it may be as well to give a short description of the existing lines of communication connecting the Oxus plains and Herat with Bamian and Kabul, before attempting to follow out their mediæval adaptation to commercial intercourse.

From Balkh, or Mazar-i-Sharif, or from Deh Dadi (the new fortified position near Mazar) the most direct routes southward either follow the Balkh Ab valley to Kupruk and the Zari affluent, and then crossing the Alakah ridge pass into the river valley again, and so reach the Band-i-Amir and the head of the river at Yakulang; or passing by the Darra Yusuf (a most important affluent of the Balkh River) attain more directly to Bamian. Balkh and Mazar lie close together on the open plain, and about 10 miles to the south of them rises the northern wall of the plateau called Elburz, through which the Balkh River, and other drainage of the plateau, forces its passage. Thus the whole course of the Balkh River, from its head to within a mile or two of Balkh, lies within a deep and narrow ditch cut out from the plateau which fills up the space from the Elburz to the great divide of Central Afghanistan. East and west of the Balkh River the plateau increases in elevation as it reaches southward, culminating in knolls or peaks 12,000 and 13,000 feet high about the latitude 35° 30′, and falling gently where it encloses the actual sources of the river. It is this plateau, or uplift, which forms the dominant topographical feature of Northern Afghanistan.

West of the Balkh Ab it is represented by the Firozkohi uplands, which contain the head valleys of the Murghab, bordered on the north by the Tirband-i-Turkistan from the foot of which stretch away towards the Oxus the endless sand-waves of the Chol, and by the highlands of Maimana and Sangcharak, and which trend northward to within a few miles of Balkh. At Balkh its northern edge is well defined by the Elburz, but between Balkh and Maimana it is more or less merged into the great loess sand sea, and its limitations become indefinite. East of the longitude of Balkh it is lost in a distance whither our surveyors have not traced its outlines, but where without doubt it fills a wide area north of the Hindu Kush, determining the nature of the Badakshan River sources and shaping itself into a vast upland region of mountain and deep sunk gully, and generally preserving the same characteristics throughout, till it overlooks the valley of the Oxus. That part of it which embraces the affluents of the Balkh Ab and the Kunduz is described as intensely wild and dreary, traversed by irregular folds and ridges which rise in more or less rounded slopes to great altitudes, hiding amongst them deep-seated valleys and gulches, wherein is to be found all that there is of cultivation and beauty. From above it presents the aspect of a huge drab-coloured, hill-encumbered desert where man's habitation is not, and Nature has sunk her brightest efforts out of sight. These efforts are to be found in the valleys, which are excavated by ages of erosion, steep sided, with precipitous cliffs overhanging, and a narrow green ribbon of fertility winding through the flat floor of them.

Across those dreary uplands, or else wandering blindfold along the bottom of the river troughs, run the roads and tracks of the country; some of them being the roads of centuries of busy traffic. A little apart from the obvious route supplied by the lower course of the Balkh Ab, and more important as leading more directly to the crest of the main divide, is the road from Mazar to the Band-i-Amir district which is practically the best road to Kabul. This strikes on to the plateau and crosses several minor passes over spurs dividing the heads of certain eastern affluents of the Balkh Ab before it drops into the trough of the Darra Yusuf. Following the course of this river, and skirting the towns of Kala Sarkari and Sadmurda, it strikes off from its head over a pass called Dandan Shikan (the "tooth-breaker") into the Kamard valley which runs eastwards into the big river of Badakshan—the Kunduz. From Kamard over three passes into the Saigan—another valley draining deeply eastwards into the Kunduz. From this again, two parallel routes and passes southward connect Saigan with the Bamian depression. Here the river of Bamian also runs east, parallel to Saigan and Kamard (the three forming three parallel depressions in the general plateau land), but meeting an affluent draining from the east, the two join and curve northward into the Kunduz.

This new affluent from the east is important, for it leads over the easy Shibar Pass into the head of the Ghorband valley and to Charikar. Finally, there is the well-travelled route from Bamian, leading southward over the Hajigak Pass into the Helmund valley at Gardandiwal, where it crosses the river and then proceeds *via* the Unai Pass and Maidan to Kabul. Such is the general system of the Balkh communications with Kabul.

From Tashkurghan, east of Mazar, there are other routes equally important. There is a direct road southward, which starts through an extraordinary defile, where perpendicular walls of slippery rock enclose a narrow cleft which hardly admits the passing of a loaded mule to Ghaznigak and Haibak. From Haibak you may follow up the Tashkurgan River to its head and then drop over the Kara Pass into Kamard at Bajgah, and so to Bamian again; or you may avoid Bamian altogether and striking off south-east from Haibak over the plateau, slip down into the Kunduz drainage at Baghlan, and then follow it to its junction with the Andarab at Dosh. This position at Dosh gives practical command of all the passes over the Hindu Kush into the Kabul basin, for the Andarab drains along the northern foot of the Hindu Kush, and commands the back doors of all passes between the Chapdara (or Chahardar) and the Khawak.

The most trodden route to-day is that which is the most direct between Kabul and Mazar, *i.e.* the route *via* Bamian and the Darra Yusuf. This is the route taken by the late Amir when he met his cousin Ishak Khan in the field of Afghan Turkistan and defeated him. It is not the route taken by the Afghan Boundary Commission in returning from the same field in 1885. They returned by Haibak and Dosh and deploying along the northern foot of the Hindu Kush, crossed by nearly every available pass either into the Ghorband valley or that of the Panjshir.

It would almost appear from mediæval geographical record that there was no way between Herat and Kabul that did not lead to the Bamian valley. This is very far from accurately representing the actual position, for Bamian lies obviously to the north of the direct line of communication. Bamian was undoubtedly a place of great significance, probably more important as a Buddhist centre than Kabul, more valuable as a centre trade-market subsequently than the Indian city, as Kabul was called. But its significance has disappeared, and it is now far more important for us to know how to reach Kabul directly from the west than how to pass through Bamian. The route to Bamian and Kabul from Herat diverges at the small deserted fort of Sofarak, and follows the Lal and the Kerman valleys at the head of the Hari Rud. Crossing the Ak Zarat Pass southward there is little difficulty in traversing the Besud route to the Helmund, from whence the road to Kabul over the Unai Pass is open. The Bakkak Pass northward is the only real difficulty between Herat and Bamian; much worse, indeed, than anything on the route between Herat and Kabul direct; so that we have determined the existence of a fairly easy route by the Hari Rud from Herat to Kabul, and another route, with but one severe pass, between Herat and Bamian. We must, however, remember that we are dealing with Alpine altitudes. Overlooking the Yakulang head of the Balkh River are magnificent peaks of 13,000 and 14,000 feet, and the passes are but a few thousand feet lower. The valley of the Bamian, deep sunk in the great plateau level, is between 8000 and 9000 feet above sea-level, and the passes leading out of it are over 10,000 feet. To the south is the magnificent snow-capped array of the Koh-i-Baba (or probably Babar, from the name of the ancient people who occupied Bamian), the culminating group of the central water-parting of Afghanistan running to 16,000 and 17,000 feet. It is altitude, nothing but sheer altitude, which is the effectual barrier to approach through the mountains which divide the Oxus and Kabul basins. Rocky and "tooth-breaking" as may be the passes of these northern hills they are all practicable at certain times and seasons, but for months they are closed by the depth of winter snows and the fierce terror of the Asiatic blizzard. The deep valleys traversing the storm-ridden plateau are often beautiful exceedingly, and form a strange contrast to the dull grey expanse of rocky ridge and treeless plain of the weird plateau land; but in order to reach them, or to pass from one to the other, high altitudes and rugged pathways must always be negotiated.

In the days before the Mahomedan conquest, the pilgrim days of devout Chinese searchers after truth, the footsteps of the Buddhist devotees can be very plainly traced. Balkh was a specially sacred centre; and the magnificence of the Bamian relics are also celebrated. We should not have known precisely the route followed by the pilgrims had they not left their traces half-way between Balkh and Bamian at Haibak. Here in the heart of this stony and rugged wilderness is an open cultivated plain, green with summer crops and streaked with the dark lines of orchard foliage. Little white houses peep out from amongst the greenery, and there is a kind of Swiss summer holiday air encompassing this mountain oasis which must have enchanted the votaries of Buddha in their time. The Buddhist architects of old were unsurpassed, even by the Roman Catholic Monks of later ages in the selection of sites for their monasteries and temples. The sweet seductions which Nature has to offer in her mountain retreats were as a thanksgiving to the pilgrim, weary footed and sore with the terrible experiences of travel which was far rougher than anything which even the most devoted Hajji can place to the credit of his account with the recording angel of the present day, and they were appreciated accordingly. Haibak, although not quite on the straight line to Bamian, was not to be overlooked as a resting-place, and here one of the quaintest of all these northern religious relics was literally unearthed by Captain Talbot[1] during the progress of the Russo-Afghan surveys. A small circular stupa was discovered cut out of solid rock below the ground level. It was surrounded by a ditch, and crowned by a small square-built chamber which was also cut out of the rock *in situ*. There was nothing

[1] Now Colonel the Hon. M. G. Talbot, R.E.

to indicate the origin or meaning of a stupa in such a position, and time was wanting for anything more than a superficial examination; but here we had the evidence of Buddhist occupation and Buddhist worship forming a distinct link between Balkh and Bamian, and marking one resting-place for the weary pilgrim. As for caves, the country round Haibak appears to be studded with them.

So long must this strange region of ditch-like valleys, carved out of the wrinkled central highlands of Afghanistan, have existed as the focus of devout pilgrimage, if not of commercial activity, under the Bamian kings, that the absence of any record descriptive of the routes across it is rather surprising. Above the surface of the plateau the long grey folds of the hills follow each other in monotonous succession, with little relief from vegetation and unmarked by forest growth. It is generally a scene of weary, stony desolation through which narrow, white worn tracks thread their way. In the valleys it is different. Cut squarely out of the plateau these intersecting valleys, cliff bound on either side with reddish walls such as border the valley of Bamian, offer fair opportunity for colonization. Where the valleys open out there is space enough for cultivation, which in early summer makes pretty contrast with the ruddy hills that hedge it. Where it spreads out from the mouth of the gorges nourished by hundreds of small channels which carry the water far afield, it is in most charming contrast to the gaunt ruggedness of the hills from whence it emerges. Such is the general outlook from the Firozkohi plateau, looking northward into the Oxus plains when the yellow dust haze, driven southward by the north-western winds, lifts sufficiently from athwart the plains to render it possible to see towards Maimana or into the valley of Astarab.

The valley of Bamian stands at a level of about 8500 feet; the passes out of it northward to Balkh or southward to Kabul rise to 11,000 and 12,000 feet. It is the mystery of its unrecorded history and the local evidences of the departed glory of Buddhism, which render Bamian the most interesting valley in Afghanistan. Massive ruins still look down from the bordering cliffs, and for six or seven miles these cliffs are pierced by an infinity of cave dwellings. Little is left of the ancient city but its acropolis (known as Ghulghula), which crowns an isolated rock in the middle of the valley. Enormous figures (170 and 120 feet high) are carved out of the conglomerate rock on the sides of the Bamian gorge. Once coated with cement, and possibly coloured, or gilt, these images must have appealed strongly to the imagination of the weary pilgrim who prostrated himself at their feet. "Their golden lines sparkle on every side," says Huen Tsang, who saw them in the year A.D. 630, when he counted ten convents and 1000 monks of the "Little Vehicle" in the valley of Bamian.

Twelve hundred and fifty years later the great idols were measured by theodolite and tape, and duly catalogued as curiosities of the world's museum. We know very little of the later history of Bamian. The city was swept off the face of the valley by Chengiz Khan; and Nadir Shah, in later times, left the marks of his artillery on the face of cliffs and images. Moslem destroyers and iconoclasts have worked their wicked will on these ancient monuments, but they witness to the strength and tenacity of a faith that still survives to sway a third of the human race.

Chahilburj and Shahr-i-Babar (31 miles above Chahilburj at the junction of the Sarikoh stream with the Band-i-Amir) with the ruined fortresses of Gawargar and Zohak, wonderful for the multiplicity of its lines of defence, all attest to the former position of Bamian in Afghan history and explain its prominence in mediæval annals. And yet there is not much said about the road thither from Balkh, or onward to the "Indian city" of Kabul.

Idrisi just mentions the road connecting Balkh with Bamian, which he describes as follows: "From Balkh to Meder (a small town in a plain not far from mountains) three days' journey. From Meder to Kah (well-populated town with bazaar and mosque) one day's journey. From Kah to Bamian three days." Bamian he describes as of about the same extent as Balkh, built on the summit of a mountain called Bamian, from which issue several rivers which join the Andarab, possessing a palace, a grand mosque, and a vast "faubourg"; and he enumerates Kabul, Ghazni, and Karwan (which we find elsewhere to be near Charikar) amongst others as dependencies of Bamian.

It is not easy to identify Meder and Kah. The total distance from Balkh to Bamian is at least 200 miles by the most direct route *via* the Darra Yusuf. Forty miles a day through such a country must be regarded as a fine performance, even for Arab travellers who would think little of 50 or 60 miles over the flats of Turkistan. However, we must take the record as we find it, and assume that the camels of those days (for the Arabs never rode horses on their journeys) were better adapted for work in the hills than they are at present.

The inference, however, is strong that not very much was really known about this mountain region south of the Balkh plain. To the pilgrim it offered no terrors; but to the merchant, with his heavily laden caravan, it is difficult to conceive that 800 or 900 years ago it could have been much easier to negotiate than it is to the Bokhara merchants of to-day, who take a much longer route between the Oxus and Kabul than that which carries them past Bamian.

The province of Badakshan to the east (the ancient Baktria) is still but indifferently explored. It is true that certain native explorers of the Indian Survey have made tracks through the country, passing from the Pamir region to the Oxus plains; but no English traveller has recently done more than touch the fringe of that section of the Hindu Kush system which includes Kafiristan and its extension northwards, encircled by the great bend of the Oxus River. Kafiristan has ever been an unexplored region—a mountain wilderness into which no call of Buddhism ever lured the pilgrim, no Moslem conquerer (excepting perhaps Timur) ever set his foot, until the late Amir Abdurrahmon essayed to reduce that region and make it part of civilized Afghanistan. Even he was content to leave it alone after a year or two of vain hammering at its southern gates. Kafiristan formed part of the mediæval province, or kingdom, of Bolor; but it is always written of as the home of an uncouth and savage race of people, with whom it was difficult to establish intercourse. Kafiristan is, however, in these modern days very much curtailed as the home of the Kafir. Undoubtedly many of the border tribes fringing the country (Dehgans, Nimchas, etc.), who are now to be numbered amongst the most fanatical of Moslem clans, are comparatively new recruits to the faith, and therefore handle the new broom with traditional ardour; but they were not so long ago members of the great mixed community of Kafirs who, driven from many directions into the most inaccessible fastnesses of the hills by the advance of stronger races north and south, have occupied remote valleys, preserving their own dialects, mixing up in strange confusion Brahman, Zoroastian, and Buddhist tenets with classical mythology, each valley with apparently a law and a language of its own, until it is impossible to unravel the threads of their complicated relationship. Here we should expect to find (and we do find) the last relics of the Greek occupation of Baktria, and here are certainly remnants of a yet more ancient Persian stock, with all the flotsam and jetsam of High Asia intermingled. They are, from the point of view of the Kabul Court, all lumped together as Kafirs under two denominations, Siahposh and Lalposh; and not till scientific investigation, such as has not yet reached Afghanistan, can touch them shall we know more than we do now. No commercial road ever ran through the heart of Kafiristan, but there were two routes touching its eastern and western limits, viz. that on the east passing by Jirm, and that on the west by Anjuman, both joining the Kokcha River, which are vaguely referred to by our Arab authorities. That by Jirm is certainly impracticable for any but travellers on foot.

Badakshan (*i.e.* the province) was apparently full of well-populated and flourishing towns 1000 years ago. The names of many of them are given by Idrisi, but it is not possible to identify more than a few. The ancient Khulm (50 miles east of Balkh) was included in Badakshan. In Idrisi's day it was a place "of which the productions and resources were very abundant: there is running water, cultivated fields, and all sorts of vegetable productions." From thence to Semenjan "a pretty town, in every way comparable to Khulm, commercial, populated, and encircled with mud walls," two days' journey. Then we have "from Balkh to Warwalin" (a town agreeable and commercial with others dependent on it), two days. From Warwalin to Talekan, two days. Talekan is described as only one-fourth the size of Balkh, on the banks of a big river in a plain where there are vineyards. And then, strangely enough, we find "from Balkh to Khulm west of Warwalin is a two-days' journey. From Semenjan to Talekan, two days."

This is a puzzle which requires some adjustment. From Balkh to Khulm is about 50 miles and may well pass as two days' journey. But from Balkh to Warwalin is also said to be a two-days' journey, and from Warwalin to Talekan two days, whilst Khulm is two days *west* of Warwalin. The difficulty lies in the fact that all these places must be on a line running almost due *east* from Balkh. It was and is the great high-road of Badakshan in the Oxus plains. Moreover, Talekan has been fixed by native surveyors at a point about 150 miles east of Balkh which fully corresponds in its physical features to the description given of that place above. If, however, we assume 150 miles to represent six days' journey instead of four, the difficulty vanishes. We then have Balkh to Khulm, two days; Khulm to

Warwalin, two days; and Warwalin to Talekan, two days. This would place Warwalin somewhere about Kunduz, which is, indeed, a very probable position for it.

Semenjan is important. Two days from Talekan; two days from Khulm; five days from Andarab.

Andarab is fortunately a fixed position. The description given of it by Idrisi places it at the junction of the Kaisan (or Kasan) stream with the Andarab, both of which retain their ancient names. Andarab is a very old and a very important position in all itineraries, from Greek times till now, and it may be important again. But seeing that Khulm is separated from Talekan by four days, it is difficult to distinguish between Semenjan and Warwalin which is also two days from each of those places. This illustrates the problems which beset the unravelling of Arab itineraries. Seeing, however, that Talekan and Warwalin have already been confused once, it is, I think, justifiable to assume that the same mistake has occurred again. Such an assumption would place Semenjan about where Haibak is, and where some central town of importance must have always been, judging from its important geographical position. Haibak is rather more than a hundred miles from Andarab by the only practicable khafila route, which is a very fair five-days' journey. This would indicate that the route followed by the English Commission for the settlement of the Russo-Afghan frontier from Balkh to Kabul was one of those recognized as trade routes in the tenth and eleventh centuries. The location of one other town in Badakshan is of interest, and that is a town called by Idrisi "Badakshan," which gave its name to the province. The first assumption to make is that the modern capital Faizabad is on or near the site of the ancient one. Let us see how it fits Idrisi's itinerary. The information is most meagre. From Talekan to Badakshan, seven days. From Andarab to the same town (going east), four days. Badakshan is described as a town "not very large but possessing many dependencies and a most fertile soil. The vine and other trees grow freely, and the country is watered by running streams. The town is defended by strong walls, and it possesses markets, caravanserais, and baths. It is a commercial centre. It is built on the west bank of the Khariab, the largest river of those which flow to the Oxus." It is elsewhere stated that the Khariab is another name for the Oxus or Jihun. It is added that horses are bred there and mules; and rubies and lapis lazuli found in the neighbourhood and distributed through the world. Musk from Wakhan is brought to Badakshan. Also Badakshan adjoins Canouj, a dependency of India. The two provinces which are found immediately beyond the Oxus (under one government) are Djil and Waksh, which lie between the Khariab (? Oxus) and Wakshab rivers, of which the first bathes the eastern part of Djil and the other the country of Waksh. The Waksh joins the Oxus from the north near the junction of the latter with the Kunduz. Then follow the names of places dependent on Waksh, of which Helawerd and Menk seem to be the chief.

Now Faizabad is about 70 miles from Talekan, and about 160 at least from Andarab. From Andarab the route strikes east at first, but after crossing the Nawak Pass, over a spur of the Hindu Kush (which is itself crossed near this point by the Khawak), it turns and passes down the valley of Anjuman to Jirm and Faizabad. Jirm is on the left bank of the Kokcha or Khariab—Faizabad being on the right,—and its altitude (4800 feet) would certainly admit of vine-growing and may be suitable for horse-breeding; but it must be admitted that in both these particulars Faizabad has the advantage, although Jirm is the centre of the mining industry in lapis lazuli, if not in rubies. Jirm is about 130 miles from Andarab, and 80 (with a well-marked road between) to Talekan. To fit Idrisi's itinerary we should have to select a spot in the Anjuman valley some sixty miles south of Jirm. This would involve an impossible altitude for either wine or horses (in that latitude), so we are forced to conclude that the itinerary is wrong. If it were exactly reversed and made seven days from Andarab and four from Talekan, Jirm would represent the site of the ancient capital exactly. Some such adjustment as this is necessary in order to meet the requirements, and Idrisi's indications of the climate.

On the whole, I am inclined to believe that Jirm represents the ancient capital. However that may be, it is important to note that the Anjuman route from the pass at the head of the Panjshir valley was a recognized route in the Middle Ages, and emphasizes the importance of the Andarab position in Afghanistan. We have seen that from the very earliest times, prior to the Greek invasion of India, this was probably the region of western settlements in Baktria. It is about here that we find the greatest number of indications (if place-names are to be trusted) of Greek colonization. It is one of the districts which are to be recognized as distinctly the theatres of Alexander's military movements during his famous expedition. It commands four, if not five of the most important passes across the Hindu Kush. The surveyor who carried his traverse up to the head of the Andarab and over the Khawak Pass into the Panjshir found a depression in the Hindu Kush range which admitted of two crossings (the Til and Khawak) at an elevation of about 11,650 feet, neither of which presented any great physical difficulty apart from that of altitude, both leading by comparatively easy grades into the upper Panjshir valley.

It is reported that since the Russo-Afghan Commission surveyors passed that way, the late Amir has constructed a passable road for commercial purposes, which can be kept open by the employment of coolie labour in removing the snow, and that khafilas pass freely between Kabul and Badakshan all the year round. In the tenth century there is ample evidence that it was a well-trodden route, for we find it stated that from Andarab to Hariana (travelling southward) is three days' journey. "Hariana is a small town built at the foot of a mountain and on the banks of a river, which, taking its source near Panjshir (Banjohir) traverses that town without being utilized for irrigation until, reaching Karwan, it enters into the territory of India and joins its waters to the Nahrwara (Kabul) River. The inhabitants of Hariana possess neither trees nor orchards. They only cultivate vegetables, but they live by mining. It is impossible to see anything more perfect than the metal which is extracted from the mines of Panjshir, a small town built on a hill at one day's distance from Hariana and of which the inhabitants are remarkable for violence and wickedness (mechanceté) of their character. The river, which issues from Panjshir, runs to Hariana as we have said." . . . "From there (? Hariana) to Karwan, southward, two days' journey." "The town of Karwan is small but pretty, its environs are agreeable, bazaars frequent, inhabitants well-off. The houses are built of mud and bricks. Situated on the banks of a river which comes from Panjshir, this town is one of the principal markets of India."

From this account it is clear that the village of Panjshir must have been somewhere near the modern Khawak, and Hariana about 20 miles lower down the stream. But the site is not identified. Karwan was obviously near the site of the modern Charikar, and might possibly be Parwan, a very ancient site. It is worthy of note that in the tenth century all the Kabul province was "India." Of all the passes traversing the Hindu Kush we have mention only of this, the Khawak, and (indirectly) of the group which connect Kabul with Bamian; and it may be doubted whether in the Middle Ages any use was made of the Shibar, Chapdara, or others that lie between the Kaoshan and Irak for commercial purposes.

There is, however, strong inference that the Greeks made use of the Kaoshan, or Parwan, which is also commanded from Andarab. The excellent military road constructed by the late Amir from Charikar, up the Ghorband valley and over the Chapdara Pass, is a modern development.

Here, however, we must take leave of the routes to India, which are sufficiently dealt with elsewhere, and returning to Badakshan see if we can unravel some of the mediæval geography of the region which stretches eastward to the Oxus affluents and the Pamirs. We know that between Khotan and Balkh there was a very well-trodden pilgrim route in the earlier days of our era (from the first century to the tenth), when both these places were full of the high-priests of Buddhism. Was it also a commercial route? The shortest way to determine its position is to examine the map and see which way it must have run at a time when (if we are to believe Mr. Ellsworthy Huntington's theories of periodic fluctuations of climate in High Asia) all that vastly elevated region was colder, less desiccated, and possibly more fertile than now, whilst its glaciers and lakes were larger and more extensive.

Before turning eastward into the highlands and plateau of Asia it is interesting to note that north of the Oxus the districts of Jil (which was the region of mountains) and Waksh were both well known, and boasted many important commercial centres. The two districts (under one government) lay between the Wakshab which joins the Oxus from the north to the north-east of Khulm, and the Khariab, which is clearly another river than the Khariab (now the Kokcha) of Badakshan, and which is probably the Oxus itself (see preceding note). These trans-Oxus regions take us afield into the Khanates of Central Asia beyond Afghanistan, and we can only note in passing that 1000 years ago Termez was the most important town on the Oxus, commanding as it did the main river crossing from Bokhara to Khulm and Balkh; Kabadian also being very ancient. Termez may yet again become significant in history.

References to the Pamir region are very scanty, and indicate that not much was known about them. The most direct road from Khotan in Chinese Turkistan to Balkh, a well-worn pilgrim route of the early centuries of our era, is that which first strikes north-west to Yarkand, and then passing by the stone fort of Tashkurghan (one of the ancient landmarks of Central Asian travel) follows the Tashkurghan River to its head, passes over the Wakhjir Pass from the Tagdumbash Pamir into the valley of the Wakhab (or Panja) River and follows that river to Zebak in Badakshan. So far it is a long, difficult, and toilsome route rising to an altitude of 15,000 to 16,000 feet, but after passing Zebak to Faizabad and so on through Badakshan to Balkh, it is a delightful road, full of picturesque beauty and incident. At certain seasons of the year no part of it would appear formidable to such earnest and determined devotees as the Chinese Buddhist pilgrims. From Huen Tsang's account, however, it would seem that a still more northerly route was usually preferred, one which involved crossing the Oxus at Termez or Kilif. It is a curious feature in connection with Buddhist records of travel (even the Arab records) that no account whatever seems to be taken of abstract altitude, *i.e.* the altitude of the plains. So long as the mountains towered above the pilgrims' heads they were content to assume that they were traversing lowlands. Never does it seem to have occurred to them that on the flat plains they might be at a higher elevation than on the summits of the Chinese or Arabian hills. The explanation undoubtedly lies in the fact that they had no means of determining elevation.

Hypsometers and aneroids were not for them. The gradual ascents leading to the Pamir valleys did not impress them, and so long as they ascended one side of a range to descend on the other, the fact that the descent did not balance the ascent was more or less unobserved. Wandering over the varied face of the earth they were content to accept it as God made it, and ask no questions. Recent investigations would lead us to suppose that in the palmy days of Buddhist occupation of Chinese Turkistan, when Lop Nor spread out its wide lake expanse to reflect a vista of towns and villages on its banks, refreshing the earth by a thousand rivulets not then impregnated with noxious salts; when high-roads traversed that which is now but a moving procession of sand-waves following each other in silent order at the bidding of the eternal wind; when men made their arrangements for posting from point to point, and forgot to pay their bills made out in the Karosthi language, the climate was very different from what it is now.

It was colder, moister, and the zones of cultivation far more extensive, but it may also be that these regions were not so highly elevated; indeed, there is good reason for believing that the eternal processes of expansion and contraction of the earth's crust, never altogether quiescent, is more marked in Central Asia than elsewhere, and that the gradual elevation, which is undoubtedly in operation now, may have also affected the levels of river-beds and intervening divides, and thrown out of gear much of the original natural possibilities for irrigation. However that may be, it is fairly certain that no great amount of trade ever crossed the Pamirs. Marco Polo crossed them, passing by Tashkurghan and making his way eastwards to Cathay, and has very little to say about them except in admiration of the magnificent pasturage which is just as abundant and as nutritious now as it was in his time. Idrisi's information beyond the regions of the Central Asian Khanates and the Oxus was very vague. He says that on the borders of Waksh and of Jil are Wakhan and Sacnia, dependencies of the country of the Turks. From Wakhan to Tibet is eighteen journeys. "Wakhan possesses silver mines, and gold is taken from the rivers. Musk and slaves are also taken from this country. Sacnia town, which belongs to the Khizilji Turks, is five days from Wakhan, and its territory adjoins China." Wakhan probably included the province of the same name that now forms the extreme north-eastern extension of Afghanistan, but the Tibet, which was eighteen days' journey distant, in no-wise corresponds with the modern Tibet. Assuming that it was "Little Tibet" (or Ladakh), which might perhaps correspond in the matter of distance, we should still have some difficulty in reconciling Idrisi's description of the "Ville de Tibet" with any place in Ladakh. He says "the town of Tibet is large, and the country of which it is the capital carries the name." This country belongs to the "Turks Tibetians." Its inhabitants entertain relations with Ferghana, Botm,[1] and with the subjects of the Wakhan; they travel over most of these countries, and they take from them their iron, silver, precious stones, leopard skins, and Tibetan musk. This town is built on a hill, at the foot of which runs a river which discharges into the lake Berwan, situated towards the east. It is surrounded with walls, and serves as the residence of a prince, who has many troops and much cavalry, who wear coats of mail and are armed *de pied en cap*. They make many things there, and export robes and stuff of which the tissue is thick, rough, and durable. These robes cost much, and one gets slaves and musk destined for Ferghana and India. There does not exist in the world creatures endowed with more beautiful complexions, with more charming figures, more perfect features, and more agreeable shape than these Turk slaves. They are disrobed and sold to merchants, and it is this class of girl who fetches 300 dinars. The country of Bagnarghar lies between Tibet and China, bounded on the north by the country of the Kirkhirs (Kiziljis in another MS.), possibly Kirghiz.

The course of the river on which the town is built, no less than the name of the lake into which that river falls and the description of the Turk

[1] The name or term Bot is locally applied now to certain Himalayan districts as well as to Tibet.

slave girls (as of the cavalry), is quite inapplicable to anything to be found in modern Tibet. I have little doubt that the Tibet of Idrisi was a town on the high-road to China, which followed the Tarim River eastward to its bourne in Lake Burhan. Lake Burhan is now a swamp distinct from Lob, but 1000 years ago it may have been a part of the Lob system, and Bagnarghar a part of Mongolia. The description of the slave girls would apply equally well to the Turkman women or to the Kirghiz, but certainly not to the flat-featured, squat-shaped Tibetan, although there are not wanting good looks amongst them. Then follows, in Idrisi's account, a list of the dependencies of Tibet and some travellers' tales about the musk-deer. It is impossible to place the ancient town of Tibet accurately. There are ruined sites in numbers on the Tarim banks, and amongst them a place called Tippak, but it would be dangerous to assume a connection between Tibet and Tippak. This is interesting (and the interest must be the excuse for the digression from Afghanistan), because it indicates that modern Chinese Turkistan was included in Tibet a thousand years ago, and it further throws a certain amount of light on the origin of the remarkable concentration of Buddhist centres in the Takla Makan.

CHAPTER VIII

ARAB EXPLORATION—MAKRAN

BETWEEN Arabia and India is the strange land of Makran, in the southern defiles and deserts of which country Alexander lost his way. Had he by chance separated himself from the coast and abandoned connection with his fleet he might have passed through Makran by more northernly routes to Persia, and have made one of those open ways which Arab occupation opened up to traffic 1000 years later. Makran is not an attractive country for the modern explorer. It is not yet a popular field for enterprise in research (though it well may become so), and a few words of further description are necessary to explain how it was that the death-trap of Alexander proved to be the road to wealth and power of the subsequent Arab.

From the sun-swept Arabian Sea a long line of white shore, with a ceaseless surf breaking on it, appears to edge it on the north. This is backed by other long lines of level-topped hills, seldom rising to conspicuous peaks or altitudes, but just stretched

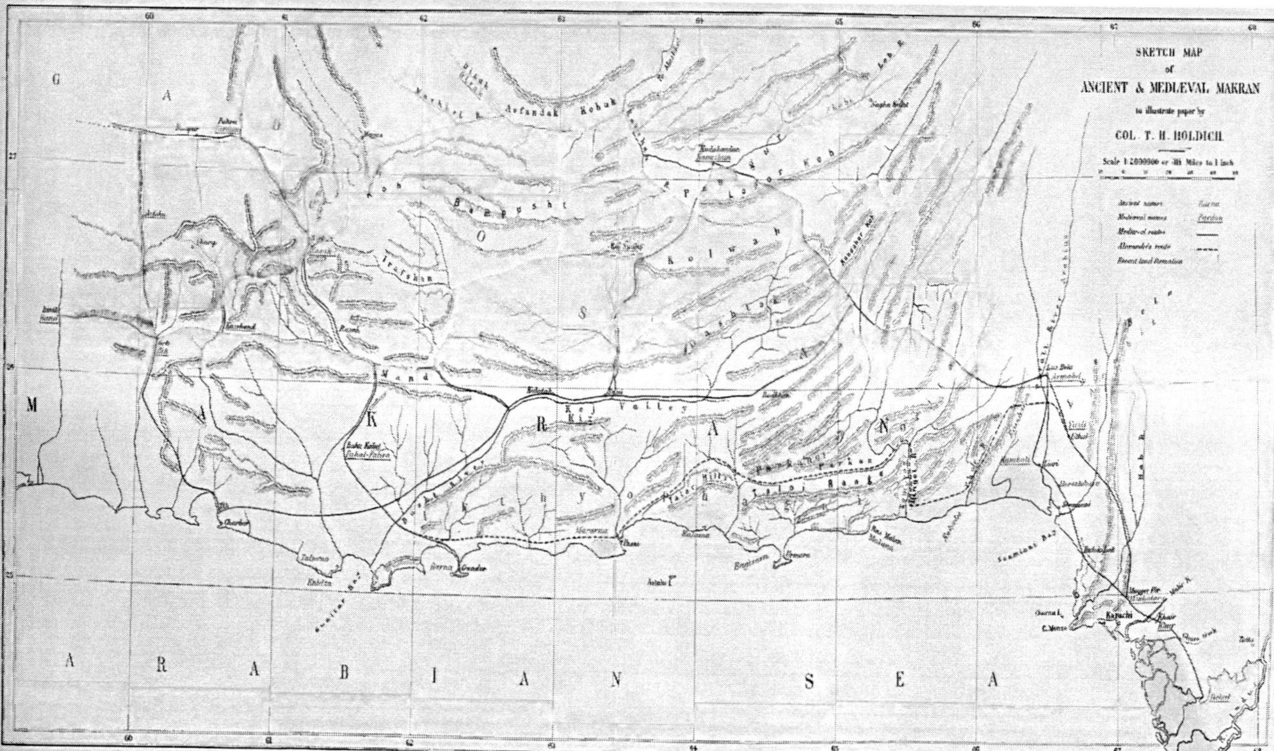
SKETCH MAP
of
ANCIENT & MEDIÆVAL MAKRAN
to illustrate paper by
COL. T. H. HOLDICH.
ARABIAN SEA
Kej Valley
Mand
Kolwah
Bampusht
Irafshan
Asfandak
Kohuk
Karachi

out in long grey and purple lines with a prominent feature here and there to serve as a useful landmark to mariners. Now and then when the shoreline is indented, the hills actually face the sea and there are clean-cut scarped cliffs presenting a square face to the waves. At such points the deep rifted mountains of the interior either extend an arm to the ocean, as at Malan, or it may be that a narrow band of ancient ridge leaves jagged sections of its length above sea-level, parallel to the coastline, and that between it and the hills of the interior is a sandy isthmus with sea indentation forming harbours on either side. This country, for a width of about 100 miles, is called Makran. It is the southernmost region of Southern Baluchistan, a country geologically of recent formation, with a coastal uplift from the sea-bottom of soft white sand strata capped here and there by laterite. Such a formation lends itself to quaint curiosities in hill structure. A protecting cap may preserve a pinnacle of soft rock, whilst all around it the persistence of weather action has cut away the soil. Gigantic cap-crowned pillars and pedestals are balanced in fantastic array about the mountain slopes; deep cuttings and gorges are formed by denudation, and from the gullies so fashioned amongst these hills there may tower up a scarped cliff edge for thousands of feet, with successive strata so well defined that it possesses all the appearance of massive masonry construction.

The sea which beats with unceasing surf on the shores of Makran is full of the wonders of the deep. From the dead silent flat surface, such as comes with an autumn calm, monstrous fish suddenly shoot out for 15 or 20 feet into the air and fall with a resounding slap almost amounting to a detonation. Whales still disport themselves close inshore, and frighten no one. It is easy, however, to understand the terror with which they inspired the Greek sailors of Nearkhos in their open Indian-built boats as they wormed their way along the coast. Occasionally a whale becomes involved with the cable of the Indo-Persian telegraph line and loops himself into it, with fatal results. There are islands off the shore, cut out from the mainland. Some of them are in process of disappearance, when they will add their quota to the bar which makes approach to the Makran shores so generally difficult; others, more remote, bid fair to last as the final remnants of a long-ago submerged ridge through ages yet to come; and one regrets that the day of their enchantment has passed. Of such is that island of Haftala, Hashtala, Nuhsala (it is difficult to account for the variety of Persian numerals which are associated with its name), which is called Nosala by Nearkhos and said by him to be sacred to the sun. In the days of the Greeks it was enveloped in a haze of mystery and tradition. The Karaks who made of this island a base for their depredations, finally drew down upon themselves the wrath of the

Arabs, and this led incidentally to one of the most successful invasions of India that have ever been conducted by sea and land.

But it is not only the historical and legendary interest of this remarkable coast which renders it a fascinating subject for exploration and romance. The physical conditions of it, the bubbling mud volcanoes which occasionally fill the sea with yellow silt from below, and always remain in a perpetual simmer of boiling activity; the weird and fantastic forms assumed by the mud strata of recent sea-making, which are the basis of the whole structure of ridge and furrow which constitute Makran conformation, no less than the extraordinary prevalence of electric phenomena,—all these offered the Arabian Sea as a promising gift to the inventive faculty of such Arab genius as revelled in stories of miraculous enterprise. On a still, warm night when the stars are all ablaze overhead the sea will, of a sudden, spread around in a sheet of milky white, and the sky become black by contrast with the blackness of ink. Then again will there be a transformation to a bright scintillating floor, with each little wavelet dropping sparks of light upon it; and from the wake of the vessel will stretch out to the horizon a shining way, like a silver path into the great unknown. Meanwhile, the ship herself will be lit up by the electric genii. Each iron rod or stanchion will gleam with a weird white light; each spar will carry a little bunch of blue flame at its point; the mast-head will be aflame, and softly through the wonders of this strange Eastern sea the ship will stalk on in solemn silence and most "excellent loneliness." Small wonder that Arab mariners were stirring story-tellers, living as they did amidst the uncounted wonders of the Persian Gulf and the Arabian Sea.

Hardly less strange is the land formation of this southern edge of Baluchistan. It is an old, old country, replete with the evidences of unwritten history, the ultimate bourne of much of the flotsam and jetsam of Asiatic humanity; a cul-de-sac where northern intruders meet and get no farther. Yet geologically it is very new—so new that one might think that the piles of sea-born shells which are to be found here and there drifted into heaps on the soft mud flats amongst the bristling ridges, were things of yesterday; so new, in fact, that it has not yet done changing its outline. There is little difficulty in marking the changes in the coast-line which must have occurred since the third century B.C. One may even count up the island formations and disappearances which have occurred within a generation; so incomplete that the changing conditions of its water-supply have left their marks everywhere over it. Desiccated forests are to be found with the trees still standing, as they will continue to stand in this dry climate for centuries. Huge masonry constructions, built as dams for the retention of water in the inland hills, testify to the existence of an abundant water-supply within historic periods; as also do the terraced slopes which reach down in orderly steps to the foot of the ridges, each step representing a formerly irrigated field. The water has failed; whether, as is most probable, from the same desiccating processes which are drying up lakes and dwindling glaciers in both northern and southern hemispheres, or whether there has been special interference with the routine of Nature and man has contributed to his own undoing, it is impossible at present to say, but the result is that Makran is now, and has been for centuries, a forgotten and almost a forsaken country. In order to understand the remarkable peculiarity of its geographical formation one requires a good map. Ridges, rather than ranges, are the predominant feature of its orography. Ridges of all degrees of altitude, extension, and rockiness, running in long lines of parallel flexure on a system of curves which sweeps them round gradually from the run of Indus frontier hills to an east and west strike through Makran, and a final trend to the north-west, where they guard the Persian coasts of the Gulf. As a rule they throw off no spurs, standing stiff, jagged, naked, and uncompromising, like the parallel walls of some gigantic system of defences, and varying in height above the plain from 5000 feet to 50. The higher ranges have been scored by weather and wet, with deep gorges and drainage lines, and their scarred sides present various degrees of angle and declivity, according to the dip of the strata that forms them. Some of the smaller ridges have their rocky backbone set up straight, forming a knife-like edge along which nothing but a squirrel could run. Across them, breaking through the axis almost at right angles run some of the main arteries of the general drainage system; but the most important features of the country are the long lateral valleys between the ridges, the streams of which feed the main rivers. These are often 8 or 10 miles in width, with a flat alluvial bottom, and one may ride for mile after mile along the open plain with clay or sand spread out on either hand, and nothing but the distant wall of the hills flanking the long and endless route. Some of these valleys are filled with a luxuriance of palm growth (the dates of Panjgur, for instance, being famous), and it is this remarkable feature of long, lateral valleys which, through all the ages, has made of Makran an avenue of approach to India from the west. The more important ranges lie to the north, facing the deserts of Central Baluchistan. It is in the solid phalanx of the coastal band of hills that the most marked adherence to the gridiron, or ridge and furrow formation, is to be found.

Exceptionally, out of this banded system arises some great mountain block forming a separate feature, such as is the massive crag-crowned cliff-lined block of Malan, west of one of the most important rivers of Makran (the Hingol), to which reference has already been made. From it an arm stretches southwards to the sea, and forms a square-headed obstruction to traffic along the coast, which almost defeated the efforts of the Indo-Persian telegraph constructors when they essayed to carry a line across it, and did entirely defeat the intentions of Alexander the Great to conduct his army within sight of his Indus-built fleet. It is within the folds of this mountain group that lies hidden that most ancient shrine of Indo-Persian worship, to which we have already referred in the story of Alexander's retreat.

It is the possibilities of Makran as an intervening link in the route from Europe to India which renders that country interesting at the present time, and it is therefore with a practical as well as historical interest that we take up the story of frontier exploration from the time when we first recognize the great commercial movements of the Arab races, centuries after the disappearance of the last remnants of ancient explorations by Assyrians, Persians, and Greeks. It is extraordinary how deep a veil of forgetfulness was drawn over Southern Baluchistan during this unrecorded interval. For a thousand years, from the withdrawal of Alexander's attenuated force to the rise and spread of Islam, we hear nothing of Makran, and we are left to the traditions of the Baluch tribes to fill up the gap in history. What the Arabs made of mediæval Makran as a gate of India may be briefly told. Recent surveys have revealed their tracks, although we have no clear record of their earliest movements. We know, however, that there was an Arab governor of Makran long previous to the historical invasion of India in A.D. 712, and that there must have been strong commercial interest and considerable traffic before his time. Arabia, indeed, had always been interested in Makran, and amongst other relics of a long dead past are those huge stone constructions for water-storage purposes to which we have referred, and which must have been of very early Arab (possibly Himyaritic) building, as well as a host of legends and traditions, all pointing to successive waves of early tribal emigration, extending from the Persian frontier to the lower Arabius —the Purali of our time.

Hajjaj, the governor of Irak, under the Kalif Walid I., projected three simultaneous expeditions into Asia for the advancement of the true faith. One was directed towards Samarkand, one against the King of Kabul, and the third was to operate directly on India through the heart of Makran. The Makran field force was organised in the first instance for the purpose of punishing certain Karak and Med pirates, who had plundered a valuable convoy sent by the ruler of Ceylon to Hajjaj and to the Kalif. These Karaks probably gave their names to the Krokala of Nearkhos, and the Karachi of to-day, and have disappeared. The Meds still exist. The expedition, which was placed under the command of an enterprising young general aged seventeen, named Mahomed Kasim, not only swept through Makran easily and successfully, but ended by establishing Mahomedan supremacy in the Indus valley, and originated a form of government which, under various phases, lasted till Mahmud of Ghazni put an end to a degenerated form of it by ousting the Karmatian rulers of Multan in A.D. 1005. The original force which invaded Sind under Mahomed Kasim, and which was drawn chiefly from Syria and Irak, consisted of 6000 camel-riders and 3000 infantry. In Makran the Arab governor (it is important to note that there was an Arab governor of Makran before that country became the high-road to India) added further reinforcements, and there was also a naval squadron, which conveyed catapults and ammunition by sea to the Indus valley port of Debal. It was with this small force that one of the most surprising invasions of India ever attempted was successfully carried through Makran—a country hitherto deemed impracticable, and associated in previous history with nothing but tales of disaster. For long, however, we find that Mahomed Kasim had both the piratical Meds, and the hardly less tractable Jats (a Skythic people still existing in the Indus valley) in his train, and the news of his successes carried to Damascus brought crowds of Arab adventurers to follow his fortunes. When he left Multan for the north, he is said to have had

50,000 men under his command. His subsequent career and tragic end are all matters of history.

The points chiefly to note in this remarkable invasion are that the Arab soldiers first engaged were chiefly recruited from Syria; that, contrary to their usual custom, they brought none of their women with them; and that none of them probably ever returned to their country again. Elliott tells us of the message sent them by the savage Kalif Suliman: "Sow and sweat, for none of you will ever see Syria again." What, then, became of all these first Arab conquerors of Western India? They must have taken Persian-speaking wives of the stock of Makran and Baluchistan, and their children, speaking their mother-tongue, lost all knowledge of their fathers' language in the course of a few generations. There are many such instances of the rapid disappearance of a language in the East. For three centuries, then, whilst a people of Arab descent ruled in Sind, there existed through Makran one of the great highways of the world, a link between West and East such as has never existed elsewhere on the Indian border, save, perhaps, through the valley of the Kabul River and its affluents. Along this highway flowed the greater part of the mighty trade of India, a trade which has never failed to give commercial predominance to that country which held the golden key to it, whether that key has been in the hands of Arab,

Turk, Venetian, Portuguese, or Englishman. And though there are traces of a rapid decline in the mediæval prosperity of Makran after the commencement of the eleventh century, yet its comparative remoteness in geographical position saved it subsequently from the ruthless destruction inflicted by Turk and Tartar in more accessible regions, and left to it cities worth despoiling even in the days of Portuguese supremacy.

It is only lately that Makran has lapsed again into a mere geographical expression. Twenty years ago our maps told us nothing about it. It might have been, and was, for all practical purposes, as unexplored and unknown as the forests of Africa. Now, however, we have found that Makran is a country of great topographical interest as well as of stirring history. And when we come to the days of Arab ascendency, when Arab merchants settled in the country; when good roads with well-marked stages were established; when, fortunately for geography, certain Western commercial travellers, following, *longo intervallo*, the example of the Chinese pilgrims—men such as Ibn Haukal of Baghdad, or Istakhri of Persepolis—first set to work to reduce geographical discovery to systematic compilation, we can take their books and maps in our hands, and verify their statements as we read. It is true that they copied a good deal from each other, and that their manner of writing geographical names was obscure, and leaves a good deal to be desired

—a fault, by the way, from which the maps of to-day are not entirely free—yet they are on the whole as much more accurate than the early Greek geographers as the area of their observations is more restricted. We may say that Makran and Sind are perhaps more fully treated of by Arab geographers than any other portion of the globe by the geographers who preceded them; and as their details are more perfect, so, for the most part, is the identification of those details rendered comparatively easy by the nature of the country and its physical characteristics. With the exception of the coast-line the topography of Makran to-day is the topography of Makran in Alexandrian days. This is very different indeed from the uncertain character of the Indus valley mediæval geography. There the extraordinary hydrographical changes that have taken place; the shifting of the great river itself from east to west, dependent on certain recognized natural laws; the drying up and total disappearance of ancient channels and river-beds; the formation of a delta, and the ever-varying alterations in the coast-line (due greatly to monsoon influences), leave large tracts almost unrecognizable as described in mediæval literature. Makran is, for the most part, a country of hills. Its valleys are narrow and sharply defined; its mountains only passable at certain well-known points, which must have been as definite before the Christian era as they are to-day; and it is consequently comparatively easy to follow up a clue to any main route passing through that country.

Makran is, in short, a country full of long narrow valleys running east and west, the longest and most important being the valley of Kej. The main drainage of the country reaches the sea by a series of main channels running south, which, inasmuch as they are driven almost at right angles across the general run of the watersheds, necessarily pass through a series of gorges of most magnificent proportions, which are far more impressive as spectacles than they are convenient for practical road-making. Thus Makran is very much easier to traverse from east to west than it is from north to south.

I have, perhaps, said enough to indicate that the old highways through Makran, however much they may have assisted trade and traffic between East and West, could only have been confined to very narrow limits indeed. It is, in fact, almost a one-road country. Given the key, then, to open the gates of such channels of communication as exist, there is no difficulty in following them up, and the identification of successive stages becomes merely a matter of local search. We know where the old Arab cities *must* have been, and we have but to look about to find their ruins. The best key, perhaps, to this mediæval system is to be found in a map given by the Baghdad traveller, Ibn Haukal, who wrote his account of Makran early in the tenth century, and though this map leaves much to be desired in clearness and accuracy, it is quite sufficient to give us the clue we require at first starting. In the written geographical accounts of the country, we labour under the disadvantage of possessing no comparative standard of distance. The Arab of mediæval days described the distance to be traversed between one point and another much as the Bedou describes it now. It is so many days' journey. Occasionally, indeed, we find a compiler of more than usual precision modifying his description of a stage as a long day's journey, or a short one. But such instances are rare, and a day's journey appears to be literally just so much as could conveniently be included in a day's work, with due regard to the character of the route traversed. Across an open desert a day's journey may be as much as 80 miles. Between the cities of a well-populated district it may be much less. Taking an average from all known distances, it is between 40 and 50 miles. Nor is it always explained whether the day's journey is by land or sea, the unit "a day's journey" being the distance traversed independent of the means of transit.

In Ibn Haukal's map, although we have very little indication of comparative distance, we have a rough idea of bearings, and the invaluable datum of a fixed starting-point that can be identified beyond doubt. The great Arab port on the Makran coast, sometimes even called the capital of

Makran, was Tiz; and Tiz is a well-known coast village to this day. About 100 miles west of the port of Gwadur there is a convenient and sheltered harbour for coast shipping, and on the shores of it there was a telegraph station of the Persian Gulf line called Charbar. The telegraph station occupied the extremity of the eastern horn of the bay, and was separated inland by some few miles of sandy waste from a low band of coarse conglomerate hills, which conceal amongst them a narrow valley, containing all that is left of the ancient port of Tiz. If you take a boat from Charbar point, and, coasting up the bay, land at the mouth of this valley, you will first of all be confronted by a picturesque little Persian fort perched on the rocks on either hand, and absolutely blocking the entrance to the valley. This fort was built, or at least renewed, in the days of General Sir F. Goldsmid's Seistan mission, to emphasize the fact that the Persian Government claimed that valley for its own. About a mile above the fort there exists a squalid little fishing village, the inhabitants of which spend their spare moments (and they have many of them) in making those palm mats which enter so largely into the house architecture of the coast villages, as they sit beneath the shade of one or two remarkably fine "banian" trees. The valley is narrow and close, and the ruins of Tiz, extending on both sides the village, are packed close together in enormous heaps of debris, so covered with broken pottery as to suggest the idea that the inhabitants of old Tiz must have once devoted themselves entirely to the production of ceramic art ware. Every heavy shower of rain washes out fragments of new curiosities in glass and china. Here may be found large quantities of an antique form of glass, the secret of the manufacture of which has (according to Venetian experts) long passed away, only to be lately rediscovered. It takes the shape of bangles chiefly, and in this form may be dug up in almost any of the recognized sites of ancient coast towns along the Makran and Persian coasts. It is apparently of Egyptian origin, and was brought to the coast in Arab ships. Here also is to be found much of a special class of pottery, of very fine texture, and usually finished with a light sage-green glaze, which appears to me to be peculiarly Arabic, but of which I have yet to learn the full history. It is well known in Afghanistan, where it is said to possess the property of detecting poison by cracking under it, but even there it is no modern importation. This is the celadon to which reference has already been made. The rocky cliffs on either side the valley are honey-combed with Mahomedan tombs, and the face of every flat-spaced eminence is scarred with them. A hundred generations of Moslems are buried there. The rocky declivities which hedge in this remarkable site may give some clue to the yet more ancient name of Talara which this place once bore. Talar in Baluchi bears the signification of a rocky band of cliffs or hills.

The obvious reason why the port of Tiz was chosen for the point of debarkation for India is that, in addition to the general convenience of the harbour, the monsoon winds do not affect the coast so far west. At seasons when the Indus delta and the port of Debal were rendered unapproachable, Tiz was an easy port to gain. There must have been a considerable local trade, too, between the coast and the highly cultivated, if restricted, valleys of Northern Makran, and it is more than probable that Tiz was the port for the commerce of Seistan in its most palmy days.

From Tiz to Kiz (or Kej, which is reckoned as the first big city on the road to India in mediæval geography) was, according to Istakhri and Idrisi, a five-days' journey. Kiz is doubtless synonymous with Kej, but the long straight valley of that name which leads eastwards towards India has no town now which exactly corresponds to the name of the valley. The distance between Tiz and the Kej district is from 160 to 170 miles. No actual ruined site can be pointed out as yet marking the position of Kiz, or (as Idrisi writes it) Kirusi, but it must have been in the close neighbourhood of Kalatak, where, indeed, there is ample room for further close investigation amongst surrounding ruins. About the city, we may note from Idrisi that it was nearly as large as Multan, and was the largest city in

Makran. "Palm trees are plentiful, and there is a large trade," says our author, who adds that it is two long days' journey west of the city of Firabuz. From all the varied forms which Arab geographical names can assume owing to omission of diacritical marks in writing, this place, Firabuz, has perhaps suffered most. The most correct reading of it would probably be Kanazbun, and this is the form adopted by Elliott, who conjectures that Kanazbun was situated near the modern Panjgur. From Kej to Panjgur is not less than 110 miles, a very long two-days' journey. Yet Istakhri supports Idrisi (if, indeed, he is not the original author of the statement) that it is two days' journey from Kiz to Kanazbun. This would lead one to place Kanazbun elsewhere than in the Panjgur district, more especially as that district lies well to the north of the direct road to India, were it not for local evidence that the fertile and flourishing Panjgur valley must certainly be included somehow in the mediæval geographical system, and that the conditions of khafila traffic in mediæval times were such as to preclude the possibility of the more direct route being utilized. To explain this fully would demand a full explanation also of the physical geography of Eastern Makran. I have no doubt whatever that Sir H. Elliott is right in his conjecture, and that amongst the many relics of ancient civilization which are to be found in Panjgur is the site of Kanazbun. Kanazbun was in existence long before the Arab invasion of Sind. The modern fort of Kudabandan probably represents the site of that more ancient fort which was built by the usurper Chach of Sind, when he marched through Makran to fix its further boundaries about the beginning of the Mahomedan era. Kanazbun was a very large city indeed. "It is a town," says Idrisi, "of which the inhabitants are rich. They carry on a great trade. They are men of their word, enemies of fraud, and they are generous and hospitable." Panjgur, I may add, is a delightfully green spot amongst many other green spots in Makran. It is not long ago that we had a small force cantoned there to preserve law and order in that lawless land. There appeared to be but one verdict on the part of the officers who lived there, and that verdict was all in its favour. In this particular, Panjgur is probably unique amongst frontier outposts.

The next important city on the road to Sind was Armail, Armabel, or Karabel, now, without doubt, Las Bela. From Kudabandan to Las Bela is from 170 to 180 miles, and there is considerable variety of opinion as to the number of days that were to be occupied in traversing the distance. Istakhri says that from Kiz to Armail is six days' journey. Deduct the two from Kiz to Kanazbun, and the distance between Kanazbun and Armail is four days. Ibn Haukal makes it fourteen marches from Kanazbun to the port of Debal, and as he reckons Armail to be six from Debal on the Kanazbun road, we get a second estimate of eight days' journey. Idrisi says that from Manhabari to Firabuz is six marches, and we know otherwise that from Manhabari to Armail was four, so the third estimate gives us two days' journey. Istakhri's estimate is more in accordance with the average that we find elsewhere, and he is the probable author of the original statements. But doubtless the number of days occupied varied with the season and the amount of supplies procurable. There were villages *en route*, and many halting-places. The *Ashkalu l' Bilad* of Ibn Haukal says: "Villages of Dahuk and Kalwan are contiguous, and are between Labi and Armail"; from which Elliott conjectures that Labi was synonymous with Kiz. Idrisi states that "between Kiz and Armail two districts touch each other, Rahun and Kalwan." I should be inclined to suggest that the districts of Dashtak and Kolwah are those referred to. They are contiguous, and they may be said to be between Kiz and Armail, though it would be more exact to place them between Kanazbun and Armail. Kolwah is a well-cultivated district lying to the south of the river, which in its upper course is known as the Lob. I should conjecture that this may be the Labi referred to by Ibn Haukal.

The city of Armail, Armabel (sometimes Karabel), or Las Bela, is of great historic interest. From the very earliest days of historical record

Armail, by right of its position commanding the high-road to India, must have been of great importance. Las Bela is but the modern name derived from the influx of the Las or Lumri tribe of Rajputs. It is at present but an insignificant little town, picturesquely perched on the banks of the Purali River, but in its immediate neighbourhood is a veritable *embarras de richesse* in ancient sites. Eleven miles north-west of Las Bela, at Gonda-kahar, are the ruins of a very ancient city, which at first sight appear to carry us back to the pre-Mahomedan era of Arab occupation, when the country was peopled by Arabii, and the Arab flag was paramount on the high seas. Not far from them are the caves of Gondrani, about which there is no room for conjecture, for they are clearly Buddhist, as can be told from their construction. We know from the Chachnama of Sind that in the middle of the eighth century the province of Las Bela was part of a Buddhist kingdom, which extended from Armabel to the modern province of Gandava in Sind. The great trade mart for the Buddhists on the frontier was a place called Kan-dabel, which Elliott identifies with Gandava, the capital of the province of Kach Gandava. It is, however, associated in the Chachnama with Kanda-har, the expression "Kandabel, that is, Kandahar" being used, an expression which Elliott condemns for its inaccuracy, as he recognizes but the one Kandahar, which is in Afghanistan. It happens that there is a Kandahar, or Gandahar, in Kach Gandava, and there are ruins enough in the neighbourhood to justify the suspicion that this was after all the original Kandabel rather than the modern town of Gandava.

The capital of this ancient Buddha—or Buddhiya—kingdom I believe to have been Armabel rather than Kandabel, it being at Armabel that Chach found a Buddhist priest reigning in the year A.H. 2, when he passed through. The curious association of names, and the undoubted Buddhist character of the Gondrani caves, would lead one to assign a Buddhist origin also to the neighbouring ruins of Gondakahar (or Gandakahar) only that direct evidence from the ruins themselves is at present wanting to confirm this conjecture. They require far closer investigation than has been found possible in the course of ordinary survey operations. The country lying between Las Bela and Kach Gandava is occupied at present by a most troublesome section of the Dravidian Brahuis, who call themselves Mingals, or Mongols, and who possibly may be a Mongolian graft on the Dravidian stock. They may prove to be modern representatives of the old Buddhist population of this land, but their objection to political control has hitherto debarred us from even exploring their country, although it is immediately on our own borders. About 8 miles north of Las Bela are the ruins of a comparatively recent Arab settlement, but they do not appear to be important. It is probable that certain other ruins, about 1½ miles east of the town, called Karia Pir, represent the latest mediæval site, the site which was adopted after the destruction of the older city by Mahomed Kasim on his way to invade Sind. Karia Pir is full of Arabic coins and pottery. So many invasions of India have been planned with varied success by the Kalifs of Baghdad since the first invasion in the days of Omar I. in A.D. 644, till the time of the final occupation of Sind in the time of the sixth Kalif Walid, about A.D. 712, that there is no difficulty in accounting for the varied sites and fortunes of any city occupying so important a strategical position as Bela.

From Armail we have a two-days' march assigned by Istakhri and Idrisi as the distance to the town of Kambali, or Yusli, towards India. These two places have, in consequence of their similarity in position, become much confused, and it has been assumed by some scholars that they are identical. But they are clearly separated in Ibn Haukal's map, and it is, in fact, the question only of which of two routes towards India is selected that will decide which of the two cities will be found on the road. There is (and always must have been) a choice of routes to the ancient port of Debal after passing the city of Armail. That route which led through Yusli in all probability passed by the modern site of Uthal. Close to this village the unmistakable ruins of a considerable Arab town have been found, and I have no hesitation in identifying them as those of Yusli. About Kambali, too, there can be very little doubt. There are certain well-known ruins called Khairokot not far to the west of the village of Liari. We know from mediæval description that Kambali was close to the sea, and the sea shaped its coast-line in mediæval days so as nearly to touch the site called Khairokot. Even now, under certain conditions of tide, it is possible to reach Liari in a coast fishing-boat, although the process of land formation at the head of the Sonmiani bay is proceeding so fast that, on the other hand, it is occasionally impossible even to reach the fishing village of Sonmiani itself. The ruins of Khairokot are so extensive, and yield such large evidences of Arab occupation that a place must certainly be found for them in the mediæval system. Kambali appears to be the only possible solution to the problem, although it was somewhat off the direct road between Armail and Debal.

From either of these towns we have a six-days' journey to Debal, passing two other cities *en route*, viz. Manabari and the "small but populous town of Khur."

The Manhanari of Istakhri, Manbatara of Ibn Haukal, or Manabari of Idrisi, again confronts us with the oft-repeated difficulty of two places with similar names, there being no one individual site which will answer all the descriptions given.

General Haig has shown that there was in all probability a Manjabari on the old channel of the Indus, nearly opposite the famous city of Mansura, some 40 miles north-east of the modern Hydrabad, which will answer certain points of Arabic description; but he shows conclusively that this could not be the Manhabari of Ibn Haukal and Idrisi, which was two days' journey from Debal on the road to Armail. As we have now decided what direction that road must have taken, after accepting General Haig's position for Debal, and bearing in mind Idrisi's description of the town as "built in a hollow," with fountains, springs, and gardens around it, there seems to me but little doubt that the site of the ancient Manhabari is to be found near that resort of all Karachi holiday-makers called Mugger Pir. Here the sacred alligators are kept, and hence the recognized name; but the real name of the place, divested of its vulgar attributes, is Manga, or Manja Pir. The affix Pir is common throughout the Bela district, and is a modern introduction. The position of Mugger Pir, with its encircling walls of hills, its adjacent hot springs and gardens (so rare as to be almost unique in this part of the country), its convenient position with respect to the coast, and, above all, its interesting architectural remains, mark it unmistakably as that Manhabari of Idrisi which was two days' march from Debal.

Whether Manhabari can be identified with that ancient capital of Indo-Skythia spoken of by

Ptolemy and the author of the *Periplus* as Minagar, or Binagar, may be open to question, though there are a good many points about it which appear to meet the description given by more ancient geographers. The question is too large to enter on now, but there is certainly reason to think that such identification may be found possible. The small but populous town of Khur has left some apparent records of its existence near the Malir waterworks of Karachi, where there is a very fine group of Arab tombs in a good state of preservation. There is a village called Khair marked on the map not far from this position, and the actual site of the old town cannot be far from it, although I have not had the opportunity of identifying it. It is directly on the road connecting Debal with Manhabari. With Manhabari and Khur our tale of buried cities closes in this direction. We have but to add that General Haig identifies Debal with a ruin-covered site 20 miles south-west of Thatta, and about 45 miles east-south-east of Karachi.

All these ancient cities eastwards from Makran are associated with one very interesting feature. Somewhat apart from the deserted and hardly recognizable ruins of the cities are groups of remarkable tombs, constructed of stone, and carved with a most minute beauty of design, which is so well preserved as to appear almost fresh from the hands of the sculptor. These tombs are locally known as "Khalmati."

Invariably placed on rising ground, with a fair command of the surrounding landscape, they are the most conspicuous witnesses yet remaining of the nature of the Saracenic style of decorative art which must have beautified those early cities. The cities themselves have long since passed away, but these stone records of dead citizens still remain to illustrate, if but with a feeble light, one of the darkest periods in the history of Indian architecture. These remains are most likely Khalmati (*not* Karmati) and belong to an Arab race who were once strong in Sind and who came from the Makran coast at Khalmat. The Karmatians were not builders.

We have so far only dealt with that route to India which combined a coasting voyage in Arab ships with an overland journey which was obviously performed on a camel, or the days' stages could never have been accomplished. But the number of cities in Western Makran and Kirman which still exist under their mediæval names, and which are thickly surrounded with evidences of their former wealth and greatness, certifies to a former trade through Persia to India which could have been nowise inferior to that from the shores of Arabia or Egypt. Indeed, the overland route to India through Persia and Makran was probably one of the best trodden trade routes that the world has ever seen. It is almost unnecessary to enumerate such names as Darak, Bih, Band, Kasrkand,

Asfaka, and Fahalfahra (all of which are to be found in Ibn Haukal's map), and to point out that they are represented in modern geography by Dizak, Geh, Binth, Kasrkand, Asfaka, and Bahu Kalat. Degenerated and narrowed as they now are, there are still evidences written large enough in surrounding ruins to satisfy the investigator of the reality and greatness of their past; whilst the present nature of the routes which connect them by river and mountain is enough to prove that they never could have been of small account in the Arab geographical system. One city in this part of Makran is, I confess, something of a riddle to me still. Rasak is ever spoken of by Arab geographers as the city of "schismatics." There is, indeed, a Rasak on the Sarbaz River road to Bampur, which might be strained to fit the position assigned it in Arab geography; but it is now a small and insignificant village, and apparently could never have been otherwise. There is no room there for a city of such world-wide fame as the ancient headquarters of heresy must have been—a city which served usefully as a link between the heretics of Persia and those of Sind.

Istakhri says that Rasak is two days' journey from Fahalfahra (which there is good reason for believing to be Bahu Kalat), but Idrisi makes it a three-days' journey from that place, and three days from Darak, so that it should be about halfway between them. Now, Darak can hardly be other than Dizak, which is described by the same authority as three days' journey from Firabuz (*i.e.* Kanazbun). It is also said to have been a populous town, and south-west of it was "a high mountain called the Mountain of Salt." South-west of Dizak are the highest mountains in Makran, called the Bampusht Koh, and there is enough salt in the neighbourhood to justify the geographer's description. It may also be said to be three days' journey from Kanazbun. Somewhere about half-way between Dizak and Bahu Kalat is the important town of Sarbaz, and from a description of contiguous ruins which has been given by Mr. E. A. Wainwright, of the Survey Department (to whom I am indebted for most of the Makran identifications), I am inclined to place the ancient Rasak at Sarbaz rather than in the position which the modern name would apply to it. It is rather significant that Ibn Haukal omits Rasak altogether from his map. Its importance may be estimated from Idrisi's description of it taken from the translation given by Elliott in the first volume of his History of India: "The inhabitants of Rasak are schismatics. Their territory is divided into two districts, one called Al Kharij, and the other Kir" (or Kiz) "Kaian. Sugar-cane is much cultivated, and a considerable trade is carried on in a sweetmeat called 'faniz,' which is made here. . . . The territory of Maskan joins that of Kirman." Maskan is probably represented by

Mashkel at the present day, Mashkel being the best date-growing district in Southern Baluchistan. It adjoins Kirman, and produces dates of such excellent quality that they compare favourably with the best products of the Euphrates. Idrisi's description of this part of Western Makran continues thus: "The inhabitants have a great reputation for courage. They have date-trees, camels, cereals, and the fruit of cold countries." He then gives a table of distances, from which we can roughly estimate the meaning of "a day's journey." After stating that Fahalfahra, Asfaka, Band, and Kasrkand are dependencies of Makran which resemble each other in point of size and extent of their trade, he goes on to say, "Fahalfahra to Rasak two days." (Istakhri makes it three days, the distance from Bahu Kalat to Sarbaz being about 80 miles.) "From Fahalfahra to Asfaka two days." (This is almost impossible, the distance being about 160 miles, and the route passing through several large towns.) "From Asfaka to Band one day towards the west." (This is about 45 miles south-west rather than west.) "From Asfaka to Darak three days." (150 to 160 miles according to the route taken.) "From Band to Kasrkand one day." (About 70 miles, passing through Bih or Geh, which is not mentioned.) "From Kasrkand to Kiz four days." This is not much over 150 miles, and is the most probable estimate of them all. It is possible, of course, that from 70 to 80 miles may have been covered on a good camel within the limits of twenty-four hours. Such distances in Arabia are not uncommon, but we are not here dealing with an absolutely desert district, devoid of water. On the contrary, halting-places must have always been frequent and convenient.

I cannot leave this corner of Makran without a short reference to what lay beyond to the north-west, on the Kirman border, as it appears to me that one or two geographical riddles of mediæval days have recently been cleared up by the results of our explorations. Idrisi says that "Tubaran is near Fahraj, which belongs to Kirman. It is a well-fortified town, and is situated on the banks of a river of the same name, which are cultivated and fertile. From hence to Fardan, a commercial town, the environs of which are well populated, four days. Kir Kaian lies to the west of Fardan, on the road to Tubaran. The country is well populated and very fertile. The vine grows here and various sorts of fruit trees, but the palm is not to be found." Elsewhere he states that "from Mansuria to Tubaran about fifteen days"; and again, "from Tubaran to Multan, on the borders of Sind, ten days." Here there is clearly the confusion which so constantly arises from the repetition of place-names in different localities. Multan and Mansuria are well-known or well-identified localities, and Turan was an equally well-recognized district of Lower Sind, of which Khozdar was the capital.

Turan may well be reckoned as ten days from Multan, or fifteen from Mansuria, but hardly the Tubaran, about which such a detailed and precise description is given. There are two places called indifferently Fahraj, Pahrag, Pahra, or Pahura, both of which are in the Kirman district; one, which is shown in St. John's map of Persia, is not very far from Regan, in the Narmashir province, and is surrounded far and wide with ruins. It has been identified by St. John as the Pahra of Arrian, the capital of Gadrosia, where Alexander rested after his retreat through Makran. The other is some 16 miles east of Bampur, to the north-west of Sarbaz. Both are on the banks of a river, "cultivated and fertile"; both are the centres of an area of ruins extending for miles; both must find a place in mediæval geography. For many reasons, into which I cannot fully enter, I am inclined to place the Pahra of Arrian in the site near Bampur. It suits the narrative in many particulars better than does the Pahra identified with Fahraj by St. John. The latter, I have very little doubt, is the Fahraj of Idrisi, and the town of Tubaran was not far from it. Fardan may well have been either Bampur itself (a very ancient town) or Pahra, 16 miles to the east of it; and between Fardan and Fahraj lay the district of Kir (or Kiz) Kaian, which has been stated to be a district of Rasak. "On Tubaran," says Idrisi, "are dependent

Mahyak, Kir Kaian, Sura" (? Suza), "Fardan" (? Bampur or Pahra), "Kashran" (? Khasrin), "and Masurjan. Masurjan is a well-peopled commercial town surrounded with villages on the banks of the Tubaran, from which town it is 42 miles distant. Masurjan to Darak Yamuna 141 miles, Darak Yamuna to Firabuz 175 miles." If we take Regan to represent the old city of Masurjan, and Yakmina as the modern representative of Darak Yamuna, we shall find Idrisi's distances most surprisingly in accordance with modern mapping. Regan is about 40 miles from Fahraj, and the other distances, though not accurate of course, are much more approximately correct than could possibly have been expected from the generality of Idrisi's compilation.

I cannot, however, now open up a fresh chapter on mediæval geography in Persia. It is Makran itself to which I wish to draw attention. In our thirst for trans-frontier knowledge farther north and farther west, we have somewhat overlooked this very remarkable country. Idrisi commences his description with the assertion that "Makran is a vast country, mostly desert." We have not altogether found it so. It is true that the voyager who might be condemned to coast his way from the Gulf of Oman to the port of Karachi in the hot weather, might wonder what of beauty, wealth, or even interest, could possibly lie beyond that brazen coast washed by that molten sea; might well recall the agonies of thirst endured during the Greek retreat; might think of the lost armies of Cyrus and Simiramis; and whilst his eye could not fail to be impressed with the grand outlines of those bold headlands which guard the coast, his nose would be far more rudely reminded of the unpleasant proximity of Ichthyophagi than delighted by soft odours of spikenard or myrrh. And yet, for century after century, the key to the golden gate of Indian commerce lay behind those Makran hills. Beyond those square-headed bluffs and precipices, hidden amongst the serrated lines of jagged ridges, was the high-road to wealth and fame, where passed along not only many a rich khafila loaded with precious merchandise, but many a stout array of troops besides. Those citizens of Makran who "loved fair dealing, who were men of their word, and enemies to fraud," who welcomed the lagging khafila, or sped on their way the swift camel-mounted soldiers of Arabia, could have little dreamed that for centuries in the undeveloped future, when trade should pass over the high seas round the southern coast of Africa, and the Western infidel should set his hated foot on Eastern shores, Makran should sink out of sight and into such forgetfulness by the world, that eventually this ancient land of the sun should become something less well known than those mountains of the moon in which lay the far-off sources of the Egyptian Nile.

Yet it is not at all impossible that Makran may

once again rise to significance in Indian Councils. Men's eyes have been so much turned to the proximity of Russia and Russian railways to the Indian frontier that they have hardly taken into serious consideration the problems of the future, which deal with the direct connection overland between India and Europe other than those which touch Seistan or Herat. That such connection will finally eventuate either through Seistan or Herat (or through both) no one who has any appreciation of the power of commercial interests to overcome purely military or political objections will doubt; but meanwhile it may be more than interesting to prove that a line through Persia is quite a practicable scheme, although it would not be practicable on any alignment that has as yet been suggested. It would not be practicable by following the coast, for instance. It would be useless to link up Teheran with Mashad, unless the Seistan line were adopted in extension; and the proposal to join Ispahan to Seistan through Central Persia would involve such a lengthening of the route to India as would seriously discount its value. The only solution of the difficulty is through Makran to Karachi. Military nervousness would thus be met by the fact that Russia could make no use of such a line for purposes of invasion, inasmuch as it would be commanded and protected from the sea. Political difficulties with Afghanistan would be absolutely avoided by a Persian line. Whether that would be better than a final agreement with Russia based on mutual interest, which would certainly make strongly for the peace of our borders, is another question. I am only concerned just now in illustrating the geography of Makran and pointing out its facilities as a land of possible routes to India, and in showing how the exploration of Baluchistan and of Western India was secured in mediæval times by means of these routes.

It will, then, be interesting to note that at the eastern extremity of Makran, dovetailed between the Makran hills as they sweep off with a curve westward and our Sind frontier hills as they continue their general strike southwards, is the little state of Las Bela. The mountain conformation which encloses it makes the flat alluvial portion of the state triangular in shape, and from the apex of the triangle to the sea runs a river now known as the Purali, which in ancient times was called the Arabis from the early Arab occupation of the region. There are relics of apparent Arabic origin which, independently of Greek records, testify to a very early interest in this corner of the Indian borderland. Las Bela has a history which is not without interest. It has been a Buddhist centre, and the caves of Gondakahar near by testify to the ascetic fervour of the Buddhist priesthood. The grave of one of the greatest of frontier political leaders, Sir Robert Sandeman, lies near this little capital. Already it forms an object of devotional pilgrimage through all the Sind countryside. Possibly once again it may happen that Las Bela will be a wayside resting-place on the road to India, as it has undoubtedly been in the centuries of the past. It is not difficult to reach Las Bela from Karachi by following the modern telegraph line. There are no great physical obstacles interposed to make the way thorny for the slow-moving train of a khafila, and where camels can take their stately way there the more lively locomotive can follow. Should the railway from Central Persia (let us say Ispahan) ever extend its iron lines to Las Bela, it will make little of the rest of its extension to Karachi. It is the actual physical arrangement of Makran topography only which really matters; and here we are but treading in the footsteps of the ubiquitous Arab when first he made his way south-eastward from Arabia, or from Syria, to the Indian frontier. He could, and he did, pass from the plateau of Persia into the very heart of Makran without encountering the impediment of a single difficult pass.

Although the chief trade route of the Arabs to India was not through Persia, but by way of the sea in coasting vessels, it is probable that both Arabs and Persians before them made good use of the geographical opportunities offered for an approach to the Indus valley and Northern India, and that the central line of Persian approach through Makran had been a world-old route for centuries. It is really a delightful route to follow, full of the interest of magnificent scenery and of varied human existence, and it is the telegraph route from Ispahan to Panjgur in Makran. With the initial process of reaching Ispahan, whether through the Kurdistan hills from Baghdad by way of Kermanshah and the ancient town of Hamadan to Kum (the mountain road selected for the telegraph line), or whether from Teheran to Kum and thence by Kashan (a line not so replete with hills), we have no concern. This part of Persia now falls by agreement under the influence of Russia, and it is only by further agreement with Russia that this link in any European connection could be forged. But from Ispahan to Karachi one may still look over the wide uplands of the Persian plateau and imagine, if we please, that it is for England to take her share in the development of these ancient highways into a modern railway. Ispahan is 5300 feet above sea-level, and from Ispahan one never descends to a lower level than 3000 feet till one enters Makran.

As Ispahan lies in a wide valley separated by a continuous line of flanking hills from the main high road of Central Persia, which connects Teheran and Kashan with Kirman, passing through Yezd, it is necessary to cross this intervening divide in order to reach Yezd. There is a waterway through the hills, near Taft, a little to the south-west of Yezd which meets this difficulty. From Yezd onwards to the south-west of Kirman, Bam, and the populous plains of Narmashir and Regan, the road is never out of sight of mountains, the long lines of the Persian ranges flanking it north and south culminating in the magnificent peak of the Koh-i-Basman, but leaving a wide space between unhindered by passes or rivers. From Narmashir the modern telegraph passes off north-eastward to Seistan, and from there follows the new trade route to Nushki and Quetta. It is probable that through all ages this palpable method of circumventing the Dasht-i-Lut (the Kirman desert) by skirting it on the south was adopted by travellers seeking Seistan and Kandahar. There is, however, the difficulty of a formidable band of mountains skirting the desert Seistan, which would be a difficulty to railway construction. From Regan to Bampur and Panjgur the normal and most convenient mountain conformation (although the ranges close in and the valleys narrow) points an open way, with no obstacle to bar the passage even of a motor; but after leaving Bampur on the east there is a divide (of about 4000 to 5000 feet) to be crossed before dropping into the final system of Mashkhel drainage, which leads straight on to Panjgur, Kalat, and Quetta. Early Arab commercial explorers did not usually make this detour to Quetta in order to reach the Indus delta country, nor should we, if we wished to take the shortest line and the easiest through Persia to Karachi or Bombay. Much depends on the objective in India.

Calcutta may be reached from the Indus valley by the north-western lines on the normal Indian gauge, or it may be reached through the Rajputana system on the metre gauge. But for the latter system and for Bombay, Karachi becomes our objective. To reach Karachi *via* Seistan and Quetta would add at least 500 unnecessary miles to our route from Central Persia, an amount which equals the total distance between the present Russian terminus of the Transcaspian line at Kushk and our own Indian terminus at New Chaman. A direct through line from Panjgur to Karachi by the old Arab caravan route, within striking distance from the sea, would apparently outflank not only all political objections, but would satisfy those military objectors who can only see in a railway the opportunity for invasion of India.

CHAPTER IX

EARLIEST ENGLISH EXPLORATION—CHRISTIE AND POTTINGER

THE Arabs of the Mediæval period, whose footsteps we have been endeavouring to trace, were after their fashion true geographers and explorers. True that with them the process of empire-making was usually a savage process in the first instance, followed by the peaceable extension of commercial interests. Trade with them (as with us) followed the flag, and the Semitic instinct for making the most of a newly-acquired property was ever the motive for wider exploration. With the Chinese, during the Buddhist period, the ecstatic bliss of pilgrimage, and the acquirement of special sanctity, were the motive power of extraordinary energies; but with this difference of impulse the result was much the same. Arab trader and Chinese pilgrim alike gave to the world a new record, a record of geographical fact which, simple and unscientific as it might be, was yet a true revelation for the time being. But when Buddhism had become a memory, and Arab domination had ceased to regulate the affairs of the Indus valley; when the devastating hordes of the Mongol swept through Afghanistan to the plains of India, geographical record no longer formed part of the programme, and exploration found no place in the scheme of conquest. The Mongol and the Turk were not geographers, such as were the Chinese pilgrim and the Arab, and one gets little or nothing from either of geographical record, in spite of the abundance of their historical literature and the really high standard of literary attainment enjoyed by many of the Turk leaders. That truly delightful historical personage Babar, for instance, "the adventurer," the founder of the Turk dynasty in India, good-looking, intellectual, possessed of great ability as a soldier, endowed with true artistic temperament as painter, poet, and author, the man who has left to all subsequent ages an autobiography which is almost unique in its power of presenting to the mind of its reader the impression of a "whole, real, live, human being," with all his faults and his fancies, his affections and aspirations, was apparently unimpressed with the value of dull details of geography. He can say much about the human interests of the scenes of his wanderings; he can describe landscape and climate, flowers and fruits (especially melons); but though he doubtless possessed the true bandit's instinct for local topography (which must, indeed, have been very necessary in many of the episodes of his remarkable career) he makes no systematic attempt to place before us a clear notion of the geographical conditions of Afghanistan as they existed in his time. His literary cousin Haidar is far more useful as a geographer. To him we owe something more than a vague outline of the elusive kingdom of Bolar and the limits of Kafiristan, but he merely touches on Afghanistan in its connection with Tibet, and says little of the country with which we are now immediately concerned.

The one pre-eminent European traveller of the thirteenth century (1272-73), the immortal Marco Polo, hardly touched Afghanistan. He and his kinsmen passed by the high valleys of Vardos and Wakhan on their way to Kashgar and Cathay, but his geographical information is so vague as to render it difficult (until the surveys of these regions were completed) to trace his footsteps. The raid of Taimur into Kafiristan early in the fifteenth century, when it is said that he reached Najil from the Khawak Pass over the Hindu Kush, will be referred to again in dealing with Masson's narrative; but even to this day it is doubtful how far he succeeded in penetrating into Kafiristan, although the geographical inference of a practicable military line of communication between Andarab and the head of the Alingar River is certain. Three hundred and thirty years after Polo's journey another European traveller passed through Badakshan and across the Pamirs. This was the lay Jesuit,

Benedict Goës, a true geographer, bent on the exploration of Cathay and the reconnaissance of its capabilities as a mission field. He crossed the Parwan Pass of the Hindu Kush from Kabul to Badakshan and journeyed thence to Yarkand; but he did not survive to tell his story in sufficient detail to leave intelligible geography. We find practically no useful geographical records of Afghanistan during many centuries of its turbulent history, so that from the time of Arab commercial enterprise to the days of our forefathers in India, when Afghanistan began to loom large on the political horizon as a factor in our relations with Russia and it became all important to know of what Afghanistan consisted, there is little to collect from the pages of its turbid history which can fairly rank as a record of geographical exploration. It took a long time to awaken an intelligent interest in trans-Indus geography in the minds of India's British administrators. But for Russia it is possible that it would have remained unawakened still; but early in the nineteenth century the shadow of Russia began to loom over the north-western horizon, and it became unpleasantly obvious that if we did not concern ourselves with Afghan politics, and secure some knowledge of Afghan territory, our northern neighbours would not fail to secure the advantages of early action.

It is strange to recall the fact that we are indebted to the Emperor Napoleon Buonaparte for the first exploration made by British officers into the trans-frontier regions of Afghanistan and Baluchistan in British political interests. Nearly a century ago (in 1810) the uneasiness created by the ambitious schemes of that most irrepressible military freebooter resulted in the nomination of two officers of Bombay Infantry to investigate the countries lying to the west of what was then British India, with a view to ascertaining the possibilities of invasion. The Punjab and Sind intervened between British India and the hinterland of the frontier, and their independence and jealous suspicion of the expansive tendency of the British Raj added greatly to the difficulties and the risks of any such trans-frontier enterprise. The Bombay Infantry has ever been a sort of nursery for explorers of the best and most famous type, and the two young gentlemen selected for this remarkable exploit were worthy forerunners of Burton and Speke. The traditions of intelligence service may almost be said to have been founded by them. The rule of exploration a century ago admitted of no elaborate preparation: a knowledge of the languages to be encountered was the one acquisition which was deemed indispensable; and there can be little doubt that the knowledge of Oriental tongues was an advantage which in those days very rapidly led to distinction. It was probably less widespread but much more thorough than it is at present. Captain Christie and Lieutenant

Pottinger started fair in the characters which they meant to assume during their travels. They embarked as natives in a native ship, and from the very outset they found it necessary to play up to their disguise. The port of Sonmiani on the north-eastern shores of the Arabian Sea was the objective in the first instance, and the rôle of horse-dealers in the service of a Bombay firm was the part they elected to play. How far it really imposed on Baluch or Afghan it is difficult to say. One cannot but recollect that when another gallant officer in later years assumed this disguise on the Persian frontier, he was regarded as a harmless but eccentric European, who injured nobody by the assumption of an expert knowledge which he did not possess. He was known locally for years after his travels had ceased as the English officer who "called himself" a horse-dealer.

Sonmiani was a more important port a century ago than it is now that Karachi has absorbed the trade of the Indus coast; but even then the mud flats which render the village so unapproachable from the coast were in process of formation, and it was only with favourable conditions of tide that this wretched and long overlooked little seaport could be reached. Sonmiani, however, may yet again rise to distinction, for it is a notable fact that the facility for reaching the interior of Baluchistan and the Afghan frontier by this route, which facility decided its selection by Christie and Pottinger, is no less nowadays than it was then. The explanation of it lies in the fact that the route practically turns the frontier hills. It follows the extraordinary alignment of their innumerable folds, passing between them from valley to valley instead of breaking crudely across the backbone of the system, and slips gently into the flat places of the plateau land which stretch from Kharan to Kandahar. The more obvious reason which presented itself to these early explorers was doubtless the avoidance of the independent buffer land of Sind. They experienced little difficulty, in spite of many warnings of the dangers in front of them, when they left Sonmiani for Bela. At Bela they interviewed an interesting and picturesque personality in the person of the Jam, and were closely questioned about the English and their proceedings. Apparently the Jam was prepared to accept their description of things European generally, until they ventured to describe a 100-gun warship and its equipment. Such an astounding creation he was unable to believe in, and he frankly said so. From Bela the great northern high-road led to the old capital, Khozdar, through a district infested with Brahui robbers; but there was no better alternative, and the two officers followed it. On the whole, the Brahui tribespeople treated them well, and there was no serious collision. Khozdar was an important centre in those days, with eight hundred houses, and certain Hindu merchants from Shikarpur drove a thriving business there. Nothing was more extraordinary in the palmy days of Sind than the widespread commercial interests of Shikarpur. Credit could be obtained at almost all the chief towns of Central Asia through the Shikarpur merchants, and it was by draft, or "hundi," on Hindu bankers far and wide that travellers were able to keep themselves supplied with cash as they journeyed through these long stages.

The route to Kalat passed by Sohrab and Rodinjo, and the two wayfarers reached Kalat on February 9, 1810. The cold was intense; they were quite unprepared for it, and suffered accordingly. Living with the natives and putting up at the Mehman Khana (the guest house) of such principal villages or towns as possessed one, they naturally were thrown very closely into contact with native life, and learned native opinions. The views of such travellers when dealing with the social details of native existence are especially valuable, and the opinions expressed by them of the character and disposition of the people amongst whom they lived, and with whom they daily conversed on every conceivable subject, are infinitely to be preferred to those of the state officials of that time who lived in an artificial atmosphere. Thus we find very considerable divergence in the opinions expressed regarding Baluch and Afghan character between such close observers as Pottinger or Masson and such eminent authorities as Burnes and Elphinstone. The splendid hospitality and the affectation of frankness which is common to all these varied types of frontier humanity, combined with their magnificent presence, and very often with a determined adherence to certain rules of guardianship and the faithful discharge of the duties which it entails, are all of them easily recognizable virtues which are much in the minds and mouths of official travellers with a mission. The counteracting vices, the spirit of fanatical hatred, of thievish malevolence, and the utter social demoralization which usually (but not always) distinguishes their domestic life and disgusts the stranger, is not so much *en evidence*, and is only to be discerned by those who mix freely with ordinary natives of the jungle and bazaar. As an instance, take Pottinger's estimate of Persian character; it is really worth recording as the impression of one of the earliest of English soldier travellers. "Among themselves, with their equals, the Persians are affable and polite; to their superiors, servile and obsequious; towards their inferiors, haughty and domineering. All ranks are equally avaricious, sordid, and dishonest. . . . Falsehood they look on . . . as highly commendable, and good faith, generosity, and gratitude are alike unknown to them. In debauchery none can exceed them, and some of their propensities are too execrable and infamous to admit of mention. . . . I feel inclined to look upon Persia, at the present day, to be the very fountainhead of every species of tyranny, cruelty, meanness, injustice, extortion, and infamy that can disgrace or pollute human nature, and have ever been found in any age or nation." These are strong terms to use about a people of whom we have been assured that the basis of their youthful education is to "ride, to shoot, and to speak the truth!" and yet who is it who knows Persia who will say even now that they are undeserved? May the Persian parliament mend their morals and reform their methods—if, indeed, such a "silk purse" as a parliament can be made out of such crude material as the Persian plebs!

In spite of endless vexations and much spiteful malevolence, which included endless attempts to trip up Pottinger in his assumed disguise (and which, it must be admitted, were met by a not too strict adherence to the actual truth on Pottinger's part), he does not condemn the Baluchi and the Afghan in such terms as he applies to the Persian; but he illustrates most forcibly the dangers arising from habitual lawlessness due to the semi-feudal system of the Baluch federation, and consequent want of administrative responsibility. In spite, however, of endless difficulties, he finally got through, and so did Christie; and for the getting through they were both largely indebted to the vicarious hospitality of village chiefs and heads of independent clans.

At Kalat they found it far easier to get into the

timber and mud fortress than to get out again, and this difficulty repeated itself at Nushki. At Nushki begins the real interest of their adventures. Christie (after the usual wrangling and procrastination which attended all arrangements for onward movement) took his way to Herat on almost the exact line of route (*via* Chagai, the Helmund, and Seistan) which was followed seventy-three years later by the Russo-Afghan Boundary Commission. Pottinger made what was really a far more venturesome journey *via* Kharan to Jalk and Persia. The meeting of these two officers eventually at Ispahan in the darkness of night, and their gradual recognition of each other, is as dramatic a story as the meeting of Nearkhos with Alexander in Makran, or of Nansen with Jackson amongst the ice-floes of the Far North.

Christie gives us but small detail of his adventures. He necessarily suffered much from thirst, but met with no serious encounters. Beyond a well-deserved tribute to the sweet beauty of that picturesque wayside town of Anardara in his careful record of his progress northward from Seistan, where he made Jalalabad (which he calls Doshak) his base for further exploration, he says very little about the country he passed through. Incidentally he mentions Pulaki (Poolki) as a very remarkable relic of past ages. He describes the ruins of this place as covering an area of 16 square miles. Ferrier mentions the same place subsequently, and locates it about a day's march to the north of Kala-i-Fath (which Christie did not visit), and it must have been one of the most famous of mediæval towns in Seistan. But as collective ruins covering an area of 500 square miles have been noted by Mr. Tate, the surveyor of the late Seistan mission, who camped in their midst to the north of Kala-i-Fath, the exact site of Pulaki may yet require careful research before it is identified. Seistan is the land of half-buried ruins. No such extent of ruins exists anywhere else in the world. It seems probable, therefore, that, like the sites of many another ancient city of Seistan, Pulaki has been either partially or absolutely absorbed in the boundless sea of desert sand, which envelops and hides away each trace of the past as its waves move forward in irresistible sequence before the howling blasts of the north-west.

Christie's route through Seistan followed the track connecting Jalalabad on the Helmund with Peshawaran on the Farah Rud in dry seasons, but which disappears in seasons of flood, when the two hamúns or lakes of Seistan become one. Pushing on to Jawani he passed Anardara on April 4, and reached Herat on the 18th. His description of Herat is of a very general character, but is sufficient to indicate that no very great change took place between the time of his visit and that of the 1883 Commission. He was fairly well received, and remained a month without any incident worthy of note, leaving on May 18 for Persia.

This century-old visit of a British officer to Herat is chiefly notable for its revelations as to the attitude of the Afghan Government and people towards the English at the time it was made. With the exception of the risk inseparable from travel in a lawless country infested with organised bands of professional robbers, there appears to have been no hostility bred by fanaticism or suspicion of the trend of British policy. Afghanistan was socially in about the same stage of development that France was in the days of Louis XI.—or England a little earlier; and it is only the solidity conferred on Afghan administration by the moral support of the British Government which has effected any real change. Were England to abandon India to-morrow there would be nothing to prevent a lapse into the same condition of social anarchy which prevailed a century ago. India would become the bait for ceaseless activity on the part of every Afghan border chief who thought he had following sufficient to make a raid effective. A thin veneer of civilization has crept into Afghanistan with motors and telegraphs, but with it also has arisen new incentives to hostility from dread of a possible loss of independence, and (in the western parts of Afghanistan) from real fanatical hatred to the infidel. Thus Afghanistan is actually more dangerous as a field of exploration to the individual European at the present moment than it was in the days of Christie and Pottinger. At the same time, British military assistance would not only be welcome nowadays in case of a conflict with a foreign enemy, but it would be claimed as the fulfilment of a political engagement and expected as a right.

Christie's stay at Herat seems to have been quite uneventful, and when he left for Persia no one barred his way. The Persian frontier then seems to have been rather more than 20 miles distant from Herat—Christie places it a mile beyond the village of "Sekhwan," 22 miles from the city. The only place which appears to correspond with the position of Sekhwan now is Shakiban, which probably represents another village. Making rapid progress westward through Persia, he eventually reached Ispahan, where he rejoined Pottinger on June 30. It must have been a hot and trying experience!

Lieutenant Pottinger's adventures after leaving Nushki (from which place he had considerable difficulty in effecting his departure) were more exciting and apparently more risky than those of Christie. He selected a route which no European has subsequently attempted, and which it would be difficult to follow from his description of it were it not that this region has now been completely surveyed. He struck southwards down the Bado river, which leads almost directly to Kharan and the desert beyond it stretching to the Mashkhel "hamún" or swamp. He did not visit Kharan itself, and he apparently misplaces its position by at least 50 miles, unless, indeed (which is quite possible), the present site of the Naoshirwani capital is far removed from that of a century ago. I am unaware, however, that any evidence exists to that effect.

Until the desert was encountered there was no great difficulty on this route, but the horror of that desert crossing fully atoned for any lack of unpleasant incident previously. It would even now be regarded as a formidable undertaking, and we can easily understand the deadly feelings that beset this pioneer explorer as he made his way in the month of April from Kharan on a south-westerly track to the border of Persia at Jalk. His description of this desert, like the rest of his narrative, is full of instructive suggestion. The scope of his observation generally, and the accuracy of the information which he collected about the infinitely complex nationality of the Baluch tribes, renders his evidence valuable as regards the natural phenomena which he encountered; and no part of this evidence is more interesting than his story of the Kharan desert, especially as no one since his time has made anything like a scientific examination of its construction and peculiarities. He describes it as a sea of red sand, "the particles of which were so light that when taken in the hand they were scarcely more than palpable; the whole is thrown into an irregular mass of waves, principally running from east to west, and varying in height from 10 to 20 feet. Most of them rise perpendicularly on the opposite side to that from which the prevailing wind blows (north-west), and might readily be fancied at a distance to resemble a new brick wall. The side facing the wind slopes off with a gradual declivity to the base (or near it) of the next windward wave." He further describes a phenomenon which he observed in the midst of this sand sea, which I think has not been described by any later traveller or surveyor. He says "the desert seemed at a distance of half a mile or less to have an elevated or flat surface from 6 to 12 inches higher than the summits of the waves. This vapour appeared to recede as we advanced, and once or twice completely encircled us, limiting the horizon to a very confined space, and conveying a most gloomy and unnatural sensation to the mind of the beholder; at the same moment we were imperceptibly covered with innumerable atoms of small sand, which, getting into our eyes, mouths and nostrils, caused excessive irritation, attended with extreme thirst that was increased in no small degree by the intense heat of the sun." This was only visible during the hottest part of the day. Pottinger's explanation of this curious phenomenon is that the fine particles of this dust-sand, which are swept into the air almost daily by the force of the north-west winds, fail to settle down at once when those winds cease, but float in the air by reason of some change in their specific gravity due to rarefaction from intense heat; and he adds that he has seen this condition of sand-haze at the same time that, in an opposite quarter, he has observed the mirage or luminous appearance of water which is common to all deserts. Crossing the bed of the Budu (the Mashkhel nullah—dry in April), he makes a curious mistake about the direction of its waters, which he says run in a south-easterly direction towards the coast. It actually runs north-west and empties itself (when there is water in it) into the Mashkhel swamps. I must admit, however, that, from personal observation, it is often exceedingly difficult to decide from a casual inspection in which direction the water of these abnormally flat nullahs runs. Shortly after passing the Mashkhel, he encountered an ordinary dust-storm, followed by heavy rain, which much modified the terrors of the awful heat.

Pottinger has something to say about the hot winds that occur between June and September in these regions, known as the Bad-i-Simun, or pestilential winds, which kill men exposed to them and destroy vegetation, but his information was not derived from actual observation, and it is difficult to get any really authentic account of these winds. Parts of the Sind desert are equally subject to them. After losing his way (which was inexcusable on the part of his guide with the hills in sight), he arrived finally at the delightful little valley of Kalagan, near Jalk, where the terrors of nature were exchanged for those of his human surroundings. Kalagan is one of the sweetest and greenest spots of the Baluch frontier, and it is easy to realize Pottinger's intense joy in its palm groves and orchards. He was now in Persia, and his subsequent proceedings do not concern our present purpose. He travelled by Sib and Magas to Pahra and Bampur, maintaining his disguise as a Pirzada, or wandering religious student, with some difficulty, as he was insufficiently versed in the tenets of Islam. However, he acted up to his Moslem professions with a certain amount of success till he reached Pahra, where he was at once recognized as an Englishman by a boy who had previously met an English officer exploring in Southern Persia. But he was excellently well treated at Pahra, in strange contrast to his subsequent treatment at Bampur, close by. He eventually reached Kirman, and passed on by the regular trade route to Ispahan.

It is impossible to take leave of these two gallant young officers without a tribute of admiration for their magnificent pluck, the tenacity with which they held to their original purpose, the forbearance and cleverness with which they met the persistent and worrying difficulties which were set in their way by truculent native officials, and the accuracy of their final statements. Pottinger really left little to be discovered about the distribution of Baluch tribes, and if his mapping exhibits some curious eccentricities, we must remember that it was practically a compilation from memory, with but the vaguest means at his disposal for the measurement of distances. It was a first map, and by the light of it the success of the subsequent explorations of Masson (which covered a good deal of the same ground in Baluchistan) is fairly accounted for. Christie died a soldier's death early in his career, but Pottinger lived to transmit an honoured name to yet later adventurers in the field of geography.

CHAPTER X

AMERICAN EXPLORATION—MASSON

IN 1832 Lord William Bentinck, then Governor-General of India, found Shah Sujah, the deposed Amir of Kabul, living as a pensioner at Ludhiana when he visited the Punjab for an interview with its ruler Ranjit Singh. At that interview the question of aiding Shah Sujah to regain his throne from the usurper Dost Mahomed, who was suspected of Russian proclivities, was mooted; and it was then, probably, that the seeds of active interference in Afghan politics were sown, although the idea of aiding Shah Sujah was negatived for the time being. The result was the mission of Alexander Burnes to Kabul, which formed a new era in Central Asian geography. From this time forward the map of Afghanistan commenced to grow. The story of Burnes' first journey to Kabul was published by Murray in 1834, and his example as a geographical observer stimulated his assistants Leech, Lord, and Wood to further enterprise during a second journey to the same capital. Indeed the geographical work of some of these explorers still remains as our standard reference for a knowledge of the configuration of Northern Badakshan. This was the beginning of official recognition of the value of trans-Indian geographical knowledge to Indian administration; but then, as now, information obtained through recognized official agents was apt to be regarded as the only information worth having; and far too little effort was made to secure the results of travellers' work, who, in a private capacity and unhindered by official red tape, were able to acquire a direct personal knowledge of Afghan geography such as was absolutely impossible to political agents or their assistants.

Before Indian administrators had seriously turned their attention to the Afghan buffer-land and set to work to fill up ".intelligence" material at second hand, there was at least one active European agent in the field who was in direct touch with the chief political actors in that strange land of everlasting unrest, and who has left behind him a record which is unsurpassed on the Indian frontier for the width of its scope of inquiry into matters political, social, economic, and scientific, and the general accuracy of his conclusions. This was the American, Masson. It must be remembered that the Punjab and Sind were almost as much *terra incognita* to us in 1830 as was Afghanistan. The approach to the latter country was through foreign territory. The Sikh chiefs of the Punjab and the Amirs of Sind were not then necessarily hostile to British interests. They watched, no doubt, the gradual extension of the red line of our maps towards the north-west and west, and were fully alive to the probability that, so far as regarded their own countries, they would all soon be "painted red." But there was no official discourtesy or intoleration shown towards European travellers, and in the Sikh-governed Punjab, at any rate, much of the military control of that most military nationality was in the hands of European leaders. Nor do we find much of the spirit of fanatical hatred to the Feringhi even in Afghanistan at that time. The European came and went, and it was only due to the disturbed state of the country and the local absence of law and order that he ran any risk of serious misadventure.

In these days it would be impossible for any European to travel as Masson or Ferrier travelled in Afghanistan, but in those days there was something to be gained by friendship with England, and the weakness of our support was hardly suspected until it was disclosed by the results of the first Afghan war. So Masson and Ferrier assumed the rôle of Afghan travellers, clothed in Afghan garments, but more or less ignorant of the Afghan language, living with the people, partaking of their hospitality, studying their ways, joining their pursuits, discussing their politics, and placing themselves on terms of familiarity, if not of intimacy, with their many hosts in a way which has never been imitated since. No one now ever assumes the dress of the Afghan and lives with him. No one joins a caravan and sits over the nightly fire discussing bazaar prices or the character of a chief. A hurried rush to Kabul, a few brief and badly conducted interviews with the Amir, and the official representative of India's foreign policy returns to India as an Afghan oracle, but with no more knowledge of the real inwardness of Afghan political aspiration, or of the trend of national thought and feeling, than is acquired during a six months' trip of a travelling M.P. in India. Consequently there is a peculiar value in the records of such a traveller as Masson. They are in many ways as valuable now as they were eighty years ago, for the character of the Afghan has not changed with his history or his politics. To some extent they are even more valuable, for it is inevitable that the story of a long travel through an unknown and unimagined world should be received with a certain amount of reservation until later experience confirms the tale and verifies localities.

Fifty years elapsed before the footsteps of Masson could be traced with certainty. Not till the conclusion of the last Afghan war, and the final reshaping of the surveys of Baluchistan, could it be said exactly where he wandered during those strenuous years of unremitting travel. And now that we can take his story in detail, and follow him stage by stage through the Indian borderlands, we can only say that, considering the circumstances under which his observations were taken and recorded, it is marvellously accurate in geographical detail. Were his long past history of those stirring times as accurate as his geography or as his antiquarian information there would be little indeed left for subsequent investigators to add.

Masson was in the field before Burnes. In the month of September 1830 the Resident in the Persian Gulf writes to the Chief Secretary to the Government of India[1] that "an American gentleman of the name of Masson" arrived at Bushire from Bassadore on the "13th June last," and that he described himself as belonging to the state of Kentucky, having been absent for ten years from his country, "which he must consequently have left when he was young, as he is now only about two-and-thirty years of age." The same letter says that previous to the breaking out of the war between Russia and Persia in 1826 Masson "appears to have visited Khorasan from Tiflis by way of Mashed and Herat, making no effort to conceal his European origin," and that from Herat he went to Kandahar, Shikarpur, and Sind.

Masson appears to have furnished some valuable information to the Indian Government regarding the Durani occupation of Herat and the political situation in Kabul and Kandahar, which, according

[1] *Selections from Travels and Journals preserved in the Bombay Secretariat*, Forrest, 1908.

to his own account, he subsequently regretted, as he obviously regarded the British attitude towards Afghanistan at that time in much the same light as certain continental nations regarded the British attitude towards the Transvaal previous to the last Boer war. "About the same time," says the same letter from the Resident at Bushire, Masson was much in the Bahawalpur country (Sind), after which he proceeded to Peshawar, Kabul, Ghazni, etc. Extracts from his reports of his journeys are forwarded with other information. In his book (*Travels in Afghanistan, Baluchistan, the Punjab, and Kalat*, published in 1842) Masson opens his story with the autumn of 1826, when he was in Bahawalpur and Sind, which he had approached through Rajputana, and not from Afghanistan. He has much to say about Bahawalpur which, however interesting and valuable as first-hand information about a foreign state in 1826, no longer concerns this story. From Bahawalpur he passed on to Peshawar and Kabul, from Kabul to Kandahar, and thence to Shikarpur. As the incidents of his remarkable journey between Kandahar and Shikarpur, described in the letter of the Bushire Resident, are obviously the same as those in his book, the inference is strong that the journey from Tiflis to Herat and Kandahar (which is not mentioned in the book) has been somehow misplaced in the Resident's record.

When Masson entered Afghanistan from

Peshawar there is certain indirect evidence that this was the first time that he crossed the Afghan border. He knew nothing of the Pashto language, which would be remarkable in the case of a man like Masson, who always lived with the people and not with the chiefs, and there is not the remotest reference to any previous visit to Herat in his subsequent history. We will at any rate follow the text of his own narrative, and surely no narrative of adventure that has ever appeared before or since in connection with Afghan exploration can rival it for interest. Peshawar was at that time held by four Pathan Sirdars, brothers, who were hardly independent, as they held their country (a small space extending to about 25 miles round Peshawar, and which included Kohat and Hangu) entirely at the pleasure of Ranjit Singh, the Sikh Chief of the Punjab. Some show of making a strike for independence had been made in connection with the Yusufzai rising led by Saiad Ahmad Shah, but it had been suppressed, and during the temporary occupation of Peshawar by the Sikhs the city had been despoiled and devastated. Masson estimated that there were about fifty or sixty thousand inhabitants in Peshawar, where he was exceedingly well treated. "People of all classes were most civil and desirous to oblige." He was an honoured guest at all entertainments.

How long Masson remained at Peshawar it is difficult to say, for there is a most lamentable absence of dates from his records, and Peshawar appears to have been the base from which he started on a good many excursions. Finally he made acquaintance with a Pathan who offered to accompany him to Kabul, and he left Peshawar for Afghanistan by the Khaibar route. He mentions two other routes as being popular in those days, *i.e.* those of Abkhana and Karapa, and he asserts that they were far more secure for traders than the Khaibar, but not so level nor so direct. Masson started with his companion, dressed as a Pathan, but taking nothing but a few pais (copper coins) and a book. His companion, however, possessed a knife tied up in a corner of his pyjamas. After cautiously crossing the plains and some intervening hills, they struck the high road of the Khaibar apparently not far from Ali Masjid, and here they fell in with the first people they had met *en route*—about twenty men sitting in the shade of a rock, "elderly, respectable, and venerable." They were hospitably received and entertained, and news of the arrival of a European quickly spread. Every European was expected to be a doctor in those days, and Masson had to assume the rôle and make the most of his limited medical knowledge. He either prescribed local remedies, or healed the sick on Christian Science principles with a certain amount of success—enough to ensure him a welcome wherever he went. It is a curious story for any one who has traversed the Khaibar in these later days to read. A European with a most limited knowledge of Pushto tramping the road in company with a Pathan, living the simple life of the people, picking up information every yard of the way, keenly interested in his rough surroundings, taking count of the ragged groups of stone-built huts clinging to the hill-sides or massed around a central citadel in the open plain, with here and there a disintegrating monument crowning the hill-top with a cupola or dome, the like of which he had never seen before.

Masson had hardly realized in these early days that he was on one of the routes most sacred to pilgrimage of all those known to the disciples of Buddha, and it was not till later years that he set about a systematic exploration of the extraordinary wealth of Buddhist relics which lie about Jalalabad and the valleys adjoining the Khaibar route to Kabul. On his journey he made his way with the varied incidents of adventure common to the time —robbed at one place, treated with hospitality at another; sitting under the mulberry trees discussing politics with all the energy of the true Afghan (who is never deficient in the power of expressing his political sentiments), and, taking it altogether, enjoying a close, if not an absolutely friendly, intimacy with the half-savage people of those wholly savage hills. An intimacy, such as no other educated European has ever attained, and which tells a tale of a totally different attitude on the part of the Afghan towards the European then, to that which has existed since. The fact that Masson was American and not English counted for nothing. The difference was not recognized by the Afghans, although it was explained by him sometimes with careful elaboration. It was the time when Dost Mahomed ruled in Kabul, but with the claims of Shah Sujah (possibly backed by both Sikh and British) on the political horizon. It was a time of political intrigue amongst Afghan Sirdars and chiefs so complicated and so widespread as to be almost unintelligible at this distance of time, and not even Masson, with all his advantages of intimate association and great powers of intuition, seems to have fathomed the position satisfactorily. Consequently it was to the interests of the Afghan Government to stand well with the British, even if it were equally their aim to keep on good terms with Russia—in short, to play the same game that has lasted during the rest of the century, and which threatens to last for many another decade yet. But this was before the mission of Burnes, and before the events of the subsequent Afghan war had taught the Afghan that British arms were not necessarily invincible, nor British promises always trustworthy.

Apart from the ordinary chances of disaster on the roads arising from the lack of law and order, any European would have met with a hospitable reception at that time, and Masson himself relates how, in Kabul, during some of the friendly gatherings which he attended, the respective probabilities of British or Russian intervention in Kabul affairs was a common subject of discussion. It is easy for one who knows the country to picture him sitting under the shade of the mulberry trees, with the soft lush of the Afghan summer in grass and flowers about him, the scent of the willow in the air, and, across the sliding blue of the Kabul River, a dim haze shadowing the rounded outlines of some ancient stupa, whilst trying to unriddle the tangle of Afghan politics or taking notes of weird stories and ancient legends. Nothing seems to have come amiss to his inquiring mind. Archæology, numismatics, botany, geology, and history—it was all new to him, and an inexhaustible opportunity lay before him. He certainly made good use of it. He busied himself, amongst other things, with an inquiry into the origin of the Siahposh Kafirs, and, although his speculations regarding them have long been discounted by the results of subsequent investigation from nearer points of view, it is interesting to note how these savages were then regarded by the nearest Mahomedan communities. Masson admits that the history of a Greek origin is supported by all natural and historical indications, but he declines to accept "so bold and welcome an inference." Why he should call it "bold and welcome" and then reject it, is not explained, but it is probable that he accepted the claim to a Greek origin on the part of the Kafirs as indicating that they claimed to be Greek and nothing but Greek. When we consider the number and extent of the Greek colonies which once existed beyond the Hindu Kush it would indeed be surprising if there were no survival of Greek blood in the veins of the people who, in the last stronghold of a conquered and hunted race, represent the debris of the once powerful Baktrian kingdom. Incidentally he discussed the interesting episode of Timur's invasion of Kafiristan, a subject on which no recent investigations have thrown any further light. The story, as told by Timur's historian, Sharifudin, says that in A.D. 1399, when Timur was at Andarab, complaints were made to him of outrage and oppression by the exaction of tribute, or "Karaj," against the idolaters of Katawar and the Siahposh. It appears that Katawar was then the general name for the northern regions of Kafiristan, although no reference to that name had been recorded lately.

Timur is said to have taken a third part of the army of the Andarab against the infidels, and to have reached Perjan (probably Parwan), from whence he detached a part of his force to act to the north of that place, whilst he himself proceeded to Kawak, which is certainly Khawak at the head of the Panjshir valley. If Perjan is Parwan (which I think most probable) this distribution of his force would indicate that he held the Panjshir valley at both ends, and thus secured his flank whilst operating in Kafiristan. From Khawak he "made the ascent" of the mountains of "Ketnev" (*i.e.* he crossed the intervening snow-covered divide between the Panjshir and the head of the Alishang) and descended upon the fortress of Najil. This was abandoned by the Siahposh Kafirs, who held a high hill on the left bank of the river. After an obstinate fight the hill was carried, and the male infidels, "whose souls were blacker than their garments," were killed, and their women and children carried away. Timur set up a marble pillar with an inscription recording the event, and it would be exceedingly interesting if that pillar could be identified. Masson thinks that a structure which he ascertained to have been in existence in his time a little to the north of Najil, known as the Timur Hissar (Timur's Fort), may be the fort which Timur destroyed after it had been abandoned by the Kafirs, and that the record of his victory would be found near by. The chief of Najil in Masson's time claimed descent from Timur, and there was (and is still) so much of Tartar tradition enveloping the valley of Najil (or the upper Alishang) as to make it fairly certain that Tartar, or Mongol, troops did actually invade that valley from the Panjshir, and that there is consequently a practicable pass from the Panjshir into the upper Alishang.

If we are correct in our assumption of the position of Farajghan and Najil in the modern maps of Afghanistan, as determined from native sources of information (for no surveyor has ever laid down the course of the upper affluents of the Alishang) this Mongol force must have crossed from about the centre of the Panjshir valley. It is a matter of interest to observe that, historically, between Afghan Turkistan and the Kabul plain the fashionable pass over the Hindu Kush until quite recently was the Parwan, and this, no doubt, was due to the fact that its altitude (12,300 feet) is less by quite 2000 feet than that of the Kaoshan which closely adjoins it, although the Kaoshan is in some other important respects the easier pass of the two. The Khawak, at the head of the Panjshir, is lower still (11,650 feet), but it offers a more circuitous route; whilst the Chahardar, the pass selected by the Amir Abdurrahmon for the construction of a high-road into Afghan Turkistan from the Kabul plain, is as high as the Kaoshan. All these routes converge on the important strategical position of Charikar, adjoining the junction of the Ghorband and Panjshir rivers; and they all lead from that ancient strategical centre of Baktria, the Andarab basin. Undoubtedly through all time the passage over the Khawak (now a well-trodden khafila route, said to be open to traffic all the year round) must have been the most attractive to the freebooters and adventurers of the north; but there appears to have been a reputation for ferocity and strength attached to the inhabitants of the Panjshir valley, which was remarkable even in the days when the only recognized right was might, and half Asia was peopled by barbarians. They were spoken of with the respect due to a condition of savage independence by the Arab writers who detail the geography of these regions, and it is probable that they shared the historical lawlessness of their Kafir neighbours (the Siahposh), even if in those days they did not share a race affinity. At the beginning of the sixteenth century the Emperor Babar notes that the Panjshir people paid tribute to their neighbours the Kafirs.

Masson's observations on this troublous corner of Asiatic geography are shrewd and interesting, and as much to the purpose to-day as they were when they were written. The explorations of McNair and Robertson over the Kafiristan border from Chitral, and the march of Lockhart's party through the Arnawai valley, added much to the geographical knowledge of the eastern fringe of Kafiristan, whilst the identification of the Koh-i-Mor with the classic Meros, and of certain sections of the eastern Kafirs as representative of the ancient Nysæans, clearly establishes the Greek connection about which Masson was so sceptical. But the Kafirs of Central and Western Kafiristan, the inhabitants of the upper basins of the Alishang and Alingar about the centre of the Hindu Kush and of the Badakshan rivers to the north, are just as unknown to us as they were to him. The only certain inference that we can draw from the total absence of history about these valleys of the Hindu

Kush is that between the Khawak Pass at the head of the Panjshir valley on the west, and the Minjan Pass leading to Chitral on the east, there is not, and never has been, a practicable route connecting the Kabul basin with Badakshan. No Arab khafilas ever passed that way; no hordes of raiding robbers from Central Asian fields ever forced a passage southward through those Kafir defiles; they are still dark and impenetrable, the home of distinct and separate valley communities, differing as widely in form of speech as in superstitious ritual, the very flotsam and jetsam of High Asia, as wild as the eagles above them or the markhor on their craggy hill-sides.

We will not follow Masson into the mazes of Afghan political history. It is all a story of the past, but a story with a moral to it. Had the Government of India in those days but troubled itself to obtain information from existing practical sources within its reach, instead of improvising a most imperfect political intelligence system, the subsequent war with Afghanistan would have been conducted on very different lines to those which were adopted, if it ever took place at all.

Masson made his way steadily to Kabul after meeting with adventures and vicissitudes enough for a two-volume novel, and passed on to Ghazni, where the army of Dost Mahomed Khan was then encamped, and with which he took up his quarters. Here he was well received, and he interviewed the great Afghan Chief (who settled his quarrel with his brothers from Kandahar without fighting), and thus records his opinion of a remarkable personage in history: "Dost Mahomed Khan has distinguished himself on various occasions by acts of personal intrepidity . . . has proved himself an able Commander, equally well skilled in stratagem and polity, and only employs the sword when other means fail. He is remarkably plain in attire. . . . I should not have conjectured him a man of ability either from his conversation or his appearance"; but "a stranger must be cautious in estimating the character of a Durani from his appearance," which caution he also found it necessary to exercise in the case of Dost Mahomed's corpulent brother, Mahomed Khan, the Governor of Ghazni. From Ghazni, Masson continued his journey to Kandahar, still trudging the weary road on foot in the doubtful company of casual Pathan wayfarers; and he accepts the savage treatment which he experienced at the hands of certain Lohanis near Ghazni as all in the day's work, never complaining of his want of luck so long as he got off with his life, and always ready to accept the chances of the most unsafe road rather than remain inactive. At Kandahar he again set himself to acquire a store of useful political information, though with what object it is difficult to say. He certainly did not mean it for the Indian Government, for he regrets later on in his career that he ever gave any of it away, and as a record of almost unintelligible Afghan intrigue it could hardly have interested his own. He was a wide observer, however, and must have been the possessor of a most remarkable memory. He was indeed a whole intelligence department in himself. After some weird and gruesome experiences in Kandahar (where, however, he was personally made welcome) he left for Shikarpur by the Quetta and Bolan route, and it was on this journey that he nearly lost his life. He committed the error of allowing the caravan with which he was to travel to precede him, trusting to his being able to catch it up *en route*. He fell amongst the Achakzai thieves of those ugly plains, and being everywhere known and recognised as a Feringhi, he passed a very rough time with them. They stripped him of his clothing after beating him and robbing him of his money, and left him "destitute, a stranger in the centre of Asia, unacquainted with the language—which would have been useful to me—and from my colour exposed on all occasions to notice, inquiry, ridicule, and insult." However, "it was some consolation to find the khafila was not far off," and eventually he joined it; but he nearly died of cold and exposure, and it took him years to recover from the rheumatism set up by crouching naked over the embers of the fire at night.

There are several points about this remarkable journey which might lead one to suspect that romance was not altogether a stranger to it, were it not that the route itself is described with surprising accuracy. It has only lately been possible to verify step by step the road described by Masson. He could hardly have carried about volumes of notes with him under such conditions as his story depicts, and it might very well have happened that he dislocated his topography or his ethnography from lapse of memory. But he does neither; and the most amazing feature of Masson's tales of travel is that in all essential features we knew little more about the country of the Afghans after the last war with Afghanistan than he could have told us before the first. Shall (or Quetta as we know it now) is described as a town of about 300 houses, surrounded by a slight crenelated wall. The "huge mound" (now the fort) is noted as supporting a ruinous citadel, the residence of the Governor. Fruit was plentiful then, and he adds that "Shall is proverbially celebrated for the excellence of its lambs." By the desolate plain of Dasht-i-bedoulat and the Bolan Pass, Masson trod the well-known route to Dadar and Shikarpur. He lived a strange life in those days. No one since his time has rubbed shoulders with Afghan and Baluch, intimately associating himself with all their simple and savage ways; reckoning every man he met on the road as a robber till he proved a friend; absolutely penniless, yet still meeting with rough hospitality and real kindness now and then, and ever absorbing with a most marvellous power of digestion all that was useful in the way of information, whether it concerned the red-hot sand-strewn plains, or the vermin-covered thieves and outcasts that disgraced them. It was quite as often with the lowest of the gang as with the leaders that he found himself most intimately associated.

In those days Sind was a country as unknown to us geographically as Afghanistan. The Indus and its capacity for navigation was a matter of supreme interest, but the deserts of Sind were eyed askance, and across those deserts came little call for exploration. The government of the country under the Sind Amirs was decrepit and loose, leaving district municipalities to look after themselves, and promoting no general scheme for the public good. Shikarpur had been a great centre of trade under the Duranis, and its financial credit extended far into Central Asia. But in Masson's time much of that credit had disappeared with the capitalists who supported it—chiefly Hindu bankers—who migrated to the cities of Multan and Amritsar as the Sikh power in the Punjab became a more and more powerful factor in frontier politics. Whether Masson is correct in his estimate of the mischief done by the reckless supply of funds from Shikarpur to the restless nobles of Afghanistan, who were thus enabled to set on foot raids and inroads into each other's territories, is, I think, doubtful. The want of money never stayed an Afghan raid—on the contrary it is more apt to instigate it. From Shikarpur he bent his steps towards the Punjab. No modern traveller, racing down the Indus valley by a north-western train, can well appreciate the amount of human interest and activity which lies hidden beyond the wide flat plains of tamarisk jungle that stretch between him and the frontier hills. This same Indus valley was Arabic India for centuries, and there were Greek settlements centuries earlier than the Arabs; none of this escaped Masson.

The vicissitudes of this weary walk were many. Masson was put to curious expedients in order to keep himself even decently clothed. From under one hospitable roof he stole out in the evening, when the ragged retinue of his host were all in a state of stupefaction from drink, in order to be spared their too familiar adieux. It is a remarkable fact that he found himself able to pass muster as a Mongol on his journey, there being a tradition in Sind that some Mongols were as fair as Englishmen. From Rohri on the Indus he made his way almost exactly along the line of the present railway, through Bhawalpur to Uch, continually losing his way in the narrow tracks that intersected the intricate jungle, with but a rupee or two in his pocket, and nothing but the saving grace of the village masjid as a refuge for the night. His experiences with wayfarers like himself, the lies that he heard (and I am afraid also told), the hospitality which he received both from men and women, and the variety of incident generally which adorns this part of Masson's tale is a refreshing contrast to the dreary monotony of the modern traveller's tale of Indian travel, the bare record of a dusty railway experience, with here and there a new impression of old and worn-out themes. He was impressed with the "contented, orderly, and hospitable" character of the people of Northern Sind, whose condition was "very respectable" notwithstanding an oppressive government. Saiads and fakirs, pirs and spiritual guides of all sorts were an abomination to him, but it is somewhat new to hear of Saiads that "they may commit any crime with impunity." At Fazilpur (in Bhawalpur) he found an old friend, one Rahmat Khan, and was once again in the lap of native luxury. Clean clothes, a bed to lie on, and good food, kept him idle for a month ere he started again northward for Lahore. Rahmat Khan was almost too generous. He spent his last rupee recklessly on a nautch, and had to borrow from the Hindus of his bazaar in order to find two rupees to present to his guest for the cost of his journey to Lahore. Of this large sum it is interesting to note that Masson had still eight annas left in his pocket on his arrival at that city. Alas for the good old days! What a modern tramp might achieve in India if he were allowed free play it is difficult to guess, but never again will any European travel 360 miles in India and feed himself for two months on a rupee and a half.

Masson notes the extraordinary extent of ancient

ruins around Uch, and correctly infers the importance of that city in the days of Arab ascendency. He has much to say that is still interesting about Multan and its surroundings. It must have been new to historians to hear that the heat of Multan is due to the maledictions of the Saint Shams Tabieri, who was flayed alive by the progenitors of the people who now venerate his shrine. Multan was in the hands of the Sikhs when Masson was there. From Multan Masson ceased to follow the modern line of railway, and adopted a route north of the Ravi River until near the city, when he recrossed to the southern bank. Lost in admiration of the luxuriance of the cultivation of this part of the Punjab, and full of the interest aroused by the fact that he was on classical ground, the ground of ancient history, he wandered into Lahore. Lahore and the Sikh administration, the character of Ranjit Singh and his policy towards British and Afghan neighbours, are all part of Indian history, but it is interesting to recall the prominence of French and Italians in the Punjab 100 years ago. General Allard was encountered quite accidentally by Masson, who was at once recognized as a European, and found himself able to talk French fluently. This naturally led to his entertainment by the General at his own splendid establishments. The beautiful tomb of Jehangir, the Shahdera, was occupied as a residence by the French general, Amise, who died, so they said, in expiation of his impiety in cleaning it up and making it tidy—which was probably very necessary. The tomb of Anarkalli, south of the city, was used as a harem by M. Ventura, the Italian general, whilst the well-known Avitabile lived in a house decorated after the fashion of Neapolitan art in cantonments to the east of the city. The lovely gardens of Shalimar had already been robbed of much of their beauty by the transfer of marble and stone from their pavilions for the building of Amritsar, the new religious capital of the Sikhs. Lahore is "a dull city in the commercial sense," says Masson, and Amritsar "has become the great mart of the Punjab." We need not follow Masson's explorations in the Punjab and Sind, further than to relate that he finally left Lahore during the rainy season (he was riding now, and in fairly easy circumstances) and made his way south again *via* Multan, Haidarabad, and Tatta, to Karachi. There is a lamentable want of dates about this narrative, and it is almost impossible to fix the month, or even the year, in which Masson visited any particular part of the frontier.

His next exploits and explorations conducted from Karachi are sufficiently remarkable in themselves to place Masson quite at the head of the list of frontier explorers. He stands, indeed, in the same relation to the Indian borderland as Livingstone does to Africa. He first made a sea trip in Arab crafts up the Persian Gulf, visiting Muskat and obtaining a passage in a cruiser of the

H.E.I. Company to Bushire. This we know from Major David Wilson's report to have been in 1830. It was then that he gave up the record of his previous travels, to which we have referred, and which he subsequently thought he had reason to regret. A month or two was passed at Tabriz, and a trip up the Tigris to Bagdad and Basrah. From Basrah he returned in a merchant vessel to Muskat, and finally made Karachi again in an Arab bagala. At Karachi he was not permitted to land, owing (as he suspected) to another party of Englishmen who were then attempting to explore the Indus. This turned out to be Captain Burnes' (afterwards Sir Alex. Burnes) party. The objection was based on a somewhat ridiculous notion of the capacity of the English to carry about regiments of soldiers concealed in *boxes*, and Masson subsequently learned that having no boxes with him, the opposition in his case had been withdrawn by the Amirs of Sind as tantamount to a breach of hospitality. However, for the time he was forced to return to Urmara on the Makran coast, from which place he hoped to reach Kalat. In this he was disappointed, but he found his way back to Sonmiani in an Arab dunghi (or bagala), which, with the monsoon wind at her back, was run in gallant style straight over the shallow bar into the harbour with hardly a foot of water below her. The practice of medicine was what sustained Masson at this period, but his reputation was slightly impaired by a crude prescription of sea water. A lady, too, who suffered from a disposition of her face to break out into white blotches, and who appealed for a remedy, was told that she would look much better all white. This again led to a lively controversy; but on the whole the practice of medicine was as useful to Masson as it has proved through all ages to explorers in all regions of the world.

The story of Masson's next journey through Las Bela and Eastern Baluchistan to Kalat and the neighbourhood of Quetta, must have been an almost unintelligible record for half a century after it was written. It is almost useless to repeat the names of the places he visited. Five-and-twenty years ago these names were absolutely unfamiliar, an empty sound signifying nothing to the dwellers on the British side of the Baluch frontier. Gradually they have emerged from the regions of the vague unknown into the ordered series of completed maps; and nothing testifies more surely to the general accuracy of Masson's narrative than the possibility which now exists of tracing his steps from point to point through these wild and desolate regions of rocky ridge and salt-edged jungle in Eastern Baluchistan. It is certainly significant that in the year 1830 more should have been known of the regions that lie between Karachi and Quetta or Kandahar, than was known fifty years later when plans were elaborated for bringing Quetta into railway communication with India.

Had Masson's information been properly digested, the most direct route to Kalat, Quetta, or Kandahar, *via* the Purali River, would surely have been weighed in administrative councils, and the advantage of direct communication with the seaport by a cheaply constructed line would have received due consideration. But Masson's work was still unproven and unchecked, and it would have been more than any Englishman's life was worth to have attempted in 1880 the task which he undertook with such light-hearted energy. His observations of the country he passed through, and the complicated tribal distribution which distinguishes it are necessarily superficial, but they are shrewd. It was clearly impossible for him to attempt any form of survey, and without some map evidence of the scene of his wanderings his explorations were deprived at the time of their chief significance. From Las Bela to Kalat he appears to have encountered no more dangerous adventure than might befall any Baluch traveller in the same regions. From Kalat he wandered at leisure northward till he overlooked the Dasht-i-bedaulat from the heights of Chahiltan. This well-known Quetta peak has probably often been ascended by Englishmen in late years, and the misty legend which is wreathed around it is familiar to every regimental mess in the Quetta garrison. It is perhaps a little disappointing to remember that the first white man who achieved its ascent and told the story of the forty heaven-sent infants who gambol about its summit to the eternal glory of the sainted Hazart Ghaos (the patron saint of Baluch children), was an American. Masson's interesting record of Chahiltan botany, however, would be more useful if he translated the native names into botanical language.

From Quetta he returned to Kalat, and, determined to see as much of the borderland as possible, he made his return journey from Kalat to Sonmiani *via* the Mulla Pass. The pass is still an interesting feature in Baluch geography. It was once the popular route from the plains to the highlands, when trade was more frequent between Kalat and Hindustan, and may serve a useful purpose again. Very few even of frontier officials know anything of it. Masson gives a capital description of the Mulla route, "easy and safe, and may be travelled at all seasons." From Jhal he went south through Sind to Sehwan, the antiquity of which place gives him room for much speculation; but from Sehwan to Sonmiani his route is not so clear. He started backwards on his tracks from Sehwan, then struck southward through lower Sind, passing on his way many ancient sites (locally known as "gôt," *i.e.* kôt, or fort), the origin of which he was apparently unable to determine, but halting at no place with a name that is still prominent, unless the modern Pokran represents his Pokar. I am not aware whether the "gôts" described by Masson in lower Sind have as yet been scientifically examined, but his description of them tallies with that of similar ruins lately found near Las Bela (especially as regards the stone-built circle), which, occurring as they do in Makran and the valley of the Purali (the ancient Arabis), are possibly relics of the building races of Arabs (Sabœan or Himyaritic) who occupied these districts in early ages before they became withered and waterless with the gradual alteration of their geographical conditions. Other constructions, such as the cylindrical heaps on the hills, are more certainly Buddhist. Masson was unaware that he was traversing a province which figured as Bodh in Arab chronicles, and is full of the traces of Buddhist occupation. Makran, Las Bela, and the Sind borderland still offer a mine of wealth for archæological research. The last two or three days' march was in company with a Bulfut (Lumri) camel-man, whose mount was shared by Masson. As the Lumri sowar was in the habit not only of taking opium himself but of giving it to his camel, the morning's ride was sometimes perilously lively.

One would have thought that after so extensive an exploration, filled, as it was, with daily risk from the hostility of fanatics, or the more common (in those days) assaults of robbers, Masson would have had enough of adventure to last him some years. It was not so. He appears to have been an irreclaimable nomadic vagabond, and his only thought, now that he had reached the West, was to be off again to Afghanistan. Kalat again was his first objective, and to reach that place he followed very much the same route as before. From Kalat, however, to Kandahar and Kabul, he opened up a new line which is worth description. There is little to record as far as Kalat. Once again he joined a mixed Afghan khafila returning from India, and followed the route which leads through Las Bela, Wad, and Khozdar. It was spring, and the country was bright with flowers, the narrow little valleys being full of the brilliance of upspringing crops. It is a mistake to regard Baluchistan as a waste corner of Asia, the dumping ground of the rubbish left over from the world's creation. Much of it, doubtless, is inexpressibly dreary, and in certain dry and sun-baked plains scarred with leprous streaks of salt eruption, it is occasionally difficult to realize the beauty of the spring and summer time in valleys where water is still fairly abundant, and the green things of the earth seem mostly to congregate. A bed of scarlet tulips, or the yellow sheen of the flowering shrub which spreads across the plain of Wad would make any landscape gay, and the long jagged lines of purple hills with chequered shadows patching their rugged spurs would be a fascinating background to any picture. "Only man is vile,"—but this is not true either.

The character of the mixed inhabitants of these valleys of Eastern Baluchistan (we have no room for ethnological disquisitions) is as rugged as their hills, and as varied with patches of brightness as their plains. Masson knew them as no one knows them now, and he evidently loved them. His life was never safe from day to day, but that did not prevent much good comradeship, some genuine friendship, and a shrewd appreciation of the straight uprightness of those who, like the patriarchs and prophets of old, seemed to be the righteous few who leaven the whole lump. Masson was not a missionary, he was only a well-educated and most observant vagabond, but what he has to say of Baluch (or Brahui) character is just what Sandeman said half a century later, and what Barnes or MacMahon[1] would say to-day.

What Masson never seemed to appreciate (any more than the Arab traders who trod the same roads in mediæval centuries) was the change of altitude that accrued after long travelling over apparently flat roads. The natural change in the character of vegetation with the increase of altitude appears, therefore, to surprise him. He reached Kalat without much incident. Here he parted with the Peshin Saiads and the Brahuis of the caravan, and proceeded with the Afghan contingent to Kandahar. The direct road from Kalat to Kandahar runs through the Mangachar valley and thence crosses the Khwaja Amran, or Kojak range, by the Kotal-i-bed into Shorawak, and runs northward to Kandahar through the eastern part

[1] Now Sir Hugh Barnes and Sir Henry MacMahon, one a past, and the other the present, Agent for the Governor-General in Baluchistan.

of the Registan, without touching the main road from Quetta till within a march or two of Kandahar itself. It is worth noting that there was no want of water on this route, and no great difficulties were experienced in passing through the hills. Irrigation canals and the intricacies of natural ravines in Shorawak seem to have been the chief obstacles. It is a route which was never made use of during the last Afghan war, nor, so far as I can discover, during the previous one. The Achakzai tribes-people (some of whom were with the khafila returning to their country from Bombay) behaved with remarkable modesty and good faith, and altogether belied their natural characteristics of truculence and treachery. The journey was made on camel-back in a kajáwa, a method of travelling which ensures a good overlook of the proceedings of the khafila and the country traversed by it, but which can have few other recommendations. Kandahar, however, was not Masson's objective on this trip. Afghanistan was in its usual state of distracted politics, and Kabul was the centre of distraction. To Kabul, therefore, Masson felt himself impelled; like the stormy petrel he preferred a troubled horizon and plenty of incident to the calmer seas of oriental existence in the flat plains of Kandahar. His journey with an Afghan khafila by the well-trodden road which leads to Ghazni was quite sufficiently full of incident, and the extraordinary rapacity of the Ghilzai tribes, who occupy the road as far as that city, leaves one astonished that enough was left of the khafila for useful business purposes in Kabul. Masson was impressed with the desolation and degradation of Ghazni. He can hardly believe that this waste wilderness of mounds around an insignificant town, with its two dreary sentinel minars standing out on the plain, and a dilapidated tomb where rests all that is left of the great conqueror Mahmud, can be the city of such former magnificence as is described in Afghan history. Every traveller to Ghazni has been touched with the same feeling of incredulity, but it only testifies to the remarkable power possessed by the destroying hordes of Chenghiz Khan and his successors of making a clean sweep of the cities which fell into their hands.

A few days before Masson's arrival in Kabul (this is one of the rare dates which we find recorded in his story) in June 1832, three Englishmen had visited the city. These were Lieutenant Burnes, Dr. Gerard, and the Rev. Joseph Wolff. He does not appear to have actually met them. Mr. Wolff had been fortunate enough to distinguish himself as a prophet, and had acquired considerable reputation. An earthquake preceding certain local disturbances between the Sunis and the Shiahs, which he foretold, had established his position, and imitators had begun to arise amongst the people. No better account of the city of Kabul, the beauty of its surroundings, its fruit and its trade, and the social customs of its people, is to be found than that of Masson. What he observed of the city and suburbs in 1832 might almost have been written of the Kabul of fifty years later; but the last twenty-five years have introduced many radical changes, and good roads for wheeled vehicles (not to mention motors) and a small local railway have done more even than the stucco palaces and fantastic halls of the late Amir Abdurrahmon to change the character of the place. The curious spirit of tolerance and liberality which still pervades Kabul and distinguishes it from other Afghan towns, which makes the life of an individual European far more secure there than it would be in Kandahar, the absence of Ghazidom and fanaticism, was even more marked then than it is now. Armenian Christians were treated with more than toleration, they intermarried with Mahomedans; the fact that Masson was known to be a Feringhi never interfered with the spirit of hospitality with which he was received and treated. Only on one occasion was he insulted in the streets, and that was when he wore a Persian cap instead of the usual lunghi. But the Jews were as much anathema as they are now, and Masson tells a curious tale of one Jew who was stoned to death by Mahomedans for denying the divinity of Jesus Christ, after the Christian community of Armenians had declined to carry out the punishment. To this day nothing arouses Afghan hatred like the cry of Yahudi (Jew), and it may very possibly be partly due to their firm conviction in their origin as Ben-i-Israel.

The summer of 1832 at Kabul must have been a delightful experience, but with the coming autumn the restlessness of the nomad again seized on Masson and he made that journey to Bamian in company with an Afghan friend, one Haji Khan, chief of Bamian, which followed the mission of Burnes to Kunduz, and proved the possibilities of the route to Afghan Turkestan by the southern passes of the Hindu Kush. Bamian was then separated from Kabul by the width of the Besud territory, which was practically controlled by a semi-independent Hazara chief, Yezdambaksh. Beyond Bamian the pass of Ak Robat defined the northern frontier of Afghanistan, beyond which again were more semi-independent chiefs, of whom by far the most powerful, south of the Oxus, was Mir Murad Beg of Kunduz. Amongst them all political intrigue was in a state of boiling effervescence. Haji Khan (a Kakar soldier of fortune) from Western Afghanistan knew himself to be unpopular with the Amir Dost Mahomed Khan, and had shrewd suspicions that spite of a long-tried friendship, he was regarded as a dangerous factor in Kabul politics. Yezdambaksh, influenced doubtless by his gallant wife, who rode and fought by his side and was ever at his elbow in council, trimmed his course to patch up a temporary alliance with Haji Khan under the pretext of suffocating the ambition of the local chief of

Saighan; whilst Murad Beg about that time was strong enough to preserve his own position unassisted and aloof. Into the seething welter of intrigue arising from the conflicting interests of these many candidates for distinction in the Afghan border field Masson plunged when he accepted Haji Khan's invitation to join him at Bamian. Across the lovely plain of Chardeh, bright with the orange blossoms of the safflower, Masson followed the well-known route to Argandi and over the Safed Khak Pass to the foot of the divide which is crossed by the Unai (called Honai by Masson), meeting with the usual demands for "karij," or duty, from the Hazaras at their border, with the usual altercations and violence on both sides. Well known as is this route, it may be doubted whether any better description of it has ever been written than that of Masson. Instead of striking straight across the Helmund at Gardandiwal by the direct route to Bamian, the party followed the course of the Helmund, then fringed with rose bushes and willows, passing through a delightfully picturesque country till they fell in with the Afghan camp, after much wandering in unknown parts on the banks of the Helmund, at a point which it is difficult to identify.

The story of the daily progress of the oriental military camp, and the daily discussions with Haji Khan, who appeared to be as frank and childlike in his disclosures of his methods as any chattering booby, is excellent. There is no doubt that Masson at this time exercised very considerable influence over his Afghan and Hazara acquaintances, and he is probably justified in his claim to have prevented more than one serious row over the everlasting demands for karij. It is to be noted that two guns were dragged along with this expedition by forced Hazara labour, eighty men being required for one, and two hundred for the other, assisted by an elephant. The calibre of the guns is not mentioned. At a place called Shaitana they were still south of the Helmund, and in the course of their progress through Besud visited the sources of the Logar. Near these sources is the Azdha of Besud, the petrified dragon slain by Hazrat Ali (not to be confused with Azdha of Bamian), a volcanic formation stretching its white length through about 170 yards, exhaling sulphurous odours. The red rock found about its head is supposed to be tinged with blood. The Azdha afterwards seen and described at Bamian is of "more imposing size."

Another long march (apparently on the road to Ghazni) brought the expedition to the frontier of Besud, at a point reckoned by Masson as three marches from the Ghazni district. From here they retraced their steps and crossed the Helmund at Ghoweh Kol (? Pai Kol), making for Bamian. This closed the Besud expedition, which, regarded as a geographical exploration, is still authoritative, no complete survey of that district having ever been made. From the Helmund they reached Bamian by the Siah Reg Pass, thus proving the possibility of traversing that district by comparatively unknown routes which were "not on the whole difficult to cavalry, though impracticable to wheeled carriages." The guns were left in Besud, to be dragged through by Hazaras. It must be remembered that this was early winter, and the frozen snow rendered the passes slippery and difficult. The aspect of the Koh-i-Baba (? Babar) mountains, and their "craggy pinnacles" (which, by reason of their similarity of outline, gave much trouble to our surveyors in 1882-83) seems to have impressed Masson greatly. The descent into the Bamian valley was "perfectly easy, and the road excellent throughout." Masson's contributions to the Asiatic Society on the subject of Bamian and its "idols" are well known. His observations were acute, and on the whole accurate. He rightly conjectured these wonderful relics to be Buddhist, although he never grasped the full extent of Buddhist influence, nor the extraordinary width of their occupation in Northern Afghanistan. His conjectures and impressions need not be repeated, but his somewhat crude sketches of Bamian and the citadel of Gulgula intensify the regret which I always feel that a thoroughly competent photographer was not attached to the long subsequent Russo-Afghan Boundary Commission.

Masson's wanderings in the company of the Afghan chief Haji Khan and his redoubtable army through the valleys and over the passes of the Hindu Kush and its western spurs is full of interest to the military reader. The Afghan force consisted largely of cavalry, as did that of the gallant Hazara chief, Yezdambaksh. Nothing is said about infantry, but it was probably little better than a badly armed mob chiefly concerned in guarding the guns which reached the valley of Bamian, but, as already stated, they could not follow the cavalry over the Siah Reg Pass from Besud. They were sent round by the "Karza" Pass, which is probably the one known as Kafza on our maps, which indicates the most direct route from Kabul to Bamian.

It is necessary to follow the ostensible policy of these military movements in order to render Masson's account of them intelligible. Haji Khan was acting in concert with Yezdambaksh and his Hazara troops, with the presumed object of crushing first Mahomed Ali, the chief of Saighan (north of Bamian), and ultimately repeating the process on Rahmatulla Khan, the chief of Kamard (north of Saighan). In order to effect this he had to pass up the Bamian valley to its northern head, marked by the Ak Robat Pass (10,200 feet high), and thence descend into the Saighan valley by the route formed by one of its southern tributaries. It was early winter (or late autumn), but still the passes seemed to have been more or less free from snow, and the Ak Robat Pass in particular appears to have given little trouble, although the valley contracts almost to a gorge in the descent. Masson noted evidences of the former existence of a considerable town near this route on the descent from Ak Robat. Much to his astonishment, instead of smashing the Saighan opposition with his superior force, Haji Khan proceeded to patch up an alliance with Mahomed Ali, which was cemented by his marrying one of the daughters of that wily chief. Here, however, he experienced a cruel disappointment. Instead of the lovely bride whom he had been led to expect, he received a squat and snub-nosed Hazara girl, who was, indeed, of very doubtful parentage. This little swindle, however, was not permitted to interfere with his politics. The alliance ought to have aroused the suspicion of Yezdambaksh, but the latter seems to have trusted to the strength of his following to meet any possible contingency.

The next step was to proceed to Kamard and repeat the process of occupation. Here, however, an unexpected difficulty arose. The easy-going, hard-drinking Tajik chief of Kamard was far too wily to put himself into Haji Khan's power, and with some of the Uzbek chiefs who owed their allegiance to that fine old border bandit Murad Khan of Kunduz (of whom we shall hear again), positively declined to permit Haji Khan to come farther. Meanwhile, however, a force had advanced over the divide between Saighan and Kamard by a pass which Masson calls the Nalpach (or horseshoe-breaking pass), which can hardly be the same as the well-known Dandan Shikan (or tooth-breaking pass), but is probably to the east of it, leading more directly to Bajgah. Before ascending the pass, Masson noted the remains of an ancient town or fort built of immense stones, and here they halted. Here also snow fell. Next day a reconnaissance in force was made over the Nalpach Pass ("long, but not difficult"), and apparently part of the force descended into Kamard and commenced hostile operations against the Kamard chieftain. Haji Khan, however, returned to camp. He had now succeeded in breaking up the Hazara force which was with him into two or three detached bodies, so the opportunity was ripe for one of the blackest acts of treachery that ever disgraced Afghan history—which is saying a good deal. He entrapped and seized the fine old Hazara chief, Yezdambaksh, and, after dragging him about with him under circumstances of great indignity, he finally executed him. The Hazara troops seem to have scattered without striking a concerted blow; their camp was looted, whilst such wretched refugees as were caught were stripped and enslaved.

The savage barbarity of these proceedings, especially of the method of the execution of Yezdambaksh (a rope being looped round the wretched victim's neck, the two ends of which were hauled tight by a mixed company of relatives and enemies), disgusted Masson deeply, and there is a very obvious disposition evinced hereafter to part company with his treacherous host, although he makes some attempt to excuse these proceedings by pointing out that Haji Khan, after meeting with an unexpected rebuff from Kamard (which he dare not resent so long as the redoubtable Murad Beg loomed in the distance as the protector of the frontier chiefs of Badakshan), would have been unable to keep and feed his troops in the winter without scattering the Hazara contingent and possessing himself of the resources of Besud.

Winter had already set in, and the subsequent story is instructive in illustration of the difficulties which beset the road between Kabul and Bamian during the winter season. The resources of Bamian were insufficient even for his diminished force (now reduced to about its original strength of eight hundred), and the Ghulam Khana contingent grew restive and impatient, demanding to go back to Kabul. The passes, however, were not only closed by snow, but the position at Karzar was held by Hazaras, who, however much they were demoralised by the execution of their chief, might well be expected to make reprisals. The Ghulam Khana men, about two hundred and twenty strong, therefore moved in force from Bamian, with the hope of being able to influence the Hazaras to let them pass through Besud. Apparently they did not rank as true Afghans. No great resistance was made at Karzar, although they were not admitted to shelter. They were freely looted, and eventually allowed to pass after three days' detention, exposed to the terrific blasts of a winter shamal (north-west wind) in snow which was then breast high. Many of them perished before reaching Kabul, and many more were permanently disabled from frostbites.

Haji Khan, meanwhile, settled down as the uninvited guest of the people of Bamian, and ensconced himself and his wives in the fort of Saidabad, a strongly built construction of burnt bricks of immense size, which Masson believed to have been built by the Arabs. Saidabad is hard by the detached position of Gulgula; it is described by Masson in considerable detail. Here, at an altitude of about 8500 feet, a winter in Bamian is endurable, and Haji Khan avowed his intention of remaining. It is interesting to note that a khafila from Bokhara for Kabul arrived about this time, and was duly looted. Even in winter the route (as a commercial route) was open.

Masson's efforts were now directed towards getting back to Kabul. His first essay was in company of two brothers of Haji Khan, who vowed to get to Kabul somehow, even if, as Afghans, they had to fight their way through Besud. The party followed up the Topchi valley from Bamian, and crossing by the Shutar Gardan Pass, they reached Karzar. Here again Masson noted extensive ruins *en route*. The road was bad and the difficulties great, "leading over precipices," but they did, nevertheless, succeed in crossing the main divide. Here Masson experienced a very bad time, and to his disgust found that he must retrace his steps to Bamian, owing to counter orders from Haji Khan recalling the escort. There appeared, however, a prospect of getting out of Bamian by the Shibar Pass (an easy pass), leading to the head of the Ghorband valley; and trusting to certain arrangements made by a Paghmani chief, Masson made a fresh attempt, passing eastward the ancient remains of Zohak, and ascending by a fairly easy open track to the valley or plain of Irak. Probably this pass is the one known as Khashka in our maps. The wind was terrific, but the comparative freedom from snow was an unexpected advantage.

Passing eastwards from Irak (still on the northern slopes of the Hindu Kush) the party made comparatively easy progress by a valley which Masson calls Bubulak (where he observed tobacco to be growing). They gradually ascended until once again they found themselves in snow, but instead of making direct for the Shibar they inclined to a more northerly pass called Bitchilik, which is separated from the Shibar by a slight kotal (or divide). Here they found the Paghmani chief whom they expected to join, but they found also that the section of Hazaras who held these passes then were determined to bar their passage. Once again Masson had to abandon the attempt (albeit the Shibar route to Kabul would have been a very devious and dangerous one), and returned to Bamian.

There are one or two circumstances about this exploration of the western Hindu Kush passes which deserve attention. For once Masson is slightly inaccurate in his geography when he states that the Irak stream drains into the Bamian valley. It joins the Bamian River after it has left the valley and turned northward. So slight an error is only a useful proof of his general accuracy. Another remarkable fact was that he, a Feringhi, was elected by the Afghan gang with which he was temporarily associated as their Khan, or chief! He was a little better dressed than most of them in European chintzes. He found himself utterly unable to restrain their looting propensities, but he made himself quite popular by his civility and his small presents to the wretched Hazaras on whom they were quartered. Incidentally he gives us a most valuable impression of the nature of an important group of Afghan passes, and I doubt if his information has ever been much improved upon.

Finally, the surrender of the Karzar position by the Hazaras reopened the road to Kabul, and Masson was enabled to reach that capital by the Topchi, Shutar Gardan, Kalu, Hajigak routes to Gardandiwal on the Helmund. The Hajigak route he describes as easy of ascent, but "steep and very troublesome" in the south. The Shutar Gardan (called Panjpilan now) was "intricate and dangerous," but the passing of it was done at night. This is, and always has been, the main khafila route between Kabul, Bamian, and Bokhara. The journey from the Helmund across the Unai (which pass was itself "difficult") was not accomplished without great distress. A winter shumal caught Masson on the road, and but for the timely shelter at Zaimuni would have terminated his career there and then. Masson describes the terrific effect of the wind with great vigour, but those who have experienced it will not accuse him of exaggeration.

CHAPTER XI

AMERICAN EXPLORATION—MASSON (*continued*)

ON Masson's return to Kabul he observed the first symptoms of active interest in Afghan politics on the part of the Indian Government, in the person of an accredited native agent (Saiad Karamat Ali) who had travelled with Lieut. Conolly to Herat. Colonel Stoddart was at that time detained in Bokhara, and was apparently under the impression that he was befriended by a "profligate adventurer," one Samad Khan, who had succeeded in establishing himself there as a pillar of the State after imposing on so astute a politician as the Amir Dost Mahomed Khan and on many of the leading Afghan Sirdars. Masson seems to have been better aware of the character of this Khan than the Indian Government, for he notes that "to be befriended by such a man is in itself calamitous."

It is quite comprehensible that the Indian Government should not duly appreciate the position of an adventurer like Masson and his intimate acquaintance with Afghanistan and its riotous rulers; but it was unfortunate; for it is not too much to say that Indian Government officials at that time were but amateurs in their knowledge of Afghan politics compared to Masson; and much of the horrors of subsequent events might have been avoided could Masson have been admitted freely and fully to their counsels. However, for a time he employed himself in collecting historical and scientific notes on Afghanistan, which we still regard as standard works for reference. No one has succeeded better in giving us an impression of the leading characteristics of the Afghan chiefs of his time, and probably there is not much improvement effected by a century of moral development. Steeped up to the eyes in treachery towards each other, debauchees, drunkards, liars, and murderers, one cannot but admire their extraordinary virility. It was truly a case of the survival of the fittest, and the fittest were certainly remarkable men.

The Amir Dost Mahomed Khan was one of the worst, and one of the best. One of the twenty-two sons of Sirafraz Khan, he worked his way upwards by truly Afghan methods; methods which in the early days of his career were utterly detestable, but which attained some sort of reflected dignity later, when there were not wanting signs that in a different environment he might have been truly great. He was illiterate and uneducated, but appreciated the advantages of elementary schooling in others. Into the strange welter of political intrigue which forms Afghan history during the period of his rise to power we need not enter; but it is necessary to note the extraordinary difference with which the stranger in the land, a Feringhi, was regarded throughout Afghanistan, then, as compared with his reception at present. It is even possible that the life of a Feringhi was then safer (*i.e.* deemed of more importance) than that of any ordinary Afghan chief. It is certain that there was a strong feeling that it was well to be on good terms with the representatives of a powerful neighbouring state. This feeling was greatly weakened by the results of the first Afghan war, and has never again been completely restored.

Although we are only dealing with Masson as an explorer, it is impossible not to express sympathy with his whole-hearted admiration for the country of the Afghan. His description of the beauties of the land, especially in early spring with the awakening of the season of flowers, the irresistible charm of the mountain scenery of the Kohistan as the gradual burst of summer bloom crept upwards over the hills—all this finds an echo in the heart of every one who has ever seen this "God granted" land; where, after all, the seething scum of Afghan politics is very much confined to a class, although it undoubtedly sinks deeper and reaches the mass of the people with more of the force of self-interest than is the case in India, where the historical pageant of kings and dynasties has passed over the great mass of India's self-absorbed people and left them profoundly unconscious of its progress.

In the year 1833 Masson resumed his researches in the neighbourhood of Kabul, commencing in the plains about 25 miles north-east from Kabul, and 8 or 10 from Charikar. These researches were continued for some years, until the failure of the mission to Kabul in 1838 obliged him to leave the country; and in his proposal to resume them again in 1840 he was opposed by "a miserable fraction of the Calcutta clique," who had recourse to "acts as unprecedented, base, and illegal as perhaps were ever perpetrated under the sanction of authority against a subject of the British Crown." So that apparently he claimed British nationality before he left Afghanistan. However that may be, it is certain that no subsequent explorer has added much that is of value to the extraordinary evidences of ancient occupation collected by Masson. Here, he maintains, once existed the city of Alexandria founded by Alexander on the Kabul plain; and a recent announcement from Kabul that the site of an ancient city has been discovered obviously refers to the same position at Begram near Charikar, and is a useful commentary on the rapidity with which the fame and name of an original explorer can disappear.

The Masson collection of coins, which totalled between 15,000 and 20,000 in 1837, and which was presented to the East India Company, proved a veritable revelation of unknown kings and dynasties, and contributed enormously to our positive knowledge of Central Asian history. The vast number of Cufic coins found at Begram show that the city must have existed for some centuries after the Mahomedan invasion. Chinese travellers tell of a city called Hupian in this neighbourhood, but Masson is inclined to place the site of Hupian near Charikar, where there was, in his time, a village called Malek Hupian. He thinks that Begram had certainly ceased to exist at the time of Timur's expedition to India; or that conqueror would not have found it necessary to construct a canal from the Ghorband stream in order to colonize this favoured corner of the Kabul plain. The canal still exists as the Mahighir, and the people of the neighbourhood talked Turki in Masson's time. Three miles east of Kabul there is another ancient site known as Begram. This was probably the precursor of Kabul itself, and other "Begrams" are known in India. The term appears to be generic and to denote a famous site. Buddhist relics lie thickly round about the Afghan Begrams, groups of them being very abundant throughout the Kabul valley.

It was after his first visit to Begram that Masson became acquainted with M. Honigberger, whom he describes as a gentleman from Lahore bent on archæological research; and at the close of the autumn Dr. Gerard, the companion of Lieut. Burnes, appeared at Kabul. Honigberger's researches, like those of Gerard, appear to have been confined to archæology, and the results of them form an interesting story which was given to the world by Eugene Jacquet; but as neither of these gentlemen can be said to have contributed to the early geographical knowledge of the country, no further reference need be made to them, beyond remarking that Honigberger very narrowly escaped being murdered on his subsequent journey to Bokhara.

Masson's extraordinary capability of dealing with every class of people with whom he came in contact, and his consequent apparent immunity from the dangers which beset the ordinary unaccredited traveller, should not lead to the assumption that Afghanistan was a safe country to travel in at the time of our first political negotiations, in spite of there being less fanaticism at that time; whilst the trans-Oxus states were then almost unapproachable. There, at least, the gradual encroachment of Russian civilization has absolutely altered the conditions of European existence, and Bokhara has become quite a favourite resort for tourists.

Masson's story of Afghan intrigue, which is the substance of Afghan history at this period, is as interesting as are his archæological investigations, for it affords us a view of events which occurred behind the scenes, shut off from India by the curtain of the frontier hills; but whilst he thus occupied his busy mind with the past and the present policy of Afghanistan, he did not lose sight of the opportunity for making fresh excursions into Afghan territory. His visits to the Kabul valley and Peshawar can hardly claim to be original explorations, though he undoubtedly acquired by them a local geographical knowledge far in advance of anything then existing on the Indian side of the border, and some of it ranks as authoritative even now. It must not be supposed that these visits and investigations were carried on without grave risk and constant difficulty, but by this time Masson had so wide and so varied a personal acquaintance with the leading chiefs and tribespeople of the country that he usually succeeded in distinguishing friend from foe, and extricated himself from positions which would have been fatal to any one less knowledgeable than himself.

During the year 1835 we learn that Masson was in Northern Afghanistan, chiefly at Kabul, gathering information; but there appears to be hardly a place which now figures in our maps with any prominence in the Kabul province which he did not succeed in visiting; and as regards some of them (Kunar, for instance) there was nothing added to his record for at least sixty years. He penetrated the Alishang valley to within 12 miles of Najil, a point which no European has succeeded in reaching since; but his sphere of observation was always too restricted to enable him to make much of his geographical opportunities. Najil is now somewhat doubtfully placed on our maps from native information gathered during the surveys executed with the Afghan campaign of 1878-80.

It was at this period in Masson's career (in 1835) that English political interest in Kabul began to take an active shape. About this time Masson accepted a proposal from the Indian Government (which reached him through Captain Wade, the political officer on the Punjab frontier) to act as British agent and keep the Government informed as to the progress of affairs in Kabul. It is rather surprising that Masson, who never misses an opportunity of asserting that he was not an Englishman, and was by no means in sympathy with the policy of the Indian Government towards Afghanistan, should have accepted this responsibility. However, he did so, for a time at least, though he subsequently requested that he might be relieved from the duties entailed by such an equivocal position. He negotiated the foundation of a commercial treaty between India and Kabul, but with scant success. This period of seething intrigue at Kabul (as also between Dost Mahomed Khan and the Sikhs) was hardly favourable to its inception. His efforts were duly acknowledged by the Government, but his position as agent became untenable when he found that it led to interference with the great object of his residence in Afghanistan, *i.e.* antiquarian research. We can only touch upon the political events of 1836-37 cursorily, in spite of their absorbing interest, in order to follow the sequence of Masson's career.

At the beginning of 1836 the Sikhs under Ranjit Singh were consolidating their position on the Western Punjab frontier, whilst Dost Mahomed Khan was working all he knew to secure men and money for military purposes. This led to a half-hearted renewal of correspondence between Masson and Wade. The commencement of the year 1837 was marked by active preparations on the part of Dost Mahomed for a campaign against the Sikhs, resulting in an equivocal victory for the Afghans near Jamrud under Akbar Khan, but no essential change in the relative position as regards the Peshawar frontier. Various were the projects set on foot at this time for the assassination of the Amir, and in the general network of bloody intrigue Masson was not overlooked; but he was discreetly absent from Kabul during the winter of 1836-37, having previously found it necessary to keep his house full of armed men. He returned to Kabul in the spring.

Towards the end of September 1837 Captain Burnes arrived in Kabul on that historical commercial mission which was to result in a disastrous misunderstanding between the Indian Government and the Amir. If we are to believe Masson, it would be difficult to conceive a more mismanaged and hopelessly bungled political function than this mission proved to be; but we must remember that in experience of the Afghan character and knowledge of intrigue the Indian Government and Council were by no means experts. It is difficult to believe that the mere fact of inadequate recognition of his services and consequent disappointment could have so affected a man of Masson's independence of character, natural ability, and clear sense of justice, as to lead him to misrepresent the position absolutely. As a commercial mission he regarded it as unnecessary.

Burnes was instructed to proceed first to Haidarabad (in Sind) for the purpose of opening up the Indus to commercial navigation, and thence to journey *via* Attok to Peshawar (held by the Sikhs), Kabul, and Kandahar, back again to Haidarabad, all in the interest of a trade which was already flourishing between Afghanistan and ports on the Indus already established. "The Governments of India and of England," says Masson, "as well as the public at large were never amused and deceived by a greater fallacy than that of opening the Indus as regards commercial objects."

The keynote of Masson's policy was non-interference, so long as interference either in trade or politics was not forced on the British Government. At that time such views were undoubtedly sound; but even then there was a stir in the political atmosphere which betokened much nervousness in high quarters on the subject of Persian and Russian intrigues with Afghanistan. So far, however, as Masson observes, "there was little notion entertained at this time of convulsing Central Asia, of deposing and setting up Kings, of carrying on wars, of lavishing treasure, and of the commission of a long train of crimes and follies." But with the arrival of Burnes at Kabul trade interests seem to have faded and those of a more active policy to have taken their place. The weak point in this change of policy appears to have been the want of definite instructions from the Government of India to their agent.

The appearance of a Russian officer (Lieut. Vektavitch) at Kabul from the Russian camp at Herat in December (he had, according to Masson, no real authority to support him, and could only have been acting as a spy on Burnes) was a source of much agitation; but nothing whatever appears to have eventuated from his residence in Kabul, except grave risk to himself. Masson never believed in the dangers arising from either Persian or Russian intrigue (and he was certainly in a position to judge), and he remarks about Vektavitch "that such a man could have been expected to defeat a British mission is too ridiculous a notion to be entertained; nor would his mere appearance have produced such a result had not the mission itself been set forth without instructions for its guidance, and had it not been conducted recklessly, and in defiance of all common sense and decorum." This, indeed, is the attitude assumed by Masson throughout towards the mission, although he was still in the service of the Indian Government and acting under Burnes.

Burnes certainly seems to have behaved with great want of dignity in the presence of the Amir and his Sirdars; making obeisance, and addressing the Amir as if he were a dependant. Nor can his private arrangements and his method of living in Kabul be commended as those of a dignified agent. European manners and customs were looser in those days in India than they are now, but with all latitude for the *autres temps autres mœurs* excuse for his conduct, his ideas of Eastern life seem to have been almost too oriental even for the approval of the dissolute Afghan. Certain it is that no proposal made by him on his own responsibility to the Amir (especially as regards the cession of Peshawar on the death of Ranjit Singh) was supported by his Government, and time after time he enjoyed the humiliation of being obliged to eat his own words. On these occasions it would appear that Masson seldom omitted the opportunity of saying "I told you so."

In the interests of geographical explorations, this mission of Burnes was important. Whatever else he was, there is no question that he was as keen a geographical observer as Masson himself, and even if the wisdom of the despatch of his assistants (Lieut. Leech to Kandahar, and Dr.

Lord with Lieut. Wood to Badakshan) may be questioned on political grounds, it led to a series of remarkable explorations, some of which even now furnish authority for Afghan map-making.

In May 1837, Lieut. Eldred Pottinger arrived on leave from India (with the interest of his father Sir Henry Pottinger to back him), and immediately made secret preparations for his adventurous journey through the Hazarajat from Kabul to Herat, which terminated in his participation in the defence of Herat against the Persians. Thus was the first authentic account received of the nature of that difficult mountain region which has subsequently been so thoroughly exploited. Afghanistan was just beginning to be known.

Masson naturally disapproved of Pottinger's exploit, for he found himself in hot water owing to the suspicion that he connived at it. He says: "I have always thought that however fortunate for Lieut. Pottinger himself, his trip to Herat was an unlucky one for his country; the place would have been fought as well without him; and his presence, which would scarcely be thought accidental, although truly it was so, must not only have irritated the Persian King, but have served as a pretext for the more prominent exertions of the Russian staff. It is certain that when he started from Kabul he had no idea that the city would be invested by a Persian army." Colonel Stoddart was then the British agent in the Persian Camp.

Incidentally it may be useful to note the results of the occupation of Seistan about this time by an Afghan army under Shah Kamran, Governor of Herat and brother to Dost Mahomed; the one brother, in fact, whom he feared the most. Kamran's army had threatened Kandahar in the early spring and had spread into Seistan. Here the cavalry horses perished from disease, and the finest force which had marched from Herat for years was placed absolutely *hors de combat.* Unable to obtain the assistance of the army in the field, the frontier fortress of Ghorian surrendered, and thus reduced Kamran to the necessity of retirement on Herat and sustaining a siege. The destructive climate of Seistan has evidently not greatly changed during the last century.

Masson's view of the policy best adapted to the tangled situation was the surrender of Peshawur to Sulṭan Mahomed Khan (the Amir's brother), who already enjoyed half its revenues, which would have been an acceptable proposition to the Sikh chief, Ranjit Singh (who found the occupation of Peshawar a most profitless undertaking), and would at the same time have reconciled the chiefs at Kandahar. The Amir Dost Mahomed would have reconciled himself to a situation which he could not avoid and the Indian Government would have enjoyed the credit of establishing order on their frontiers on a tolerably sure basis without committing themselves to any alliance, for (he writes) "my experience has brought me to the decided opinion that any strict alliance with powers so constituted would prove only productive of mischief and embarrassment, while I still thought that British influence might be usefully exerted in preserving the integrity of the several states and putting their rulers on their good behaviour." Subsequent events proved the soundness of these views, but we must remember that Masson wrote "after the event." That he did, however, strongly counsel Burnes to make no promise in the name of his Government of the cession of Peshawar to the Amir on the death of Ranjit Singh, is clear, and it is impossible to say how far the disappointment felt by the Amir at the refusal of the Indian Government to ratify this promise may have affected his subsequent actions. Masson thinks that Burnes should have been recalled, but he admits the difficulty that beset him owing to want of instructions. "The folly of sending such a man as Captain Burnes without the fullest and clearest instructions was now shown," etc. etc. It is surprising that with his confidence in the ability of his immediate Chief so absolutely destroyed, he should have continued to serve under him.

Finally, on April 26, Burnes and Masson left Kabul together in a hurry and were subsequently joined by Lord and Wood, and "thus closed a mission, one of the most extraordinary ever sent forth by a Government, whether as to the singular manner in which it was conducted, or as to the results." Shortly after Masson resigned an appointment under the Government of India which he stigmatises as "disagreeable and dishonourable." It was a pity that he held it so long.

When Masson reached India he found that the Government had already decided to restore the refugee Shah Sujah to the throne of Kabul, and that a military expedition to Kandahar had been arranged. What he has to say about the manner of this arrangement and the nature of the influence brought to bear on Lord Auckland to bring it about is not more pleasant reading than is his story of the Kabul Mission. This tale, indeed, does not belong to the history of exploration any further than to indicate under what conditions the first military geographical knowledge of Farther Afghanistan was gained by such true explorers as Pottinger, Lord, and Wood; and what amount of actually new information was attained by Burnes' mission. This was very considerable, as we shall see when we follow Burnes' assistants into the field. Meanwhile we have not quite done with Masson.

The closing incidents of the career of this remarkable man, as an explorer, call for little more comment. Once again, in the year preceding the disastrous termination to our first occupation of Kabul, did he make Karachi and Sonmiani his base of departure for a fresh venture in behalf of archæological research in Afghanistan. It was his intention to proceed to Kandahar and Kabul, but his plans were frustrated by as remarkable a series of incidents as could well have barred the progress of any traveller. The Government of India, instigated by reports which (according to Masson) were the results of local intrigue and were palpably false, considered itself justified in an expedition to Kalat and the deposition of its Brahui chief, Mehrab Khan. This expedition was successfully carried out by General Wiltshire, and Mehrab Khan was killed in the defence of his citadel. Subsequently a British agent, Lieut. Loveday, was appointed to Kalat, and Masson found him there on his arrival from Sonmiani. Masson's description of him and of his crude political methods is not flattering, and his weak surrender of Kalat to the badly armed Brahui rabble who attacked the place in the interests of the late Khan's son was certainly disgraceful. That surrender, which was only wiped out by Nott's advance on Kalat, and the final suppression of the Brahui revolt, cost Loveday his life, and placed Masson in deadly peril. He, however, succeeded in reaching Quetta, where Captain Bean was in political charge; but this officer not only put him into confinement but treated him with positive barbarity.

It is difficult to understand the political view of Masson's existence in Baluchistan. If any man was capable of unriddling the network of intrigue that occupied all the Baluch chiefs at this time, or could bring anything of personal influence to bear on them, it was undoubtedly Masson, and something of his history was at any rate known. But he had resigned service under the Indian Government as "disagreeable and dishonourable," and his reappearance at a time when all Baluchistan was in the ferment of seething revolt was perhaps regarded with suspicion. It is also quite conceivable that the local political officer regarded him simply as an interloping loafer, and, until he became better acquianted with Masson's character and ability, would be no more likely to pay him attention than would any political officer on the frontier to-day who suddenly found himself confronted with a European in native dress with no valid explanation of his appearance under very ambiguous circumstances. The days were not long past when European loafers of any nationality whatsoever could, and did, find not only service, but distinction, in the courts and armies of native chiefs who were hostile to British interests. One can only gather from Masson's strange story that there was no officer in the British political service at that time with intuition sufficient to enable him to appraise the situation correctly, or make use of other experience than his own.

Here, however, we must leave Masson. As an explorer in Afghanistan he stands alone. His work has never been equalled; but owing to the very unsatisfactory methods adopted by all explorers in those days for the recording of geographical observations it cannot be said that his contribution to exact geographical knowledge was commensurate with his extraordinary capacity as an observant traveller, or his remarkable industry.

It is as a critic on the political methods of the Government of India that Masson's records are chiefly instructive. Hostile critics of Indian administrative methods usually belong to one of two classes. They are either uninformed, notoriety-seeking demagogues playing to a certain party gallery at home, or they are disappointed servants of the Government, by whom they consider that their merits have been overlooked. To this latter class it must be conceded that Masson belonged, in spite of his expressed contempt for government service. Thus the virulence of his attacks on the ignorance and fatuity of the political officials with whom he was brought in contact must be freely discounted, because of the obvious animus which pervades them. Still it is to be feared there is too much reason to believe that private interest was the recommendation which carried most weight in the appointment of unfledged officers, both civil and military, to political duty on the Indian frontier. These gentlemen took the field without experience, and without that which might to a certain extent take the place of experience, viz. an education in the main principles both social and economical which govern the conditions of existence of the people with whom they had to deal. A knowledge of political economy, law, and languages is not enough to enable the young administrator to take his place on the frontier, if he knows not enough of the characteristics of the frontier tribes-people to enable him to maintain the dignity of his position. Even physically there are qualifications which are not always regarded as useful, which make for strong influence and good government. A man may be physically powerful enough to use his strength in fair contest to the immense enhancement of his personal prestige, but he must not strike a blow where the blow cannot be returned; and above all he must not endeavour to conciliate by a silly display of obsequious attention, unless he is prepared to sacrifice all his personal influence and destroy the respect due to his office.

Setting aside Masson's sentiments of disgust and horror (which he really felt) that the fate of men should have been placed at the mercy of the political officers in whom, at that time, Lord Auckland was pleased to repose confidence, and his assertions that "on me developed the task to obtain satisfaction for the insults some of these shallow and misguided men thought fit to practise," his own account of the extraordinary complexity of intrigue, and the unfathomable abyss of deceit and crime which distinguished the political field of native Baluchistan, is quite enough to account for much of their failure to deal with the situation. At the same time, it is a strong indication of the necessity for a sounder system of political education than any which now exists. Possibly a time may come when we shall cease to see systems of administration suitable to the plains applied to frontier mountaineers, or, for that matter, the foreign methods of India hammered into the nomadic pastoral peoples of other continents than Asia, where they are wholly inapplicable.

CHAPTER XII

ENGLISH OFFICIAL EXPLORATION—LORD AND WOOD

THEN followed the Afghan Campaign of 1839-40, a campaign which was in many ways disastrous to our credit in Afghanistan both as diplomats and soldiers, but which undoubtedly opened out an opportunity for acquiring a general knowledge of the conformation of the country which was not altogether neglected. With the political methods attending the inception of the campaign (treated with such scathing scorn by Masson), and the strange bungling of an overweighted and unwieldy force armed with antique weapons we have nothing to do. The question is whether, apart from the acquisition of route sketches and intelligence reports dependent on the movements of the army in the field, was there anything that could rank as original exploration in new geographical fields? Lieut. North's excellent traverse and report of the route to Kandahar, which still supplies data for an integral part of our maps, was distinguished for more accuracy of detail and observation than most efforts of a similar character made at that time; but it can hardly be regarded as an illustration of new and original exploration, the route itself being well enough known to British Missions, although never before surveyed. It is undoubtedly one of the best map contributions of the period.

The adventures of Dr. Lord and Lieut. Wood in Badakshan, and the remarkable journey of Broadfoot across Central Afghanistan, however, belong to another category. These explorations covered new ground, much of which has never since been visited by European travellers, and they are authoritative records still. There were missed opportunities in abundance. Also opportunities which were not missed, but of which our records are so incomplete and obscure that the modern map-maker can extract but little useful information from them.

When Burnes was in Kabul on his first commercial mission, Dr. Lord and Lieut. Leech of the Bombay Engineers were attached to his staff, and both these gentlemen, with Lieut. Wood of the Indian Navy, distinguished themselves by much original research, and have left records the value of which has been proved by subsequent observations. In the middle of October 1837 Dr. Lord left Kabul on an expedition into the plains of the Koh Daman, to the north of that city, which was to be extended to the passes of the Hindu Kush leading into Badakshan, when he was subsequently invited to attend the court of Murad Beg, the chief of Kunduz, in his professional capacity. Murad Beg was one of the strongest chiefs of that time. As a bold and astute freebooter and successful warrior he had made his name great amongst the Uzbeks south of the Oxus, and had consolidated their scattered clans for the time being into a formidable cohesion, the strength of which made itself felt and respected at Kabul. Where Dost Mahomed's influence ceased on the north there commenced that of Murad Beg, and the line of division may be said to have extended from Ak Robat at the head of the Bamian valley on the west, to the passes and foot-hills of the Hindu Kush above Andarab on the east. It was late in the year for Lord to attempt the passing of the Hindu Kush, and he appears to have lingered too long amongst the delightful autumn scenes of that land of enchantment, the Koh Daman. He selected the passes which strike off from Charikar, near the junction of the Ghorband with the Panjshir rivers. There has always been a slight confusion in the naming of this group of passes, owing to the universal habit in Afghanistan of bestowing the name of some possibly insignificant village site on rivers, passes, and roads, without attaching any distinct and definite name to these features themselves.

From that break in the hills which gives passage to the Ghorband from the south-west and the Panjshir from the north-east there strikes off one well-known route across the backbone of the Hindu Kush, which is marked near the southern foot of the mountains by the ancient town of Parwan—a commercial site more ancient than that of Kabul—the headquarters of Sabaktagin, the Ghuri conqueror, when he wrested Kabul from the Hindu kings, and of Timur the Tartar in later ages. Consequently, the pass which bears north from that point is often called the Parwan. It was, according to Lord, the chief khafila route from Badakshan (although it may be doubted whether it was ever as popular as the Khawak when the Panjshir route was not closed by tribal hostility), notwithstanding that far less traffic passed that way than by Bamian and the Unai. The head of the pass was known as Sar Alang, so that it figures in geographical records frequently under this name also, whilst the local name acquired for it in the course of surveying in 1883 was Bajgah. To the west of this is the Kaoshan Pass, which is also known *par excellence* as the pass of "Hindu Kush"; and farther west again is the Gwalian (or Walian), an alternative to the Kaoshan when the latter is in flood. Lord selected the Parwan or Sar Alang Pass, narrow, rocky, and uneven, with a fall of about 200 feet per mile, and was fairly defeated in his attempt to cross, on October 19, by snow. This is about the closing time of the passes generally, the Parwan being only 12,300 feet in altitude, although Lord estimated it at 15,000. It is worth noting here that the Russo-Afghan Boundary Commission party crossed by the Chahardar Pass (a pass to the west again of the Walian) in the same month of October without encountering any insuperable difficulty from snow, although the Chahardar is more than 1000 feet higher than the Parwan. The fact that Lord met a khafila snow-bound near the top of the pass indicates that it was closed rather unexpectedly. Valuable observations were, however, the result of this reconnaissance. It revealed the fact that snow lies lower and deeper on the northern side of the Hindu Kush than on the southern, a fact which is in direct opposition to the general characteristics of the Himalayas. The explanation is, however, simple. In both cases the snow lies lowest on that side which reaches down to low humid plains and much precipitation of moisture. Where the barrier of the mountains breaks the upward sweep of vapour-bearing currents, there snowfall is arrested, and the highlands become desiccated. Lord's observation as a geologist also determined the constitution of these mountains. He noted the rugged uplift (beautiful from the admixture of pure white felspar and glossy black hornblende) of the central granite peaks through the overlying gneiss, schists, and slate, which thus revealed the extension of one of the great primeval folds of Himalayan conformation.

Returning from his attempt to cross the pass, Lord had the good fortune to be able to extend his researches for a day's march up the Ghorband valley, and to explore the ancient lead mines of Ferengal, which have been sunk in the Ghorband conglomerates, but had long been abandoned by the Afghans. These he found to have been worked on "knowledge and principle, not on blind chance,"—as might have been expected in a country which still possesses some of the best practical mining and irrigation engineers in the world; and he testifies, *inter alia*, to the extraordinary effect of the exceeding dryness of the interior, as evidenced by the preservation from decay of dead animals. Similar phenomena have been observed in many parts of the world both before and since, and it would appear that a satisfactory scientific explanation is still wanting for this preservative tendency of caves and mines; the atmosphere, in some cases where well-preserved remains are found, being subject to exactly the same conditions of humidity as the outer air.

It was during this interesting exploratory trip that Dr. Lord received a welcome invitation to visit Murad Beg in the Uzbek capital of Kunduz, where his professional advice was in urgent demand. Although the northern passes of the Hindu Kush were closed, the route to Badakshan was still open *via* Bamian and Khulm, and it was by this route that for the first (and apparently the last) time the journey from Kabul to Kunduz was made by European officers. Lord was accompanied by Lieut. Wood, and it is to Wood's summary of the conditions of the route that we now refer. As far as Bamian it was already beginning to be a well-known road (well known, that is, to European travellers); but beyond that point it was a new venture then, nor can any record be traced of subsequent investigations on it.

Wood summarises the route by first enumerating the seven passes which have to be negotiated before reaching Kunduz (or Khulm), and gives us a slight description of them all. Four of these passes were in Afghan territory, and three beyond. Of the passes of Ispahak and Unai he merely remarks that a mail-coach might be driven over them. The Hajigak group he regards as the "Key-guide to the Bamian line," the Hajigak being the highest pass encountered (about 11,000 feet). A little to the north is the Irak, and to the south is the Pushti Hajigak (Kafzur in modern maps); the Hajigak, or Irak, being open to khafilas for ten months of the year, but for a considerably less period to the passage of troops. The next pass Wood calls Kalloo (Panjpilan in our maps), which he regards as being lower than Hajigak. Then follows the descent into Bamian. Next is the Ak Robat Pass (10,200 feet), between the valleys of Bamian and Saighan, of which Wood reports that "it is open to wheeled traffic of all description." As far as this (the then frontier of Afghanistan) Wood refers to the fact, already recorded, that the Amir's Lieutenant—Haji Khan—was able to take field-pieces "of a size between 12- and 18-pounders." We already know the conditions under which this passage of artillery was effected. It is also on record that Nadir Shah took guns as far as Saighan. What is not so generally known is that the Uzbek chief, Murad Beg, took an 18-pounder over the rest of the route from Saighan to Kunduz. The three remaining passes are (1) the Dandan Shikan, between Saighan and Kamard, of which Wood reports the north face to be exceedingly difficult, and where he would never have believed that a gun could pass, had it not been actually traversed by the 18-pounder of Murad Beg. It may be mentioned here that it took 1100 men to drag that gun up the northern face of the pass, so that Wood is quite justified in classing it as only fit for camels. Then follows (2) the Kara Pass, leading from Kamard into the valley of the Tashkurghan River, about which the only remark made by Wood is that it may be turned by the pass of Surkh Kila (which involves a considerable detour). As Wood does not definitely state which is (3) the seventh pass, we may assume that it is the Shamsuddin, which is merely a detour to avoid an awkward reach of the Tashkurghan valley.

This is probably the first clear exposition which has ever been made of the general nature of the route connecting Kabul with Afghan Turkistan, and for it we must give Lieut. Wood all the credit that is fully due; for no subsequent surveys and investigations have materially altered his opinion. It must not be forgotten that in dealing with the story of Afghan exploration we are touching on past records. The far-sighted policy of public works development, which distinguished the late Amir Abdurrahmon, led to the extension of roads for facilitating commerce between the Oxus and Kabul, the full effect of which we have yet to learn. To the north of Kabul the roads opened to khafila traffic, *via* the Chahardar Pass and the Khawak, have introduced a new and important feature into the system of Afghan communications; and it is more than probable that the facilities for wheeled traffic between Kabul and Tashkurghan have lately been largely increased.[1] It is well also to remember that it is not the physical difficulties of rough roads and narrow passes which form the chief obstacle to the movement of large bodies of troops. Roads can be made, and crooked places straightened with comparative ease, but altitude, sheer altitude, still remains a formidable barrier, which no modern ingenuity has taught us to overcome. Deep impassable snow-drifts, and the fierce killing blasts of the north-westers of Afghanistan close these highland fields for months together; and neither roads nor railways (still less air-ships) can prevail against them.

[1] The latest reports indicate that there is now a road fit for motor traffic between Kabul and Afghan Turkistan, as well as between Kabul and Badakshan.

When Wood and Lord turned eastward from Khulm, and passed on to Kunduz and Badakshan, they were treading ground which was absolutely new to the European explorer, and which has seldom been reached even by the ubiquitous native surveyor. Lord gives us but a scanty account of Kunduz and northern Badakshan in his report, and we must turn to the immortal Wood (the discoverer of one of the Oxus' sources) for fuller and more picturesque detail. Wood left Kunduz for the upper Oxus in the early spring of 1838, and it is somewhat remarkable that he should have effected an important exploration successfully in regions so highly elevated at the worst season of the year. Before following Wood to the Oxus, we may add a few further details of that important march from Kabul to Kunduz.

It was in November 1837 that Wood and Lord were again in Kabul after their unsuccessful attempt to cross the Parwan Pass, and losing no time they started on the 15th for Badakshan by the Bamian route, crossing the Unai Pass and the elevated plain which separates it from the Helmund without difficulty. They encountered large parties of half-starved Hazaras seeking the plains on their annual pilgrimage to warm quarters for the winter. They crossed the Hajigak Pass on the 19th "with great ease," then passing the divide between the Afghan and Turkistan drainage; but they had to make a considerable detour to avoid the direct Kalu Pass, and entered Bamian by the precipitous Pimuri defile and the volcanic valley of Zohak. The Ak Robat Pass presented no difficulty. In Saighan they encountered the slave-gang of wretched Hazara people who were being then conducted to Kunduz as yearly contribution. Not much is said about the Dandan Shikan Pass dividing Saighan from Kamurd, where they were welcomed by the drunken old chief Rahmatulla Khan, whose character for reckless hospitality seems to have been a well-known feature in Badakshan. He is mentioned by every traveller who passed that way since Burnes' mission in 1832. On the 28th they reached Kuram, where they found another slave-gang being conducted by Afghans from Kabul, who had the grace to appear much ashamed of being caught red-handed in a traffic which has never commended itself to Afghan public opinion. Amongst Uzbeks it is different, the custom of man-stealing appears to have smothered every better feeling, and the traffic in human beings extends even into their domestic arrangements. Their wives are just as much "property" as their slaves. A little below Kuram they struck off to the right by a direct route to Kunduz, and passing over a district which had "a wavy surface," "affording excellent pasturage," which involved the crossing of the pass of Archa, they finally crossed the Kunduz River, and making their way through the swampy district of Baglan and Aliabad, reached Kunduz on December 4.

Wood is not enthusiastic about Kunduz. He calls it one of the most wretched towns in Murad Beg's dominions. "The appearance of Kunduz accords with the habits of an Uzbek; and by its manner, poverty and filth, may be estimated the moral worth of its inhabitants." He thought a good deal of Murad Beg all the same, and could not deny his great abilities. "But with all his high qualifications Murad Beg is but the head of an organised banditti, a nation of plunderers, whom, however, none of the neighbouring states can exterminate." Murad Beg has joined his fathers long ago, but no recent account of Kunduz much alters Wood's opinion of it. The wretched Badakshanis whom Murad Beg conquered, and whom he set to live or die in the dank pestilential marshes which fill up the space between the Badakshan highlands and the Oxus, have since then been restored to their own country; and of Badakshan we heard enough from the Amir's officials connected with the Pamir Boundary Commission to lead us to believe in it as a veritable land of promise, a land whose natural beauty and fertility may be compared to that of Kashmir—but this was told of the mountain regions, not of the Oxus flats.

When Wood got away from Kunduz and travelled eastwards to Faizabad and Jirm he does rise to enthusiasm, and tells us of scenes of natural beauty which no European eye has seen since he passed that way. On December 11, in mid-winter, Wood started from Kunduz with the permission of

Murad Beg to trace the "Jihun" to its source, and the story of this historical exploration will always be most excellent reading.

First crossing an open plain with a southern background of mountains, a plain of jungle grass, moist and unfavourable to human life, with stifling mists of vapour flitting uneasily before them, the party reached higher ground and the town of Khanabad. Behind Khanabad rises the isolated peak of Koh Umbar, 2500 feet above the plain, which appears to be a remarkable landmark in this region. It has never yet been fixed geographically. Passing through the low foot-hills surrounding this mountain, Wood emerged into the plain of Talikhan, and reached the ancient town of that name in a heavy downpour of winter rain. Here at once he encountered reminiscences of Greek occupation and claimants to the lineage of Alexander the Great. The trail of the Greek occupation of Baktria clings to Badakshan as does that of Nysa to the valleys of Kafiristan. The impression of Talikhan is summed up by Wood in the statement that it is a most disagreeable place in rainy weather. He might say the same of every town in Afghan Turkistan. He has much to say of Uzbek character and idiosyncrasies. In one respect he says that the habits of Uzbek children are superior to those of young Britons. They do not rob sparrows' nests! Here, too, Wood found himself on the track of Moorcroft. Striking eastward he crossed the

Lataband Pass (since fixed at 5650 feet in height) and first encountered snow. From the pass he describes the surrounding view as glorious: "In every quarter snowclad peaks shot up into the sky," and he gives the name Khoja Mahomed to the range (unnamed in our maps) which crosses Badakshan from north-east to south-west and forms the chief water-parting of the country. Before him the Kokcha "rolled its green waters through the rugged valley of Duvanah." The summit of Lataband is wide and level and the descent eastwards comparatively easy.

Through the pretty vale of Mashad (where Wood's party crossed the Varsach River) to Teshkhan the road led generally over hilly country covered with snow; but leaving Teshkhan it rises over the pass of Junasdara (fixed by Wood at 6600 feet), crossing one of the great spurs of the Khoja Mahomed system, and descended to Daraim, "a valley scarce a bowshot across, but watered, as all the valleys in Badakshan are, by a beautiful stream of the purest water, and bordered, wherever there is soil, by a soft velvet turf." To Daraim succeeded the plain of Argu and the "wavy" district of Reishkhan, which reached to the valley of the Kokcha. So far, since leaving Talikhan, they had met with "no sign of man or beast," but the latter were occasionally in close proximity, for the path was made easy by hog tracks, and Wood has some grisly tales to tell about the ferocity of the wolves of the country.

Junasdara he describes as a difficult or steep pass, but he notes the fact that Murad Beg had crossed it with artillery which left evidence in wheel tracks.

Of Faizabad, when Wood was there, "scarcely a vestige was left," and Jirm had become the capital of the country. But Faizabad has risen to importance since, and according to the reports of subsequent native explorers, has regained a good deal of its commercial importance. "Behind the site of the town the mountains are in successive ridges to a height of at least 2000 feet" (*i.e.* above the plain); "before it rolls the Kokcha in a rocky trench-like bed sufficiently deep to preclude all danger of inundation. Looking up the valley, the ruined and uncultivated gardens are seen to fringe the stream for a distance of two miles above the town." Faizabad is about 3950 feet above sea-level. Wood makes it about 500 feet lower, and his original observations were probably of more than equal value with those of subsequent native explorers. But certain recent improvements in exploring instruments, and certain refinements in computing the value of such observations, render the balance of probability in favour of the later records. Wood (as a sailor) was a professional observer, and where observations alone are concerned his own are excellent.

From Faizabad Wood went to Jirm, which he regarded as a more important position than

Faizabad. Elsewhere an opinion has been expressed that Jirm was the ancient capital of the country. Wood took the shortest road to Jirm which leaves the Kokcha valley and passes over the Kasur spur, winding by a high and slippery path for some distance along the face of the hill. It was a two days' march. The fort at Jirm he describes as the most important in Murad Beg's dominions. His stay at Jirm gave him the opportunity of visiting the lapis-lazuli mines near the head of the Kokcha River under the shadow of the Hindu Kush just bordering Kafiristan. This experience was useful, for Wood not only contributes a most interesting account of the working of the mines, but places on record the impracticable nature of the route which follows the Kokcha River from its source above the mines to Jirm. Near the assumed source, and not far south of the mines, there are two passes across the Hindu Kush, viz. the Minjan, which connects with the well-known Dorah and leads to Chitral, and the Mandal, which unites the head of the Bashgol valley of Kafiristan with the Minjan sources of the Kokcha. The upper reaches of the Kokcha River form the Minjan valley. Sir George Robertson crossed the Mandal in 1889 and fixed its height at over 15,000 feet, and he places the head of the Minjan (or Kokcha) much farther south than it appears in our maps. As the Mandal Pass connects Kafiristan with the Minjan valley of the Kokcha (pronounced by Wood to be almost impracticable above Jirm), it is of no great geographical importance; nor, owing to the same impracticability, is the Minjan Pass itself of any great consequence, although it connects with Chitral. The Dorah (14,800 feet), on the other hand, links up Chitral with another branch of the Kokcha, passing by the populous commercial town of Zebak, and is consequently a pass to be reckoned with in spite of its altitude. It is, in short, the chief pass over the Hindu Kush directly connecting India with Badakshan; but a pass which is nearly as high as Mont Blanc affords no royal gateway through the mountains.

Wood had sufficiently indicated the nature of the Kokcha valley between Jirm and Minjan. At the point where the mines occur it is about 200 yards wide. On both sides the mountains are "high and naked," and the river flows in a trough 70 feet below the bed of the valley. We know that it is not a practicable route. It is, however, much to be regretted that no modern explorer has touched the valley of Anjuman to the west of Minjan, which, whilst it is perhaps the main contributor to the waters of the Kokcha, also appears to have contained a recognised route in mediæval times. "If you wish not to go to destruction, avoid the narrow valley of Koran," is a native warning quoted by Wood, which seems to apply to the upper Kokcha. As a passable khafila route, Idrisi writes that from Andarab to Badakshan *towards the east* is a four days' journey. Andarab (the ancient site) being fixed at the junction of the Kasan stream with the Andarab River, the only possible route eastwards would be to the head of the Andarab at Khawak, and thence over the Nawak Pass into the Anjuman valley. Nor can the Nawak (which is as well known a pass as the Khawak) have any *raison d'être* unless it connects with that valley. There is, however, the possibility of a wrong inference from Idrisi's vague statement. "Badakshan" (which was represented by either Jirm or Faizabad) is actually east of Andarab, but to reach it by the obvious route of the lowlands, following the Kunduz River and ultimately striking eastwards, would involve starting from Andarab to the west of north. But just as the Mandal leading into the Minjan valley opens up no useful route in spite of being a well-known pass, so may the Nawak lead to nothing really practicable in Anjuman. This, indeed, is probably the case, but Anjuman remains to be explored.

Returning to Jirm, Wood awaited the opportunity for his historic exploration of the Oxus. This occurred at the end of January 1838, when news came to Jirm that the Oxus was frozen above Darwaz. The only route open to travellers in the snow time of that region is the bed of the frozen river, and Wood determined to make the best use of the opportunity. He was anxious to visit the ruby mines of the Oxus valley, but in this he did not succeed, owing to the extreme difficulties of the route following the river from its great bend northward to the district of Gharan, in which these mines are situated. He met the remnants of a party returning from Gharan which had lost nearly half its numbers from an avalanche when he reached Zebak, and wisely determined to expend his efforts in following up the course of the river to its source, rather than tempt Providence by a dangerous detour. To reach Zebak from Jirm it was necessary to follow the Kokcha to its junction with the Wardoj and then turn up that valley to Zebak. This journey in winter, with the biting blasts of the glacier-bred winds of the Hindu Kush in their teeth, was sufficiently trying. These devastated regions seem to be never free from the plague of wind. It is bad enough in the Pamirs in summer, but in winter when superadded to the effects of a cold registering 6° below zero it must have been maddening. There was no great difficulty in crossing the divide between Zebak (a small but not unimportant town) and the elbow of the Oxus River at Ishkashm.

Once again since the days of Wood a party of Europeans, which included two well-known geographers (Lockhart and Woodthorpe, both of whom have since gone to their rest), reached Ishkashm in 1886, and they were treated there with anything but hospitality. Wood seemed to have fared better. With the authority of Murad Beg to back him, and his own tact and determination to carry him through, he succeeded in overcoming all obstacles, and from point to point he made his way to where the Oxus forks at Kila Panja. From Ishkashm to Kila Panja the valley was fairly wide and open, and here for the first time he met those interesting nomadic folk the Kirghiz.

Wood's observations on the people he met are always acute and interesting, but he seems rather to have been influenced (as he admits that he may have been) by his Badakshani guides in framing his estimate of Kirghiz character. Thieves and liars they may be. These characteristics are common in High Asia, but even in these particulars they compare favourably with Uzbeks and Afghans generally. At any rate he trusted them, and it was with their assistance that he reached the source of the Oxus. Without them in a world of snow-covered hills and depressions, with every halting-place buried deep and not a trace of a track to be seen, he would have fared badly. At Kila Panja he was faced with a difficulty which gave him anxious consideration. Could he have guessed what issues would thereafter hang on a decision to that momentous question—which branch of the Oxus led to its real source—it would have caused him even greater anxiety. Ultimately he followed the northern branch which waters the Great Pamir, and after almost incredible exertion in floundering through snowdrifts and scratching his way along the ice road of the river surface, on February 19, 1838, he overlooked that long narrow expanse of frozen water which is now known as Victoria Lake.

We may discuss the question of the source, or sources, of the Oxus still, and trace them to the great glaciers from which the lakes north and south of the Nicolas range are fed, or to the ice caverns of the Hindu Kush as we please—there are many sources, and it is not in the power of mortal man to measure their relative profundity—but Wood still lives in geographical history as the first explorer of the upper Oxus, and will rank with Speke and Grant as the author of a solution to one of the great riddles of the world's hydrography. With infinite labour he dug a hole through the ice and found the depth of the lake at its centre to be only 9 feet. Were he to plumb it again in these days he would find it even less, for the lake (like all Central Asian lakes) is growing smaller and shallower year by year. The information which he absorbed about the high regions of Asia, the Pamirs (the Bam-i-dunya), was wonderfully correct on the whole, and is strong evidence of his ability in sifting the mass of miscellaneous matter with which the Asiatic usually conceals a geographical truth. He is incorrect only in the matter of altitude, which he fixes too high by more than a thousand feet, and he makes rather a strange mistake in recording that the Kunar (the Chitral River) rises north of the Hindu Kush and breaks through that range. Otherwise it would be difficult to add to or to correct his information by the light of subsequent surveys. With his return journey surrounded by all the enchantment of bursting spring in those regions we need not concern ourselves. After a three months' absence he rejoined Dr. Lord at Kunduz.

Wood's return to Kunduz was but the prelude to another journey of exploration into the northern regions of Badakshan which, in some respects, was the most important of all his investigations, for it is to the information obtained on this journey that we are still indebted for what little knowledge we possess of the general characteristics of the Oxus valley above Termez. Dr. Lord was summoned in his medical capacity to visit a chief at Hazrat Imam on the Oxus River, and Wood seized the opportunity to explore the Oxus basin from Hazrat Imam upwards through Darwaz.

Kunduz itself has been described by both authorities as a miserable swamp-bound town, with pestilential low-lying flats stretching beyond it towards the Oxus. This low country is, however, productive, and is probably by this time largely reclaimed from the grass and reed beds which covered it. Into this poisonous swamp country the Uzbek chief had imported the wretched Badakshani Tajiks whom he had captured during his extensive raids, for the purpose of colonizing. Wood reckons that 100,000 people must have originally been dumped into this swamp land, of whom barely 6000 were left when he was at Kunduz. Between the swamp and the Oxus was a splendid stretch of prairie or pasture land, reaching to the tangled jungle which immediately fringed the river below the Darwaz mountains, and this naturally excited his admiration. "Eastward" of Khulm "to the rocky barriers of Darwaz all the high-lying portion of the valley is at this season (March) a wild prairie of sweets, a verdant carpet enamelled with flowers"; and he describes the "low swelling" hills fringing these plains as "soft to the eye as the verdant sod which carpets them is to the foot." This is very pretty, and quite accords with the general description of country which forms part of the Oxus valley much farther west. The Oxus jungles, however, only occur at intervals. In Wood's time (1838) they were a thick tangle of low-growing scrub, which formed the haunts of wild beasts which were a terror to the dwellers in the plains. Tigers are found in those patches of Oxus jungle still. Hazrat Imam then ranked with Zebak and Jirm as one of the most important towns of Badakshan. East of Hazrat Imam were the traces of a gigantic canal system with its head about Sherwan, from which point to the foot-hills of Darwaz the river is (or was) fordable in almost any part. Wood forded it at a point near Yang Kila, opposite Saib in Kolab, in March, and found the river running in three channels, only one of which was really difficult. In this one, however, the current was running 4 miles an hour and the width of the channel was about 200 yards. It was only by uniting the forces of the party to oppose the stream that they were able to effect the passage. Thus was Wood probably the first European to set his foot in Kolab north of the Oxus. The river-bottom in this part of its course is generally pebbly, and at the Sherwan ford guns had been taken across. Near the mouth of the Kokcha (here a sluggish muddy stream) Wood found the site of an ancient city which he calls Barbarra, and which I think is probably the Mabara of Idrisi.

Wood's next excursion from Kunduz was by the direct high road westward to Mazar, where he and Lord hoped to find relics of Moorcroft (in which quest they were successful), and back again. This only confirmed what was previously known of the facility of that route, one of the most ancient in the world, and the attention which had been paid to it by the construction of covered tanks (they would be called Haoz farther west) at intervals for the convenience of travellers. The final recall of these two explorers to Kabul afforded them the opportunity for investigating the route which runs directly south from Kunduz by the river valley of that name to the junction with the Baghlan. Thence, following the Baghlan to its head, they crossed by the Murgh Pass into the valley of Andarab, and diverging eastward they adopted the Khawak Pass to reach the Panjshir valley, and so to Kabul. No great difficulties were encountered on this route (which has only been partially explored since), involving only two passes between the Oxus and Kabul, *i.e.* the Murgh (7400 feet) which is barely mentioned by Wood, and the Khawak (11,650 feet—Wood makes it 1500 feet higher), and it undoubtedly possesses many advantages as the modern popular route between Kabul and Badakshan. It is not the high-road to Mazar (the capital of Afghan Turkistan), which will always be represented by the Bamian route, but it must be recognised as a fairly easy means of communication in summer between the chief fords of the Oxus and the Kabul valley. The Greek settlements were about Baghlan and Andarab, and undoubtedly this was the road best known to them across the Hindu Kush, and probably as much used as the Kaoshan or Parwan passes, which were more direct. For many centuries, however, in mediæval history the Panjshir valley possessed such an evil reputation as the home of the worst robbers in Asia, that a wide berth was given to it by casual travellers. Timur Shah made good use of it for military purposes, as we have seen, and latterly it has been improved into a fair commercial high-road under Afghan engineers. The Panjshir inhabitants (once Kafirs—now truculent Mohamedans) have been reduced to reason, and it will be in the future what it has been in the ancient past—one of the great khafila routes of Asia. When Wood crossed it in May it was not really practicable for horses, and the party made their way across with considerable difficulty. It is the altitude, and the altitude alone, which renders it a formidable military barrier, and thus will it remain as part of that great Hindu Kush wall which forms the central obstruction of a buffer state.

Before taking leave of these two most successful (and most trustworthy) explorers of Afghanistan, it may be useful to sum up their views on that little-known region, Badakshan. The plains, the useful and beautiful valleys of Badakshan, lie in the embrace of a kind of mountain horse-shoe, which shuts them off from the Oxus on the north-east and east and winds round to the Hindu Kush on the south. The weak point of the semicircular barrier occurs at the junction with the Hindu Kush, where the pass between Zebak and Ishkashm is only 8700 feet high. From the slopes of the Hindu Kush mountain torrents drain down through the valleys of Zebak (called the Wardoj by Wood), the Minjan (or Kokcha) and the Anjuman into the great central river of Kokcha. Of these valleys, so far as we know, only the Wardoj is really practicable as a northerly route to the Oxus. Shutting off the head of the Kokcha system, a lateral range called Khoja Mahomed by Wood (a name which ought to be preserved), in which are many magnificent peaks, sends down its contributions north-west to the Kunduz. We know nothing about these valleys, and Wood tells us nothing, but the geographical inference is strong that all this part of upper Badakshan, including the heads of the Kokcha and Kunduz affluents, is but a wide inhospitable upland plateau of a conformation similar to that which lies east and west of it, cut into deep furrows and impassable gorges by the mountain streams which run thousands of feet below the plateau level. Within it will almost certainly be traced in due course of time the evidences of those primeval parallel folds, or wrinkles, which form the basis of Himalayan construction. Probably the Khoja Mahomed represents one of them, and the heads of the streams which feed the Kokcha and the eastern affluents of the Kunduz will be found (as already indicated in the Wardoj, or Zebak, stream) to take their source in deep, lateral, ditch-like valleys, which, closely underlying these folds, have been reshaped and altered by ages of denudation and seismic destruction.

The few inhabitants who are hidden away in remote villages and hamlets belong to the great Kafir community. This is a part of unexplored Kafiristan rather than Badakshan, and he will be a bold man indeed who undertakes its investigation. No Asiatic secret now held back from view will command so much vivid interest in its unfolding as will the ethnographical conditions of these people when we can really get at them. This mountain region occupies a large share of Badakshan. The rest of the plateau land to the west we know fairly well and have sufficiently described. The wonder of the world is that the deeply recessed valleys of it, the Bamian, Saighan, Kamard, Baghlan, and

Andarab depressions should have figured so largely in the world's history. That a confined narrow ribbon of space such as Bamian, difficult of access, placed by nature in the heart of a wilderness, should have been the centre not only of a great kingdom but the focus of a great religion, would be inexplicable if we did not remember that through it runs the connecting link between the wealth of India and the great cities of the Oxus plains and Central Asia.

The northern slopes and plains of Badakshan, between the mountains and the Oxus, form part of a region which once represented the wealth of civilization in Asia. The whole region was dotted with towns of importance in mediæval times, and the fame of its beauty and wealth had passed down the ages from the days of Assyria and Greece to those of the destroying Mongol hordes. From prehistoric times nations of the west had planted colonies in Baktria, and here are to be gathered together the threads of so many ethnographical survivals as may be represented by the successive Empires of the West. Baktria is the cradle of a marvellously mixed ethnography, and to all who have seen the weird beauty of that strange land, the fascination which it has ever possessed for the explorer and pilgrims is no matter of surprise.

A word or two must be added here about that previous explorer (Moorcroft) in Northern Afghanistan whose fate was ascertained by Lord. It is most unfortunate that some of the most important manuscripts of this unfortunate Asiatic traveller were never recovered, but his story has been written and will be referred to in further detail. We have direct testimony to the fate which finally overtook him in Dr. Lord's report of his visit to Mazar-i-Sharif, which was made with the express purpose of recovering all the records that might be traced of Moorcroft's travels in Afghan Turkistan.

A previous story of Moorcroft is highly interesting. An early Tibetan explorer (the celebrated Abbé Huc) told a tale of a certain Englishman named Moorcroft, who was reported to have lived in Lhasa for twelve years previous to the year 1838 and who was supposed to have been assassinated on his way back to India *via* Ladak. The story was circumstantial and attracted considerable attention. We know now from a memorandum of Dr. Lord written in May 1838, that in the early spring of that year when he and Lieut. Wood visited Mazar-i-Sharif they discovered that the German companion of Moorcroft (Trebeck) had died in that city, leaving amongst many loose records a slip of paper, with the date September 6, 1825, thereon, noting the fact that "Mr. M." (Moorcroft) "died on August 27th." Dr. Lord's investigations led him to the conclusion that Moorcroft died at Andkhui, a victim "not more to the baneful effects of the climate than to the web of treachery and intrigue with which he found himself surrounded and his return cut off." Trebeck, who seems to have been held in great estimation by the Afghans, died soon after; neither traveller leaving any substantial account of his adventures. Moorcroft's books (thirty volumes) were recovered, and the list of them would surprise any modern traveller who believes in a light and handy equipment. Dr. Lord's inquiries, in my opinion, effectually dispose of the venerable Abbé's story of Moorcroft's residence at Lhasa; although, of course, the record of his visit to Western Tibet and the Manasarawar Lakes earlier in the century must have been well enough known; and the Tibetans may possibly have believed in a reincarnation of their one and only European visitor in their own capital.

This chapter cannot be closed without a tribute of respect to those most able and enterprising geographers who (chiefly as assistants to Burnes) were the means of first giving to the world a reasonable knowledge of the geography of Afghanistan. The names of Leech, Lord, and Wood will always remain great in geographical story, and although none of them individually (nor, indeed, all of them collectively) covered anything like as wide an area as the American Masson, they effected a far greater change in the maps of the period—for Masson was no map-maker. As regards Sir Alexander Burnes, his initiative in all that pertained to geographical exploration was great and valuable, but he was individually more connected with the exploitation of Central Asian and Persian geography than with that of Afghanistan. Previous to the year 1836, when he undertook his political mission to Kabul (and when he was travelling over comparatively old ground), he had already extended his journeys across the Hindu Kush to the Oxus, Bokhara, and Persia; and the book which he published in 1834 was a revelation in Central Asian physiography and policy. But as an explorer in Afghanistan he owed his information chiefly to his assistants, and undoubtedly he was splendidly well served. The ridiculous and costly impedimenta which seemed to be recognised as a necessary accompaniment to a campaign or "an occupation" in those days—the magnificent tents, the elephants, wives and nurseries and retinue of military officers—found no place whatever in the explorers' camps. Men were content to make their way from point to point and take their chance of native hospitality. They lived with the people amongst whom they moved, and they gradually became almost as much of them as with them. Perhaps their views, political and social, became somewhat too warmly tinted with local colour by these methods, but undoubtedly they learned more and they saw more, and they acquired a wider, deeper sympathy with native aspirations and native character than is possible to travellers who move *en prince* amongst a people who only interest them as races dominating a certain section of the mountains and plains of a strange world. All honour to the names of Leech, Lord, and Wood—especially Wood.

CHAPTER XIII

ACROSS AFGHANISTAN TO BOKHARA—MOORCROFT

One of the most disappointing of the early British explorers of our Indian trans-frontier was Moorcroft. Disappointing, because he got so little geographical information out of so large an area of adventure. Moorcroft was a veterinary surgeon blessed with an unusually good education and all the impulse of a nomadic wanderer. He was Superintendent of the H.E.I. Company's stud at Calcutta, and his views on agricultural subjects generally, especially the improvement of stock, were certainly in advance of his time, although it seems extraordinary that he should have sought further inspiration in the wilds of the then unexplored trans-Himalayas or in Central Asia. The Government of India were evidently sceptical as to the value of such researches, and he received but cold comfort from their grudging spirit of support, which ended in a threat to cut off his pay altogether after a few years' sojourn in Ladak whilst studying the elementary principles of Tibetan farming. Neither would they supply him with the ample stock of merchandise which he asked for as a means of opening up trade with those chilly countries; and when, finally, he assumed the position of a high political functionary, and became the vehicle of an offer to the Government of India of the sovereignty of Ladak (which certainly might have led to complications with the Sikh Government of the Punjab) he was rather curtly told to mind his own business.

On the whole, it is tolerably clear that the Government represented by old John Company was not much more favourable to irresponsible travelling over the border and political intermeddling than is our modern Imperial institution. However, the fact remains that Moorcroft showed a spirit of daring enterprise, which led to the acquirement of a vast amount of most important information about countries and peoples contiguous to India of whom the Government of the time must have been in utter ignorance. When he first exploited Ladak, Leh was the *ultima thule* of geographical investigation. What lay beyond it was almost blank conjecture, and a residence of two years must have ended in the amassing of a vast fund of useful information. Unfortunately, much of that information was lost at his death, and the correspondence and notes which came into the hands of his biographer were of such a character—so extraordinarily discursive and frequently so little relevant to the subject of his investigation—as to leave an impression that Moorcroft was certainly eccentric in his correspondence if not in more material ways. We get very little original geographical suggestion from him; but his constant and faithful companion Trebeck is much more consistent and careful in such detail as we find due to his personal observation, and it is to Trebeck rather than Moorcroft that the thanks of the Asiatic map-maker are due. With the Ladak episodes of Moorcroft's career we have nothing to do here, beyond noting that there is ample evidence that he never reached Lhasa, and never resided there, in spite of the persistent rumours which prevailed (even in Tibet) that a traveller of his name had lived in the city. It is exceedingly difficult to account for this rumour, unless indeed we credit the authors of it with a confusion of ideas between Lhasa, the capital of Tibet proper, and Leh, the capital of little Tibet.

The interest of Moorcroft's adventures so far as we are now concerned commences with his journey from Peshawar to Kabul, Badakshan and Bokhara in 1824, when he was undoubtedly the first in the field of British Central Asiatic exploration. He owed his safe conduct from Peshawar (which place he reached only after some most unpleasant experiences in passing through the Sikh dominions of the Punjab) to a political crisis. Dost Mahomed Khan was consolidating his power at Kabul, but he had not then squared accounts with Habibullah the son of the former governor, his deceased elder brother Mahomed Azim Khan; and certain other members of his family (his brothers, Yar Mahomed, Pir Mahomed, and Sultan Mahomed), who were governors in the Indus provinces, thought it as well to step in and effect an arrangement. It was their stately march to Kabul which was Moorcroft's opportunity. Those were days when an Englishman was yet of interest to the Afghan potentate, who knew not what turn of fortune's wheel might necessitate an appeal for the intervention of the English.

Moorcroft did not love the Afghans, and between the unauthorised robbers of the Kabul road and the official despoilers of the city he paid dearly for the right of transit through Afghanistan of himself and his merchandise. It was this assumed rôle of merchant (if indeed it was assumed) that hampered Moorcroft from first to last in his journeys beyond the frontier of British India. There was something to be made out of him, either by fair means or foul, and the rapacious exactions to which he was subjected were probably not in the least modified by his obstinate refusals to meet what he considered unjust demands. Invariably he had to pay in the end. His account of the road to Kabul is interesting from the keen observation which he brought to bear on his surroundings. He has much to say about the groups of Buddhist buildings which are so marked a feature at various points of the route, and his previous experiences in Tibet left him little room for doubt as to the nature of them. It is strange that locally there was not a tale to be told, not even a legend about them, which even indefinitely maintained their Buddhist origin.

From Kabul Moorcroft succeeded in getting free with surprisingly little difficulty, though several members of his party declined to go farther. He gradually made his way by the Unai and Hajigak passes to Bamian, and thence to Haibak and Balkh. He was not slow to recognize the connection between the obvious Buddhist relics of Bamian and those which he had seen on the Kabul road; and at Haibak he visited a tope called Takht-i-Rustam (a generic name for these topes in Central Asia) of which his description tallies more or less with that of Captain Talbot, R.E., who unearthed what is probably the same relic some sixty years later. To Moorcroft we owe the identification of Haibak with the old mediæval town of Semenjan, and he states that he was told on the spot that this was its ancient name. No such name was recognised sixty years later, but the evidence of Idrisi's records confirms the fact beyond dispute.

We need not enter into details of this well-worn and often described route. Moorcroft's best efforts were not directed to gazetteering, and we have much abler and more complete accounts of it than his. After passing the Ak Robat divide, Moorcroft found himself beyond Afghan jurisdiction and within the reach of that historic Uzbek chieftain, Murad Beg of Kunduz. Although Murad Beg was little better than a successful freebooter, he is a personage who has left his own definite mark on the history of days when British interest was just dawning on the Oxus banks. Moorcroft fell into his hands, and in spite of introductions he fared exceedingly badly. Indeed there can be little doubt that the cupidity excited by the possibility of so much plunder would have ended fatally for him, but for a happy inspiration which occurred to him when his affairs appeared to be *in extremis*. With great difficulty and at the peril of his life he made his way eastward to Talikhan, where resided a saintly Pirzada, uncle of Murad Beg, the one righteous man whose upright and dignified character redeemed his people from the taint of utter barbarism and treachery. He had discrimination enough to read Moorcroft aright, and at once discountenanced the tales that had been assiduously set abroad of his being a British spy upon the land; and he had firmness and authority sufficient to deliver him from the rapacity of his truculent nephew, and procure him freedom to depart after months of delay in the pestilential atmosphere of Kunduz. Yet this grand old Mahomedan saint patronised the institution of slavery, and was not above making a profit out of it, though at the same time he firmly declined to receive presents or have bribes for his good offices.

As other travellers following in Moorcroft's footsteps at no great distance of time fell also into the hands of Murad Beg, and experienced very different treatment, it is useful just to note Moorcroft's description of him. He says: "I scarcely ever beheld a more forbidding countenance. His extremely high cheekbones gave the appearance to the skin of the face of its being unnaturally stretched, whilst the narrowness of the lower jaw left scarcely room for the teeth which were standing in all directions; he was extremely near-sighted." Not an attractive description! The spring had well advanced, and it was not till the middle of February 1825 that Moorcroft was able to resume his journey to the Oxus. He travelled from Kunduz to Tashkurghan and Mazar, and from the latter place he followed the most direct route to Bokhara *via* the Khwaja Salar ferry across the Oxus, reaching Bokhara on February 25. Here his narrative ends, and we only know from Dr. Lord and Wood that he returned from Bokhara to Andkhui, and died there apparently of fever contracted in Kunduz. He was buried near Balkh. Trebeck died soon after, and was buried at Mazar-i-Sharif. Burnes visited and described the tombs of both travellers, but they have long since disappeared.

As a geographer there is much that is wanting in the methods of this most enterprising traveller, who at least pioneered the way to High Asia from British India but who never made geographical exploration a primary object of his labours. He was true to the last to his trade as a student of agriculture, and it is in this particular, rather than in the regions of geography or history, that the value of his studies chiefly lies. He was the first to point out the general character of that disastrous road to Kabul which has cost England so dear, and he is still, with Burnes and Lord and Wood, our chief authority for the general characteristics of Badakshan and of the Oxus valley east of Balkh. He did not, however, touch the Oxus east of Khwaja Salar, and consequently did not see or appreciate the great spread of splendid pastoral country which lies between the pestilential marsh lands of Kunduz and the river.

One would be apt to gather a pessimistic idea of lower Badakshan from the pages of Moorcroft's story, which are undoubtedly tinted strongly with the gloomy and grey colouring of his own unhappy experiences. Of Balkh he has very little to say; he noted no antiquities about Balkh, but he calls attention to the wide spaces covered with ruins which are to be found at intervals scattered over the plains between Balkh and the Oxus. It is a little difficult to follow his exact route across the Oxus plains by the light of modern maps, but his Feruckabad is probably our Feruk, and I gather that his Akbarabad is Akcha or Akcha-abad. The condition of Balkh, of Akcha, and of the ruin-studded plains of the Oxus were evidently much the same in 1824 as they were in 1884 Khwaja Salar (where Moorcroft crossed the Oxus in ferry-boats drawn by horses) has since become historical. It was accepted in the Anglo-Russian protocols defining the Afghan boundary as an important point in the Russo-Afghan boundary delimitation, but it was not to be found. Moorcroft gives a very good reason for its disappearance, by stating that the place was razed to the ground just the day before he arrived there. Since then the ruins of the old village have been devoured by the shifting Oxus, and nothing but a ziarat at some distance from the river remains as a record of the distinguished saint who gave it its name.

CHAPTER XIV

BURNES

No traveller who ever returned to his country with tales of stirring adventure ever attracted more interest, or even astonishment, than Lieut. Alexander Burnes. He published his story in 1835, when the Oxus regions of Asia were but vaguely outlined and shadowy geography. It did not matter that they had been the scene of classical history for more than 2000 years, and that the whole network of Oxus roads and rivers had been written about and traversed by European hosts for centuries before our era. That story belonged to a buried past, and the British occupation of India had come about in modern history by way of the sea. England and Russia were then searching forward into Central Asia like two blind wrestlers in the dark, feeling their ground before them ere they came to grips. A veil of mystery hung over these highlands, a geographical fog that had thickened up, with just a thinner space in it here and there, where a gleam of light had penetrated, but never dispersed it, since the days when Assyrian and Persian, Skyth, Greek, and Mongul wandered through the highest of Asiatic highways at their own sweet will.

In the present year of grace and of red tape bindings to most books of Asiatic travels, when the best of the geographical information accumulated by the few who bear with them the seal of officialdom is pigeon-holed for a use that never will be made of it, it is quite refreshing to fall back on these most entertaining records of men who (whether official or otherwise) all travelled under the same conditions of association with the natives of the country they traversed, accepting their hospitality, speaking their language, assuming their manners and dress, and passing with the crowd (and with the crowd only) as casual wayfarers. The fact of their European origin was almost always suspected, if not known, to certain of the better informed of their Asiatic hosts, but they were seldom given away. It was nobody's business to quarrel with England then. A hundred years ago the military credit of England stood high, and the irrepressible advance of the red line of the British India-border impressed the mind of the Asiatic of the highlands beyond the plains as evidence of an irresistible power. Russia then made no such impression. She was still far off, and the ties of commerce bound the Oxus Khanates to India, even when Russian goods were in Asiatic markets. The bankers of the country were Hindus —traders from the great commercial centre of

Shikarpur. It is strange to read of this constant contact with Hindus in every part of Central Asia in those days, when the *hundi* (or bill) of a Shikarpur banker was as good as a letter of credit in any bazaar as far as the Russian border. The power of England in India undoubtedly loomed much larger in Asiatic eyes before the disasters of the first Afghan war, and Englishmen of the type of Burnes, Christie, Pottinger, Vigne, and Broadfoot were able to carry out prolonged journeys through districts that are certainly not open to English exploration now. Even were English officers to-day free under existing political conditions to travel beyond the British border at all, it is doubtful whether any disguise would serve as a protection.

The day has passed for such ventures as those of Burnes, and we must turn back a page or two in geographical history if we wish to appreciate the full value of British enterprise in exploring Afghanistan. Undoubtedly Burnes ranks high as a geographer and original pioneer. The fact that there is little or nothing left of the scene of his travels in 1830-32 and 1833 which has not been reduced to scientific mapping now, does not in any way detract from the merit of his early work; although it must be confessed that the perils of disguise prevented the use of any but the very crudest methods of ascertaining position and distance, and his map results would, in these days, be regarded as disappointing. Sind and the Punjab being trans-border lands, there were always useful and handy opportunities for teaching the enterprising subaltern of Bombay Infantry how to travel intelligently; with the natural result that no corps in the world possessed a more splendid record of geographical achievement than the Bombay N.I.

Burnes began well in the Quartermaster-General's department, and was soon entrusted with political power. Full early in his career he was despatched with an enterprising sailor, Lieut. Wood, on a voyage up the Indus which was to determine the commercial possibilities of its navigation, and which did in fact lead to the formation of the Indus flotilla—some fragments of which possibly exist still. It is most interesting to read the able reports compiled by these young officers; and one might speculate idly as to the feelings with which they would now learn that within half a century their flotilla had come and gone, superseded by one of the best paying of Indian railways. Their feelings would probably be much the same as ours could we see fifty years hence a well-established electric train service between Kabul and Peshawar, and a double or treble line of rails linking up Russia with India *via* Herat. We shall not see it. It will be left to another generation to write of its accomplishment.

Searching the archives of the Royal Geographical Society for the story of Burnes the traveller (apart from the voluminous records of Burnes the diplomat), I came across a book with this simple inscription on the title-page: "To the Royal Geographical Society of London, with the best wishes for its prosperity by the Author." This is Vol. I. of Burnes' Travels. It is written in the attenuated, pointed, and ladylike style which was the style of the very early Victorian era. It hardly leads to an impression of forceful and enterprising character.

On January 2, 1831, Burnes made his first plunge into the wilderness which lay between him and Lahore, the capital of the Sikh kingdom, and he entered that city on the 17th. There he was most hospitably received by the French officers in the service of Ranjit Singh, Messieurs Allard and Court, and was welcomed by the Maharaja Ranjit Singh, who treated him with "marked affability." Burnes was accompanied by Dr. Gerard, and the two travellers were taken by Ranjit Singh to a hunting party in the Punjab; a description of which serves as a forcible illustration of the changes which less than one century of British administration has effected in the plains of India. Never will its like be seen again in the Land of the Five Rivers. The guests' tents were made of Kashmir shawls, and were about 14 feet square. One tent was red and the other white, and they were connected by tent-walls of the same material, shaded by a *Shamiana* supported on silver-mounted poles. In each tent stood a camp-bed with Kashmir shawl curtains. It was, as Burnes remarks, not an encampment suited to the Punjab jungles; and the hunting procession headed by the Maharaja, dressed in a tunic of green shawls, lined with fur, his dagger studded with the richest brilliants, and a light metal shield, the gift of the ex-king of Kabul (Shah Sujah, who, it will be remembered, also surrendered the Koh-i-Nor diamond to Ranjit Singh about this time), as the finishing touch to his equipment, must have been quite melodramatic in its effects of colour and movement. It was, as a matter of fact, a pig-sticking expedition, but the game fell to the sword rather than to the spear; such of it, that is to say, as was not caught in traps. The party was terminated by a hog-baiting exhibition, in which dogs were used to worry the captive pigs, after the latter were tied by one leg to a stake. When the pigs were sufficiently infuriated, the entertainment concluded with letting them loose through the camp, in order, as Ranjit said, "that men might praise his humanity."

Such episodes, however they might beguile the journey to the Afghan frontier, belong to other histories than that of Afghan exploration, and little more need be said of Burnes' experiences before reaching the Afghan city of Peshawar, than that he experienced very different treatment *en route* to that which made Moorcroft's journey both perilous and disheartening. In Peshawar the two brothers of Dost Mahomed Khan (Sultan Mahomed and Pir Mahomed) seem to have rivalled each other in courtly attentions to their guests, and Burnes was as much enchanted with this garden of the North-West as any traveller of to-day would be, provided that his visit were suitably timed. Burnes thus sums up his impression of Ranjit Singh: "I never quitted the presence of a native of Asia with such impressions as I left this man; without education, and without a guide, he conducts all the affairs of his kingdom with surpassing energy and vigour, and yet he wields his power with a moderation quite unprecedented in an Eastern prince."

On leaving Lahore Burnes received this salutary advice from M. Court, packed in a French proverb, "Si tu veux vivre en paix en voyageant, fais en sorte de hurler comme les loups avec qui tu te trouves." And he set himself to conform to this text (and to the excellent sermon which accompanied it) with a determination which undoubtedly served as the foundation of his remarkable success as a traveller. It cannot be too often insisted that the experiences of intelligent and cultivated Europeans in the days of close association with the Asiatic led to an appreciation of native character and to an intimacy with native methods, which is only to be found in India now amongst missionaries and police officers, if it is to be found at all. But even with all the advantages possessed by such experiences as those of Burnes and of the intrepid school of Asiatic travellers of his time, it required an intuitive discernment almost amounting to genius to detect the motive springs of Eastern political action.

It may be doubted (as Masson doubted) whether to the day of his death Burnes himself quite understood either the Afghan or the Sikh. But he vigorously conformed to native usages in all outward show: "We threw away all our European clothes and adopted without reserve the costume of the Asiatic. We gave away our tents, beds, and boxes, and broke our tables and chairs—a blanket serves to cover the saddle and to sleep under. . . . The greater portion of my now limited wardrobe found a place in the 'kurjin.' A single mule carried the whole of the baggage." Armed with letters of introduction from a holy man (Fazl Haq), who boasted a horde of disciples in Bokhara, and with all the graceful good wishes which an Afghan potentate knows how to bestow, Burnes left Peshawar and the two Afghan sirdars, and started for Kabul. It is instructive to note that he avoided the Khaibar route, which had an evil reputation.

It would be interesting to trace Burnes' route from Peshawar to Bokhara, *via* Kabul and Bamian, were it not that we are dealing with ground already sufficiently well discussed in these pages. Moreover, Burnes travelled to Kabul in company which permitted him to make little or no use of his opportunities for original geographical research. After he left Kabul the vicissitudes and difficulties that beset him were only such as might be experienced by any recognised official political mission, and he experienced none of the vexatious opposition and delay which was so fatal to Moorcroft. *En route* he passed through Bamian, Haibak, Khulm, and Balkh; he visited Kunduz, and identified the tomb of Trebeck at Mazar; and by the light of a brilliant moon he stood by the grave of Moorcroft, which he found under a wall outside the city, apart from the Mussulman cemeteries. The three days passed at Balkh were assiduously employed in local investigation and the collection of coins and relics. He found coins, or tokens, dating from early Persian occupation to the Mogul dynasties, and he notes the size of the bricks and their shape, which he describes as oblong approaching to square; but he mentions no inscriptions.

At this time Balkh was in the hands of the Bokhara chief, and Burnes was already in Bokhara territory. The journey across the plains to the Oxus was made on camels, Burnes being seated in a kajawa, and balancing his servant on the other side. It was slow, but it gave him the opportunity of overlooking the broad Oxus plain and noting the general accuracy of the description given of it by Quintus Curtius. As they approached the Oxus it was found necessary to employ a Turkman guard. Burnes does not say from what Turkman tribe his guard was taken, but from his description of them, their dress, equipment, and steeds, they were clearly men of the same Ersari tribe that was found fifty years later in the same neighbourhood by the Russo-Afghan Boundary

Commission. "They rode good horses and were armed with a sword and long spear. They were not encumbered with shields and powder-horns like other Asiatics, and only a few had matchlocks. . . . They never use more than a single rein, which sets off their horses to advantage."

On the banks of the river they halted near the small village of Khwaja Salar. This was the same place evidently that Moorcroft visited, and which he described as destroyed in a raid; and it was here that Burnes made use of the peculiar horse-drawn ferry which has already been described. Fifty years later the ferry was at Kilif, and nothing was to be found of the "village" of Khwaja Salar. Burnes' astonishment at the quaint, but most efficient, method of utilizing the power of swimming horses to haul the great ferry-boats has been shared by every one who has seen them since; but he noted a fact which has not been observed by other travellers, viz. that *any* horse was taken for the purpose, no matter whether trained or not; and he states that the horses were yoked to the boat by a rope fixed to the hair of the mane. If so, this method was improved on during the next half-century, for the rope is now attached to a surcingle. "One of the boats was dragged over by two of our jaded ponies; and the vessel which attempted to follow us without them was carried so far down the stream as to detain us a whole day on the banks till it could be brought up to the camp of our caravan." The river at this point is about 800 yards wide, and runs at the rate of three to four miles an hour. The crossing was effected in fifteen minutes. Burnes adds: "I see nothing to prevent the general adoption of this expeditious mode of crossing a river. . . . I had never before seen the horse converted to such a use; and in my travels through India I had always considered that noble animal as a great encumbrance in crossing a river." And yet after two centuries of military training in the plains of India, we English have not yet arrived at this economical use of this great motive power always at our command in a campaign!

After passing the Oxus the chief interest of Burnes' story commences. His life at Bokhara and his subsequent journey through the Turkman deserts to Persia form a record which, combined with his own physical capability, his energy, and his unfailing tact, good humour, and modesty, stamp him as one of the greatest of English travellers. His name has its own high place in geographical annals. We shall never cease to admire the traveller, whatever we may think of the diplomat. But once over the Oxus his story hardly concerns the gates of India. He was beyond them, he had passed through, and was now on the far landward side, still on a road to India; but it is a road over which it no longer concerns us to follow him.

CHAPTER XV

THE GATES OF GHAZNI—VIGNE

AMONGST original explorers of Afghanistan place must be found for G. T. Vigne, who made in 1836 a venturesome, and, as it proved, a most successful exploration of the Gomul route from the Indus to Ghazni. Vigne was not a professional geographer so much as a botanist and geologist, and the value of his work lies chiefly in the results of his researches in those two branches of science, although he has left on record a map of his journey which quite sufficiently illustrates his route. He had previously visited Ladak (Little Tibet) and Kashmir, and had made passing acquaintance with the Chief of the Punjab, Ranjit Singh, in whose service foreigners found honourable employment. Masson was in the field at the same time as Vigne, and the success of his antiquarian researches in Northern Afghanistan, as well as those of Honigberger and other archæologists during the time that Dost Mahomed ruled in Kabul, and whilst the Amir's brother, Jabar Khan, befriended

Europeans, indicated a very different political atmosphere from that which has subsequently clouded the Afghan horizon, so far as European travellers are concerned.

Vigne found no difficulty whatever in passing through Punjab territory to the Indus Valley near Dera Ismail Khan, where he joined a Lohani khafila which was making its annual journey to Ghazni with a valuable stock of merchandise consisting chiefly of English goods. In the genial month of May the khafila left Draband and took the world-old Gomul route through the frontier hills to the central uplands of Afghanistan. The heat must have been awful, and as Vigne lived the life of the Lohani merchants, and shared their primitive shelter from day to day, it is not surprising that we find him complaining gently of the climate. The Lohanis treated him with the utmost kindness and consideration from first to last; and the story of his travels is in pleasing contrast to the tale told by Masson about the same time, of his adventures on the Kandahar side. This was due chiefly, no doubt, to Vigne's success as a doctor. It is always the doctors who make the best way amongst uncivilized peoples, and India especially (or rather the British Ráj in India) owes almost as much to doctors as to politicians. There is also a fellow-feeling which binds together travellers of all sorts and conditions when bound for the same bourne, taking together the same risks, experiencing the same trials and difficulties, and enjoying unrestrained intercourse. This kind of fellowship is world wide. One can trace a genial spirit of *camaraderie* pervading the wanderings of Chinese pilgrims, the tracks of mediæval Arab merchants, the ways of modern missionaries, or the ocean paths of sailors. Once on the move, with the sweet influences of primitive nature pervading earth and air around, we may find, even in these days, that the Afghan becomes quite a sociable companion, and that he is to be trusted so far as he gives his word.

Vigne seems to have had no trouble whatever except such as arose from the persistent neglect of his medical instructions in cases of severe illness. As the khafila followed the Gomul River closely, it was, of course, subject to attack from the irrepressible Waziris on its flank, and had to pay heavy duties to the Suliman Khel Ghilzais as soon as it touched their country. There is little change in these respects since 1836, except that the Gomul route has been made plain and easy through the first bands of frontier hills till it reaches the plateau, and the Waziris are under better control. The interest of the journey lies in that section of it which connects Domandi (the junction of the Gomul and the Kundar Rivers) with Ghazni. This central part of Afghanistan has never yet been surveyed. From the Takht-i-Suliman a few peaks have been indifferently fixed on the ridges which form the divide between the Gomul and the Ghazni drainage, but the hilly country beyond, stretching to the Ghazni plain, is absolutely unreconnoitred. We have still to appeal to Broadfoot and Vigne for geographical authority in these regions, although native information (but not native surveyors) has furnished details of a route which sufficiently corresponds with that of both these enterprising travellers.

There is some confusion about dates in Vigne's account, but it appears that the khafila reached the Sarwandi Pass (which he calls Sir-i-koll—7200 feet) over the central divide on the 12th June, and thence descended into the Kattawaz country on the Ghazni side of this central water-parting. About this region we have no accurate geographical knowledge. Beyond the Sarwandi ridge, and intervening between it and Ghazni, is a secondary pass, called Gazdarra in our maps, crossing a ridge near the northern foot of which is Dihsai (the nearest approach to Vigne's Dshara), which was reached by Vigne on the 16th June. Probably the two names represent the same place.

Vigne's description of the central Sarwandi ridge corresponds generally with what we know in other parts of the nature of those long sweeping folds which traverse the central plateau from north-east to south-west, preserving more or less a direction parallel to the frontier. He writes of it as a broken and tumbled mass of sandstone, but about "Dshara" he speaks of gently undulating hills exhibiting small peaks of limestone and denuded patches of shingle. Between the Sarwandi and the Dshara ridge the plain was covered with glittering sand and was sweet with the scent of wild thyme. Somewhere on the "level-topped" Sarwandi ridge there was said to be the ruins of an ancient city called Zohaka, with gates of burnt brick, which Vigne did not see, but in his map he indicates a position for it a long way to the east of the ridge. It is quite probable that the ruins of more than one ancient city are to be found in the neighbourhood of this very ancient highway. Ancient as it is, however, it formed no part of the mediæval commercial system of the Arabs — a system which apparently did not include the frontier passes into India; and I have failed to identify Vigne's Zohaka with any previous indications. These uplands to the south of Ghazni evidently partake of the general characteristics of the Wardak and Logar Valleys beyond them, intervening between Ghazni and Kabul. Vigne was enchanted with the prospect around him, and with the clear sweet atmosphere filled with the aroma of wild thyme, wormwood, and the scented willow. It has charmed many a weary soldier since his time.

At Dshara, finding that the Lohani khafila was not going to Ghazni but intended to follow a straighter route to Kabul, whilst at the same time a very ready and profitable business was being done in the well-populated valleys around, Vigne set off by himself with one Kizzilbash guide for Ghazni. He says many hard things of the Lohanis for breaking their promise of escort to Ghazni, remarks which seem scarcely to accord with his free acknowledgments of their great kindness to him elsewhere. As the opinion of so observant a traveller, sharing the trials of the road with a band of native merchants, is always interesting when it concerns the company with which he was associated, I will quote his opinion of the Lohanis. "Taking them altogether, I look on the Lohanis as the most respectable of the Mahomedans and the most worthy of the notice and assistance of our countrymen. The Turkish gentleman is said to be a man of his word; he must be an enviable exception; but I otherwise solemnly believe that there is not a Mahomedan—Sunni or Shiah—between Constantinople and Yarkand who would hesitate to cheat a Feringi, Frank or European, and who would not lie and scheme and try to deceive when the temptation was worth his doing so," etc. This, of course, includes the Lohanis.

At Ghazni, Vigne found a servant of Moorcroft's, who gave him interesting information about the travels of that unfortunate explorer; and he takes some useful notes of the present military position and former condition of that city before its utter destruction by Allah-u-din, Ghuri. He determined to depart somewhat from the regular route to

Kabul, and diverged from the straight road which runs to the Sher-i-dahan in order to visit the "bund-i-sultan," or reservoir, which had been constructed by Mahmud on the Ghazni River for the proper water-supply of the town in its palmy days. As his last day's travel took him to Lungar and Maidan before reaching Kabul he evidently made a considerable detour westward. He inspected a copper mine (with which he was greatly disappointed) at a place called Shibar *en route*. To reach Shibar he made a long day's march from Ser-ab (? Sar-i-ab), near the head of the Logar River. It is difficult to trace this part of his route by the light of the map which he borrowed from Honigberger. He clearly followed up the Ghazni River nearly to its source, and then struck across to the head of the Logar, where he correctly places Ser-ab, and where he found an agent of Masson's engaged in excavating a tope. He next visited Shibar, and finally marched by Lungar to Maidan and Kabul. He must, therefore, have crossed the divide between the Ghazni River and the Logar, but we fail to follow him to the Shibar copper mine.

Shibar is the name of the pass which divides the Turkistan drainage from the Ghorband, or Kabul, system; but it would be totally impracticable to reach that point in a day's excursion from Ser-ab. We must, therefore, conclude that there is another Shibar somewhere, undetected by our surveyors.

At Kabul he received a hospitable welcome from

the Nawab Jabar Khan, brother of the Amir Dost Mahomed, and here he fell in with Masson. We need not trace his journey farther, for his subsequent footsteps only followed the well-worn tracks to the Punjab. To Vigne we owe a vague reference to a yet earlier English traveller in Afghanistan, one Hicks, who died and was buried near the Peshawar gate of the old city. The inscription on his tomb in English was—

HICKS, SON OF WILLIAM AND ELIZABETH HICKS,

and Vigne adds that "by its date he must have lived a hundred and fifty years ago." This is the earliest record we have of an English traveller reaching Kabul, and it is strange that nothing is known about Hicks, who certainly could not have inscribed his own epitaph! The remarkable feature about the tomb is that such a memorial of a Christian burial should have remained so long unmolested in a Moslem country. No vestige of the tomb was discovered during the occupation of Kabul in 1879–80.

CHAPTER XVI

ENGLISH OFFICIAL EXPLORATION—BROADFOOT

In the year 1839 and in the month of October Lieut. J. S. Broadfoot of the Indian Engineers made a memorable excursion across Central Afghanistan, intervening between Ghazni and the Indus Valley, which resulted in the acquisition of much information about one of the gates of India which is too little known. No one has followed his tracks since with any means of making a better reconnaissance, nor has any one added much to the information obtained by him. It is true that Vigne had been over the ground before him, but there is no comparison between the use which Broadfoot made of his opportunities and the geography which Vigne secured. Both took their lives in their hands, but Vigne passed along with his Lohani khafila in days preceding the British occupation of Afghanistan. There was no fanatical hostility displayed towards him. On the contrary, his medical profession was a recommendation which won him friends and good fellowship all along the line. A few years had much changed the national (if one can use such a word with regard to Afghanistan) feeling towards the European. From day to day, and almost from hour to hour, Broadfoot felt that his life hung on the chances of the moment. He was told by friends and enemies alike that he would most certainly be killed. Yet he survived to do good service in other fields, and to maintain the reputation of that most distinguished branch of the military service, the Indian Engineers. Broadfoot was but typical of his corps, even in the scientific ability displayed in his researches, the clearness and the soundness of the views he expresses, the determined pluck of his enterprise, and his knowledge of native life and character. Durand, North, Leach, and Broadfoot were Lieutenants of Engineers at the same time, and their reports and their work are all historical records.

Previously to his start on the Gomul reconnaissance Broadfoot had the opportunity of reconnoitring much of the country to the south of Ghazni bordering the Kandahar-Ghazni route. He had, therefore, a very fair acquaintance with the people with whom he had to deal, and a fairly well fixed point of departure for his work. His methods were the time-honoured methods of many past generations of explorers. He took his bearings with the prismatic compass, and he reckoned his distance by the mean values obtained from three men pacing. Consequently, he could not pretend, in such circumstances as he was placed (being hardly able to leave his tent in spite of his disguise), to complete much in the way of topography; but his clear description of the ground he passed over, and the people he passed amongst, furnishes nearly all that is necessary to enable us to realise the practical value and the political difficulty of that important line of communication with Central Afghanistan.

From Ghazni southwards to Pannah there is nothing but open plain. From near Pannah to the Sarwandi Pass, which crosses the main divide (the Kohnak range) between the Helmund and the Indus basins, there is much of the ridge and furrow formation which distinguishes the north-western frontier, the alignment of the ridges being from N.E. to S.W., but the Gazdarra Pass over the Kattawaz ridge is not formidable, and the road along the plain of Kattawaz is open. In Kattawaz were groups of villages, denoting a settled population, and as much cultivation as might be possible amidst a lawless, crop-destroying, and raiding generation of Ghilzais.

"Kattasang, as viewed from Dand" (on the northern side) "appears a mass of undulating hills, and as bare as a desert; it is the resort in summer of some pastoral families of Suliman Khels." Approaching the main divide of Sarwandi by the Sargo Pass two forts are passed near Sargo, which sufficiently well illustrate the characteristics of perpetual feud common to clans or families of the

Ghilzai fraternity. The forts are close to each other; one of them is known as Ghlo kala (thieves' fort), but they are probably both equally worthy of the name. The inhabitants of these forts absolutely destroyed each other in a family feud, so that nothing now remains. Their very waters have dried up.

Near the Sargo, on the Ghazni side of the Sarwandi Pass, is Schintza, at which place Vigne also halted, and from Schintza commences the real ascent to the Sarwandi. The ascent, and indeed the crossing altogether, are described by Broadfoot as easy. Vigne does not say much about this. From the foot of the Sarwandi one branch of the Gomul takes off, and from that point to the Indus the great trade route practically follows the Gomul on a gradually descending grade. It is a stony, rough, and broken hill route, now expanding into a broad track of river-bed, now contracting into a cliff-bordered gully, occasionally leaving the river and running parallel over adjoining cliffs, but more often involving the worry of perpetual crossing and re-crossing of the stream. Here and there is an expansion (such as the "flower-bed," Gulkatz) into a reed-covered flat, and occasionally there occurs a level open border space which the blackened stones of previous khafilas denote as a camping-ground. Wild and dreary, carving its way beneath the heat-cracked and rain-seared foot-hills of Waziristan, strewn with stones and boulders, and disfigured by leprous outbreaks of streaky white efflorescence, the Gomul in the hot weather is not an attractive river. In flood-time it is dangerous, and it is in the hottest of the hot weather months that the route is fullest of the moving khafila crowds.

In Broadfoot's time the worst part of the route was between the plateau and the Indus plains. This is no longer so, for a trade-developing and road-making Government has made the rough places plain, and engineered a first-class high-road thus far. And there is this to be noted about that section of it which still lies beyond the ken of the frontier officer and which as yet the surveyor has not mapped. Not a single camel-load in Broadfoot's khafila had to be shifted on account of the roughness of the route between Ghazni and the Indus, and not a space of any great length occurred over which guns might not easily pass. The drawback to the route as a high-road for trade has ever been the blackmailing propensities of Waziris and cognate tribes who flank the route on either side. Broadfoot's khafila lost no less than 100 men in transit; but this was at a time when the country was generally disturbed. In more peaceful days previously Vigne refers to constant losses both of men and property, but to nothing like so great an extent.

Broadfoot still stands for our authority in all that pertains to the central Afghan tribes-people —chiefly the Suliman Khel clan of Ghilzais—

who occupy the Highlands between Waziristan and Ghazni. Under the iron heel of the late Amir of Afghanistan no doubt much of their turbulent and feud-loving propensities has been repressed, and with its repression has followed a development of agriculture, and a general improvement throughout the favoured districts of Kattawaz and the Ghazni plain. Here the climate is exceptionally invigorating, and much of the sweet landscape beauty of the adjoining districts of Wardak and Logar (two of the loveliest valleys of Afghanistan) is evidently repeated. Several fine rivers traverse these uplands, the Jilgu and the Dwa Gomul (both rising from the central divide near to the sources of the Tochi) having much local reputation, and claiming a crude sort of reverence from the wild tribes of the plateau which is only accorded to the gifts of Allah. The Suliman Khel are not nomads—though like all Afghans they love tents—and their villages, clinging to wall-sides or clustering round a central tower, are well built and often exceedingly picturesque. The Ghilzai skill at the construction of these underground irrigation channels called karez is famous throughout Afghanistan. It is, however, the more westerly clans who especially excel in the development of water-supply. The Suliman Khel and the Nasirs take more kindly to the khafila and "povindah" form of life, and this Gomul route is the very backbone of their existence. It is a pity that we know so little about it.

CHAPTER XVII

FRENCH EXPLORATION—FERRIER

AMONGST modern explorers of Afghanistan who have earned distinction by their capacity for single-handed geographical research and ability in recording their experiences, the French officer M. Ferrier is one of the most interesting and one of the most disappointing. He is interesting in all that relates to the historical and political aspects of Afghanistan at a date when England was specially concerned with that country, and so far and so long as his footsteps can now be traced with certainty on our recent maps, he is clearly to be credited with powers of accurate observation and a fairly retentive memory. It is just where, as a geographer, he leaves the known for the unknown, and makes a plunge into a part of the country which no European has actually traversed before or since, that he becomes disappointing. He is the only known wanderer from the west who has traversed the uplands of the Firozkohi plateau from north to south; and it is just that region of the Upper

Murghab basin which our surveyors were unable to reach during the progress of the Russo-Afghan Boundary mapping. The rapidity of the movements of the Commission when once it got to work precluded the possibility, with only a weak staff of topographers, of detailing native assistants to map every corner of that most interesting district, and naturally the more important section of the country received the first attention. But they closed round it so nearly as to leave but little room for pure conjecture, and it is quite possible to verify by local evidence the facts stated by Ferrier, if not actually to trace out his route and map it.

M. Ferrier's career was a sufficiently remarkable one. He served with the French army in Africa, and was delegated with other officers to organise the Persian army. Here he was regarded by the Russian Ambassador as hostile to Russian interests, and the result was his return to France in 1843, where he obtained no satisfaction for his grievances. Deciding to take service with the Punjab Government under the Regency which succeeded Ranjit Singh, he left France for Bagdad and set out from that city in 1845 for a journey through Persia and Afghanistan to India.

Ferrier reached Herat seven years after the siege of that place by the Persians, and four years after the British evacuation of Afghanistan, and his story of interviews with that wily politician, Yar Mahomed Khan, are most entertaining. It is satisfactory to note that the English left on the whole a good reputation behind them. His attempt to reach Lahore *via* Balkh and Kabul was frustrated, and he was forced off the line of route connecting Balkh with Kabul at what was then the Afghan frontier. It was at this period of his travels that his records become most interesting, as he was compelled to pass through the Hazara country to the west of Kabul by an unknown route not exactly recognisable, crossing the Firozkohi plateau and descending through the Taimani country to Ghur. From Ghur he was sent back to Herat, and so ended a very remarkable tour through an absolutely unexplored part of Afghanistan. His final effort to reach the Punjab by the already well-worn roads which lead by Kandahar and Shikarpur was unsuccessful. Considering the risks of the journey, it was a surprising attempt. It was in the course of this adventure that he came across some of the ill-starred remnants of the disasters which attended the British arms during the evacuation of Afghanistan. There were apparently Englishmen in captivity in other parts of Afghanistan than the north, and the fate of those unfortunate victims to the extraordinary combination of political and military blundering which marked those eventful years is left to conjecture.

Such in brief outline was the story of Afghan exploration as it concerned this gallant French officer, and from it we obtain some useful geographical and antiquarian suggestions. The province of Herat he regards as coincident with the Aria of the Greek historians, and the Aria metropolis (or Artakoana) he considers might be represented either by Kuhsan or by Herat itself. He expends a little useless argument in refuting the common Afghan tradition that any part of modern Herat was built by Alexander. Between the twelfth century and the commencement of the seventeenth Herat has been sacked and rebuilt at least seven times, and its previous history must have involved many other radical changes since the days of Alexander. It is, however, probable that the city has been built time after time on the site which it now occupies, or very near it. The vast extent of mounds and other evidences of ancient occupation to the north of it, together with its very obvious strategic importance, give this position a precedence in the district which could never have been overlooked by any conqueror; but the other cities of Greek geography, Sousa and Candace, are not so easy to place. Ferrier may be right in his suggestion that Tous (north-west of Mashad) represents the Greek Sousa, but he is unable to place Candace. To the west of Herat are three very ancient sites, Kardozan, Zindajan (which Ferrier rightly identified with the Arab city of Bouchinj), and Kuhsan, and Candace might have stood where any of them now stand.

Ferrier's description of Herat and its environment fully sustains Sir Henry Rawlinson's opinion of him as an observant traveller. For a simple soldier of fortune he displays remarkable erudition, as well as careful observation, and there is hardly a suggestion which he makes about the Herat of 1845 which subsequent examination did not justify in 1885. It was the custom during the residence of the English Mission under Major d'Arcy Todd in Herat for some, at least, of the leading Afghan chiefs to accept invitations to dinner with the English officers, a custom which promoted a certain amount of mutual good-fellowship between Afghans and English, of which the effects had not worn off when Ferrier was there. When, finally, Yar Mahomed was convinced that Ferrier had no ulterior political motive for his visit, and was persuaded to let him proceed on his journey, a final dinner was arranged, at which Ferrier was the principal guest. It appears to have been a success. "At the close of the repast the guests were incapable of sitting upright, and at two in the morning I left these worthy Mussulmans rolling on the carpet! The following day I prepared for my departure." In 1885 manners and methods had changed for the better. The English officers employed on the reorganisation of the defences of the city were occasionally entertained at modest tea-parties by the Afghan military commandant, but no such rollicking proceedings as those recounted by Ferrier would ever have been countenanced; and it must be confessed that Ferrier's accounts, both here and elsewhere, of the social manners and customs of the Afghan people are a little difficult to accept without reservation. We must, however, make allowances for the times and the loose quality of Afghan government. He left Herat by the northerly route, passing Parwana, the Baba Pass, and the Kashan valley to Bala Murghab and Maimana.

Ferrier has much to say that is interesting about the tribal communities through which he passed, especially about the Chahar Aimak, or wandering tent-living tribes, which include the Hazaras, Jamshidis, Taimanis, and Firozkohis. He is, I think, the first to draw attention to the fact that the Firozkohis are of Persian origin, a people whose forefathers were driven by Tamerlane into the mountains south of Mazanderan, and were eventually transported into the Herat district. They spring from several different Persian tribes, and take the name Firozkohi from "a village in the neighbourhood of which they were surrounded and captured." The origin of the name Ferozkohi has always been something of a geographical puzzle, and it is doubtful whether there was ever a city originally of that name in Afghanistan, although it may have been applied to the chief habitat of this agglomeration of Persian refugees and colonists.

Ferrier's account of his progress includes no geographical data worthy of remark. Politically, this part of Afghan Turkistan has remained much the same during the last seventy years, and geographically one can only say that his account of the route is generally correct, although it indicates that it is compiled from memory. For instance, there is a steep watershed to be crossed between Torashekh and Mingal, but it is not of the nature of a "rugged mountain," nor could there have ever been space enough for the extent of cultivation which he describes in the Murghab valley. He is very much at fault in his description of the road from Nimlik (which he calls Meilik) to Balkh. The hills are on the right (not left) of the road, and are much higher than those previously described as rugged mountains. No water from these hills could possibly reach the road, for there is a canal between them, the overflow of which, however, might possibly swamp the road. Balkh hardly responds to his description of it. There is no mosque to the north of Balkh, nor is the citadel square.

The road from Khulm to Bamian passes through Tashkurghan (which is due east of Mazar—not south) and Haibak, and changes very much in character before reaching Haibak. From Haibak to Kuram the description of the road is fairly correct, but no amount of research on the part of later surveyors has revealed the position of "Kartchoo" (which apparently means locally a market); nor could Ferrier possibly have encountered snow in July on any part of this route, even if he saw any. We must, however, consider the conditions under which he was travelling, and make allowances for the impossibility of keeping anything of the nature of a systematic record. At Kuram, a well-known point above Haibak on the road to Kabul, he reached the Uzbek frontier. Beyond this point —into Afghanistan—no Uzbek would venture, and it was impossible to proceed farther on the direct route to Kabul. Yielding to the pressure of friendly advice, he made a retrograde detour to Saripul, through districts occupied by Hazaras, and "Kart-choo" was but a nomadic camp that he encountered during his first day out from Kuram. Clearly he was making for the Yusuf Darra route to Saripul; and his next camp, Dehao, marks the river. It may possibly be the point marked Dehi on modern maps. At Saripul he was not only well received by the Uzbek Governor, Mahomed Khan, but the extraordinary influence which this man possessed with the Hazaras, Firozkohis, and other Aimak tribes of northern Afghanistan enabled Ferrier to procure food and horses at irregular stages which carried him to Ghur in the Taimani land.

It is this part of Ferrier's journey which is so tantalizing and so difficult to follow. He must have travelled both far and fast. Leaving Saripul on July 11, he rode "ten parasangs," over country very varied in character, to Boodhi. Now this country has been surveyed, and there can be no reasonable doubt about the route he took southwards. But no such place as Boodhi has ever been identified, nor have the remarkable sculptures which were observed *en route*, fashioned on an "enormous block of rock," been found again, although careful inquiries were made about them. They may, of course, have been missed, and information may have been purposely withheld, for geographical surveys do not permit of lengthy halts for inquiry on any line of route. Ferrier's description of them is so full of detail that it is difficult to believe that it is imaginary. He mentions that on the plain on which Boodhi stood, "two parasangs to the right," there were the "ruins of a large town," which might very possibly be the ruins identified by Imam Sharif (a surveyor of the Afghan Boundary Commission), and which would fix the position of "Boodhi" somewhere near Belchirag on the main route southward to Ghur. Belchirag is about 55 miles from Saripul. The next day's ride must have carried him into the valley of the Upper Murghab on the Firozkohi plateau, crossing the Band-i-Turkistan *en route*, and it was here that he met with such a remarkable welcome at the fortress of Dev Hissar.

Ferrier describes the valley of the Upper Murghab in terms of rapture which appear to be a trifle extravagant to those who know that country. No systematic survey of it, however, has ever been possible, and to this day the position of Dev Hissar is a matter of conjecture, and the charming manners of its inhabitants (so unlike the ordinary rough hospitality of the men and the unobtrusive character of the women of the Firozkohi Aimak) are experiences such as our surveyors sighed for in vain! As a mere guess, I should be inclined to place Dev Hissar near Kila Gaohar, or to identify it with that fort. At any rate, I prefer this solution of the puzzle to the suggestion that Dev Hissar and its delightful inhabitants, like the previous sculptures, were but an effort of imagination on the part of this volatile and fascinating Frenchman.

There is always an element of suspicion as to the value of Ferrier's information when he deals with the feminine side of Hazara human nature. For instance, he asserts that the Hazara women fight in their tribal battles side by side with their husbands. This is a feature in their character for independence which the Hazara men absolutely deny, and it is hardly necessary to add that no confirmation could be obtained anywhere of the remarkable familiarity with which the ladies of Hissar are said by Ferrier customarily to treat their guests.

The next long day's ride terminated at Singlak (another unknown place), which was found deserted owing to a feud between the Hazaras and Firozkohis. It was evidently within the Murghab basin and short of the crest of the line of watershed bordering the Hari Rud valley on the north, for the following day Ferrier crossed these hills, and the

Hari Rud valley beneath them (avoiding Daolatyar), at a point which he fixes as "six parasangs S.W. of Sheherek." Again it is impossible to locate the position. Kila Safarak is at the head of the Hari Rud, and Kila Shaharak is in another valley (that of the Tagao Ishlan), so that it will perhaps be safe to assume that it was nowhere near either of these places, but at a point some 10 miles west of Daolatyar, which marks the regular route for Ghur from the north.

Ferrier's description of this part of his journey is vague and unsatisfactory. No such place as Kohistani, "situated on a high plain in the midst of the Siah Koh," is known any more than is Singlak. The divide, or ridge, which he crossed in passing from the Murghab valley to the narrow trough of the Hari Rud is lower than the hills on the south of the river. He could not possibly have crossed snow nor overlooked the landscape to Saripul. It is doubtful if Chalapdalan, the mountain which impressed him so mightily, is visible from any part of the broken watershed north of the Hari Rud. Chalapdalan is only 13,600 feet high, and there would have been no snow on it in July. As we proceed farther we fail to identify Ferrier's Tingelab River, unless he means the Ab-i-lal. The Hari Rud does not flow through Shaharak, and no one has found a village called Jaor in the Hari Rud valley. Continuing to cross the Band-i-Baian (which he calls Siah Koh) from Kohistani Baba, a very long day's ride brought him to Deria-dereh, also called "Dereh Mustapha Khan," which was evidently a place of importance and the headquarters of a powerful section of either Hazaras or Taimanis under a Chief, Mustapha Khan. Here, in a small oblong valley entirely closed by mountains, was a little lake of azure colour and transparent clearness which lay like a vast gem embedded in surrounding verdure . . . "around which were somewhat irregularly pitched a number of Taimani tents, separated from each other by little patches of cultivation and gardens enclosed by stone walls breast high. . . . The luxuriance of the vegetation in this valley might compare with any that I had ever seen in Europe. On the summits of the surrounding mountains were several ruins, etc. etc." Ash and oak trees were there. Fishermen were dragging the lake, women were leading flocks to the water, and young girls sat outside the tents weaving bereks (barak, or camel-hair cloth), and contentment was depicted on every face.

From Deria-dereh another long day's ride brought him to Zirni, which he describes as the ancient capital of Ghur. From the Band-i-Baian (or Koh Siah, as he calls it) to Zirni is at least 100 miles by the very straightest road, and that would pass by Taiwara. It is clear that he did not take that road, or he could hardly have ignored so important a position as Taiwara. If he made a detour eastward he would pass through Hazara country—

very mountainous, very high and difficult, and the length of the two days' journey would be nearer 150 miles than 100. To the first day's journey (as far as Deria-dereh) he gives ten hours on horseback, which in that country might represent 60 miles; but no such place as he describes, no lake with Arcadian surroundings, has been either seen or heard of by subsequent surveyors within the recognized limits of Taimani country. If it exists at all, it is to the east of the great watershed from which spring the Ghur River and the Farah Rud, hidden within the spurs of the Hazara mountains. This is just possible, for this wild and weatherbeaten country has not been so fully reconnoitred as that farther west; but it makes Ferrier's journey extraordinary for the distances covered, and fully accounts for the fact that he has preserved so little detail of this eventful ride that, practically, there is nothing of geographical interest to be learnt from it.

Ferrier's description of the ruins which are to be found in the neighbourhood of Zirni and Taiwara, especially his reference to a "paved" road leading towards Ghazni, is very interesting. He is fully impressed with the beauty of the surrounding country, and what he has to say about this centre of an historical Afghan kingdom has been more or less confirmed by subsequent explorers. Only the "Ghebers" have disappeared; and the magnificent altitude of the "Chalap Dalan" mountain, described by him as one of the "highest in the world," has been reduced to comparatively humble proportions. Its isolated position, however, undoubtedly entitles it to rank as a remarkable geographical feature.

At Zirni Ferrier found that his further progress towards Kandahar was arrested, and from that point, to his bitter disgust, he was compelled to return to Herat. From Zirni to Herat was, in his day, an unmapped region, and he is the first European to give us even a glimpse of that once well-trodden highway. His conjectures about the origin of the Aimak tribes which people Central Afghanistan are worthy of study, as they are based on original inquiry from the people themselves; but it is very clear that either time has modified the manners of these people, or that popular sources of information are not always to be trusted. He repeats the story of the fighting propensities of Hazara women when dealing with the Taimanis, and adds, as regards the latter, that "a girl does not marry until she has performed some feat of arms." It may be that "feats of arms" are not so easy of achievement in these days, but it is certain that such an inducement to marry would fail to be effective now. It might even prove detrimental to a girl's chances.

Once again we can only regard with astonishment Ferrier's record of a ride from "Tarsi" (Parsi) to Herat, at least 90 miles, in one night. A district Chief told Captain (now Colonel) the Hon. M. G.

Talbot, who conducted the surveys of the country in 1883, that "a good Taimani on a good horse" might accomplish the feat, but that nobody else could. Ferrier, with his considerable escort, seemed to have found no difficulty, but undoubtedly he was in excellent training. His general description of the country that he passed through accords with the pace at which he swept through it, and nothing is to be gained by criticising his hasty observations. At Herat he was fortunate in securing the consent of Yar Mahomed Khan to his project for reaching the Punjab *via* Kandahar and Kabul; and with letters from that wily potentate to the Amir Dost Mahomed Khan and his son-in-law Mahomed Akbar Khan this "Lord of the Kingdom of France, General Ferrier" set out on another attempt to reach India. In this he was unsuccessful, and his path was a thorny one. He travelled by the road which had been adopted as the post-road between Herat and Kandahar, during the residence of the English Mission at Herat—a route which, leaving Farah to the west, approaches Kandahar by Washir and Girishk, and which is still undoubtedly the most direct road between the two capitals. But the particularly truculent character of the Durani Afghan tribes of Western Afghanistan rendered this journey most dangerous for a single European moving without an armed escort, and he was robbed and maltreated with fiendish persistency. It was a well-known and much-trodden old road, but it has always been, and it is still, about the worst road in all Afghanistan for the fanatical unpleasantness of its Achakzai and Nurzai environment.

After leaving Washir Ferrier was imprisoned at Mahmudabad, and again when he reached Girishk, and the story of the treatment he received at both places says much for the natural soundness of his constitution. Luckily he fell in with a friendly Munshi who had been in English service, who, whilst warning Ferrier that he might consider the position of his head on his shoulders as "wonderfully shaky," did a good deal to dissipate the notion that he was an English spy, and helped him through what was indeed a very tight place. It was at this point of his journey that Ferrier heard of an English prisoner in Zamindawar,—a traveller with "green eyes and red hair,"—and the fact that he actually received a note from this man (which he could not read as it was written in English) seems to confirm that fact. He could do nothing to help him, and no one knows what may have been the ultimate fate of this unfortunate captive.

Ferrier is naturally indignant with Sir Alexander Burnes for describing the Afghans as "a sober, simple steady people" (Burnes' *Travels in Bokhara*, vol. i. pp. 143, 144). How Burnes could ever have arrived at such an extraordinary estimate of Afghan character is hard to imagine, and it says little for those perceptive faculties for which Masson has such contempt. But it not inaptly points the great contrast that does really exist between the Kabuli and the Kandahari to this day. When the English officers of the Afghan Boundary Commission in 1883 were occupied in putting Herat into a state of defence, their personal escort was carefully chosen from soldiers of the northern province, who, by no means either "sober or simple," were at any rate far less fanatical and truculent than the men of the west, and they were, on the whole, a pleasant and friendly contingent to deal with.

At Girishk, and subsequently, Ferrier has certain geographical facts of interest to record. Some of them still want verification, but they are valuable indications. He notes the immense ruins and mounds on both sides the Helmund at Girishk. He was in confinement at Girishk for eight days, where he suffered much from "the vermin which I could not prevent from getting into my clothes, and the rattling of my inside from the scantiness of my daily ration." However, his trials came to an end at last, and he left Girishk "with a heart full of hatred for its inhabitants and a lively joy at his departure," fording the Helmund at some little distance from the town. He remarks on the vast ruins at Kushk-i-Nakhud, where there is a huge artificial mound. A similar one exists at Sangusar, about 3 miles south-east of Kushk-i-Nakhud. At Kandahar the final result of a short residence that was certainly full of lively incident, and an interview with the Governor Kohendil Khan (brother of the Amir Dost Mahomed), was a return to Girishk. This must have been sickening; but it resulted in a series of excursions into Baluch territory which are not uninstructive. The ill-treatment (amounting to the actual infliction of torture) which Ferrier endured at the hands of the Girishk Governor (Sadik Khan, a son of Kohendil Khan) on this second visit to Girishk, was even worse than the first, and it was only by signing away his veracity and giving a false certificate of friendship with the brute that he finally got free again. He was to follow the Helmund to Lash Jowain in Seistan, but the attempt was frustrated by a local disturbance at Binadur, on the Helmund. So far, however, this abortive excursion was of certain geographical interest as covering new ground. The places mentioned by Ferrier *en route* are all still in existence, but he gives no detailed account of them.

Once more a start was made from Girishk, and this time our explorer succeeded in reaching Farah by the direct route through Washir. It was in the month of October, and the fiery heat of the Bakwa plain was sufficiently trying even to this case-hardened Frenchman. About Farah he has much to say that still requires confirmation. Of the exceeding antiquity of this place there is ample evidence; but no one since Ferrier has identified the site of the second and later town of Farah "an hour" farther north or "half an hour" from the Farah Rud (river), where bricks were seen "three feet long and four inches thick," with inscriptions on them in cuneiform character, amidst the ruins. This town was abandoned in favour of the older (and present) site when Shah Abbas the Great besieged and destroyed it, but there can be no doubt that the bricks seen by Ferrier must have possessed an origin long anterior to the town, which only dates from the time of Chenghiz Khan. The existence of such evidence of the ancient and long-continued connection between Assyria and Western Afghanistan would be exceedingly interesting were it confirmed by modern observation. Farah is by all accounts a most remarkable town, and it undoubtedly contains secrets of the past which for interest could only be surpassed by those of Balkh. At Farah Ferrier was lodged in a "hole over the north gate of the town, open to the violent winds of Seistan, which rushed in at eight enormous holes, through which also came the rays of the sun." Here wasps, scorpions, and mice were his companions, and it must be admitted that Ferrier's account of the horrors of Farah residence have been more or less confirmed by all subsequent travellers to Seistan. But he finally succeeded in obtaining, through the not inhospitable governor, the necessary permission from Yar Mahomed Khan of Herat (whose policy in his dealings with Ferrier it is quite impossible to decipher) to pass on to Shikarpur and Sind; and the permission is couched in such pious and affectionate terms, that the "very noble, very exalted, the companion of honour, of fortune, and of happiness, my kind friend, General Ferrier," really thought there was a chance of escaping from his clutches. He was, by the way, invited back again to Herat, but he was told that he might please himself.

Here follows a most interesting exploration into a stretch of territory then utterly unreconnoitred and unknown, and it is unfortunate that this most trying route through the flats and wastes which stretch away eastwards of the Helmund lagoons should still be but sketchily indicated in our maps. It is, however, from Farah to Khash (where the Khash Rud is crossed), and from Khash to the Helmund, but a track through a straight region of desolation and heat, relieved, however (like the desert region to the south of the Helmund), by strips of occasional tamarisk vegetation, where grass is to be found in the spring and nomads collect with their flocks. Watering-places might be developed here by digging wells, and the route rendered practicable across the Dasht-i-Margo as it has been between Nushki and Seistan, but when Ferrier crossed it it was a dangerous route to attempt on tired and ill-fed horses. The existence of troops of wild asses was sufficient evidence of its life-supporting capabilities if properly developed. Ferrier struck the Helmund about Khan Nashin. Here a most ill-timed and ill-advised fight with a Baluch clan ended in a disastrous flight of the whole party down the Helmund to Rudbar, and it would perhaps be unkind to criticise too closely the heroics of this part of Ferrier's story.

At Rudbar Ferrier again noticed bricks a yard square in an old dyke, whilst hiding. Rudbar was well known to the Arab geographers, but this record of Ferrier's carries it back (and with it the course of the Helmund) to very ancient times indeed. Continuing to follow the river, they passed Kala-i-Fath and reached "Poulka"—a place which no longer exists under that name. This is all surveyed country; but no investigator since Ferrier has observed the same ancient bricks at Kala-i-Fath which Ferrier noted there as at Farah and Rudbar. There is every probability, however, of their existence. All this part of the Helmund valley abounds in antiquities which are as old as Asiatic civilization, but nothing short of systematic antiquarian exploration will lead to further discoveries of any value.

Ferrier was now in Seistan, and we may pass over his record of interesting observations on the wealth of antiquarian remains which surrounded him. It is enough to point out that he was one of the first to call public attention to them from the point of view of actual contact. It must be accepted as much to the credit of Ferrier's narrative that the latest surveys of Seistan (*i.e.* those completed during the work of the Commission under Sir H. MacMahon in 1903-5) entirely support the account given in his *Caravan Journeys* as he wandered through that historic land. By the light of the older maps, completed during the Afghan Boundary Commission some twenty years previously, it would have been difficult to have traced his steps. We know now that the lake of Seistan should, with all due regard to its extraordinary capacity for expansion and contraction, be represented as in MacMahon's map, extending southwards to a level with the great bend of the Helmund. Ferrier's narrative very conclusively illustrates this position of it, and proves that such an expansion must be regarded as normal. We can no longer accurately locate the positions of Pulaki and Galjin, but from his own statements it seems more than probable that the first place is already sand-buried. They were not far north of Kala-i-Fath. From there he went northward to Jahanabad, and north-west (not south-west) to Jalalabad. It was at Jahanabad that he nearly fell into the hands of Ali Khan, the chief of Chakansur (Sheikh Nassoor of Ferrier), the scoundrel who had previously murdered Dr. Forbes and hung his body up to be carefully watered and watched till it fell to pieces in gold ducats. There was an unfortunate superstition current in Baluchistan to the effect that this was the normal end of European existence! Luckily it has passed away. Escaping such a calamity, he turned the lake at its southern extremity, passing through Sekoha, and travelled up its western banks till, after crossing the Harat Rud, he reached Lash Jowain. From here to Farah and from Farah once again to Herat, his road was made straight for him, and we need only note what he has to say about the extent of the ruins near Sabzawar to be convinced that here was the mediæval provincial capital of Parwana. At Herat he was enabled to to do what would have saved him a most adventurous journey (and lost us the pleasure of recording his work as that of a notable explorer of Afghanistan), *i.e.* take the straight road back to Teheran from whence he came.

With this we may bid adieu to Ferrier, but it is only fair to do tardy justice to his remarkable work. I confess that after the regions of Central Afghanistan had been fairly well reconnoitred by the surveyors of the Russo-Afghan Boundary Commission, considerable doubt remained in my mind as to the veracity of Ferrier's statements. I still think he was imposed upon now and then by what he *heard*, but I have little doubt that he adhered on the whole (and the conditions under which he travelled must be remembered) to a truthful description of what he *saw*. It is true that there still remains wanting an explanation of his experiences at that restful island in the sea of difficulty and danger which surrounded him—Dev Hissar—but I have already pointed out that it may exist beyond the limits of actual subsequent observation; and as regards the stupendous bricks with cuneiform inscription, it can only be said that their existence in the localities which he mentions has been rendered so probable by recent investigation, that nothing short of serious and systematic excavation, conducted in the spirit which animated the discovery of Nineveh, will finally disprove this most interesting evidence of the extreme antiquity of the cities of Afghanistan, and their relation to the cities of Mesopotamia.

CHAPTER XVIII

SUMMARY

THE close of the Afghan war of 1839-40 left a great deal to be desired in the matter of practical geography. It was not the men but the methods that were wanting. The commencement of the second and last Afghan war in 1878 saw the initiation of a system of field survey of a practical geographical nature, which combined the accuracy of mathematical deduction with the rapidity of plane table topography. It was the perfecting of the smaller class of triangulating instruments that made this system possible, quite as much as the unique opportunity afforded to a survey department in such a country as India for training topographers. It worked well from the very first, and wherever a force could march or a political mission be launched into such a region of open hill and valley as the Indian trans-frontier, there could the surveyors hold their own (no matter what the nature of the movement might be) and make a "square" survey in fairly accurate detail, with the certainty that it

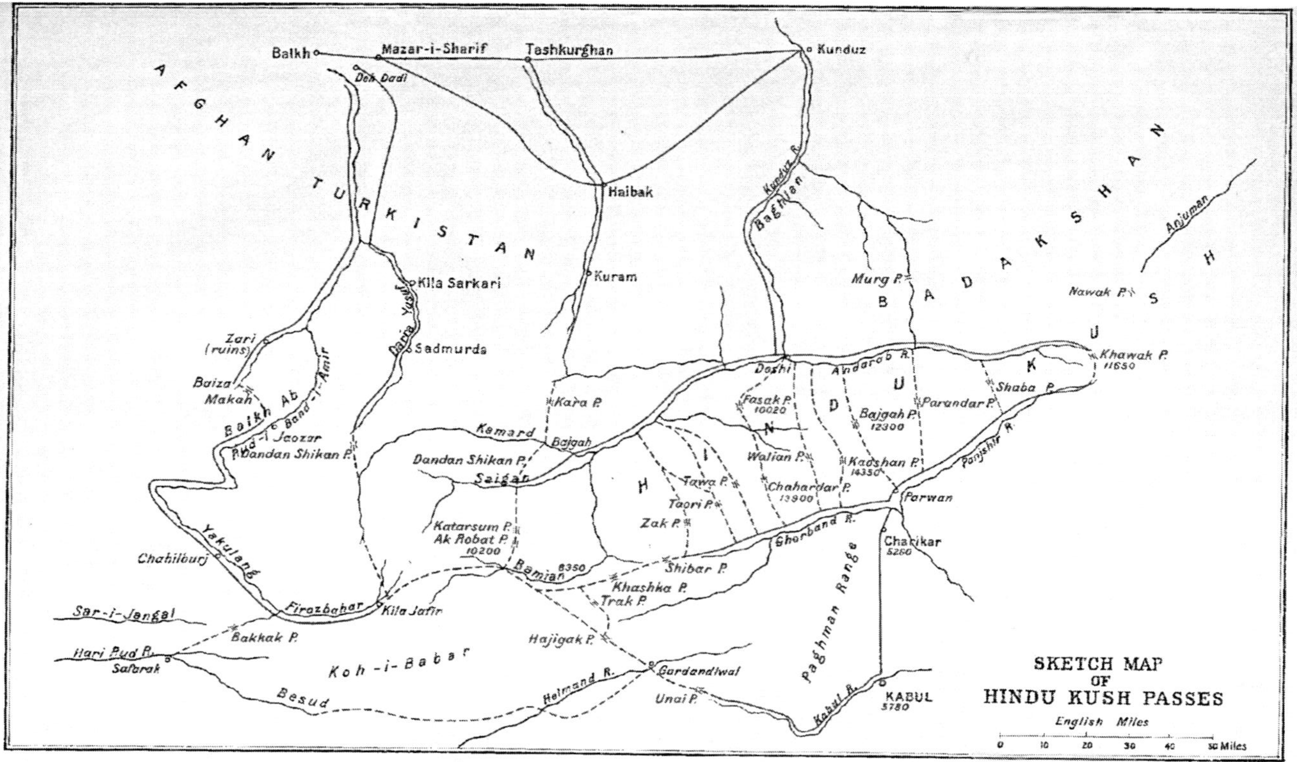
SKETCH MAP OF HINDU KUSH PASSES
English Miles
0 10 20 30 40 50 Miles
AFGHAN TURKISTAN
BADAKSHAN
HINDU KUSH
Balkh
Mazar-i-Sharif
Tashkurghan
Kunduz
Deh Dadi
Haibak
Kuram
Kila Sarkari
Sadmurda
Zari (ruins)
Baiza
Makah
Balkh Ab
Band-i-Amir
Rud-i Jaozar
Dandan Shikan P.
Kamard
Bajgah
Kara P.
Saigan
Kunduz R.
Baghlan
Murg P.
Nawak P.
Anjuman
Khawak P. 11650
Doshi
Andarob R.
Fasak P. 10020
Shaba P.
Parandar P.
Bajgah P. 12300
Walian P.
Kadshan P. 14350
Tawa P.
Chahardar P. 13900
Taori P.
Zak P.
Panjshir R.
Parwan
Charikar 5260
Ghorband R.
Shibar P.
Khashka P.
Trak P.
Katarsum P.
Ak Robat P. 10200
Bamian 8350
Yakulang
Chahilburj
Firozbahar
Kila Jafir
Sar-i-Jangal
Bakkak P.
Hari Rud R.
Safarak
Koh-i-Babar
Besud
Hajigak P.
Gardandiwal
Helmand R.
Unai P.
Paghman Range
Kabul R.
KABUL 5780

would take its final place without squeezing or distortion in the general map of Asia. This was of course very different from the plodding traverse work of former days, and it rapidly placed quite a new complexion on our trans-frontier maps. Since then regular systematic surveys in extension of those of India have been carried far afield, and it may safely be said now that no country in the world is better provided with military maps of its frontiers than India. In Baluchistan, indeed, there is little left to the imagination. A country which forty years ago was an ugly blank in our maps, with a doubtful locality indicated here and there, is now almost as well surveyed as Scotland. Afghanistan, however, is beyond our line, "out of bounds," and the result is that there are serious gaps in our map knowledge of the country of the Amir, gaps which there seems little probability of investigating under the present closure of the frontier to explorers.

By far the most important of these gaps are the uplands of Badakshan, stretching from the Oxus plains to the Hindu Kush. The plains of Balkh, as far east as Khulm and Tashkurghan, from whence the high-road leads to Haibak, Bamian, and the Hindu Kush passes, are fairly well mapped. The Oxus, to the north of Balkh, is well known, and the fords and passages of that river have been reckoned up with fair accuracy. From time immemorial every horde of Skythic origin, Nagas, Sakas, or Jatas, must have passed these fords from the hills and valleys of the Central Asian divide on their way to India. The Oxus fords have seen men in millions making south for the valleys of Badakshan and the Golden Gates of Central Asiatic ideal which lay yet farther south beyond the grim line of Hindu Kush. Balkh (the city) must have stood like a rock in the human tide which flowed from north to south. From the west, too, from Asia Minor and the Persian provinces, as well as from the Caspian steppes to the north-west, must have come many a weary band of tear-stained captives, transported across half a continent by their conquerors to colonize, build cities, and gradually amalgamate with the indigenous people, and so to disappear from history. From the west came Parthians, Medes, Assyrians, and Greeks, who did not altogether disappear. But no such human tide ever flowed into Badakshan from the east nor yet from the south. To the east are the barrier heights of the Pamirs. No crowd of fugitives or captives ever faced those bleak, inhospitable, wind-torn valleys that we know of. Nor can we find any trace of emigration from India. Yet routes were known across the Pamirs, and in due time, as we have seen, small parties of pilgrims from China made use of these routes, seeking for religious truth in Balkh when, as a Buddhist centre, Balkh was in direct connection with the Buddhist cities of Eastern Turkistan. And Buddhism itself, when it left India, went northward and flourished exceedingly in those same cities of the sandy plain, where the people talked and wrote a language of India for centuries after the birth of Christ. Balkh, however, never stayed the tide which overlapped it and, passing on, lost itself in the valleys under the Hindu Kush, or else, surmounting that range, streamed over into the Kabul basin. Whether the tide set in from north or west, the overflow was forced by purely geographical conditions into precisely the same channels, and in many cases it drifted into the hills and stayed there. What we should expect to find in Balkh, then (whenever Dr. Stein can get there), are records in brick, records in writing, and records in coin, of nearly every great Asiatic movement which has influenced the destinies of India from the days of Assyria to those of Mohamed. What a history to unfold!

Of the Badakshan uplands south and south-east of Balkh, we have but most unsatisfying geographical record. In the days preceding the first Afghan war when Burnes, Moorcroft, Lord, and Wood were in the field, we certainly acquired much useful information which is still all that we have for scientific reference. Moorcroft, as we have seen, made several hurried journeys between Balkh and Kunduz under most perilous conditions, when endeavouring to escape from the clutches of the border chief, Murad Beg. But Moorcroft's opportunities of scientific observation were small, and his means of ascertaining his geographical position were crude, and we gain little or nothing from his thrilling story of adventure, beyond a general description of a desolate region of swamp and upland which forms the main features of Northern Badakshan.

Lord and Wood, who followed Moorcroft at no great interval, and who were also in direct personal touch with Murad Beg under much the same political circumstances, have furnished much more useful information of the routes and passes between Haibak and Kunduz, and given us a very fair idea of the physical configuration of that desolate district. Lord's memoir on the *Uzbek State of Kundooz* (published at Simla in July 1838) is indeed the best, if not the only, authoritative document concerning the history and policy of Badakshan, giving us a fair idea of the conditions under which Murad Beg established and consolidated his position as the paramount chief of that country, and the guardian of the great commercial route between Kabul and Bokhara; but there is little geographical information in the memoir. The four fortified towns of the Kunduz state, Kunduz, Rustak, Talikhan, and Hazrat Imam, are described rather as depositories for plunder than as positions of any great importance, and the real strength of Murad Beg's military force lay in the quality of his hordes of irregular Uzbek horsemen and the extraordinary hardiness and endurance of the Kataghani horses. So highly esteemed is this particular breed that the late Amir of Afghanistan would permit of no export of horses from Kataghan, reserving them especially for the purpose of mounting his own cavalry.

We learn incidentally of the waste and desolation caused by the poisonous climate of the fens and marshes between Hazrat Imam and Kunduin, to which Murad Beg had transported 20,000 Badakshani families for purposes of colonization, and where Dr. Lord was told that barely 1000 individuals had survived; but Wood tells us much more than this in his charming book on the Oxus. From the point where he left the main road from Kabul to Bokhara (a little below Kuram north of the Saighan valley) till he reached Kunduz, he was passing over country and by-ways which have never been revisited by any European geographer. He tells us that "the plain between the streams that water Kunduz and Kuram has a wavy surface, and though unsuited to agriculture has an excellent pasturage. The only village on the road is Hazrat Baba Kamur. On the eastern side the plain is supported by a ridge of hills sloping down from the mountains to the south. We crossed it by the pass of Archa (so called from the fir trees which cover its crest), from the top of which we had a noble view of the snowy mountains to the east, the outliers of Hindu Kush. Next day we forded the river of Kunduz, and continuing to journey along its right bank, through the swampy district of Baghlan and Aliabad, reached the capital of Murad Beg on Monday the 4th Dec. (1837)." The story of Wood's travels in Badakshan has already been told; the moonlit march from Kunduz through the dense jungle grass and swamp, often knee-deep in water; the gradual rise to higher ground above; the floating vapour screen that hovered over the fens; Khanabad and its quaint array of colleges and students, and the Koh Umber mountain, isolated and conspicuous, dividing the plains of Kunduz and Talikhan—all these are features which will indicate the general character of that part of Badakshan but leave us no fixed and determined position. The Koh Umber in particular must be a remarkable topographical landmark, as it towers 2500 feet above the surrounding plain with a snow-covered summit. Wood says of it that it is central to the districts of Talikhan, Kunduz, and Hazrat Imam, and its pasturage is common to the flocks of all three plains. But it is an undetermined geographical feature, and still remains in its solitary grandeur, a position to be won by future explorers.

From Khanabad to Talikhan, Faizabad, and Jirm (which, it will be recollected, was once the capital of Badakshan—probably the "Badakshan" of Arab geography), we have the description of a mountainous country supporting the conjectural topography of our maps, which indicate that this route borders and occasionally crosses a series of gigantic spurs or offshoots of a central range (which Wood calls the Khoja) which must itself be a north-easterly arm of the Hindu Kush, taking off from the latter range somewhere near the Khawak Pass. Here, then, is one of the most important blanks in the map of our frontier. Inconceivably rugged and difficult of access, it seems probable that it is more accessible from Badakshan than from the south. We know from Wood's account of the extraordinary difficulty that beset his efforts to reach the lapis-lazuli mines above Jirm in the Kokcha River something of the general nature of these northern valleys and defiles of Kafiristan reaching down to lower Badakshan. It would, indeed, be a splendid geographical feat to fix the position and illustrate the topography of this roughest section of Asia.

Between the Khawak Pass of the Hindu Kush which leads to Andarab, and the Mandal, or Minjan, passes, some 70 miles to the east, we have never solved the problem of the Hindu Kush divide. What lies behind Wood's Khoja range, between it and the main divide? We have the valley called Anjuman, which is believed to lead as directly to Jirm from the Khawak Pass as Andarab does to Kunduz. It is an important feature in Hindu Kush topography, but we know nothing of it. We may, however, safely conjecture that the Minjan River, reached by Sir George Robertson in one of his gallant attempts to explore Kafiristan, is the upper Kokcha flowing past the lapis-lazuli mines to Jirm. But where does it rise? And where on the southern slopes of the Hindu Kush do the small affluents of the Alingar and Alishang have their beginning?

These are the hidden secrets of Kafiristan. It is here that those turbulent people (who, by the way, seem to exhibit the same characteristics from whatever valley of Kafiristan they come, and to be much more homogeneous than is usually supposed) hide themselves in their upland villages, amidst their magnificent woods and forests, untroubled by either Afghan or European visitors. Here they live their primitive lives, enlivened with quaint ceremonies and a heathenism equally reminiscent of the mythology of Greece, the ritual of Zoroaster, and the beliefs of the Hindu. Who will unravel the secrets of this inhabited outland, which appears at present to be more impracticable to the explorer than either of the poles? Yule, in his preface to the last edition of Wood's *Oxus*, remarks that Colonel Walker, the late Surveyor-General of India (and one of the greatest of Asiatic geographers) repeatedly expressed his opinion that there is no well-defined range where the Hindu Kush is represented in our maps, and he adds that such an expression of opinion can only apply to that part of the Hindu Kush which lies east of the Khawak Pass. Sir Henry Yule refers to Wood's incidental notices of the mountains which he saw towering to the south of him, "rising to a vast height and bearing far below their summits the snow of ages," in refutation of such an opinion; and he further quotes the "havildar's" (native surveyor) report of the Nuksan and Dorah passes in confirmation of Wood.

Since Yule wrote, Woodthorpe's surveys of the Nuksan and Dorah passes during the Lockhart mission leave little doubt as to the nature of the Hindu Kush as far west as those passes, but it is precisely between those passes and the Khawak, along the backbone of Kafiristan, that we have yet to learn the actual facts of mountain conformation. And here possibly there may be something in Walker's suggestion. The mountains to which Wood looked up from Talikhan or Kishm, towering to the south of him and covered with perpetual snow, certainly formed no part of the main Hindu Kush divide. Between them and the Hindu Kush is either the deep valley of Anjuman, or more probably the upper drainage of the Minjan, which, rising not far east of Khawak, repeats the almost universal Himalayan feature of a long, lateral, ditch-like valley in continuation of the Andarab depression, marking the base of the connecting link in the primeval fold formed by the Hindu Kush east and west of it. We should expect to find the Kafiristan mountain conformation to be an integral part of the now recognised Himalayan system of parallel mountain folds, with deep lateral valleys fed by a transverse drainage. The long valley of the Alingar will prove to be another such parallel depression, and we shall find when the map is finished that the dominating structural feature of all this wild hinterland of mountains is the north-east to south-west trend of mountain and valley which marks the Ḳunar (or

Chitral) valley on the one side and the Panjshir on the other. The reason why it is more probable that the Minjan River takes the direct drainage of the northern slopes of this Kafiristan backbone into a lateral trough than that the Anjuman spreads its head into a fan, is that Sir George Robertson found the Minjan, below the pass of Mandal, to be a far more considerable river than its assumed origin in the official maps would make it. He accordingly makes a deep indentation in the Hindu Kush divide (on the map which illustrates his captivating book, *The Kafirs of the Hindu Kush*), bringing it down southward nearly half a degree to an acute angle, so as to afford room for the Minjan to rise and follow a course in direct line with its northerly run (as the Kokcha) in Badakshan. This is a serious disturbance of the laws which govern the structure of Asiatic mountain systems, as now recognized, and it is indeed far more likely that the Minjan (Kokcha) follows those laws which have placed the Andarab and the Panjshir (or for that matter the Indus and the Brahmaputra) in their parallel mountain troughs, than that the primeval fold of the Hindu Kush has become disjointed and indented by some agency which it would be impossible to explain. Who is going to complete the map and solve the question?

We are still very far from possessing a satisfactory geographical knowledge of even the more accessible districts of Badakshan. We still depend on Wood for the best that we know of the route between Faizabad and Zebak; and of those Eastern mountains which border the Oxus as it bends northward to Kila Khum we know positively nothing at all.

But beyond all contention the hidden jewels to be acquired by scientific research in Badakshan are archæological and antiquarian rather than geographical. Now that Nineveh and Babylon have yielded up their secrets, there is no such field out of Egypt for the antiquarian and his spade as the plains of Balkh. But enough has been said of what may be hidden beneath the unsightly bazaars and crumbling ruins of modern Balkh. Whilst Badakshan literally teems with opportunities for investigation, certain features of ancient Baktria appear to be especially associated with certain sites; such, for instance, as the sites of Semenjan (Haibak), Baghlan, Andarab, and particularly the junction of the rivers at Kasan. That Andarab (Ariaspa) held the capital of the Greek colonies there can be as little doubt as that Haibak and its neighbourhood formed the great Buddhist centre between Balkh and Kabul. Again, who is going to make friends with the Amir of Afghanistan and try his luck? It must be a foreigner, for no Englishman would be permitted by his own government to pass that way at present.

The wild and savage altitudes of Badakshan and Kafiristan by no means exhaust the unexplored tracts of Afghanistan. We have the curious feature of a well-surveyed route connecting Ghazni with Kandahar, one of the straightest and best of military routes trodden by armies uncountable from the days of Alexander to those of Roberts, a narrow ribbon of well-ascertained topography, dividing the two most important of the unexplored regions of Afghanistan. North-west of this road lies the great basin of the central Helmund. South-east is a broken land of plain, ribbed and streaked with sharp ridges of frontier formation, about which we ought to know a great deal more than we do. Up the frontier staircases and on to this plain run many important routes from India. The Kuram route strikes it at its northern extremity and leaves it to the southward. The Tochi valley route, and the great mercantile Gomal highway strike into the middle of it, and yet no one of our modern frontier explorers has ever reached it from one side or the other. We still depend on Broadfoot's and Vigne's account of what they saw there, although it is only just on the far side of the rocky band of hills which face the Indus.

About midway between Ghazni and Bannu is the water-parting which separates the Indus drainage from that of the Helmund, and at this point there are some formidable peaks, well over 12,000 feet in height, to distinguish it. The Tochi passage is easy enough as far as the Sheranni group of villages near the head of its long cultivated ramp, but beyond that point the traveller becomes involved in the narrow lateral valleys which follow the trend of the ridges which traverse his path, where streams curl up from the Birmal hills to the south and from the high altitudes which shelter the Kharotis on the north. It is a perpetual wriggle through steep-sided rocky waterways, until one emerges into more open country after crossing the main divide by the Kotanni Pass. The hills here are called Jadran, and it is probable that the Jadran divide and that of the Kohnak farther south are one and the same. Beyond the Kotanni Pass to Ghazni the way is fairly open, but we know very little about it beyond the historical fact that the arch-raider, Mahmud of Ghazni, used to follow this route for his cavalry descents on the Indian frontier with most remarkable success. The remains of old encampments are to be seen in the plain at the foot of the Tochi, and disjointed indications of an ancient high-road were found on the hill slopes to the north of the stream by our surveyors.

Of the actual physical facts of the Gomul route we have only the details gathered by Broadfoot under great difficulties, and a traveller's account by Vigne. What they found has already been described, and the frontier expedition to the Takht-i-Suliman in 1882 sufficiently well determined the position of the Kohnak water-parting to give a fixed geographical value to their narratives. But we have no topography beyond Domandi and Wana. We know that the ever-present repellent band of rocky ridge and furrow, the hill and valley distribution which is distinctive, has to be encountered and passed; but the route does not bristle with the difficulties of narrow ways and stony footpaths as does the Tochi, and there is no doubt that it could soon be reduced to a very practicable artillery road. The important point is that we do not know here (any more than as regards the upper Tochi) a great deal that it concerns us very much to know. We have no mapping of the country which lies between the Baluch frontier and Lake Abistada, the land of the stalwart Suliman Khel tribes-people, and it is a country of which the possible resources might be of great value to us if ever we are driven again to take military stock of Afghanistan.

But the importance of good mapping in this part of Afghanistan is due solely to its position in geographical relation to the Indian frontier. It is different when we turn to the stupendous altitudes of the high Hazara plateau land to the north of the Ghazni-Kandahar route. With this we are not likely to have any future concern, except that which may be called academic. In spite of the reputation for sterile wind-scoured desolation which the uplands hiding the upper Helmund valleys have always enjoyed, it is not to be forgotten that there are summer ways about them, and strong indications that some of these ways are distinctly useful. Our knowledge of the Helmund River (such knowledge, that is to say, as justifies us in mapping the course of the river with a firm line) from its sources ends almost exactly at the intersection of the parallel of 34° of North latitude with the meridian of 67° East longitude. For the next 120 miles we really know nothing about its course, except that it is said to run nearly straight through the heart of the Hazara highlands.

Two very considerable, but nameless, rivers run more or less parallel to the Helmund to the south of it, draining the valleys of Ujaristan and Urusgan, the upper part of the latter being called Malistan. What these valleys are like, or what may be the nature of the dividing water-parting, we do not know, nor have we any authentic description of the valley of Nawar, which lies under the Gulkoh mountain at the head of the Arghandab, but apparently unconnected with it. Native information on the subject of these highly elevated valleys is excessively meagre, nor are they of any special interest from either the strategic or economic point of view. Far more interesting would it be to secure a geographical map of those northern branches of the Helmund, the Khud Rud, and the Kokhar Ab, which drain the mountain districts to the east of Taiwara above the undetermined position of Ghizao on the Helmund. These mountain streams must rush their waters through magnificent gorges, for the peaks which soar above them rise to 13,000 feet in altitude, and the country is described as inconceivably rugged and wild. This is the real centre and home of the Hazara communities, and, in spite of the fact that there are certain well-ascertained tracks traversing the country and connecting the Helmund with the valley of the Hari Rud, we know that for the greater part of the year they must be closed to all traffic. They are of no importance outside purely local interests. The comparatively small area yet unexplored which lies to the north of the Hazara mountains, shut off from them by the straight trough of the Hari Rud and embracing the head of the Murghab River of Turkistan, is almost equally unimportant, although it would be a matter of great interest to investigate a little more closely the remarkable statements of Ferrier which bear on this region.

When we have finally struck a balance between our knowledge and our ignorance of that which concerns the landward gates of India, we shall recognize the fact that we know all that it is really essential that we should know of these uplifted approaches. They are inconceivably old—as old as the very mountains which they traverse. What use may be made of them has been made long ago. We have but to turn back the pages of history and we find abundant indications which may enable us to gauge their real value as highways from Central Asia to India. History says that none of the tracks which lead from China and Tibet have ever been utilized for the passage of large bodies of people either as emigrants, troops, commercial travellers, or pilgrims into India, although there exists a direct connection between China and the Brahmaputra in Assam, and although we know that the difficulties of the road between Lhasa and India are by no means insuperable. Nor by the Kashmir passes from Turkistan or the Pamirs is it possible to find any record of a formidable passing of large bodies of people, although the Karakoram has been a trade route through all time, and although the Chinese have left their mark below Chitral. Yet we have had explorers over the passes connecting the upper Oxus affluents with Gilgit and Chitral who have not failed, some of them, to sound a solemn note of warning.

Before the settlement of the Oxus extension of the northern boundary of Afghanistan, something of a scare was started by a demonstration of the fact that it is occasionally quite easy to cross the Kilik Pass from the Taghdumbash Pamir into the Gilgit basin, or to climb over the comparatively easy slopes of the flat-backed Hindu Kush by the Baroghel Pass and slip down into the valley of the Chitral. There was, however, always a certain amount of geographical controversy as to the value of the Chitral or of the Kilik approach after the crossing of the Hindu Kush had been effected. Much of the difference of opinion expressed by exploring experts was due to the different conditions under which those undesirable, troublesome approaches to India were viewed. Where one explorer might find a protruding glacier blocking his path and terminating his excursions, another would speak of an open roadway.

From season to season in these high altitudes local conditions vary to an extent which makes it impossible to forecast the difficulties which may obtrude themselves during any one month or even for any one summer. In winter, *i.e.* for at least eight months of the year, all are equally ice-bound and impracticable, and although the general spirit of desiccation, which reigns over High Asia and is tending to reduce the glaciers and diminish the snowfall, may eventually change the conditions of mountain passages to an appreciable extent (and for a period), it would be idle to speculate on any really important modification of these difficulties from such natural climatic causes. We must take these mountain passes as we find them now, and as the Chinese pilgrim of old found them, placed by Nature in positions demanding a stout heart and an earnest purpose, determined to wrest from inhospitable Nature the merit of a victorious encounter with her worst and most detestable moods, ere we surmount them. To the pilgrim they represented the "strait gate" and "narrow way" which ever leads to salvation, and he accepted the horrors as a part of the sacrifice. To us they represent troublesome breaks in the stern continuity of our natural defences which can be made to serve no useful purpose, but which may nevertheless afford the opportunity to an aggressive and enterprising enemy to spy out the land and raise trouble on the border. We cannot altogether leave them alone. They have to be watched by the official guardians of our frontier, and all the gathered threads of them converging on Leh or Gilgit must be held by hands that are alert and strong. It is just as dangerous an error to regard such approaches to India as negligible quantities in the military and political field of Indian defence, as to take a serious view of their practicability for purposes of invasion.

Beyond this scattered series of rugged and elevated by-ways of the mountains crossing the great Asiatic divide from regions of Tibet and the Pamirs, to the west of them, we find on the edge of the unsurveyed regions of Kafiristan that group of passages, the Mandal and Minjan, the Nuksan and the Dorah which converge on Chitral as they pass southward over the Hindu Kush from the rugged uplands of Badakshan. None of these appear to have been pilgrim routes, nor does history help us in estimating their value as gateways in the mountains. They are practicable at certain seasons, and one of them, the Dorah, is a much-trodden route, connecting what is probably the best road traversing upper Badakshan from Faizabad to the Hindu Kush with the Chitral valley, and it enjoys the comparatively moderate altitude of about 14,500 feet above sea-level. A pass of this altitude is a pass to be reckoned with, and nothing but its remote geographical position, and the extreme difficulty of its approaches on either side (from Badakshan or Chitral), can justify the curious absence of any historical evidence proving it to have witnessed the crossing of troops or the incursions of emigrants. For the latter purpose, indeed, it may have served, but we know too little about the ethnography or derivation of the Chitral valley tribes to be able to indulge in speculation on the subject.

What we know of the Dorah is that it is the connecting commercial link between Badakshan and the Kunar valley during the summer months (July to September), when mules and donkeys carry over wood and cloth goods to be exchanged for firearms and cutlery with other produce of a more local nature, including (so it is said) Badakshi slaves. It has been crossed in early November in face of a bitter blizzard and piercing cold, but it is not normally open then. The Nuksan Pass, which is not far removed from it, is much higher (16,100 feet) and is frequently blocked by glacial ice; but the Dorah, which steals its way through rugged defiles from the Chitral valley over the dip in the Hindu Kush down past the little blue lake of Dufferin into the depths of the gorges which enclose the upper reaches of the Zebak affluent of the great Kokcha River of Badakshan, (about which we have heard from Wood), is the one gateway which is normally open from year to year, and its existence renders necessary an advanced watch-tower at Chitral. Like the Baroghel and other passes to the east of it, it is not the Dorah itself but the extreme difficulty of the narrow ways which lead to it, the wildness and sterility of the remote regions which encompass it on either side, which lock this door to anything in the shape of serious military enterprise.

Beyond the Dorah to the westward, following the Kafiristan divide of the Hindu Kush, we may well leave unassisted Nature to maintain her own work of perfect defence, for there is not a track that we can discover to exist, nor a by-way that we can hear of which passes through that inconceivably grand and savage wilderness of untamed mountains. Undoubtedly such tracks exist, but judging from the remarkable physical constitution of the Kafir, they are such as to demand an exceptional type of mountaineer to deal with them. It is only when we work our way farther westward to those passes which lead into the valleys of the upper Kabul River affluents, from the Khawak Pass at the head of the Panjshir valley to the Unai which points the way from Kabul to Bamian, that we find material for sober reflection derived from the records of the past.

The general characteristics of these passes have been described already—and something of their history. We have seen that they have been more or less open doors to India through the ages. Men literally "in nations" have passed through them; the dynasties of India have been changed and her destinies reshaped time after time by the facilities of approach which they have afforded; and if the modern conditions of things military were now what they were in the days of Alexander or of Baber, there would be no reason why her destinies should not once again be changed through use of them. We must remember that they are not what they have been. How far they have been opened up by artificial means, or which of them, besides the Nuksan and the Chahardar, have been so improved, we have no means of knowing, but we may take it for granted that the Public Works Department of Afghanistan has not been idle; for we know that that department was very closely directed by the late Amir, and that his staff of engineers is most eminent and most practical.[1]

The base of all this group of passes lies in Badakshan, so that the chief characteristics as gates of India are common to all. It has been too often pointed out to require repetition that the plains of Balkh—all Afghan Turkistan in short—lie at the mercy of any well-organized force which crosses the Oxus southwards; but once that force enters the gorges and surmounts the passes of the Badakshan ramparts a totally new set of military problems would

[1] Afghan Turkistan and Badakshan are now said to be connected with Kabul by good motor roads.

be presented. The narrowness and the isolation of its cultivated valleys; the vast spaces of dreary, rugged desolation which part them; the roughness and the altitude of the intervening ranges—in short, the passive hostility of the uplands and their blank sterility would create the necessity for some artificial means of importing supplies from the plains before any formidable force could be kept alive at the front. Modern methods point to military railways, for the ancient methods which included the occupation of the country by well-planted military colonies are no longer available. All military engineers nowadays believe in a line, more or less perfect, of railway connection between the front of a field force and its base of supply. But it would be a long and weary, if not absolutely hopeless, task to bring a railway across the highlands of Badakshan to the foot of the Hindu Kush from the Oxus plains.

We have read what Wood has to say of the routes from Kunduz southward to Bamian and Kabul. This is the recognized trade route; the great highway to Afghan Turkistan. Seven passes to be negotiated over as many rough mountain divides, plunges innumerable into the deep-rifted valleys by ways that are short and sharp, a series of physical obstacles to be encountered, to surmount any one of which would be a triumph of engineering enterprise. Amongst the scientific devices which altitude renders absolutely necessary, would be a repeated process of tunnelling. No railway yet has been carried over a sharp divide of 10,000 or 11,000 feet altitude, subject to sudden and severe climatic conditions, without the protection of a tunnel. As a work of peaceful enterprise alone, this would be a line probably without a parallel for the proportion of difficulty compared to its length in the whole wide world. As a military enterprise, a rapid construction for the support of a field army, it is but a childish chimera. Yet we are writing of Badakshan's best road!

It is true that by the Haibak route to Ghori and that ancient military base of the Greeks, Andarab, the difficulty of the sheer physical altitude of great passes is not encountered, and there are spaces which might be pointed out where a light line could be engineered with comparative facility. Even to reach thus far from the Oxus plains would be a great advantage to a force that could spend a year or two, like a Chinese army, in devising its route, but this comparative facility terminates at the base of the Hindu Kush foot-hills; and it matters not beyond that point whether the way be rough or plain, for the wall of the mountains never drops to less than 12,500 feet, and no railway has ever been carried in the open over such altitudes. Tunnelling here would be found impossible, owing to the flat-backed nature of the wide divide. With what may happen in future military developments; whether a fleet of air-ships should in the farther future sail over the snow-crested mountain tops and settle, replete with all military devices in gunnery and stores, on the plains of the Kohistan of Kabul we need hardly concern ourselves. It is at least an eventuality of which the risk seems remote at present, and we may rest content with the Hindu Kush barrier as a defensive line which cannot be violated in the future as it has been in the past by any formidable force cutting through Badakshan, without years of preparation and forewarning.

For any serious menace to the line of India's north-western defence we must look farther west—much farther west—for enough has been said of the great swelling highlands of the Firozkohi plateau, and of the Hazara regions south of the Hari Rud sources, to indicate their impracticable nature as the scene of military movement. It is, after all, the highways of Herat and Seistan that form the only avenues for military approach to the Indian frontier that are not barred by difficulties of Nature's own providing, or commanded from the sea. Once on these western fields we are touching on matter which has been so worn threadbare by controversy that it might seem almost useless to add further opinions. Historically it seems strange at first sight that, compared with the northern approaches to which Kabul gives the command, so very little use has been made of this open way. It was not till the eighteenth century saw the foundation laid for the Afghan kingdom that the more direct routes between Eastern Persia and the Indus became alive with marching troops. The reason is, obviously, geographical. Neither trade, nor the flag which preceded it from the west, cared to face the dreary wastes of sand to the south of the Helmund, backed, as they are, by the terrible band of the Sind frontier hills full of untamed and untameable tribes, merely for the purpose of dropping into the narrow riverain of the lower Indus, beyond which, again, the deserts of Rajputana parted them from the rich plains of Central India. When the Indus delta and Sind were the objective of a military expedition, the conquerors came by way of the sea, or by approaches within command of the sea—never from Herat. Herat was but the gateway to Kandahar, and to Kabul in the days when Kabul was "India."

It was not, so far as we can tell, till Nadir Shah, after ravaging Seistan and the rich towns of the Helmund valley, found a narrow passage across the Sind frontier hills that any practical use was ever made of the gates of Baluchistan. Although there are ethnological evidences that a remnant of the Mongol hordes of Chenghis Khan settled in those same Sind hills, there is no evidence that they crossed them by any of the Baluch passes. It seems certain that in prehistoric times, when the geographical conditions of Western India were different from what they are now, Turanian peoples in tribal crowds must have made their way into India southwards from Western Asia, but they drifted by routes that hugged the coast-line. We have now, however, replaced the old natural geographical conditions by an artificial system which totally alters the strategic properties of this part of the frontier. We have revolutionised the savage wilderness of Baluchistan, and made highways not only from the Indus to the Helmund, but from Central India to the Indus. The old barriers have been broken down and new gateways thrown open. We could not help breaking them down, if we were to have peace on our borders; but the process has been attended with the disadvantage that it obliges us to take anxious note of the roads through Eastern Persia and Western Afghanistan which lead to them.

For just about one century since the first scare arose concerning an Indian invasion by Napoleon Bonaparte, have we been alternating between periods of intense apprehension and of equally foolish apathy concerning these Western Indian gateways. The rise and fall of public apprehension might be expressed by a series of curves of curious regularity. At present we are at the bottom of a curve, for reasons which it is hardly necessary to enter into; but it is not an inapt position for a calm review of the subject. There is, then, one great highway after passing through Herat (which city is about 60 miles from the nearest Russian military post), a highway which has been quite sufficiently well described already, of about 360 miles in length between Herat and

Kandahar; Kandahar, again, being about 80 miles from our frontier—say 500 miles in all; and the distinguishing feature of this highway between Russia and India is the comparative ease with which that great Asiatic divide which extends all the way from the Hindu Kush to the Persian frontier (or beyond) can be crossed on the north of Herat. There, this great central water-parting, so formidable in its altitudes for many hundreds of miles, sinks to insignificant levels and the comparatively gentle gradients of a debased and disintegrated range. This divide is parted and split by the passage of the Hari Rud River; but the passage of the river is hill-enclosed and narrow, with many a rock-bound gorge which would not readily lend itself to railway-making (although by no means precluding it), so that the ridges of the divide could be better passed elsewhere.

We must concede that, taking it for all in all, that 500 miles of railway gap which still yawns between the Indian and Russian systems is an easy gap to fill up, and that it affords a road for advance which (apart from the question of supplies) can only be regarded as an open highway. Then there is also that other parallel road to Seistan from the Russian Transcaspian line across the Elburz mountains (which here represents the great divide) *via* Mashad—a route infinitely more difficult, but still practicable—which leads by a longer way to the Helmund and Kandahar. Were it not for the political considerations arising from the respective geographical positions of these two routes, one lying within Persian territory and the other being Afghan, they might be regarded as practically one and the same. Neither of them could be used (in the aggressive sense) without the occupation of Herat, and most assuredly should circumstances arise in which either of the two should be used (in the same aggressive sense) the other would be utilized at the same time.

This is, then, the chief problem of Indian defence so far as the shutting of the gate is concerned, and there are no two ways of dealing with it. We must have men and material sufficient in both quantity and quality to guard these gates when open, or to close them if we wish them shut. The question whether these western gates should remain as they are, easily traversable, or should yield (as they must do sooner or later) to commercial interests and admit of an iron way to link up the Russian and Indian railway systems is really immaterial. In the latter case they might be the more readily closed, for such a connection would serve the purposes of a defence better than those for offence; but in any case in order to be secure we must be strong.

INDEX

THE END

MACMILLAN AND CO.'S NEW WORKS

IN THE GRIP OF THE NYIKA. Further Adventures in British East Africa. By Lieut.-Colonel J. H. PATTERSON, D.S.O., Author of "The Man-Eaters of Tsavo." With Illustrations. 8vo. 7s. 6d. net.

THE LIFE OF WILLIAM THOMSON, BARON KELVIN OF LARGS. By SILVANUS P. THOMPSON, D.Sc., F.R.S. With numerous Photogravure Portraits and other Illustrations. 2 vols. 8vo.

LORD KELVIN'S EARLY HOME. Being the Recollections of his Sister, the late Mrs. ELIZABETH KING; together with some Family Letters and a Supplementary Chapter by the Editor, ELIZABETH THOMSON KING. With Illustrations. 8vo. 8s. 6d. net.

LIGHT COME, LIGHT GO. Gambling—Gamesters—Wagers—The Turf. By RALPH NEVILL. With 9 Coloured Plates and other Illustrations. 8vo. 15s. net.

ACTIONS AND REACTIONS. By RUDYARD KIPLING. Uniform Edition. Extra Crown 8vo. 6s.

Pocket Edition. On India Paper. Limp leather. Fcap. 8vo. 5s. net.

Edition de Luxe. In Sateen cloth, with embossed gilt back, and monogram on side. 8vo. 10s. 6d. net.

A HISTORY OF THE BRITISH ARMY. By the Hon. JOHN W. FORTESCUE. Volumes V. and VI. From the Peace of Amiens (1802) to the Evacuation of Spain by the British Troops (1809). With Maps. 8vo.

A PROJECT OF EMPIRE. A Critical Study of the Economics of Imperialism, with Special Reference to the Ideas of Adam Smith. By J. SHIELD NICHOLSON, M.A., D.Sc., Professor of Political Economy in the University of Edinburgh. 8vo. 7s. 6d. net.

LAND AND LABOUR: LESSONS FROM BELGIUM. By B. SEEBOHM ROWNTREE, Author of "Poverty: A Study of Town Life." 8vo.

HIGHWAYS AND BYWAYS IN BUCKINGHAMSHIRE. By CLEMENT K. SHORTER. With Illustrations by FREDERICK L. GRIGGS. Extra Crown 8vo. Gilt top. 6s.

[*Highways and Byways Series.*